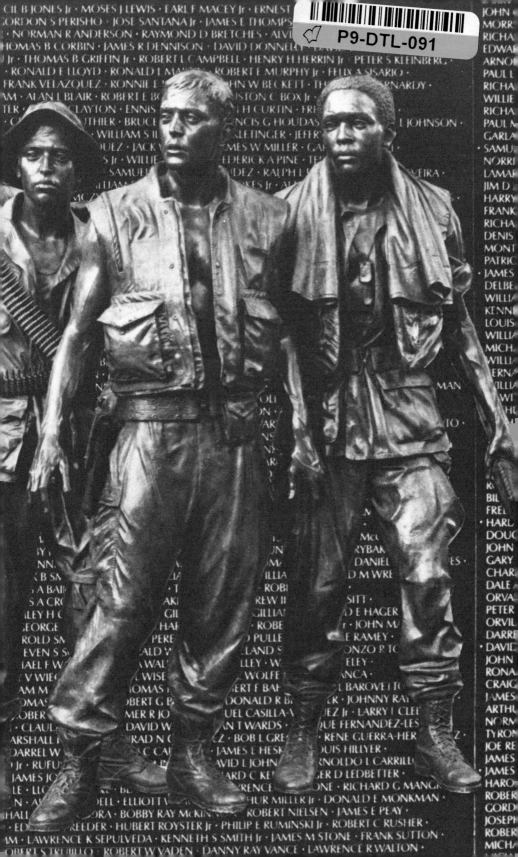

Rice Paddy GRUNT

Unfading Memories of the
Vietnam Generation

Rice Paddy GRUNT

Unfading Memories of the
Vietnam Generation

JOHN M.G. BROWN

For Phil and Nancy with memories of Drew + Amanda's wedding — August 2003 Mattole Valley

John + Josie

Regnery Books

Regnery Books is a imprint of Regnery Gateway, Inc. All inquiries concerning this book should be directed to Regnery Gateway, Inc., 950 North Shore Drive, Lake Bluff, IL 60044.

Library of Congress Cataloging-in-Publication Data

Brown, John M. G., 1947-
  Rice paddy grunt: unfading memories of the vietnam generation.

  1. Brown, John M. G., 1947-
2. Vietnamese Conflict, 1961-1975—Personal narratives, American.
3. Soldiers—United States—Biography.
4. United States Army—Biography.
I. Title.
DS559.5.B76   1986   959.704′38   85-14415
ISBN 0-89526-589-3

Contents

Acknowledgments

With thanks to Mr. Paul Taborn and the staff of the Washington National Records Center, John Slonaker of the U.S. Military History Institute, Carlisle Barracks, PA, Publications of the Society of the 1st Division, Philadelphia, PA, the 9th Infantry Division Museum, Ft. Lewis, Washington, interviews with several veteran comrades portrayed within the book, Mr. Henry Regnery, and most especially, my beloved wife Josie, for living and working with Vietnam these many years.

The three original maps for this volume were prepared by Allan Thomas.

Dedicated to:

Those Americans who gave their lives in service to our country in Indochina and to those who serve our Republic today.

Introduction

This book is the view of a witness to, and participant in, one of the great tragedies of American history, the Vietnam War. Since the founding of our Republic, the tradition of American military history has been one of citizen soldiers answering the call to arms when needed. Even with a standing military force, this continued to be necessary at the time of Vietnam and hopefully will always be so.

My objective is to demonstrate that the long record of American citizen soldiers to quickly and clearly penetrate overall problems, see through veils of official mystery and make quick judgements based on fact, continued in Vietnam. This was reflected in the morale of all the services. The record of daring, commitment and overall performance declined a long way from the operations of 1965-1968 to the withdrawal in 1972. This closely paralleled a failure in our highest leadership to equal the sacrifice and courage of the fighting men. It is perhaps not coincidental though, that most of the seriously considered criticism and analysis of "what went wrong" is coming from the same class who directed, managed and reported on the War. Is this a manifestation of continued growth away from our traditions of support in crisis by intelligent, independent citizen-soldiers? No matter how brilliant or penetrating such criticism or analysis is as seen by their fellow politicians, bureaucrats, officers and correspondents, it should be continually balanced by the ideas and memories of the enlisted soldiers who dealt first-hand with the day to day realities of the war, and who faced angry generational peers upon returning home.

At the same time the former student protestors have gone on to claim positions in government, business, or the bureaucracy of the modern American social-welfare state. They have had to carry with them through the same succeeding years the memories of watching millions of their peers serve in and live through a war effort that they themselves attempted to undermine or avoid. For many in this category that the author has known, this has led to a continued justification of their cause. It has led to a seemingly permanent generational division about proper American response to anti-U.S. aggression or Communist guerilla wars that threaten our interests. It is to this division that I dedicate my work, that through greater understanding the two sides of my generation might achieve some kind of reconciliation that is genuine. We must reach this objective to be able to work together in preserving the traditions of our democratic-republic and insure the survival of our free society for our children.

I ask of former soldiers who read this book to remember your own bitterness and sense of waste while in 'Nam, as memories of rage rise at the words and actions of the protestors. I ask of former protestors who read this book and who feel anger or shame at references to their class by fighting GIs, to remember the labels and names flung at the soldiers in meetings or protest rallies, and the disgraceful treatment many of them received at the hands of their peers upon returning home . We must understand each other, for in a time of danger we must be prepared to work together. Our children demand it. We, of both groups, are those who acted, one way or another, in the great events of our youth. We are the present day inheritors of the leadership for America.

There is a widespread belief in intellectual and sophisticated circles that the common soldiers in Vietnam were the uneducated, under-privileged of the nation, "mostly minority race," or boys incapable of knowing why they went to serve. The fact is that those who responded to the call, from all types of family backgrounds, did so primarily because they were told their country needed them. While blacks formed a disproportionately higher number in combat units in the beginning, the Army purposefully reduced their number in front line units year by year. In 1968, their numbers were approaching a proportion close to their population at home. Thirteen percent of American deaths in Vietnam were black GIs, a proportionate number of the total to serve there. The majority of combatants who served in Vietnam were, contrary to media criticisms, volunteers from average white American families, supplemented by representatives of all the other minorities that make up the "great American experience."

In political terms, the war divided the United States in a manner unseen since the time of the Civil War, and like that War, the wounds of divisiveness have been slow to heal and in fact are still present. Looking back now, I believe that America went to the defense of South Vietnam with relatively good, honorable intentions. There was, however, no national dialogue or consensus before the action was taken, only an arbitrary and thoughtless continuation of "free world leadership in opposing Communist advances everywhere."

As an observer who both served in combat in Vietnam and was active later in the antiwar movement, I feel a responsibility to write on both subjects in an attempt to create better understanding. It is important for former and present soldiers to understand the very real reasons for the anti-Vietnam War feeling. It is just as important for former and present protestors to understand something of the true nature of the day-to-day war, rather than remembering only preconceived notions of what occurred there. The knowledge (to all but the most blind) of what happened throughout Indochina following withdrawal of American support demands it. The future possibility for unity of purpose and survival of our country in any future crisis also demands it.

There was a definite lack of forethought and overall strategic planning by our political and military leaders which led us into a nearly impossible situation. Whether this was due partially to perceptive strategic planning by our enemies or totally the fault of our own leadership is no longer of prime importance. The issue for the future should be: When do we commit U.S. troops to battle on a massive scale and at the same time insure a complete victory? Defeat and shame are unacceptable to most Americans and Vietnam has had a resounding effect on our nation.

The Communist strategy of taking some basic civil dissatisfaction in an under-developed country and, by combining it with guerilla attacks and terrorism, winning control of the population, has proven to be highly successful. If America is to counter this trend for its own future self-interest, the effect of this strategy on our military forces and population must be analyzed from the highest strategic level to the lowest common soldier's experiences. It is the common soldier, after all, who must carry out military policy to its conclusion and deal with all inherent difficulties of a given situation in a guerilla war where personal initiative and responsibility by individual soldiers is particularly important. Our success as a nation in the future will depend largely on how well we understand our failure in Vietnam.

When reading the wartime experiences recorded here, the reader should bear in mind that this book deals primarily with a small, two-thousand-square-mile area of South Vietnam stretching 100 miles from the Song Be-Loc Ninh area in the north to My Tho on the Mekong River in the south and about 20 miles wide, east to west. This is a relatively miniscule portion of the land area of South Vietnam and about equivalent to our own small state of Delaware. Thousands of American soldiers died within this area during the War. Perhaps it would assist the reader to gain a broader perspective of the War to multiply the incidents recorded here day after day by 30 times, all occuring over South Vietnam at the same time.

Due to the nature of this Communist-directed guerilla war, the combat actions, enemy shelling attacks and American counter-attacks often present a very difficult situation to recount. In concentrating this narrative on the author's own area of operation, it is hoped the reader can better understand the confusing localized course of the War, its impact upon American soldiers on the scene and on our population at home. When one attempts to summarize only a particular platoon, company or battalion's operations in Vietnam the result is often so apparently unconnected to an overall campaign or strategy as to seem incomprehensible to those who weren't there. Hence, I have tied into the narrative related or adjacent units' actions that I witnessed or which directly affected the units in which I served.

It is not my intention to imply that I saw the worst of the fighting. That would be a great disservice to thousands of others who bore heavier burdens and scars than I, who lost their lives or were abandoned by our country after the American withdrawal. Nor do I profess to be an "expert" on the history of the War. I will leave that to those who constantly interpret and change things that occurred to suit their purposes or espouse some particular philosophy. Rather, I attempt to focus on the common American citizen soldier in frontline combat in an undeclared, unpopular, no-win war, and the personal and political developments created at home by that experience.

In this book I remember and honor the Americans who went to war, put their lives on the line and did their time in the old tradition. I also remember the millions who did not do so. Many of these fellow Americans had valid and understandable reasons for their stand, including concern for the killing and wounding of Americans for what seemed to them an obscure purpose.

This narrative does not contain a complete roster of the members of units I served with or a complete record of casualties. Any omissions are the fault of my own memory or lack of records. Neither is it a complete record of combat actions which occurred in the vicinity. It is a compilation from letters written home after the events, my eyewitness memories, and a journal kept while in the U.S. Army. The summarizing of these presents the reader with the experience of the war in one area.

It is a factual, essential recording of one citizen's share of, and interpretation of, American history.

—John Brown

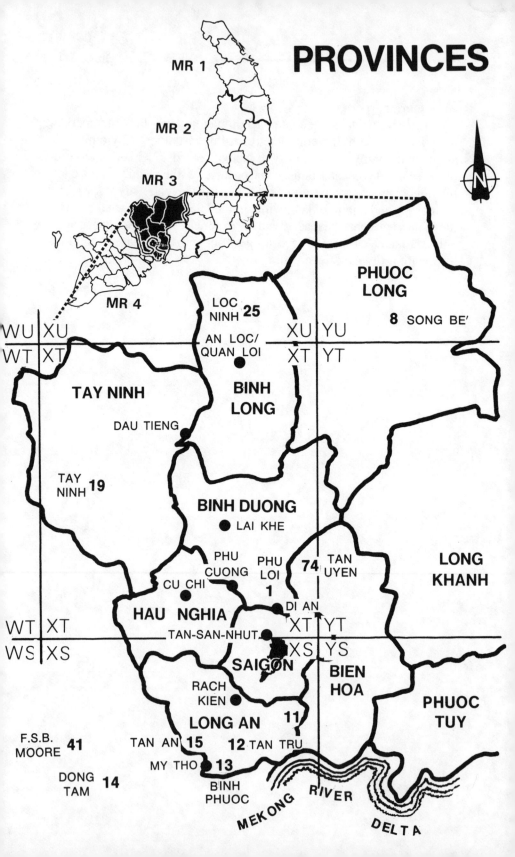

1   Memories

Once you were a strange, alien name...
Then you were a small, damp green
hostile land
where...I...nearly died
Now you are...a part of me
—Jan Barry, "Vietnam"

The diesel engine throbs with a humming rumble below the deck under my feet. I coil the line as it comes through the block with a fast, practiced motion. Coiling line's a habit that's hard to break once it becomes second nature. I learned it king-crab fishing at 125 fathoms; with 750 feet of line coming up fast, you have to coil it fast and do it right. With these Dungeness crab pots I've only got ten fathoms on, but I coil automatically. The pot explodes out of the water and up to the block. I ease off the power and reach out with a jerking twist and slam the ninety pounds of steel and wire down on the deck. It's a nice pot. A writhing, clicking mass of fat, hard keepers, maybe twenty of them.

I catch Josie's eye as she glances back at me while spinning the wheel to keep the boat into the current. She's grinning. There's a smear of fish blood all the way down the side of her face from cutting bait and a ribbon of kelp drying in her hair. She doesn't know or care about either. She's happy with the pot full of crabs, happy with our work everyday, and happy seeing the kids working with us.

The oldest boys—Jack, Moses, and Earl—have been peering over the side of the boat as they do every time. Now they rush forward as I throw open the pot door. One has the hanging bait on a hook, another pulls out the old hook and bait jug, another has the new bait jug. I'm throwing crabs into the live box. The whole operation is smooth, the whole family one. Even the two youngest, Cordelia and Ben, are cooperating by sleeping below on a bunk.

The water around us is still and calm, a deep greenish-blue. The sun is blazing down on this bay of Kodiak Island, Alaska, this hot summer day. The dense alder thickets rising from the shore nearby are like a tropical jungle this time of year. So much like the jungle. I've hunted brown bear in those alder jungles. Sometimes on hands and knees in there, following the blood trail of a wounded bear where it's so thick you can hardly see your hand held out in front of you, and he's right up ahead somewhere close, waiting. It's like back then in that other jungle a long time ago.

A helicopter clatters and thumps overhead on its way to Terror Lake and the dam construction site. I still flinch at that sound, and that completes the memory circuit. I'm back again, for the thousandth time. Back in 'Nam again. I shake my head, "Goddamn, won't it ever go away?" No, I'm there again, the hot sun, that stifling, wet, soggy heat, water everywhere, pinned down under fire, "choppers comin', airstrike!"

The burning sun of Indochina glares down on another scene of horror in a nameless swamp of the Plain of Reeds in the Mekong Delta. It is near the end of November, 1968. My platoon of infantry soldiers in a thin line, is fighting off one more ambush attack.

I'm flat in the deep, slimy mud, exhausted, when the AK-47 bullets come *Pop! Pop! Pop! — Craack! Craack!—ZZZZZ*, snapping around me again in a burst of enemy fire. Green and red tracers fly and ricochet in all directions, grenades explode, and clouds of colored smoke mark the edge of the American line. I can hear my buddies around me, other wounded GIs, screaming, "Medic! Medic!" Some of the other grunts flat on their bellies in the muck are still shooting into the Viet Cong positions. A couple more also stretched out near me are face down, the water red with their blood. The air around is being torn apart by a huge, *BRRRRRRRPPPPP!* I roll over and over in the deep muck to camouflage myself black, my right arm aching and bleeding from a ragged bullet hole. They've got me zeroed, bullets spatter in the water, shred my jungle fatigues, and shoot off my bush hat. I pull the pin on another frag-grenade. With my good left arm, I throw it in a high arc over the prostrate form of my shot-up partner, Pancho Carrera.

Phiiing! Ka-Boom! It explodes directly on the closest Viet Cong NVA position, silencing it, as I roll again, dodging bullets from another direction.

I'm working my way forward to drag Pancho out of there; I've given up trying to find the M-16 rifle shot out of my hands by enemy fire. A clattering roar behind causes me to glance back at the beautiful sight of our first helicopter-gunships diving in low over us. Then I see the body of Sergeant Wilbur Gordon, my new squad leader, badly wounded and down in the swamp, too. Under enemy anti-aircraft fire themselves, the gunships let loose their first rockets and machine-gun bullets. They are so close over me I feel I can touch them. The world around me erupts at an even higher pitch, the flashing explosions deafen me. I start crawling forward again.

"Where d'ya want it?" It's Josie's face that appears before me. She's in the wheelhouse.

I say, "Starboard a little," and wait 'til she's straightened the boat out, to shove the pot over with a splash. "So, it's fifteen years later again, huh? It's all over with, man. It was all fer nothin', jus' ferget it." Still, almost every day I hear the repetition in my mind: "Why were we there? How did it happen? What's it mean now?"

The day's work done, we're in our cabin on this remote, hidden bay of Kodiak Island. It's built out of dock planks, old lumber, and logs cut from the forest. Around the walls are framed pictures and mementos going back those fifteen years, mountain goat horns, seashells and glass-ball net floats, a string of brown- and grizzly-bear claws. They've been moved around, to different log cabins and homesteads, but our life has stayed the same. It's the only way we seem to have found freedom or contentment.

Our fishing boat rides at anchor, as a late afternoon thermal wind comes up. The vast North Pacific Ocean that's always moving starts booming now on the outside beaches with the west wind. The Sitka spruce trees stand in tall, silent rows, ringing the grassy meadow where our horses graze. Blacktail deer browse on the hills and steep mountains above. That greatest of grizzlies, the Kodiak brown bear, lurks in the alder thickets. The sea around this island is alive with ducks, sea lions, otters, salmon, halibut, crabs, and a multitude of other creatures. Birds of many species revolve in the air above us the year around.

It's been a long odyssey, searching for this peaceful place, but still I am not at rest. Those memories, dreams, and nightmares keep intruding. They mingle with remembered echoes of mass demonstrations, thousands of my peers chanting, "Uncle Sam, out of 'Nam, and Ho! Ho! Ho Chi Minh, NLF is gonna win!" I see the enemy Viet Cong flags waving in the streets of Washington and New Haven again. Visions of the part of my generation that saw their responsibilities differently.

I look across the cabin to the other half of my soul, my wife Josie. Josie, the mother of five, the fisherman, the farmer, but one of the protest leaders back then. Our torn-up, divided generation is together now long years later bonded by memories and the four noisy boys and their pretty little sister clattering around, laughing, happy.

So many memories between then and now. The patriotism and blind obedience, the long bitter combat, the veterans and protesters, the long years on the edge of the wilderness.

We're listening to National Public Radio tonight here on this far northwest border of the nation. The commentator is talking about the guerilla war in El Salvador and inteviewing a correspondent on the scene of the latest attack. They're saying basically that the Communist guerillas are right again. "The corrupt government supported by the United States" is wrong. The Communists aren't really Communists, they're a "coalition of moderates, progressives, and socialists." They're fighting for a "just cause" and America is backing the wrong side again. ("Just like Vietnam.") The government of El Salvador, which recently held successful free elections (in which most citizens voiced opposition to the Soviet- and Cuban-backed insurgency) is still "hopelessly reactionary." The high pitched voice of Marcus Raskin, director of the radical "Institute for Policy Studies" whines out over the airwaves in sympathy with Communists somewhere. To me it is a modern version of the 1960's propaganda line.

It seems as though I've heard the same carefully worded phrases a lot in recent years in comments or reports on Rhodesia-Zimbabwe, El Salvador, Grenada, Nicaragua, Angola, Ethiopia, Afghanistan, or Cuba. Our national radio, financed by us, so freely uses the words "liberation forces" when they speak of those overthrowing a government formerly friendly to us. It's another echo of the past, a continuation of the anti-America movement of the late '60s, but now it's become the standard line for much of our media and intelligentsia.

Each time the same hopes and promises are voiced that this will be the perfect "new socialist society." Each time the fine words and dreams crumble and a new "Marxist" or "socialist" or "Communist" dictatorship is forced into place and the Soviets and Cubans move in with their weapons and their methods. Weapons and methods that are somehow nobler and purer than the ones we supply to our former friends.

Only a short time ago we were being asked to share in the "burden and sacrifice" and "fight for the freedom of South Vietnam." A war that was to involve millions of Americans, in suffering and death. A war that ended in the total conquest of Vietnam, Cambodia, and Laos by a Communist enemy with the result that millions of people fled by any means to escape this fate. If we were so terribly wrong, why then did they flee? Why do they flee in millions from other beacons of socialism: Eastern Europe, Cuba, Afghanistan, or Ethiopia?

Josie yells, "Shut the damn thing off, we gotta get some kindling for tomorrow morning!"

I pull on my boots and go outside to the chopping block, mumbling to myself, "There it is, gotta work anyway."

She follows me out to the chopping block and grabs my hand, holding it tightly. We stare out past the beach at the Straits. Fishing boats are chugging by, big and small, the fleet of Kodiak is heading for another salmon opening. A group of tough men and women who make their living from a wild sea against a mountain of government rules, regulations, paper, and foreign competition.

"We can't do anything about it," she's saying. "I don't know why we always listen to the news. All it does is get us stirred up. The decisions are made by people who know nothing about any of it. They just sit up there and eat our crab and sell us and all our friends down the river. You've got to try and not think about 'Nam—it only puts you into a depression."

"It's too real to me, I can't forget it. Yesterday they were talking about the 101st Airborne Division going to Honduras. It's gonna happen again, and they haven't learned nothin'. They're gonna make the same mistakes over in those villages and jungles, and they've still got no unity here at home. An' the news media's still so quick to say everything we say an' do is wrong."

"What about that letter from Congressman John LeBoutillier on U.S. prisoners who are still held in Vietnam by the Communists? What about that report on the radio we heard a few months ago when that team of Scandinavians in North Vietnam saw a group of captured Americans under guard and heard them yelling 'Don't forget us!'?"

She rubs the back of my neck briefly and walks away. I set up the logs and start splitting, slamming the maul down clean and true, over and over.

"Done it thousands of times, years and years, at least I don't burn any damn oil." All of a sudden, I'm thinking about rockets again.

It's February 18th, 1968, the Tet Offensive. *Whoosh! Craaack! Boom!* White-orange flash, shouts: "Incoming! Hit it!" *SSSSH! BBOOM!* Buildings are blowing up and burning, helicopters blasted over on their sides. *Whooosh! Craaack! Boom!*

Screams, cries: "I'm hit! Oh Jesus, I'm hit, help me, somebody, I can't feel my legs! Oh, mama!"

"Man, I don't wanna move, that dude's hit. Goddamn, I gotta go anyway." Tensing, get ready, go! Running, running. There he is! Flop down next to him in the dust and blood. Other guys are coming. *Whoosh! Craaack! Boom!* Huge white flash, close. Like a bolt of lightning hitting. Our artillery's firing back. *Ka-Boom-ZZZ* over our heads. Blood sprays from him.

"It's a dude from Division Artillery, man. Jesus God, his legs are gone!"

"Getta 'nother belt for the other stump, we gotta stop this bleeding!"

Other GIs are flopping belly-down, frantic hands straining to help. He's screaming again.

"Oh Jesus. Oh, my God! What happened to me? I can't feel nothin'! God, oh God!"

"Let's get 'im to the medics, man. We done all we can. He's fucked up!" *Whoosh! Craaack! Boom! Ka — Boom — ZZZZZ!* Legs bunching, arms tensing, lifting in unison, "Let's go! Now!"

I keep on chopping and chopping; I've got a pretty good pile of wood here.

"All right, you boys, get out here now an' haul this wood into the house!" I watch them as they come so willing and strong; eleven, ten, and seven years old. I look at their clear trusting faces, smiling and laughing as they run up.

"How'd you like one of 'em to die in a rice paddy or a jungle with a bullet in him like all those boys that died over there?" I think. They each grab up huge armloads, as much as they can carry and stagger into the cabin. I watch them go, wondering.

"Well, what about El Salvador or Lebanon, or some other damn place. You want one of them to go? No, not if it's like 'Nam was, I don't. They've wasted 'em over there, our clean, smooth, smart politicians. They never even knew what they were doing, and they wasted 58,000 young boys, and they even left a couple of thousand over there when they walked away. They did such a bad job with the whole thing it just started a snowball rolling both here at home and overseas, and maybe now they're gonna end up in another no-win war somewhere else.

"We all gotta talk, tell 'em the plain, true story; it's our last mission of the 'Nam. We gotta make it count for somethin'. Tell 'em what Earl would've told 'em if he was alive. Earl, Art McQuade, Smitty, Bennett, Welch, Norris, Bartel, Novak, and all those other guys who never came home. It's the least I can do."

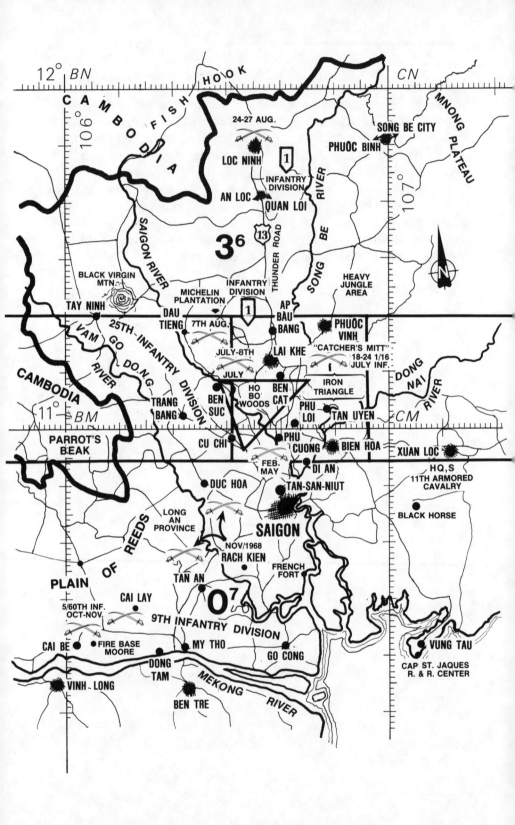

2   Traditions

"Can one part of humanity learn from the bitter experience of another, or can it not? Is it possible or impossible to warn someone of danger?"
— *Alexander Solzhenitsyn*

I came out of Pennsylvania, like many other citizen-soldiers before me. On my father's side, the Browns had first emigrated to Massachusetts from West-country Britain in 1638. On my mother's side, the Sculls were a Quaker family that had been part of William Penn's first settlement on the Delaware River in the 1680s. My father's side of the family has a long tradition of middle class solidness, having started out in the new world as farmers and tanners of leather. As early settlers of Salisbury, Massachusetts, my ancestors had fought the Indians and served in the Revolutionary War at Bunker Hill, Bennington, and Saratoga. My father served in hospitals of the Army Medical Corps in France during World War II. The Quaker side of my mother's family had been conscientious objectors to war service. The Second World War brought changes in attitudes: her brother David served in the Army in the battle of Attu in Alaska's Aleutian chain. As for me, I was raised in the tradition of service to the country if the call came.

The Pennsylvania I grew up in was a state of cities, steel mills, coal mines, and farming country, all linked by railroads and highways. It was also a state in which history was alive everywhere—in stone and wood and blood-soaked earth. The sites my father took me to, the huts of the freezing Revolutionary soldiers at Valley Forge and the rows of gravestones at Gettysburg, were part of my education.

As a young boy, I always dreamed of wild country and far-away places. For about fifteen years, our family went north in the summer to our small Vermont farm on a lake near the Canadian border. There we grew vegetable gardens, put up pickles and canned goods, sawed and chopped firewood, went hunting and fishing in the forested hills, and cut and stacked hay with our neighbors, using horse-drawn mowers, rakes, and wagons. Our hayfields were leased to neighboring farmers, and we children joined in the work each year. We rode horses on the dirt roads around East Charlestown and Island Pond and went to the county fair with its races and ox-pulling contests. Those were the best memories of my childhood.

During the winters I went through a series of schools in Pennsylvania, including one run by the Quakers, and ended up in a large public high school with several thousand other students: boys from steel mill families mixed with middle class kids and blacks from poor neighborhoods. The impression I got from my formal education was that the world was made up of the good people—America and its friends—and the enemy, the Communist nations. My father was interested in politics and current events, and we talked regularly. This practice and his large library of books on history contributed more to my view of the world than did school.

About the time of my sixteenth birthday in January of 1963 I first heard of Vietnam. President John F. Kennedy had captured the imagination of many young people with his call to "bear any burden and share any sacrifice in the defense of freedom." His support of the concept of counter-insurgency warfare units like the Army's Green Berets signaled a change in American policy. The Cuban Communist takeover had evidenced a need for a new strategy, instead of the earlier concept of massive retaliation. Trained American advisors had been sent to Vietnam to prevent "another communist victory." Several thousand U.S. advisors and support troops were in Vietnam when I heard of three U.S. Army advisors being killed in the battle of Ap Bac in the Mekong Delta in January of 1963. At that time, I had no idea that a large scale war would soon develop that would disrupt my generation. I only remember saying the name: Vietnam, and wondering about it. President Kennedy's assassination in November of 1963 was a great shock, for I had admired his ideals of service and action, and the words he spoke.

Hints of involvement in the assassination "by our Communist enemies," gradually faded away. As for me, I quit school on my seventeenth birthday in January of 1964, enlisted in the Marine Corps, and was shipped to Parris Island boot camp. Because of vision problems compounded by eye damage in an automobile accident (my head had gone through the windshield), I received a medical discharge six months after my enlistment. Bitterly disappointed because the boys I had trained with went to Santo Domingo and later to Vietnam, I decided to try frontier life as an alternative.

In July of 1964, still seventeen years old, I emigrated to Australia. At a woolbrokers warehouse in Brisbane on the coast of Queensland, I landed a job on a sheep and cattle station far to the interior of the state. A month later, I was a different person. Harder-muscled, tanned brown by the sun, wearing a broad-brimmed Aussie bush hat, khaki work clothes and jodphur boots, I was working in the hot, dusty corral with fellow station-hand Peter, castrating hundreds of young rams. Grab 'em, flip 'em, cut 'em, over and over, to the accompaniment of bleating, blood, and dust.

"D'you hear about what yer America's up to, John, me-mate?"

"No, Peter, what's up?"

"Your blokes are bombing the hell out of some silly, bloody country called Vietnam, up in French Indochina. They're talking about your ships being hit in something called the Tonkin Gulf."

I felt vaguely uneasy at the news, a sudden sense of being far from home. I tried to shrug off the feeling and went back to work. Peter was a strange character, a white African from Rhodesia. He was a tough, skinny man. As a boy, he had hunted crocodiles on the Zambezi for their hides with his father, fought in the desert war against Rommel's Germans, and then took off wandering. He'd left a chain of wives and children extending around the world from South Africa to New Zealand and Australia. We rode horseback together, herding sheep and cattle and hunting dingos, emus, and kangaroos. I ended up with a pet wallaby-roo of my own that lived under my shack.

It was Peter who introduced me to outback-style drinking in the pubs of the Queensland bush. When he got the urge to tie one on, off we'd go in his 1940 Chevrolet held together by wire. During one drinking bout I heard about the U.S. elections in the fall of '64.

"That Goldwater bloke's a crazy one, he is. He'll be startin' another war if he gets in."

"That's too bloody true, mate."

All the Aussie stockmen looked to me for an opinion but I had none. I couldn't understand the reason for fighting in Vietnam. Still, I couldn't argue against it, either. I did start listening to the radio news, however, and heard words by President Johnson about "not sending American boys to do the fighting for Asian boys.'' After a final, wild carouse with Peter, that ended with a huge barroom brawl, I left the ranch and resumed wandering.

Covering the outback from the Northern Territory to New South Wales, I got to know station hands, buffalo and crocodile hide hunters, and lived for a time with a group of full- and half-blooded Aborigines in a run-down communal shack. Later I stayed with a family of Italian immigrants who were cutting farm and vineyard out of desolate bush. I finally ended up on the docks of Sydney.

I worked as a day laborer and spent most of my nights in pubs with sailors and longshoremen. Belting down schooners and middies of beer with the best of them, my American ways still drew attention and references to Vietnam.

''I 'ear the Yanks are sendin' in troops up there, eh? Thousands of 'em, Army and Marines is wot I 'ear.''

''Wot d'you think, Johnny boy, wot's your blokes up to?''

''I don't know, mates, I've been away so long I'm wonderin' myself, now.'' I'd heard of a big Viet Cong mortar attack on an American camp at a place called Pleiku, with over a hundred American casualties, and President Johnson ordering a heavy bombing of North Vietnam in March of that year, 1965. Now they were sending in battalions of U.S. combat troops, not merely advisors. The Americans would take the war over from this ''South Vietnam.''

I got the same feeling as I had the previous fall, this time a strong feeling of homesickness. With a little bit of luck and some fast talking, I got a job as a wiper in the engine room of a German freighter, the *Cap Vilano*, 7,000 tons. We spent the next month or so steaming across the Pacific, stopping at various ports and islands for cargo. I jumped ship in Long Beach, California, in July of 1965, after about a year in Australia.

Having had enough ocean for a while, I headed straight inland to the Mojave Desert near the California-Arizona border. I found work right away on the farms that mostly hired braceros from Old Mexico. These people taught me about chopping okra, picking grapefruit, oranges, and other fruit, all over Southern California. I learned to hop the freights of the Southern Pacific too, and spent all my time either on the ranches at hard labor or traveling on boxcars. For three months it seemed natural until one night in a rough camp near Brawley, in the Imperial Valley, a Mexican, José, who had partnered with me and was sharing a bottle of wine, turned to me suddenly and said:

"Why you here, Juan? Why an Anglo boy like you stay in thees shitty place with us? We have to, there's nothing else for us. But you, you can do anything."

All the rest of that night I thought about it while we lay against an adobe wall drinking wine and shooting rats with a flashlight and a .22 pistol. In the morning, I rolled up my bedding, said a soft goodbye to him, and pulled out. I headed for Berkeley, where my high school girl-friend was attending the University of California.

The contrast between my last year-and-a-half of rugged life with the Berkeley campus was astonishing. I found my pretty, blonde Amy in a clean, luxurious dormitory. She welcomed me; pretty soon we rented a room in Berkeley and I was wandering around the campus taking in the scene. The big thing had been the "Free Speech Movement's" student challenge to a California law forbidding Communist speakers in state colleges. The idea of resisting it had been growing and the local hero was Mario Savio, a young radical who preached the Communist line openly. My impression was that he was just creating an uproar and trying to make himself famous. The Free Speech Movement was being steered by Savio toward an anti-Vietnam war stand for American students. It was the first time I discovered politics.

Tables were set up around the campus displaying literature against U.S. involvement in Vietnam and defending the rights of Communist speakers. The current civil rights movement in the South was also given space but was not regarded as a local issue.

One person at a table challenged me as I was looking through the pamphlets, "Well, would you be a tool of the government and go fight in Vietnam?"

"I guess I would if they needed me, but I already have a medical discharge."

"That's no excuse not to take a stand. You have to see it's wrong, that the Vietnamese have a right to solve their own problems and have the kind of government they want—including communism, without us forcing a military dictatorship like Thieu and Ky on them."

I'd heard these names as the Vietnamese leaders who had taken over the government in another coup. I was still loyal to my beliefs that communism was the enemy and had to be fought by America, if necessary. I didn't understand the point of view of the Berkeley student activists. Why was a pro-American dictatorship so much more evil than a Communist one? It seemed anti-American to me because my belief then was that fighting communism was ultimately fighting for freedom, and my country could never be wrong.

The only thing I could think of in response was, ''The Russians and the Chinese are supplying the Viet Cong with weapons and equipment to overthrow a government we have a treaty of assistance with, aren't they?'' He sneered and raised his eyes in an exaggerated gesture of exasperation because he had to deal with a fool.

The last thing he said before I left was: ''Can't you see this isn't America's war? This is Johnson and McNamara's war. And all the upper class snobs that run your life like Dean Rusk and McGeorge Bundy! They don't care about you or me or the people of South Vietnam. Besides, communism and socialism are the future of the world for the poor, oppressed people, and they'll never stop it!''

All this was too much for me and I shouted back at him, ''In a Communist country you wouldn't be able to sit at any table and preach against the government!''

Now he was shouting back, ''What do you know about communism? Real, pure communism is for the people. It's freedom from starvation, freedom from worrying about what you're going to do. Everything will be planned, considered, and implemented fairly by the party!''

I backed away, snarling, ''You son-of-a-bitch, you're too far out for me!'' I dimly knew there was a huge difference between Communist theory and practice, but I didn't care enough to argue. I'd already made up my mind the whole bunch of these radicals were Communists—and pretty plump, well-fed ones too.

Huddled together with Amy later in our room overlooking Telegraph Avenue, we compared thoughts. She was an intellectual with a natural belief in freedom for the individual above all. So was I. Communism was the antithesis of everything we valued. She told me, however, of the antagonism toward her beliefs in the climate of embryonic radicalism developing at Berkeley.

During the several weeks we spent together, the most exciting event we witnessed was our first antiwar demonstration. It started with the usual leaflets and fiery speeches that were to become commonplace later. It ended as a march on the Oakland Army Terminal, where troops were being gathered for shipment to Vietnam at this time of the big American buildup there. We were there as spectators. Demonstrators shouted and stomped, hundreds and hundreds of people waving signs and banners demanding that America leave Vietnam alone and get out. It was a moving sight to me this first time and I was both curious and tense.

Police cordons, threatening Hell's Angels, the hippies...all made an eyeful. Suddenly right in front of me, a protest group threw an American flag on the street, jumping and stamping on it to the accompaniment of curses and jeers. I felt a feeling of rage come over me, all of my suspicions were confirmed. I flung myself between the police guards at them and landed a solid right fist in the face of the nearest man involved. This precipitated a battle, and other bystanders jumped into the fight to assist me. In October of 1965 my commitment was made. It was still, "my country right or wrong," and though I was arrested and jailed after the fight, I still felt good. The memory of the desecration of the flag and my commitment that day were to carry me through the next few years of decisions and a long dose of war—before I began to doubt what I believed in.

Meanwhile, I became disgusted with the atmosphere of Berkeley and told Amy I was going on the road again. The feeling was still in me that my service discharge showed my good intention of serving even though I wasn't needed. I left that crazy place and headed back to the world of working men. During the next year, I covered the West from northern California to the mountains of Washington and Idaho. I rode freights of the Southern Pacific, the S.P. & S., and the Northern Pacific with old hobos from the '30s, lived in "jungles," cooked over open fires and learned how to get by and to defend myself. I put in a long stretch of time in the Klamath River country on the Oregon-California border, from the Rivers mouth to the upper headwaters of the mountain lakes. For several months I worked for contractors to the U.S. Forest Service, planting Douglas firs near the old U.S. Indian Agency and army post of Fort Klamath. I lived for a while with Klamath, Modoc, and Paiute Indians in the area, listening to tales of when all the land was theirs and their grandfathers had fought the white soldiers and settlers for it in the 1860s and '70s. I had an Indian girl friend and some wild times between there and the Fort Bidwell-Goose Lake country.

After felling timber on Puget Sound in a logging operation, I landed a job with Boeing Aircraft Corporation, building 707 jets at their big Renton, Washington plant. I lived on skidrow in Seattle, near the Alaska docks, before moving in with a young red-haired mother of several children who worked with me at Boeing. Jeanie's ex-husband was fighting in Vietnam, and she'd decided to go it alone. On weekends I'd explore around the Olympic Peninsula, and after work drink beer in the saloons of Seattle. Here, I started meeting young soldiers from Fort Lewis, just back from a year in combat. Some had gone through the Ia Drang Valley battles in Vietnam. It was the fall of 1966.

I'd be sitting in a bar after a long day of clanging and whining, drilling metal and banging rivets, feeling pretty good about myself and my wages. The door of the saloon would fly open and a bunch of young GIs my own age in khaki uniforms would swagger in. The first thing I'd see was a row of ribbons over the left chest pocket with the Vietnam campaign medal in the middle, a yellow field with three parallel red stripes and green-edged borders. Then I'd notice their faces, young-old looking, eyes hard or glinting, the eyes of age. They'd take over the barroom with their presence, and even the old men who'd hardly pay any attention to me would swing half around and listen when their stories started.

"Just got back from the war myself, yeah, back from 'Nam. What outfit was you in, buddy?"

"The best, man, 1st Cavalry Division."

"Yeah, that's where it's at, huh? I was in the Cav, too. Got hit near Plei Me in the Ia Drang myself last October. Goddamn, I'm glad I got outta that place alive."

I'd sit and listen to them next to me, their presence electric. I'd buy them a beer and say: "What was it like over there? What's the Ia Drang you're talking about?"

"It ain't nothin' like the movies, buddy. Ia Drang is where we first run into the NVA regulars. It wasn't like no big Civil War battle, just a whole bunch of firefights spread all over the jungle at once, like a big lousy nightmare. We took over a thousand casualties in the 1st Cav, and ended up with nothin' to show for it but empty bush. All ya can see is right around yer own little area an' maybe hear what happened later."

I got the feeling he was talking to me as though I were a little child. I knew then my time was approaching, my turn was coming. I'd have to go back into the service and "over there," before I could understand all this talk about "'Nam" and "firefights," "NVA Regulars" and "Communist oppression." It felt like the time was cinching down and the moment of decision was coming closer. There was a war on and the recruiting posters seemed to stare out at me, "Your country needs you!"

I knew what I had to do, but the knowledge brought back memories of boot camp at Parris Island and gave me the urge to wander once again. I decided to have one more fling. Quitting my job at Boeing, I headed my 1949 Plymouth on a journey south through the length of Old Mexico, 2,000 miles to the Yucatan peninsula of Central America where Guatemala, Mexico, and Honduras come together. Winter was coming, anyway. The old hobos had taught me to head south like a bird before the snow flew. I partnered up with a black Belize smuggler named Lloyd, whose stolen car had broken down. We lived and traveled together, drinking wine and crawling up and down the ancient Aztec and Maya pyramids at my insistence and staying in the poverty-stricken Indian and Mestizo villages at night. I became involved in his business in British Honduras, and we ended up in a sorry jail together. When I was finally released by a dignified black judge in a white powdered British wig, I was ordered out of the country. They dumped me across the river in Quintana Roo, Yucatan, flat broke. It was a long haul to Reynosa, Texas, on the cattle and freight trucks.

By now it was early January, 1967. I worked my way back across the deep South, intending to enlist. Enlistment required a special medical waiver because of my earlier medical discharge. I ended up signing papers for three years of Regular Army service, with a guarantee for training as a UH-1 helicopter crew chief/gunner. I had wanted to be a Ranger but my eyes wouldn't meet the vision requirements. I shipped out immediately, having just turned 20. Two months of basic combat training at Fort Bragg, North Carolina, went by quickly. The lineups, hair shaving, discipline, running, and rifle practice seemed easy after my preparation three years before at Parris Island.

During the training period the only thing that bothered me was a couple of talks I'd had with my platoon sergeant and drill instructor, Staff Sergeant Price. He had just returned from a year with the Special Forces, or Green Berets, in the Vietnam-Laotian border area—a wild wilderness of 6,000- and 7,000-foot jungle-covered mountains extending hundreds of miles north to Yunnan Province in China. Here the Viet Cong and North Vietnamese transported their weapons, ammunition, and supplies around the so-called DMZ over the Ho Chi Minh Trail, to carry on the war in South Vietnam. He was the first person I respected who told me the massive U.S. troop buildup to fight the war for the South Vietnamese wasn't going to work. It was a rare thing for a lifer drill sergeant even to pass the time of day with a buck private, but Sergeant Price seemed to like me. He'd invite me into his room at the end of the squad bay occasionally. He had the same lean, tough, expressionless face of many professional soldiers; sometimes he'd sit and stare, muttering to himself or at me.

"Brown, yer just a kid. You been around more than most of the boys in this platoon, but yer still green and ya don't know what yer headin' into. Where I been the last year, we don't belong. It's a whole 'nother world. Our plans and solutions don't apply to the situation there, an' we're headin' into trouble. Besides that, those Viet Cong are ready to fight us forever. They're dug in underground for hundreds of miles in every direction in that country. There ain't no one front line either; there's hundreds of 'em. They been fightin' foreigners for a thousand years. They think different than we do about time, and our politicians don't have any idea what they've gotten us into. I pity you kids for what you're gonna see and feel, and I pity our country for what's gonna happen."

At the end of basic training, I said goodbye to him and he just nodded, looking sad. It was almost as though he could see the future. During the summer in helicopter crew-chief training, I remember hearing of a big mortar attack by the enemy on the American air base at Danang, with over a hundred and fifty Americans killed and wounded. I remember really wondering what "mortars" were and asking a returned veteran.

"They're just 82mm Chinese shells, man. You'll get used to 'em, no sweat."

The U.S. Army had sucked me into its great green machine and spat me out with thousands of others ready for Indochina. My family, like most Americans, was hardly aware of a war going on at all, and wished me the best of luck and goodbye. My father's feeling was that he'd done his time and I should do mine—it would be good for me. Besides, I'd been running around for three years, accomplishing nothing, and he wanted to see me become something. The few friends and relatives my age still around at home were smug about the situation. Most of them were going to college, and their feeling was: Only idiots and suckers are in the service and going to Vietnam.

Little patriotic feeling had been aroused by committing combat troops to an Asian mainland war again. Not enough study had been given to the recent history of Vietnam by our "leaders." No one paid much attention to the fact the only a year before he died, General Douglas MacArthur warned President Kennedy not to send in an army there. The endless jungle, swamps, mountains, and plateaus, and thousands of miles of open wilderness frontiers of Indochina and its neighbors were looked upon as unimportant lines on a small map. As for my teacher, Staff Sergeant Price, his experience, wisdom—and the faraway look in his eyes told me he knew what he was talking about.

There seemed to be little reason to remain at home, so I cut my pre-overseas thirty day leave short. In San Francisco, a few days before my shipment date, some soldiers and I got detoured into the "Summer of Love of 1967" in Haight-Ashbury. Wandering around in our uniforms with somewhat naive patriotism, we were accosted by hippies and student peers.

"Hey, look at that, it's GIs, soldiers, man!"

"What 'cha gonna do, 'serve your country'?"

"I hear all yer gonna do over there is burn villages and murder peasants."

The Berkeley of '65 was spreading. The students were more radical and sure of themselves, the hippies more "spaced-out" and beyond it all. We GIs sat in the warm September grass of Golden Gate Park among a stoned crowd of the other half of our generation. Rock music drifted over the air. The songs were about self-gratification, getting high on drugs, and the absurdity of serving one's country in war. The odd thing was that we, the young soldiers on our own "strange trip," loved those songs, too. We were the same kids of America, but we were on our way to the "battlefront against Communism," while the other half of our generational peers were on their way to greater heights of mind-exploration and rejection of traditional values.

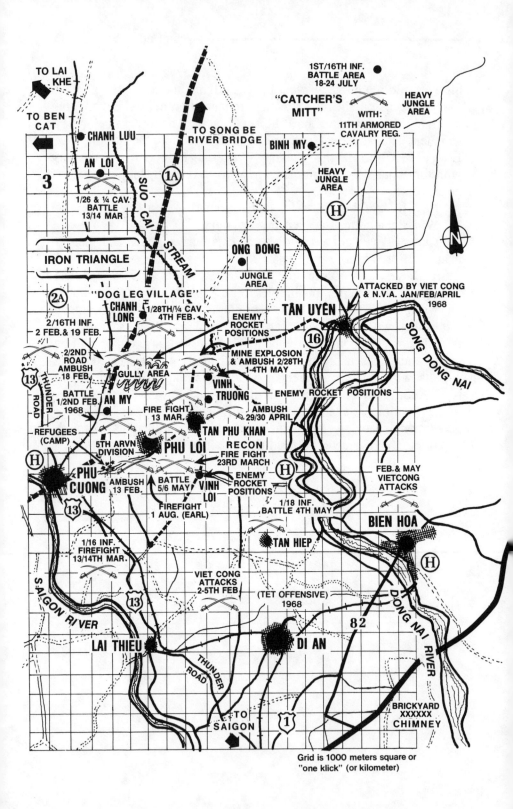

3   War Zone

"Ask not what your country can do for you,
but what you can do for your country."
—John F. Kennedy
President of the United States
1960-1963

The big transport plane eased down and hit the runway. We were in Vietnam for our "year of war." It was about the 20th of September, 1967. When the plane came to a halt and the door was thrown open, warm tropical air flooded into the cabin; the whole planeload of new cannon fodder sat nervously. A lot of us expected an enemy attack momentarily, but instead a shiny-looking MP with a .45 automatic on his belt swung in and soon had us filing towards some waiting trucks and buses.

A group of veteran soldiers going home stood staring at us. A few shouted insults or called, "You'll be sorreeee!" Most stood silent, staring at their plane, their "freedom bird" that would carry them home. We were part of the third wave of replacements since the big buildup in '65.

On the convoy to the replacement depot at Long Binh, peering through windows protected by wire mesh against grenades, I could see the dirt roads lined with shacks and hovels, and see smoke rising from cooking fires. The darkness was lit by flares hanging in the night sky. The country had a look that reminded me of Old Mexico. Artillery was firing H and I in the distance and muffled shell explosions could be heard far away. After going through paperwork processing at the huge logistics and rear-support base of Long Binh, we enlisted men stood or leaned behind a building, waiting.

A couple of strutting sergeants approached us smirking, "All right, you cherries, yer going to yer hootches!" Number this, number that, blah, blah, blah.

"Now do it. Now!"

They kept up their tough-guy, GI-Joe routine as though we were new recruits, following us, shouting all the way to the door of the barracks. Evidently, anything in Vietnam from a grass-thatched hut on up was a "hootch." Inside my "hootch" by the door lay one soldier. He was staring out at the sergeants with an evil glare.

"Fuckin' pigs! Stinkin', slimy bastards!" He rolled over mumbling, "Only reason I'm by this door where I have to look at 'em is there's a bunker right over there. An' if the gooks mortar us, I'm gonna be the first one in it."

His voice suddenly changed from a monotone to a screech.

"I'm short, you assholes! You REMF pigs can't fuck with me no more; I'm going home!"

I sat nervously at the edge of a rack, eyeing this maniac out of the corner of my eye. I'd never heard the word "REMF," and I'd never heard any soldier talk like that to an E-6 staff sergeant, let alone two of them.

"Hey man, can I ask you something?" He turned slowly and his eyes met mine. They were those same old-looking eyes I'd seen in kids back from 'Nam.

"What's a REMF?"

He let out a low, snarling chuckle that sounded fake, with no mirth in it at all.

"A REMF? Those're REMFs," he said, pointing at the two sergeants who were walking away, one of them shaking his head as though he'd seen something unbelievable.

"REMF is R, E, M, F, Romeo, Echo, Mike, Foxtrot. It means rear-echelon-mother-fucker, man. Somebody who don't know shit an' acts like he does. A pig that talks to combat soldiers like he's an' equal when he ain't."

He turned away again to face the wall, staring at it, not inviting further conversation. I lay back thinking to myself, "This place is weird, people talkin' like that to staff sergeants and gettin away with it. They didn't even look this guy in the eye—just walked away. I wonder what goes on over here that turns things upside down like that?" Other new guys in the hootch were staring at the veteran, too, but he paid no attention to anyone. I felt uncomfortable, uneasy with the sudden glaring reversal of all my training of respect for superiors. I finally got up and shuffled out into the dusty heat and climbed up on the sandbagged bunker beyond the doorway. I lay on that bunker for hours that night, staring at the flares hanging in the sky, wondering what fate had in store for me in the year to come.

The following morning my name was called out in a formation, and I found myself in front of a bored-looking clerk. My attitude had already gone through subtle change in one night because when the clean-looking "dude" behind the desk spoke to me, I was already thinking, "This is a REMF."

"Yer not goin' too far up country, dude, just to the Big Red One."

"Big Red One, huh?" I'd heard that name before: The First Infantry Division, the famous fighting outfit of World Wars I and II. The name took me aback. Things seemed as though they were getting more real all the time. I mumbled back at the clerk, "I'm glad I'm not goin' way up north."

"Yer goin' to the Iron Triangle, dude, an' there's plenty of places further north a lot quieter than that is. The Big Red One at Phu Loi and Lai Khe is what keeps the VC off our ass here. Have a nice year, man."

Orders in hand, I turned away from the smirking REMF, and picked up my gear to stand with the other replacements for the same unit waiting for transport. Along with the rest of the new troops for the Division, I rode in a truck convoy guarded by troopers in jeeps with mounted machine guns to Di An, the southernmost base camp of the 1st Division. Here I was immediately assigned to Alpha (A) Co., 1st Aviation Battalion. This turned out to be an assault helicopter unit. The other men with me drew various other outfits of the Division, including line battalions of the 2nd Infantry, 16th Infantry, 18th, 26th or 28th, 1st Squadron/4th Cav. (armored) units of the 1st Division Artillery, or 1st Engineers, supply, and maintenance. I ended up shortly on another guarded truck convoy, heading north through alternating jungle and rice paddy country with scattered villages. We passed the town of Phu Cuong and the sandbagged, bunkered barbed wire gate of my new home, Phu Loi. I was dumped off at my company area near the airstrip and reported to my First Sergeant.

Co. A., 1st Aviation Bn.
1st Infantry Division
Phu Loi, R.V.N.
28 September, 1967

Dear Family,
I've been in Phu Loi now for a few days and I'll tell you something

about it. It's headquarters for the 1st Infantry Division Artillery, and also stationed here are the 1st Aviation Battalion (Helicopters), 11th Combat Aviation, 1st Squadron/4th Cavalry (Armored), Engineers and Maintenance. It is a large, fortified camp in the southern part of Vietnam, between Saigon and the Cambodian border. This is where the Viet Cong and North Vietnamese regulars cross over to attack government outposts, troops and U.S. outfits. The Big Red One covers from the Cambodian border to the Bien Hoa-Di An Area, just north of the capital. On this camp we are fairly secure and have not been attacked on the ground (I am told) for 8 weeks (?). I heard the last mortar attack caused one killed and ten wounded. There seems to be plenty of protection in case we are attacked: bunkers, barbed wire, and watchtowers around the perimeter. We of the helicopter ground crews all pull guard on the perimeter with rifles every few days. I was told I will stay on the ground crew here until I prove myself good enough to take care of a helicopter as a permanent crew chief/gunner. We have one platoon of attack helicopters called "gunships"—heavily armed with mini-guns, rockets and two M-60 machine-guns. There are also two platoons of "slicks" which are also UH-1 Hueys but used to carry infantry troops, ammunition and supplies armed only with two M-60 machine-guns, one on each side door. It is very difficult to keep all these twenty-four ships flying. Most of the men here have the desire to get the job done. There are a lot of RA volunteers like myself, some of the best young guys I've known. We have to work seven days a week, ten to fifteen hours a day to keep the choppers flying.

I'm getting used to the Vietnamese people. They're everywhere like ants, on and off the base camp but they seem nice on the surface. The villages look like frontier forts out of the Wild West.

I have to go now.
Love,
John

Phu Loi was a big assault helicopter, artillery, and armored cavalry base supporting the American war effort, surrounded by Vietnamese villages. To the soldiers stationed there, it seemed like a dusty shack town of startlingly contrasting sights. Battle-scarred tanks and armored personnel carriers with dirty, exhausted-looking crews clanked and roared past buildings full of rear echelon troops who worked at support jobs almost oblivious to their surroundings. Relatively decent barracks or supply warehouses stood newly built alongside sagging platoon-size tents and makeshift hootch-shacks. The airfield had been built originally by the Japanese during World War II. A maze of dirt roads and tracks swirled up clouds of dust on dry days and became muddy quagmires jammed with stuck 2½- and 5-ton army trucks when the monsoon rains came. Lean, tough-looking scout-recon or infantry troops, ''grunts,'' brushed shoulders with spotless, spit-shined clerks and higher ranking officers. Phu Loi looked the same as Dong Tam for the 9th Division, Cu Chi for the 25th Division, and Lai Khe, Xuan Loc, or any other U.S. base camp. Each day crowds of Vietnamese workers were permitted inside the camp to work at various jobs, including everything from KP duty and filling sandbags to clerks and interpreters.

Just about every Vietnamese I saw seemed to grin at me when I said hello or nodded. For a while, I thought they were being friendly until I later realized they would also grin at a shotup helicopter, a mortar-blasted hootch, or an American casualty. By then what I thought of them didn't matter anymore. I didn't care that their frozen grins weren't really smirks; they were the Vietnamese reaction to the craziness of the mysterious ''American barbarians.''

My first unit was a cross between a combat unit and a rear-support unit, depending on one's job. My own first job was to work on our helicopters, on damage from overwork or enemy fire. The engineers were constructing a hangar, but for now we still did a lot of work out in the open. After having our repair work inspected, we would go up on test flights. The axiom was ''If you won't fly in it, it ain't fixed.'' Sitting in the crew chief's or gunner's seats, I got to really look over the lay of the land in Binh Duong Province and the zone called ''The Iron Triangle'' adjoining Phu Loi to the north. The base camp below appeared as a huge, dusty dirt scar on the land. The cleared defense perimeter, where we stood guard duty with rifles in bunkers at night, looked like a landscape of World War I with its long rolls of concertina barbed wire. Beyond, in every direction, were the rice paddies, jungle, and villages—the real Vietnam that we were here to ''save.''

My squad leader was a Specialist 5, equivalent of Sergeant, and nick-named Smitty. He was in the middle of his second tour in 'Nam and seemed to be on his way towards a ''lifer'' career in the service. He was intense and dedicated to keeping the choppers flying—not a bad guy to work for. He had flown a lot of hours as a crew chief on 1st Division operations. He laughed when I asked him where all the action was.

"You stay around here long enough an' you'll see the elephant, an' you won't like it, either."

At the time, I'd never heard this old army expression for living through close combat. He'd also tell me stories while we worked:

"You shoulda' been here during Operation Junction City or Cedar Falls earlier this year in the Iron Triangle. There was plenty of fighting for anyone. The grunts hitting ambushes, choppers gettin' shot down, and hundreds of casualties. They just cleared out one whole damn area of it around Ben Suc, thousands of people, livestock, chickens, and all. Then the army burned out the villages and plowed or defoliated the area. The amount of bombing gets unbelievable, too. They figure if the people hide or support the VC at all, well, just waste 'em. The crazy thing is, all the villages out there are like that, they all hide the Vietcong. This thing's gonna go on forever."

"Well, don't the Vietnamese know that they're being moved out to safe locations so they won't be caught up in the war or ruled by the Communists?"

"No, hell no, man. See, these villages from Phu Cuong, Tan Phu Khan, An My, and Chanh Long around here, over west to Cu Chi and Trang Bang, twenty miles or so, and north to Ben Suc and Ben Cat, are an old Viet Cong base area called the 'Iron Triangle.' They're full of underground tunnels and bunkers that go back to the Viet Minh and the French war. The more we try to root them out with search and destroy and clearing operations, the more the people listen to the Communists. The Viet Cong are right in there with them all the time. They tell the people every day the Americans are here to conquer the country and keep it as a colony as the French did. It's also the area from which the Viet Cong Phu Loi Battalion's been recruited for years. We've taken over the offensive fighting of the war from the Vietnamese non-Communists, too, the ARVNs. They're not stupid. They'd just as soon lay back and let us fight our way into a Viet Cong base camp instead of them. Besides, there's practically no Americans who can speak their language or even try learning it. Most Americans have no respect for the Vietnamese, and the gooks know it. Even the anti-Communists feel dominated by us. So you can see why I say it's gonna' go on forever."

"Yeah, I'm beginning to see what you mean. It's a lot different than the Korean War."

"It is. There ain't no one front line. The enemy are everywhere, in a VC uniform or out of it. They're right here on this base camp this minute, plotting out ranges and targets for their next mortar attack, and there's nothing we can do about it with the rules we have to fight by.''

I went back to repairing bullet holes in sheet metal and changing rotor-heads. The education I was getting from old hands like Smitty and a few others made me look at all Vietnamese as being potential enemies, or as hypocrites who wouldn't fight for their freedom, or simply as pawns in a big play between the Communists and us. It was the beginning of my loss of illusions about our mission of "saving South Vietnam."

That fall during a break, I saw Smitty holding a stateside magazine and laughing.

"What's so funny?"

"This here, yeah, what a sorry joke. That idiot McNamara, the Secretary of Defense, he's announcing the construction of an electronic-magnetic barrier through the jungle on the borders of South Vietnam to stop the Communist invasion. Millions and millions of dollars! My God, those people are gullible, or insane fools. They have no idea of what's going on over here in these villages under Viet Cong control. And they're the ones who sent us over here to fight. And the 'borders,' thousands of miles of jungles and mountains with North Vietnamese regulars filtering in by the battalion and regiment, with all their weapons and supplies. My God, the Ho Chi Minh trail is half of Laos and half of Cambodia. Oh, Jesus, what's gonna happen with this thing when we've got fools like this for 'leaders'?"

On nights when I had alternating guard duty in bunkers of the outer defense perimeter, I could sit and think. I was already learning something about why the war had gone on so long with so little progress. The policiticans and generals were seeing it one way and the lower echelon working troops another. Staring out past the sandbags between the flares, I could see the dim kerosene lamps of the village of An My in the distance. A whole different world. Vietnamese there looked out at us in this military encampment of foreigners, filled with great machines. I wondered what they thought, who they listened to, and what they believed in.

About the beginning of October, I made my first trip into the big Vietnamese town of Phu Cuong on the Saigon River. It was wide open that autumn before the Tet Offensive. Late one afternoon, carrying my M-16 rifle I rode the four or five kilometers in a ¾-ton truck with my buddy Chuck. We were both out on a pass. We had to drive slowly through the dusty, crowded streets. Hundreds of "ARVNs" in uniform, from the nearby 5th Vietnamese Army Division, women wearing long, flowing Ao Dai dresses, and crowds of children could be seen. Many of the latter were orphans or children of refugees; some of the smaller ones were half-breed American children. When we stopped the truck, a shrieking pack surrounded us, grabbing at our hands and yelling, "Hey GI, you gib me chop-chop? You souvenir me cigarette? You wanna boom-boom my sistah?"

We motioned them away, but they followed relentlessly as we walked along. The population of the town had been swollen by an influx of refugees, some of the thousands of peasants uprooted by search and destroy operations in the Iron Triangle during 1967. They squatted in groups along the walls of building, some holding out their hands, others clutching bundles containing all their worldly possessions. Ox-drawn carts creaked, while Lambretta motor scooters and overloaded trucks roared and clattered by, adding to the screeches of prostitutes in front of shacklike bar-whorehouses. On the corners, young slicked-up Vietnamese "cowboys," often draft dodgers, eyed us like birds of prey. Chuck and I got drunk in one of the shacks and I tried manhandling one of the girls who kept pushing herself all over me while her blank eyes looked right through and beyond me. Chuck was leering.

"See, didn't I tell you this place was good fer a laugh? You wanted to know what the 'Nam was like, man, well here it is. Heh, heh."

I finally got so tired of the whole scene that I wandered out alone to the edge of the town and sat on a muddy dike overlooking the rice paddies. I wondered why we would want to fight with anybody or for anybody over this place. I was to learn that this kind of town existed wherever there was a U.S. military camp. I was also to learn that these big, military-oriented market towns were as different as night and day from the thousands of small rural farming villages like An My.

Back at the base camp the next day, I was detailed to ride as a guard on a truck to Saigon and wrote about it in a letter home:

> *Phu Loi, R.V.N.*
> *9 Oct., 1967*

Dear Family,

Well, I rode shotgun on a truck on a convoy to get some helicopter parts at Tan San Nhut airbase, outside of Saigon. We had to spend two extra days and a night there because the Viet Cong started ambushing trucks on Highway 13, called Thunder Road, but it was worth it because

I got to spend all that time in the "Paris of the Orient." All the Americans stationed in and around Saigon live like kings, compared to the rest of the GIs. We did steal a brand new generator from the Air Force when nobody was looking. The company needs them, so the First Sergeant didn't mind us being gone for this time.

Saigon still has a large, French-type quarter with a beautiful Catholic cathedral and palaces. I also went through the Chinese quarter of Cholon and all the rest. The women wear long, flowing silk or cotton dresses called Ao Dais, and many of them are beautiful. Some are part French.

The guy I was with, Simmonds or Symonds or whatever, has been here over two years and sure knows his way around. He is married to a Vietnamese, which is unthinkable to a lot of the guys here. He owns a house in Saigon, speaks the language, and is planning to stay here permanently. It was sad to me being in his house and hearing the way he has rejected our way of life and doesn't want to go home; a real interesting person, though.

There was another big enemy attack at a place sixteen miles north of Phu Loi last night. Our choppers all scrambled to try and help them. The guys who went said it was pretty rough. When I was on guard on the perimeter wire two nights ago, we saw green enemy tracer bullets shooting up at one of our choppers. The Division artillery opened fire and cleaned them out.

I'm sending you a picture of the chopper I work on. You can see the six barrelled gatling or mini-gun, 4,000 rpm, pointing down, the rocket pods pointing forward, and the M-60 machine-gun in the door. The gunship platoon is all like this and called "the Rebels." They only fly when scrambled by the Division during operations or enemy attacks in our own AO. Our other two flight platoons of "slicks" that carry troops, ammo, or supplies into action are: first, the "Champagnes" and second, "the Commancheros."

Our company name is the "Bulldogs," and we have for a mascot a real old, ill-mannered bulldog. That's about all the news, I guess.

Love,

John

Simmonds was the American who was to have the greatest influence on my understanding of the Vietnamese and the U.S. conduct of the war. He had been in the country since the big American buildup in '65 and had become Vietnamized to a rare degree. He was a tall, fair-haired, intelligent person, something of a philosopher. It was unusual to meet any American who actually spoke fluent Vietnamese, let alone who had married into the community, owned a home, and beyond that, still was a member of an army helicopter company. After I had known Simmonds and learned from him and a few other old hands for several months, I ended up in a combat infantry unit, but my opinions were already formed. Subsequent combat experiences only hardened these opinions.

During the trip south and on the first day in Saigon, Simmonds was quiet and let me form my own view of the city. Stealing the generator had been easy at the huge Tan San Nhut airbase while we were requisitioning helicopter parts. It was just a matter of quickly grabbing and loading the crated thing while the supply sergeant was away getting us a few last items on our list. Up country away from the big parts depots, generators became as valuable as gold for emergency power or as trading material. As we started north toward Lai Thieu on Thunder Road, we were stopped suddenly in a cloud of dust by an MP gun jeep. Two troopers approached wearing heavy flak jackets and carrying M-16s like us.

"Ya can't go on right now. There's been an ambush by the gooks up the road. Yer gonna' hafta wait 'til the damned VC settle down again."

I looked over at Simmonds wondering what we were going to do. I could have sworn he was almost smiling.

"I guess we'll have to go and stay at my house. I'll be glad to be with my wife for a while anyway."

I was astonished.

"You've got...a wife, over here?"

"Yeah, my wife is Vietnamese, we have a home here, and I'm going to stay here when I get out of the service. I don't want to go back to America. It's crazy back there. They really don't know anything about the real meaning of life, the things that truly matter."

I sat in the shotgun seat thinking about the implications of what he'd said. It was the very opposite of those radicals back home who believed no Americans should be here at all, even for a short time to assist the Vietnamese in defeating this Communist insurrection. Here was an American who had come as part of the military assistance and gotten so enamoured of the country that he married and planned to remain here! He was the opposite of so many other GIs I'd met who could only talk about how "short" they were, how many days they had left until they could get out of this "hell hole."

We turned the truck around and headed back south into the teeming center of Saigon, a gigantic, spread-out version of Phu Cuong. Grinding our way through the mass of vehicles, carts, and bicycles, past crowds of Vietnamese and Americans, I could feel the vitality of a war-inflated economy. The bars with their prostitutes, the "cowboys," and off-duty servicemen were apparently numberless—all spending money chasing the same pleasures and services.

Simmond's large, two-story stucco house was like an oasis of calm. His wife welcomed him in Vietnamese, along with several young children and other relatives, apparently his wife's family. She politely made me welcome in Vietnamese, as did other members of the family. I tried to settle unobtrusively in a corner and watched this domestic scene. It was my first up-close view of the Vietnamese in their own homes. They were not shrill and demanding with each other as the Vietnamese I had observed in Phu Cuong and Phu Loi. After a dinner of rice, vegetables, and fish, I asked a few questions of Simmonds and his wife.

"Why do the Vietcong guerillas keep fighting so long and so hard?"

He translated my question for her and they talked together a little longer in Vietnamese before he answered me.

"Probably the main reason is that about 75 percent of the peasant farmers of the entire country are landless sharecroppers. That's most of the population, in fact. They live and work on land that belongs to absentee owners and are forced to pay half or more of a whole year's crop just for the right to work. It has been going on so long that they are ready and willing to believe the promises by the Viet Cong that the Communists will give them land. Anyone will fight for land if they've had nothing and have been poor long enough."

I asked, "Well, why don't they work within the governmental system already here and change things?"

"They've given up believing in government promises because they're never kept. When Diem was president he made a big announcement of land reform, but the number of people who actually got an acre each was pitiful, almost nothing, after years and years of talk."

Simmonds and his wife talked again in Vietnamese before he went on.

"After the French left, over a million people came down from North Vietnam to get away from the Communists, and they had to be fitted in somewhere. After that happened, the peasants in the South really didn't know what came of the Communist's promises in Hanoi. The fact that Ho Chi Minh's party forced most of the peasants onto collective farms instead of giving them their own land and shot those who objected was unknown to the peasants here in the South. The farmers of North Vietnam still give up half of everything they produce, except that now, it's to the "state" instead of to one landowner. When the Viet Cong started to agitate in 1960, the rice paddy villagers believed these same promises of land and justice; the only thing they had for comparison was their treatment as nobodys under the Diem dictatorship. I think that's what has kept the Viet Cong going, although now the North is also sending thousands of regular troops down here to reinforce the Viet Cong.

"Well, how do they survive against both the Americans and the ARVN?"

I got the same answer that I'd gotten from Smitty: "The village and hamlet peasants protect them, support them, and hide them if they have to. Even if the peasants don't believe the Communist promises, Viet Cong terror is so effective that they control most of the villages. Every year, the Viet Cong assassinate thousands of village chiefs and officials who support the Saigon government. They also murder any peasant who betrays their military movements to us or the ARVNs. It's almost totally effective because the ARVN army is simply not big enough to control every hamlet or village.

"In most places it has gotten to the point that the only village chiefs left have been corrupted by the Viet Cong, or are scared of them and are totally under their orders. If not, they are so bad to the people that the Viet Cong leave them alone to reinforce their propaganda about 'the corrupt lackeys of the Americans who run Saigon.' The Viet Cong also try to increase the division between the Catholics and the Buddhists, even though as Communists, they are supposed to be against all religions. Most of the government leaders are Catholic, so they try any way they can to stir up the Buddhists to disobedience or violence, even encouraging them to burn themselves alive."

I leaned back in the bamboo chair thinking, "There's no end to all this for us unless we force reform of everything on the Saigon government. It sounds so impossibly complex, I can't believe we're in the middle of a war here."

We talked late into the night about Vietnamese customs, the Chinese population of merchants and traders in Cholon, and the ways Americans were making mistakes in most of their dealings with the people of the country. All the next day I was exposed to the concentrated knowledge of Simmonds about Vietnam. On the road to Phu Loi, I reflected on the waste it was to the army and Vietnam that he was stuck in a supply job in an aviation battalion. He could have contributed more to the understanding between Americans and Vietnamese and to the will to win the war against the Communists than most field-grade officers. It was additional insight for me as to why and how things weren't going right. During the next year I was to hear many of the same ideas from other soliders, advisors, and civil action members who worked in the villages. I eventually saw the results first hand, but like a few other curious and interested American soldiers, I learned a lot early, and most of it was from old hands like Smitty, Simmonds, and others.

On the 13th of October, 1967 I came under enemy fire for the first time. As they usually were, at that stage of the war, it was a night attack. When the Viet Cong mortar shells began to explode, *Carump! Carump! Carump!* with flashes and shrapnel zinging around our hootches, I rolled out of my rack, hit the deck and started scrabbling towards the door. "So, here's the war!" I thought. A string of three or four came in close.

"*SSSSh—Boom! Boom! Boom!*"

Somebody yelled, "Incoming!"

A siren went off, sounding an attack alert, and we ran for the bunkers. The 1st Division Artillery returned fire at the suspected firing positions. Each round was a loud *"Crack-Boom—Zzzzzzzzzzzz"* overhead, followed by far off muffled, *"Wumps!"* We crouched under the dark, damp sandbags muttering, "We don't need no direct hits now." We heard later of guys hit by shrapnel, but that time I didn't see any casualties myself. All it did was give me a little quick fear for a minute and remind me there was definitely an enemy waiting out there. After a while the siren blew an all-clear signal and we climbed out. Here and there were small craters from the explosions, metal splinter holes in the buildings, and pieces of shrapnel or tailfins lying around. I finally knew what "mortars" meant, but still not how bad they could be. We took a lot of trouble to protect the helicopters and our ammo dump with sandbagged revetments and checked everything after any attack.

The enemy kept up mortar attacks on the main base camps, and ambushes of troops in an attempt to control the nights. At this stage of the war the 1st Infantry Division was still into large-scale "search and destroy operations." These sometimes involved thousands of troops surrounding and assaulting old enemy hide-outs over a wide area. Some of their base camps in the wild areas dated back to the war with the French and the days of the Viet Minh.

Co. A, 1st Avn. Bn.
Phu Loi, R.V.N.
19 October 1967

Dear Mom and Dad,
  Now that the rainy season is over, the division is moving out after the enemy some more. Two days ago, on "Operation Shennandoah," the Viet Cong 272nd or 273rd Regiment, reinforced with NVA ambushed our troops. The usual tactics of the Americans are to make contact, maul them, then pull back fast and crush them with artillery and airpower. This time, though, the enemy refused to break contact and followed our troops every step. There were intermingled and we couldn't use enough airpower. Our company's choppers were flying overhead throughout the whole thing, but couldn't do much to help. One of our company's helicopters got shot down and a group of several infantry battalions lost a battalion commander, Colonel Allen, killed two company commanders, and about 125 troops killed and wounded.
  Last night about eleven o'clock out in a watchtower on our perimeter, I sat on guard duty and thought—on the one hand you have us, the Americans sitting in forts after some 100,000 U.S. soldiers killed and wounded, still unable to safely walk 50 yards beyond our perimeter. And a few hundred yards further out, where the flares are going off, there are the enemy guerillas biding their time, as they have for years. They own the night and the day, too, if half the country. The ultimate irony to me is that late at night you can hear a Psy-ops plane drone by overhead, garbled Vietnamese words streaming out behind it. A loudspeaker is blaring a tape recording to the Viet Cong, "Surrender, lay down your arms," etc. The trouble is with the noise and aircraft vibration, the tape sounds like a broken record player. Like everything else about this war, it's real hard to understand. The enemy must laugh. As for me there is nothing to really worry about.

Love,
John

  This was the first time I'd heard the names of the enemy regiments that were part of the 9th Viet Cong Division. Originally recruited locally, they were now being reinforced by infiltration of North Vietnamese regulars down the Ho Chi Minh Trail. I was to hear the name of one again, 273rd Regiment, and eventually would see them face to face.

About this time, the news media were trumpeting the first public draft-card burning by students in Boston. The magazines we got also reported large antiwar demonstrations back home and a protest march by thousands on the Pentagon. My father wrote me angry letters complaining about the protests and about the actions of Bishops of our own diocese in Pennsylvania who encouraged the burning of draft cards and refusal to serve in the war. In response, I wrote a letter to the Governor of Pennsylvania that was signed by many of the men in my company and published in the newspapers back home. It defended our service in Vietnam and "protested the attempted Communist takeover of South Vietnam." This caused an uproar in my battalion, but it was smoothed out when Major-General John Hay, the 1st Division Commander, lent his verbal and written support to my political activism. The incident was unusual for the Army and reflected just how political the war was becoming, both at home and in the service.

I had already made a few flights as a gunner on choppers to Ben Cat, Lai Khe, and Quan Loi. Now, after a month or more of hoping, I tried to get a full-time gunner's or crew chief's job. After going over my medical records, the battalion surgeon informed me that my vision would not permit a permanent assignment in one of those positions. I was bitter and disappointed over his decision, but I was told I could fly as a standby gunner if a replacement was needed for someone wounded, sick, or worn-out from long hours. I got my first chance to fly during a period of intense activity at the end of October and early November of '67. The NVA had crossed the Cambodian border around Song Be-Phuoc Binh and Loc Ninh. It was on the "slicks" for me, hauling ammo and supplies or troops. It was the first time I felt as though I was really doing something.

The only warning I'd get would be, "Hey, Brown, ya wanna go out fer me today? It's just a milk run."

"Yeah, yer damn right I do—if Smitty will let me go."

"Well, O.K., we're all right here today, you can go."

I'd run to the Commanchero or Champagne hootch and tell the gunner, and he'd go with me to pick up the M-60 aircraft machine-gun for hanging on the mount. The pilots would come, young warrant officers mostly, a couple of years older than us. We addressed them as "Mister" instead of "Sir." One of them would eyeball me for a second, sitting behind the gun:

"Ya know how to handle that thing if we hit some fire?"

"Oh yeah, Mister. I shot expert on an M-60. I can handle it O.K."

A trust always developed between the pilots and gunners; any new person in a chopper created a question mark. We'd put on the air crew helmets and test our radio communications inside the aircraft before taking off. Then the pilot put the power to the rotor head; a storm of dust swirled up inside the sandbag revetment and up we'd go. I craved the free feeling of leaving the base camp to head out over the intense green of the rice paddies and jungle. We never knew when or where we might receive enemy fire. Sometimes it might be just a few random tracers arcing up at us, slowly below, then suddenly whizzing by.

"D'you see that! You gunners mark that spot, keep yer eyes on it!"

I'd swing the gun around but usually that's all it would be before we were far past it with no chance to open fire and hit them. Hoping for a lucky hit, the Viet Cong kept their bursts short. This reduced our chances of getting an accurate fix on their position and bringing in a heavy airstrike on them. We'd sometimes stop at Lai Khe or Quan Loi before going to the "NDPs" in the field to bring in whatever we were hauling and take out people. Most casualties were carried by the special medevac or "dust-off" choppers, but sometimes regular slicks like ours would fill in. In the NDPs, or firebases, which looked like dirty anthills from the air, the infantry would crowd around the chopper for supplies, mail, or news. The faces of these grunts were haunting. Always tired or gaunt-looking, with eyes that were different, that said, "I've seen plenty, man, I've seen it all."

A few times we came under long enough bursts of enemy fire for me to get a fix on their position and shoot back. I'd fire off a 50- or 100-round belt into the jungle below, adjusting my aim by the tracers. I never knew if I killed any enemy from the choppers—it was too fast and far away, but plenty of gunners in the company got "confirmed kills." Most of the action was in the Rebel gunship platoon and they never had any shortage of gunners willing to go. This was the elite, high-morale platoon of the company. About this time we heard reports that about 400 GIs had been killed and wounded around Loc Ninh and Song Be and 1,000 NVA had been killed in the fighting. We also heard rumors of other heavy fighting involving the 4th Division and the 173rd Airborne further north along the Cambodian border near Dak To. Later, when I ended up out in the jungle as a grunt myself, I discovered that people in the base camps usually heard far more information and statistics about overall operations than men on the scene in the field.

Phu Loi, R.V.N.
10 Nov. '67

Dear Mom and Dad,

Well, I was out on the perimeter last night and we had another enemy mortar attack on the base camp. It wasn't too bad; we had only two GIs killed and seven WIA in Phu Loi. We also had sniper fire coming in at us on the perimeter where I was in a bunker. One round hit about 6 inches from where we were behind sandbags. We fired a few M-79 40mm grenades and bursts from our M-16s and ran them off. I don't think I hit anybody. I'm still not doing as much flying as I'd like to, but I was on two resupply flights near Loc Ninh and Quan Loi a week ago as a door gunner and came under fire. There was a big battle going on around there; a lot of GIs were killed and wounded. Not much more news.

Thanks for the letters from everyone,

Love,
John.

I was generally working long hours on the choppers amid the constant smell of oil and JP-4 jet fuel, changing rotor heads or engines and fixing bullet damage. Most of the time I was bored; I pulled a lot of all-night perimeter guard duty and every so often dodged enemy mortar shells.

Late one night, while drinking beer as usual with a friend named Stone, I mentioned that a lot of the dudes in the company looked "stoned" every night.

Stone took a long look at me and said, "Well, hey, my man, I guess we can trust you now. It's about time!"

He shuffled outside, beer in hand and led the way out beyond the company hootches, tents, and bunkers to an empty field. All around us in the dark I could see little groups of GIs spread out in all directions. There were ground crews, crew chiefs, gunners, and visitors from other companies. A sweet unmistakable odor was in the air and I smiled and sat down with Stone's group. They turned me on to some weed I'd never dreamed of before: Cambodian Red. As the pipe went around and around, I just took off. The occasional pop and burst of flares in the night sky beyond the perimeter only added a light show. The boom of outgoing shells from the division artillery was like a weird black rumble. I had discovered another of the secrets of Vietnam. Over the next year, I was to learn that the use of "dinky-dau smoke" had spread to every unit in the service I came into contact with. It eventually involved most of the men I knew there. The really religious or southern crackers sometimes resisted it the longest, but loneliness, danger, and fear usually won out. The cut-off feeling which became more and more evident as the American population became opposed to the War increased its use. So did the availability of such large, cheap quantities through the Vietnamese people.

There was one thing every dude in Vietnam had to learn, however. That was when to get mellow and when to stay cool. I was lucky to learn this inside a base camp before going into an infantry platoon. It was late one night; I was in a mellow state of mind with a buddy, sitting behind a hootch. We were just getting into the warm tropic night and sailing when detonations were suddenly going off really close. Loud *Carumps! Booms!* and orange flashes with white shrapnel streaks shooting out of them all around us. Another Viet Cong mortar attack! In my condition, the fact that those people out there were trying to kill me hit home like never before. GIs were yelling and running, and sirens were wailing again. Our division artillery was firing their cannons over our heads. And we just sat there staring, our mouths hanging open, unmoving, "our minds blown" in the truest sense of the words. Then and there I began to develop the surviving combat soldier's safety-instinct of knowing when to get laid back and when not to. Later, in the jungle, it gradually became a sixth sense. "Naw, man, not now, huh? There's gooks around."

Late at night with the flying or the repair work done, I'd shuffle over to the Rebel or Commanchero hootch and sit around listening to the jungle tales of the gunners. Unlike the crew chiefs, they were mostly ex-grunts from infantry or recon units who had voluntarily extended their time in Vietnam to get out of the field into a better job.

"Yeah, well, Brown, you've gotten in a little flyin' time now, but it ain't nothin' like bein' out in the boonies. We come back ta nice hootches every night. We ain't livin' in no slimy mudhole in the jungle with gooks crawlin' around in the dark, huh? Hey, six months ago, in April, I was in the 1st of the 26th under Colonel Haig on Operation Junction City. We had a whole regiment of VC pull a ground attack on us. It was close, man; I mean, those howlin' gooks overran our perimeter and we was blastin' 'em point blank. That went on like three hours straight an' we had a body count of hundreds."

Another gunner who'd been lying on his rack staring at the ceiling sat up now, "Uh huh, yeah, I remember that son-of-a-bitch, man. I was in the 1st of the 16th on that operation, man. We got in on some of that too, but most of the time it's just the jungle, the weird noises, the goddamn bugs, and snakes, and spiders. The thing I hated was how you never know where you are or where yer goin'. It's like bein' lost in the middle of Africa a hundred years ago.

"This place here, Phu Loi, it's jus' like bein' back in the U.S. of A. compared to steppin' out through that perimeter wire. Soon as you hump about two hundred meters outta this base camp, man, yer in the 'Nam! You got mud, you got bamboo, you got rotten jungle, you got rice paddies, an' you got gooks. Gooks in their villages lookin' at you like yer a piece of dirt, gooks sneakin' around in the jungle settin' up booby traps, or settin' up a goddamn ambush in the dark. You got big gooks, little gooks, smart ones, and dumb ones but you better figure every damned one wants to blow you away!"

On the war stories would go, full of advice, hidden meanings, and lessons. When I got tired enough, I'd slip on out and go back to my rack.

"Damn, I feel like a cherry. I gotta get outta here an' see what it's like in the boonies. If I don't see that, then I ain't seen nothin' over here."

Christmas came.

> *Bob Hope Show*
> *Lai Khe, 25-26 Dec.*

Dear Family,

Thanks a lot for the Christmas presents. They were great. Yesterday I went up Thunder Road on a guarded truck convoy to see the Bob Hope-USO Christmas show. It was really a good time and very moving. One of the girls started crying while she was singing "Silent Night" to us and got interrupted by a barrage of artillery going off nearby. If you see pictures of it I'll be sitting just to the left of two tanks with "Merry Christmas" painted on them. I spent Christmas Eve guarding our ammo bunkers because the "truce" over here is a joke. The Viet Cong use it to step up their mortar attacks, terrorism, ambushes, etc. During the first hour of the "truce" one of our company's helicopters was shot down and the pilot and one of the gunners, a friend of mine named David Bell from Pennsylvania, are wounded in the hospital at Lai Khe. I visited Bell. He was hit by a Chinese .51 caliber machine-gun bullet but he's going to be okay.

Other than that, things are pretty slow around here and there's not much else to write about.

I hope you all had a nice Christmas.
                                        Love,
                                        John.

The year 1967 came to a close as I was getting broken in and beginning to be Vietnamized. I'd been under enemy fire and seen some shooting and casualties, but was still naive and heading for trouble.

At the same time, at home in America the antiwar feeling was spreading. At the Ivy League colleges and big universities the student movement was growing and their disaffection was percolating back home to many middle class families. Liberal faculty members were speaking out against America's involvement, along with influential clergymen, actors, and celebrities. Many of the more radical students and professors openly admired the Viet Cong guerillas. "Doves" in Congress, such as Wayne Morse and William Fulbright, added legitimacy to the antiwar movement and contributed to the uneasiness among soldiers, a feeling that our country would never go all the way to win a victory. This attitude prompted a question heard frequently in the Army, "If they don't want us to win, why the hell are we over here?"

During 1967, 9,378 Americans were killed and 60,000 wounded in Vietnam.

4   The Tet Offensive

*"We are easy riders to the fields of grace,
A bomb shell in the gut.*
— Richard Eberhart

Early in January 1968, one of the gunners told me about the combat recon platoon of Phu Loi.

"Hey, Brown, if you wanna see what the boonies are like, there's a recon platoon over on the east side of the perimeter. You oughta volunteer for it, man." I asked around and found out it was a non-T.O. & E. "wartime-expediency unit" under operational control of the 2nd Brigade, 1st Infantry Division, S-2 or G-2 (intelligence). It operated as an infantry recon platoon on ambush and scout patrols in the jungles, rice paddies, and hamlets of Binh Duong province surrounding Phu Loi. It sounded like a better place for me, and I requested a transfer. My company already had one man named Quinn serving in the recon platoon, so they scheduled me for transfer when his time was up. I continued to work on the choppers, occasionally flying as a standby gunner, and waited.

Through January of 1968, the Viet Cong began moving troops south from hideouts on the border, in the Iron Triangle, and along the Song Be River to the northeast of us. They converged on the area around Saigon being protected by the 1st, 9th, and 25th Infantry Divisions. Our 1st Division base camps of Phu Loi, Lai Khe, and Quan Loi came under increasing mortar and 122mm Soviet rocket attacks. This was the enemy buildup for the coming Tet Offensive. Although we didn't know what they were planning, it became obvious that something big was coming, because of the increasing number of alerts and warnings by our commanders.

In one attack in the dark before dawn on the 6th of January, I was guarding our ammo bunkers with my rifle. This huge mass of aircraft rockets and machine-gun ammo was a prime target. When the VC shells started exploding around me, all I could do was crouch down and pray. *SSSSShh Wham! SSSSShhh Wham! Boom! Boom! Boom!* Each explosion blew out a shower of shrapnel and sparks. From where I lay, I could see them steadily hitting closer to me and helicopters getting hit.

"God, lemme outta here an' I won't ever guard no ammo dump again, I promise."

I prayed and sweated until the shells and rockets finally stopped coming. When it was over, I stood up shaking. One 6½ foot long rocket, a dud, was rammed into some sandbags not 15 feet from me. I could see guys from the company running towards me to check the choppers in their revetments. Several had been hit, and a total 46 aircraft in Phu Loi were damaged or destroyed. There were U.S. casualties, too, from the 125 incoming shells. All I could think of was how thankful I was that not a single live one had hit that ammo dump. Later that morning, ARVN patrols operating out of their nearby base camp found the Viet Cong firing positions and made contact with the enemy Phu Loi Battalion. U.S. troops, including the 2nd/2nd Infantry also got into combat nearby, with eighteen killed and wounded. On the 8th of January, Ben Cat and Lai Khe came under fire. Shortly after this, reports came of a major Viet Cong attack about 20 miles west of Phu Loi in adjoining Hau Nghia Province. They had overrun and captured the provincial capital town of Khiem Cuong (or Bao Trai). It was a propaganda victory for them just to hold a government town briefly, and it was also a warning to us.

Other enemy shelling attacks on Phu Loi came on the 12th and 13th, and the 22nd and 23rd, and probably others that I have forgotten. The VC strategy was to damage or destroy as many helicopters as possible in preparation for an all-out offensive. The mortar and rocket-launching positions were north of our base camp in half-wild bush country between the villages of An My and Chanh Long (called "Dog Leg" by the grunts). Sometimes out in perimeter bunkers, we could see the flashes of firing in the dark, at other times they would be pinpointed by radar, and our division artillery would return fire on them. It was obvious that the villagers we were supposed to be defending from the Communists were in on these attacks. Seven or eight miles to the northeast of our base camp, the Viet Cong also attacked and overran the town of Tan

Uyen on the Dong Nai River. They only held it briefly, as they had at Khiem Cuong. While in control of Tan Uyen, they burned and destroyed 110 homes and publicly executed some government supporters. Such demonstrations of power sent signals to the Vietnamese for miles around that the revolutionaries were still strong and capable of attacking or taking vengeance anywhere, anytime. The action was picking up all over Vietnam and went practically unnoticed by the news media, now almost totally preoccupied with Khe Sanh and the beseiged Marines there.

On the 23rd of January, North Korean patrol boats captured the *USS Pueblo,* an intelligence ship, and imprisoned its crew. President Johnson put the armed forces on alert and called up some reserves. Even where we were, tension increased. Many felt that it was part of a plan coordinated with a Viet Cong offensive in Vietnam. The day before the *Pueblo* incident, an intelligence estimate had reported, "Two Viet Cong mainforce units with rockets, mortars, RPGs, machine-guns, and automatic weapons planning to attack Phu Loi on the ground to disrupt the entire 1st Infantry Division operations with aircraft destruction. Regimental or larger size ground assault is highly probable along with rockets and mortars between 22 Jan. and 2 Feb., 1968."

The Phu Loi Base, at coordinates XT 8615, was put on high alert. We pulled guard on the outer perimeter twice as often, and I pulled even more because I had volunteered and was heading for an infantry unit. My first sergeant probably thought I was insane. As the situation became more real and serious, I started paying closer attention to my M-16 rifle, web gear, ammo, and equipment. We lined up for inspection before going into the perimeter bunkers, and they began checking our weapons and ammo to make sure we were ready. The perimeter guards gradually became a little dustier, more tired but more alert.

Phu Loi, R.V.N.
(?) Jan. 1968

Dear Family,

Nothing much to say. I got Joan's letter today and Ma's and the tape recorder a few days ago.

We had another enemy mortar and rocket attack last night. It started at midnight and lasted about half an hour. A lot of shells. We've been having a lot of them lately. We had seven men wounded in our own company, most slightly. I don't know how many other casualties happened in Phu Loi. We lost four of our own helicopters damaged by shrapnel and disabled for a while. Our fueling truck was also hit, and there was numerous other minor damage. The 1st Squad/4th Cavalry across the strip from us had eleven of their choppers hit. Their armored tracks and tanks are out in the field most of the time. The enemy fire was extremely accurate and aimed almost entirely at helicopters (although they hit other things). The VC hate helicopters. The tail fins blown clear of the mortar shells showed that some of their ammunition was American-made and the rest Russian or Chinese, including some 122mm rockets. There are more attack warnings now, so I'm pulling a lot of guard in bunkers on the perimeter.

This place is a blank compared to the rest of the world. It's starting to affect me strangely. I've lost interest in girls, history, music, or whatever. I see-saw back and forth between worrying and trying to point to something good about this mess, or times of not caring about or noticing anything. It's not that I have it bad, or anything. It's just that there is so much here that's false, useless or dishonest, both in our army and the "Republic of Vietnam."

I'll see you in a while,

Love,
John

I'd been reading news reports of the "progress campaign" by Johnson and his cabinet officers throughout the late fall of '67. The government was doing everything it could to counter the increasing criticism of the war. This included claims that "67 percent of the Vietnamese population was living securely under government control" and only 17 percent of the people were "controlled by the Viet Cong." Even low-ranking soldiers on the scene couldn't believe this kind of propaganda. If enemy ground action or shelling attacks came out of villages immediately adjacent to American and ARVN Bases in the most heavily controlled areas, how could figures like that be believable? What about the vast areas I'd flown over where there were practically no American troops and the ARVNs were only secure in and around their little militia forts? Even then I could sense the pressure being put on our military leaders by the politicians to sound optimistic. General Westmoreland had been called back to Washington to report that "the enemy is losing" and that he thought it might be "possible to begin withdrawing U.S. troops in two years" (or late 1969). Although this is what eventually happened, I knew that two years more of what had been going on for three years or more wasn't going to make much difference. We were only coming up against the protective front line of a whole segment of the population. I couldn't see the sense in not carrying the full power of our military into North Vietnam if we were indeed committed to forcing them out of South Vietnam's civil war, cutting off all reinforcements and supplies. While I had my own ideas about what was wrong, I still felt as though we could win eventually.

One of the things that bothered me most was a widespread cynicism among rear-support troops and officers. There was an undercurrent expressed in remarks or jokes about "gettin' all the bennies" (benefits, easy duty, comfortable quarters, clubs with beer and jukeboxes). Instead of admiration or respect, the grunts who were actually fighting the Viet Cong out in the bush were the butt of constant scorn or abuse. As if they didn't care about the cases of beer and Coke that were stolen by club NCOs for profit before they could be sent out to the field. This was another facet of a war being fought as a limited holding action rather than a serious struggle for victory and survival. It created a mood with the objective of getting through one's time with a minimum of discomfort or sacrifice, and "to hell with the fools out there humping a rifle in the jungle." The growing antiwar movement at home only lent weight to the selfishness in the rear and the feeling of uselessness and despair out on the fighting lines.

On the evening of the 31st of January, I was on perimeter guard duty again. We lined up for the Officer of the Day to check us out after chow. We had already heard reports of a Viet Cong attack on the U.S. Embassy in Saigon and against the Bien Hoa and Tan San Nhut airbases. Other attacks were occuring further north at Da Nang, Hoi An, Pleiku, Kontum, Qui Nhon, Ban Me Thout, Nha Trang, and Dak To. With so much going on at once, we were expecting trouble in Phu Loi. The word was out that the "truce" declared for the Tet Lunar New Year celebration had already been cancelled. We stood in the stifling, dusty heat waiting the OD and gave our weapons a last once-over. A couple of guys had M-60 machine-guns, some had M-79 grenade launchers, and the rest, like myself, had M-16 rifles. We cursed and grumbled to each other as we waited.

"Son-of-a-bitch is probably havin' himself a nice suck of whiskey or somethin', huh?"

Finally, the man was there to give us the once-over, and we jumped up into the deuce and halves—the 2½-ton army trucks. The last thing we heard was, "All right, you men, you look sharp and stay awake. There's gooks out there for real tonight! There's fighting going on all over Saigon and the VC are attacking Tan San Nhut, Bien Hoa, and all over the Mekong Delta. We have reports of at least two enemy battalions coming toward Phu Loi." We moved out in a roaring cloud of dust and finally reached the perimeter, where I was dumped off at a sandbag bunker with two other guys opposite the village of An My.

Meanwhile, the 1st Division, reacting to the threat of attack, was moving HQs and Companies C and D of the 1st/28th Infantry, the Black Lions, inside the Phu Loi perimeter. Part of the armored forces of the 1st/4th Cavalry were in, too. In our bunker, with a PRC-25 radio for communication, we took turns watching for enemy movement. The bunker had a back room area sectioned off by a sandbag wall and a front defense position with slits and a firing step. From radio transmissions, my own recollections, and later research, the next thirty-six hours went like this:

At 22:05 on the night of 31st (10:05 p.m.), the Phu Loi Combat Recon patrol spotted a dozen or more enemy, and an hour later LRRPS spotted more than a hundred enemy with weapons, approaching An My and Phu Loi from the north. They called in artillery fire on the Viet Cong and retreated into the perimeter. The big guns opening fire behind us and over us was enough to keep me wide awake.

For the next two hours, I waited for something to happen, and at midnight our perimeter came under small arms and automatic weapons fire. The green tracers came flying in at us and bullets began popping, thudding, and ricocheting into and around the bunker. Next came some *whoosh-crack-booms* of RPGs or rockets and the flashes lit up the area around us. Whoever I was with was saying, "Hey man, something big's comin' down!" I fired a few bursts from my rifle into the enemy tracers. Firing felt good, the empty shells spewing out, the rifle warm.

The dude next to me was yelling, "Wait, man! They'll give us a whole bunch of hell for firing without permission!"

I turned to him and said, "Fuck 'em. Those're real gooks out there!"

Just after that the HQ called on the radio to say that the base camp was on the highest alert; I told them we were receiving and returning enemy fire. Sniper rounds and occasional bursts of automatic fire kept coming in until almost 2 a.m. on the 1st of February. Suddenly heavy machine-gun fire opened up from bunkers 3 and 4. They had spotted and shot into a group of a half dozen or more Viet Cong advancing towards them. About this time, twenty other Viet Cong were spotted moving towards our bunker line between An My and Phu Loi. In our bunker we kept taking incoming rounds, and several times I spotted movement out in front.

"My God! Those are Viet Cong out there!"

I opened fire in the wierd, surreal light of flares. Because of clumps of bushes and uneven ground, it was hard to tell whether I was hitting them. At 2:05 a.m. a helicopter overhead spotted seventy-five more heavily-armed enemy lying face down to avoid being seen, and called in artillery and airstrikes on them. All around us, the night was erupting with the artillery's high explosive shells, the firing machine-guns and rockets of the gunships, and the enemy tracers flying every which way.

Meanwhile, we were still under sniper fire in our bunker and about 5 a.m. came under more RPG explosions, cracking blue-white blasts. We had no idea what was happening other than that the enemy was out there. I could see scuttling movement out in front in the light from flares, and I fired bursts as accurately as I could. Other bunkers were returning fire down the line, and rocket or RPG explosions mixed with bursts of AK-47 fire, which went on until at least seven in the morning. At the same time, Tan Phu Khan outpost was under a ground assault from a VC company, and the town of Phu Cuong received incoming rockets and a ground attack, also. At about 7:30 in the morning, the 1st/4th Cavalry and Charlie Company of the 1st/28th moved out through the wire near our bunker towards An My. They found blood trails and equipment in front of our bunkers, where enemy bodies had been dragged off. A little later, Delta company of the 1st/28th advanced outside the wire and found two dead enemy soldiers and an AK-47. They moved towards Tan Phu Khan as the 1/4 Cav and Charlie Company of the 1/28 moved towards An My. From our bunker, I saw the force moving towards An My suddenly come under a long ripping roar of enemy fire. They had run into a whole battalion of VC/NVA that had pulled back into the village and dug in. The volume of fire swelled to an incredible pitch from the automatic weapons, combined with tank guns, artillery, and enemy RPGs and rockets.

The company headquarters called us on the PRC-25 in the middle of this battle and told us we would not be relieved from the bunkers but would remain in position, and that the battalion and company CPs were conducting operations from bunkers themselves. All our helicopter light fire teams were off the ground and in contact with the enemy.

Infantry recon and cavalry were pulling back from the enemy position at An My and calling in concentrated artillery fire and air support on the Viet Cong. The aerial rifle platoon of the 1/4 Cav's D Troop and four self-propelled 40mm automatic duster-guns of the 5th Battalion /2nd Artillery were sent out from our perimeter to reinforce them. Tac Air was screaming in overhead; jet fighter bombers dropped bombs and cannisters of napalm, the ground shaking from the explosions. Delta Company of the 1st/28th was also diverted from Tan Phu Khan to reinforce the An My fighting, along with the Phu Loi Combat Recon platoon that I was to join.

After a tremedous barrage of artillery and airstrikes, that caused heavy casualties on the VC/NVA, the combined American forces advanced again towards An My under heavy enemy fire. I stared out at the exploding horror of it, wondering to myself what I was heading for in the recon platoon engaged in the battle in front of me. The enemy were refusing to retreat, fighting from buildings, bunkers, and holes, destroying one APC and damaging several more. Secondary explosions blew up behind the enemy line from their ammo dumps being hit. The 1st Division Artillery had fired more than 3,000 rounds into An My, with shooting going on until 5:00 p.m. Over 150 Viet Cong were killed that day alone. I still don't know why we weren't relieved; perhaps the men of the company who weren't in the air or at HQs had been sent to reinforce the perimeter. C-rations were brought to us along the wire, and we were told to remain in position and take turns sleeping, with one man always awake and watching from the bunker.

I was so tired by then that I slept for about six hours straight; when I was awakened for relief, it was night again.

In the middle of that night, the base camp behind us came under a barrage of Soviet 122mm rockets, and we on the perimeter line came under small arms fire again. I only shot back when I thought I had the source of enemy green tracers pinpointed. At about one in the morning, the Big Red One artillery firing into An My caused other secondary explosions in the enemy positions in front of us. As the helicopter gunships took off behind us, we could see them coming under anti-aircraft fire as they approached the perimeter, and out over the battle ground. We heard by radio that Thu Duc, near Di An, was under fire from mortars and RPG plus a ground attack, and that their ammo dump had been blown up by the Viet Cong.

Early in the morning, the 1/28, 1/4 Cav/Recon, and 5/2nd Artillery duster-guns advanced into An My again. Heavy fighting broke out immediately, and about thirty more American troops were killed and wounded. Seven tanks and APCs were destroyed or damaged. Meanwhile, Alpha Company of the 2nd/16th Infantry, which had been brought in as a blocking force some 600 meters northwest of An My, advanced into a brush-filled ravine. They immediately came under heavy fire with 13 killed and wounded. Thirty-five of the enemy were killed. Heavy fighting also occurred in Tan Phu Khan village in sight of Phu Loi. On the Phu Loi base camp perimeter, we came under shellfire from Viet Cong 75mm recoiless rifles originating in that village, where another enemy battalion was fighting.

More trucks came out along the perimeter road towards our bunker, even as occasional enemy rocket shells exploded around them. We were finally relieved and loaded up, sweating, tired, filthy, and wide-eyed at everything we'd seen in about forty hours on the perimeter line. The fighting out there was still going on as we roared back towards the center of the camp. There had already been seventy-seven American soldiers killed and wounded.

The battle cost the Viet Cong and their NVA reinforcements a body count of 287 killed. The enemy battalions involved turned out to be from the 273rd VC regiment, the Dong Ngai Regiment, and the Phu Loi Battalion.

As I sat holding my rifle in the truck, bouncing and swaying along, I had plenty of time to think about what I'd just seen. A feeling of dread rose in me that I'd perhaps volunteered to trade boredom for a quick, nasty death. Back at the company area, I was ordered to report to the first sergeant immediately. He told me to get my field gear together and my rifle. After I'd gotten some sleep I was to move out to the HQ hootch of the Combat Recon Platoon. He told me that Quinn, the man I was waiting to replace, had been wounded in the An My battle. I had my gear together in a few minutes, and lay down on my rack to get a little sleep. I was awakend by my buddy Chuck Sollish, who would be at my wedding years later. He had a present for me—a machete.

"Hey, my man, here ya go. I gotcha a present, just the thing you'll be needin' for cuttin' through all them jungle vines, while I'm in here layin' back, gettin' mellow. Heh, heh."

After what I'd seen from that bunker, I wasn't laughing. With my gear loaded in a rucksack and my rifle in hand, I shuffled my way across the base camp to the Recon Platoon's hootches on the far side of the perimeter wire. That part of the line faced the large Vietnamese village of Tan Phu Khan, where fighting had been going on for two days. It was the 3rd of February.

So began the Tet Offensive of 1968 for me; the same thing was happening all over Vietman. In the first wave of enemy assaults, approximately a thousand Americans were killed and about 7,500 wounded, including about a hundred casualties in the Phu Loi area alone. On the morning of February 3rd, we were under another rocket attack, and so were Thu Duc, Lai Khe, Ben Cat, Cu Chi, and Quan Loi, which was also fighting off a ground attack. Viet Cong units were also moving into villages south of us, and heavy fighting continued in the Cho Lon and Tan San Nhut areas around Saigon. 1st Division troops were involved in heavy fighting both in the Saigon and Ben Cat areas. The 1st/28th and the 1/4th Cav were still in heavy contact with an entrenched Viet Cong force east of Tan Phu Khan. Between five hundred and a thousand Vietnamese civilian refugees from the fighting were being collected south of the village, beyond the Phu Loi perimeter. Eventually they were herded into the huge refugee camp between Phu Loi and Phu Cuong. The sounds of fighting and exploding shells could be heard as I humped along. By midday, our artillery was firing barrages overhead into the Tan Phu Khan enemy positions, while helicopter gunships clattered and roared overhead on scramble missions.

5   Recon Platoon

*"What would become of us if
everything that happens out
there were quite clear
to us?*
— Erich Maria Remarque
(in All Quiet on the
Western Front)

I stood in the dust outside the hootch, with my gear hanging, and my rifle slung, all of a sudden feeling unsure of myself. Finally, I shuffled up and peeked in the door. There were dudes laying all around, some sleeping in camouflaged jungle uniforms, others cleaning weapons or checking the cartridges in magazines. A Mexican-looking guy was slowly sharpening a knife; nobody seemed to notice me. Still, I could feel their eyes on me, taking in details, checking me out, without appearing even to be looking. The silence grew until I blurted out, "I'm Quinn's replacement."

Finally, one dude looked right up at me and said, "Say what? You replacin' Quinn, man? Oh, O.K., no sweat. Lieutenant's over there somewhere, man. Just tell'm yer here." Then he looked back down at some book mumbling incoherently to himself. Nobody else even nodded or raised their eyes. They all looked tired, bored, or blown out. They also looked old. All kinds of strange-looking equipment could be seen. Weapons, both American and Soviet, claymore mines, belts of machine-gun bullets, grenades, NVA bandoliers, knives, dirty pictures, poncho liners, mud-covered boots, and empty bottles. I thought to myself, "Uh-huh! This is one weird-looking bunch of dudes, but it's gonna' be a hell of a lot better then the crap I came from." I just dropped my equipment in a pile, and went to find the lieutenent, with my rifle still slung.

I stuck my head in the door of the only other hootch, and took in another practically identical scene. Two rows of exhausted-looking men, all with their small arms and ammo spread around them, were giving me the blankest-looking stares, warily registering me somewhere, and then letting their eyes wander off. Nevertheless, this was the right hootch, as raggedy and dilapidated as the other, but housing the CP and radio at one end in a sectioned-off area.

I walked in, feeling clean and virgin, despite my last few days in the bunker line. These dudes were just so worn out and different looking. I went through the ordeal of meeting the platoon leader, Lieutenant Michael Marano from Binghampton, New York, and the platoon sergeant, Robert Carlisle, from Alabama. Like the others, they lay on racks, staring at me briefly, sizing me up, before saying a word. Finally the lieutenant heaved himself up, followed by Carlisle; they stuck their hands out, and said hello. The lieutenant was young, sort of pleasant-looking in a worn kind of way, with black hair cut short. Carlisle was regular infantry, from a battalion of the 16th, one of those rare, really good lifer-sergeants—the lean, tight, emotionless, tough kind who appear to be any age or ageless, and who make an infantry unit good.

The lieutenant gave me kind of a tight-lipped, not unfriendly little smile, and said, "Okay, Brown, glad to have you. You'll be O.K." He turned to Sergeant Carlisle and said, "O.K., Sarge, put'm in a squad. We've got a patrol going out again today, so get'm squared away." He nodded at me once more and lay back down on the bunk, and appeared to go to sleep.

Sergeant Carlisle eyed me for a minute with his light, penetrating gaze, and said, "O.K., you can have Quinn's rack, and you'll be in Rock's squad. Let's go." He walked between the resting soldiers and scattered combat junk, quickly and easily, without any noise at all, heading straight for the hootch I'd gone to first. While we walked, he told me: "The lieutenant just got back from two weeks in the hospital. He got hit by shrapnel from a booby trap out by check point 84. He's gonna take it easy for another week or so, but he's a good platoon leader." Inside the door I noticed all the blanked-out looking dudes stirred when we entered, riveting their eyes on him listening and watching.

A tall, high-waisted guy got up and strode over, looking important, sticking his hands on his hips. Carlisle eyed him, nodded in his tight kind of way, and said, "O.K., Rock, this is Brown. Brown, this is Rock Rheiner. He's yours—Quinn's replacement. Show'm his rack, square away his shit, and get'm ready for a patrol." He hardly waited for any acknowledgement, "total-command-presence," sure of himself. He nodded at us and disappeared with hardly a sound.

Sergeant Rock remained standing there, his hands still on his hips, glorying in his importance. He gave me a look that said, "you're a piece of dirt. I'll hafta wait an' see if yer gonna be any use at all."

I found out later that his name wasn't Rock at all, but everybody called him that in a permanent joking reference to the comic book war hero character. He finally lowered his challenging stare from behind thick glasses when he noticed everyone else in the hootch had slipped back into his comatose position and was not paying any attention. It was because Carlisle had left. Well, Rock led me over to an empty cot, with no mattress, all my gear in my hands, and said, "Here it is, Quinn's rack. It's yours. Okumura, this is Brown. He's in our squad. Show him how to get his shit together for going out today." He looked at me once more and added, "You just follow my orders and do what you're told." Then he turned and stalked away.

So I came to meet my buddy and future field partner, Earl Okumura. Shy, handsome, Japanese-Hawaiian, with long black hair, he's small compared to me, but tight and tough looking. He stuck out his hand and we shook, his grip firm and warm. His eyes were alert and bright, but had a gentle look to them. Smiling, he said, "Rock's O.K., man. He's here doin' his time, too; he's just into his own trip, don't worry about it, it don't mean nothin'. Lieutenant Marano's a good dude, too. We call him Dago 6 on the radio; it means 'Italian-in-charge.' He's real mellow an' doesn't mess with us. Carlisle's number one; he got us through An My with nobody killed." Another guy had come over, so quiet I hadn't heard him 'til he slid down next to Earl. It was the Mexican-looking dude who had been sharpening a knife when I first came into the Hootch.

Earl said, "This is Baca, my main man from New Mexico, Ernesto Baca. Wha'd you say yer name was?"

"John Brown," I said. "Good to meet you guys." Baca eyed me for a minute and said, "You have to get your equipment ready for going out in the bush on a combat patrol." He spoke precise, accented English, and seemed concerned and friendly. He started picking through my relatively clean, unstained, REMF-looking field gear distastefully, as though it was totally worthless. He began a non-stop instruction while Earl nodded approvingly.

"You must tape up all this loose stuff so it doesn't rattle, or make the slightest noise. You've got to tie down everything you can't tape—or get rid of it." He was picking up my M-16 rifle magazines now, pushing down on the bullets; testing the spring tension under them to make sure they would feed without jamming. "You've got to learn quick," he was saying. "Got to do everything right the first time, you won't get any second chance. You screw up, you might screw all of us up."

Earl spoke up softly. "We've been into some bad shit the last few days; everybody's kind of uptight." I knew he was talking about the first day of the battle of An My that they'd fought through. This Recon platoon under Sergeant Carlisle was the unit that had first spotted large groups of enemy moving into the area the night before the battle erupted, and then had been called out to support the Black Lions. On the second day, the platoon had been kept inside the wire by the brass as a ready-reaction force. I told them about being in that bunker on the outer perimeter facing the village, during the battle. I didn't want them thinking I was a complete cherry. They just nodded, taking it in, until I said tentatively, "What was it like out there man, in the middle of it? What's it like out past the wire, with the gooks and all?"

Earl and Baca looked at each other slyly, then looked at me, and smiled, small, wolfish smiles. Earl said, "It's just there, man, it's what it is, it's real."

Baca smirked, "It's just them and you, nothin' between. You've got to be ready." He kept on picking through my gear, fiddling with it, separating a few things, combining others. He snatched on OD bag off the wall and handed it to me." "Here's a claymore man, you've gotta have it." I laid the rounded, rectangular, anti-personnel mine next to my ammo belt.

Some other men were kind of sliding or shuffling over around now, listening and eyeing me. One of them, carrying some long metal-linked bandoliers of M-60 machine-gun ammo, dumped them next to my claymore, nodded curtly, and went back to his bunk. He went back to carefully cleaning his long, heavy, squad machine-gun.

Earl said, "That's Tommy Donaghue, man. He's our gunner, an' damn good; he shot the hell out of those VC at An My. When we were moving into the village behind the Dusters and 1/4 Cav tracks, a VC sniper in a tree shot a lieutenent down through the head with an AK-47 and killed 'im—knocked him right off the track. It was Donaghue who saw the gook first an' blew him outta the tree with a fifty-round burst. A little later, he machine-gunned a VC recoilless-rifle gunner who was firing into the tanks. Probably saved a few guys that day the way he shoots." I looked at the man out of the corner of my eye. He was one of those stocky, tough-looking Jersey City Irish guys. "You've got to hump this ammo for Donaghue; in case we get into some shit, you get it to him, or his AG," Baca said, pointing at the linked belts. Donaghue was sitting on the bunk with another stocky-looking white guy who was going through a large, OD bag with straps and a red cross on it.

"That's our medic, Rocky Allen," said Earl. "He's Donaghue's best buddy and a good dude, too. He'll take care of you. When the grunts from the 1st of the 28th were gettin' shot to pieces, Rocky went nuts. He didn't pay no attention to those RPDs and Chi-Comm .51 cals. hittin' all around him. He crawled from one guy to the next patchin' them up, shootin' morphine, and draggin' 'em to cover. When he ran outta compresses, he used his own uniform for bandages, an' he finished up the battle wearin' a few torn-up rags."

Now another dude headed over to appraise me, strutting in an exaggerated street shuffle. He was a tall black dude, really tan-faced, and handsome. "I'm Joe Miller, man, from Philly; what's happenin'?" I stuck my hand out to shake, but he slapped it away, flipped his palm up 'til I slapped down on it, then made a fist and we tapped knuckles in a "dap." "That's it man, that's where it is. I'm from the Black Lions, man, the 28th Infantry, and the Pathfinders, too. I just got into this platoon, too. I replaced Pete MacDonald yesterday; he's goin' home in a little while." I told him what unit I'd been in and that I was also from Pennsylvania. He said, "You'll make it man," and went back to lie on his bunk, rapping with another black brother whose name I later found out was MacQueston.

So I met them all, the sly, the bold, the short, and the tall. Reynaldo Garcia, a Chicano dude from California, nicknamed "Pancho Villa," and who, like Earl, wore sunglasses day or night. "Monty" Montieth was from Vermont, tall, thin, and nervous, with acneed face, tough and true-blue. Bell, our droopy-mustached Tennessee hillbilly from the mountains of Appalachia, carried an old, wooden-stocked M-14 rifle. "I like this weapon, man. It's like a BAR and has some knock-down to it." Oddie was a short, steady dude who'd already been an advisor to the ARVNs in the Mekong Delta. Tom Hines had a pet dog named Heinrich who acted as our scout. "The Kid," Ritchie Evans, also from Philly: foxy, sharp, and bright, always saying, "I'm half-Dago, man. I'm gonna join the Mafia when I get outta here." He had come to us from the Army in Belgium, where he had been bored and restless and volunteered for 'Nam.

Two boys named Alexander, about as opposite as can be: fair, blue-eyed, golden-haired Alexander, the half-crazy, all-American boy, decorated five times for valor and wounded while serving in the 199th Light Infantry Brigade; Olly Alexandros, another Hawaiian, little and brown, hard as a nut, tight with my man Earl, and on his second tour in 'Nam after a year with the 2nd Infantry of our division, where he'd also been wounded. Don Gould, from Chicago, bright, smooth and careful. He and I ended up going on a strange journey together a few months later. Steve Hustler was from San Francisco, good-looking, and proud. You'd sometimes catch him preening. Art MacQuade was from Rhode Island, the youngest dude in the platoon. He was Irish, looking for combat, always ready for a fight. I think he was only seventeen, and had just hit the 'Nam. Another strong, stocky dude named Don Dunce ended up as a machine-gunner, and always carried his own revolver on his hip: a six-shooter as a last resort. Those are some whose faces and eyes are the main things I remember now. They were all volunteers, as brave and tough as any American soldiers ever.

The platoon had been started in October, 1967, by Colonel Henry Schroeder, after he took over command of both the 1st Infantry Division Artillery and the Phu Loi base camp. The 1st Division commander, Major-General Hay, had told him to "take care of his own problems" when he'd asked for a security force for combat Recon patrols and ambushes around the area to give warning of enemy attacks. In the beginning it was limited to short patrols and ambushes, but a tradition of daring had begun to grow in response to remarks about it being a "bastard unit."

That long morning wore on for me. The hot sun beat down on the tin roof of the hootch, flies and mosquitos buzzed around, and most of the men were asleep. Artillery and mortar shells continued to explode in the distance with *Carrumps!* and *Booms!*. I lay on my rack next to Earl's, waiting in nervous anticipation. "I'm fuckin' in it now," I'm mumbling to myself. "Wonder what it's like out there? I hope I can make it O.K. These guys seem like they're all half-crazy." They'd been talking and laughing about killing this gook, or how funny that one looked crawling along, dragging his guts behind him just before somebody shot him again to finish him off.

Suddenly I'm awake. It's early afternoon and the hootch is full of fast, sure, shuffling movement. I didn't even know I was asleep. I jump up and start hustling, putting on my web gear, bandoliers of ammo, canteen, claymore, first aid pouch, checking my rifle and grenades. We

wear soft camouflaged bush hats or helmets, according to our prefer-
ence. Rock is taking it easy after a shrapnel wound at An My, but he
comes to see how I'm fitted out. He checks me out quickly, and sur-
prisingly seems satisfied, thanks to Baca and Earl. We assemble outside the hootches and the "Ell Tee" and Sergeant Carlisle brief us on
where we're going and what to expect. "Alright, you men listen up.
Yer gonna pull security for some 1/4 Cav tanks and tracks on a reconnaissance patrol into Phu Cuong. The VC have been hitting the 5th
ARVN Division, and they've overrun part of the town. We've been
informed six Americans were killed there. They've mostly pulled back
now from around Phu Cuong and the base camp, but we still don't know
what to expect. The ARVNs have their hands full, and we gotta be damn
careful about possible ambushes." One man says something about
"heavy fighting and enemy attacks going on all over Vietnam." It's still
the first week of February, in the middle of the Tet Offensive.

Carlisle was told to pick about fifteen of us to go; the rest of the platoon remained in Phu Loi in case they were needed elsewhere. We lined
up in a file and marched out to the western gate where we met a line
of armored tracks and tanks.

"Alright, mount up! If we hit anything and the tracks start firing, you
guys get off and down fast!"

I pulled myself up on the same M-48 tank as Tommy Donaghue and
Earl. Rock Allen may have been with us, too. We headed down the dusty
road toward Phu Cuong and the junction with Highway 13. On the right
was the big South Vietnamese fortress-base camp of the 5th ARVN
Division. They were still recovering from a heavy enemy attack at the
same time that An My was hit. On the left we passed a rubber plantation and groves of banana trees. A little farther on were the Vietnamese
laundry and bar-whorehouse I'd been in a few times before the offensive. Everything seemed different now, hostile. After two or three days
of incoming rounds and casualties, the huge teeming refugee camp on
the right was quiet as a graveyard. We clanked along, watching the tree-
lines, the track gunners hunched-poised over their weapons, ready to
blow. Coming into Phu Cuong I felt like we were invaders entering a
hostile country. What had been a frenzied boom town living off the
American presence a few days before now appeared still and deserted.
At the north-south junction of Thunder Road, we dismounted (with the
other infantry unit pulling security for the Cav) and began patrolling
through the town.

Earl and I walked spread out behind Donaghue, our point-man. He carried the M-60 tight against his side with a 75-round belt hooked up and draped over his shoulder. I have my M-16 pointing in the opposite direction, safety off. Earl had his M-79 grenade launcher pointing up, the butt against his hip.

The other guys were spread out behind us, with Rocky back towards the center. Here and there we passed dead bodies of Viet Cong soldiers. We came out into a huge fish market, now empty, and headed towards a boat landing, water straight ahead. Eyes darting left-right, O.K. water-way down there, we're in a center square like a plaza, silent buildings all around, feeling that other eyes were watching us. All our fingers were on the triggers, looking quickly down empty streets left and right, across a barrier in the middle of the square. A sudden *Crack! Ping!* One shot! Off to the left. We swung around, down, ready to fire, nothing else came.

"Who the hell was that? What's goin' on? Sniper?"

"Aw, they're just fuckin' with us."

We moved out again and came upon some great big baskets scattered around.

"What's this here? Don't touch 'em, man. I don't know what they are, but they might be booby-trapped."

We gave the baskets a wide berth and keep moving. Something weird-lookin' was up ahead near the end of the square towards the river. It was like a raggedy pyramid-monument.

We moved forward cautiously and suddenly it was clear what it was. I felt a gagging vomit rush rising. Earl Okumura had stopped in mid-stride. Tommy Donaghue was shaking his head, still holding the gun pointing straight out. It was a large pile of chopped-off human heads, many of them young girls with long hair. Their dead eyes stared in all directions. Under and around the obscene pile was a puddle of dried blood, and flies were buzzing in and out of their open mouths.

We stopped in shock three or four yards from them. It looked like at least twenty-five heads in the heap. I didn't look at anyone else in the area except Earl and Tommy. Shock had taken over my reflexes. Suddenly Donaghue let out a snarling scream and ran straight down the road to the boat landing on the river.

"Fuckin' Cong! C'mon out, mothafuckahs, an' fight me today! C'mon, motha fuckahs, I'm heah, I'm ready. C'mon, Cong."

He's shaking his machine gun at the river and the vegetation on the other side.

"Come an' fight, Cong, I'm heah today!"

I kept jerking my eyes from him to the pile of heads, back and forth, and every so often in a circle around me. The real meaning of terrorism, what had been going on here for years, had suddenly hit me. Earl was still standing in the same spot, as if rooted there, still holding his grenade launcher ready to fire, shaking his head slowly. Other guys came up from behind looking at the severed heads, at Earl and me, and Donaghue still screaming down by the river bank. I didn't look at their faces.

The rest of the day was a blur, eventually ending with us back in Phu Loi, unable or unwilling to convey to those who hadn't gone out with us what we had seen.

Much later, somebody near me said authoritatively, "It's the girls, man, it's the hootch girls that worked for the Americans in the base here at Phu Loi, doin' laundry an' cleaning. The VC are teachin' the people to stay away from us, man."

I could barely hear him, I was just going through the motions. I kept thinking, "You wanted to be a grunt, you wanted to see the real thing. Well, now you're seeing it, fool; how do you like it?"

On the way through the wire, we'd heard the sound of combat to the northeast where C Troop of the 1/4 Cav and the 1/28th were still fighting it out with the Viet Cong, both at Tan Phu Khan and farther north around Dog Leg village. On February 4th, we came under another rocket attack in Phu Loi with more American casualties. Tan Uyen was also under attack again by both rockets and ground troops. For us, the next few days had with the same routine of patrols and ambushes. We divided up the platoon and took turns with the operations and some guard duty. With heavy fighting all over 'Nam, many infantry and recon units were being kept in pretty close to protect and defend major camps and towns. Thousands of Vietnamese refugees in our Lam Son area were fleeing from the fighting and congregating in refugee camps like the one outside Phu Loi.

While I was in that perimeter bunker during the Battle of An My and getting broken-in to my new recon patrol, the Tet Offensive of 1968 was raging up and down the country. Thirty-six out of forty-four provincial capitals, five out of six autonomous cities, twenty-three major military bases and airfields, and hundreds of district capitals, villages, and military camps were attacked by local Viet Cong battalions and large reinforcing-NVA regular units.

In Phu Loi, we felt as though we were under siege with rocket and mortar attacks, by sometimes hundreds of shells. Instead of just night-time attacks, we were getting hit in broad daylight, too. The enemy was trying to destroy our helicopters to help their fighting units and to keep our own combat units inside and under cover. Phu Loi was taking casualties and so were the other 1st Infantry Division camps of Di An, Lai Khe, and Quan Loi. The NVA regulars, who had been infiltrating in from the Cambodian border in nighttime marches since before the offensive, were now trying to reinforce the Viet Cong around Saigon, Cholon, Bien Hoa, and other nearby striking points farther north. I was stepping very lightly on my first combat patrols. We made long patrol sweeps around Phu Loi each day, looking for signs of enemy troops or booby traps. My senses were getting as tuned up as those of the men around me. As long as I had my M-16 loaded and ready, I liked humping through the little hamlets and villages watching the older peasants staring silently and the little kids running along yelling, "Hey, No. 1 GI, you give me chop-chop, you wanna buy dinky-dau smoke?" The kids would appear from nowhere out of the bush, packing sodas or bags of weed, following us and yelling as long as we'd let them.

It was the dry season, and a lot of the rice paddies were easy to walk although we were constantly tense, looking for signs of booby-trapped grenades set in the dikes dividing them. It was thick green jungle bordering everything that held the danger: snipers, enemy hide-outs, and base camps. On one of my first patrols, I stumbled over a large curved piece of metal during a long day between Tan Phu Khan and An My. We scraped and dug around it and uncovered a French tank, mostly buried, blown up in the first Indochina war fifteen years before. It made us look at these people around us with an even clearer understanding of what we were up against. Old men, working with their water buffalo at different jobs, would stare at us, sometimes surlily as we passed. You couldn't help but feel they've seen so much, they could know it all. By now I'm totally meshing in with the platoon and feeling like I'm most definitely part of the war in Vietnam.

The oldtimers in the platoon like Sergeant Lewis from Arizona, and Carlisle, didn't pay much attention to new guys like me. I made my friendships with newer dudes like Art McQuade, Monty, and Dave Clarke, who was from Wyoming or someplace out West, and was so friendly and light I called him "Smiley."

The main attacking forces of the Viet Cong by now had pulled back from the ARVN and militia forts in the towns and villages, but isolated raids continued. Assassinations of South Vietnamese who'd cooperated with us or the government continued after the initial Tet attacks. Throughout the Republic, tremendous psychological damage was done and helped the enemy leadership offset heavy Viet Cong losses in the major battles like An My. The people must have found it hard to believe the government could ever defeat the VC.

On my second patrol into Phu Cuong the pile of severed heads in the square was gone, but there were still some dead bodies, perhaps shot later and left like discarded refuse. We were looking for suspects, young Viets of military age with no I.D.s who might be enemy infiltrators. Any that we grabbed were turned over to MI or the ARVNs. While searching a house in the big town, I took a break after our long day of marching and talked in broken French-English-Vietnamese and sign language with the old white-haired man who owned it. He told me how two members of his family had just been killed by the Communists —executed at the beginning of the offensive. I stared at him, wondering if their heads had been in the pile we'd found. He showed me his family Bible (he was Catholic), and some old pictures and scrolls. He pointed out on a wall map how he had fled with his family from Hanoi, almost a thousand miles over foot-trails and on trucks when the Communists took over in 1954. They had been part of an exodus numbering close to a million persons. He looked so sad and blown out, I was speechless.

Pretty soon I heard the dudes yelling and forming up out in the street. I fall in with Earl and we start moving out, and I'm saying to him, "This war's gonna' be goin' on a long time after we've marched away for good." One of the civilians who had been murdered was a pretty hootch girl named Lee. I'd gotten to like her on the Phu Loi base when I was in the helicopter company. Another was a girl Tommy Donaghue knew as "Sweet Pea."

We marched along the dusty road, sweating, OD GI towels around our necks and shoulders. We were still spread out with our weapons ready. The army transport trucks, weird Vietnamese buses, Lambretta motor scooters, and old, beat-up French sedans roared by, leaving us in clouds of dust and stinking exhaust. Every gook we saw passing us or those beyond the road was a potential enemy. We eyeballed everyone. As loose and casual as we might have appeared, we were always looking for a sudden weapon or ready for a thrown grenade. There were no real behind-the-lines or safe areas, unless it's the ground you're standing on with your rifle ready.

Back in Phu Loi the next afternoon, we get orders to prepare for a night ambush out near An My. The brass wants to monitor enemy activity in the area of the battle. We get a briefing from Lieutenant Marano and Sergeant Carlisle again, as usual. I don't listen too well because I'm mostly thinking about my weapon and equipment, and whether I was a fool for ever volunteering for Recon in the first place. Next, I am standing in a jungle camouflage uniform, part of a group that has volunteered to hunt out and kill the enemy.

I'm in a long file of men in the dust of the gate at the camp perimeter. There's some APC tracks and tanks of the 1/4 Cav, in from the field, bullet-scarred and scratched up by shrapnel. The armored Cav dudes eyeball us in a bored kind of way, glad they're getting a rest and don't have to go out themselves. The bunker guards open a barbed wire gate quietly, and we move out in a long file, into the pitch blackness of gook territory, heading for a position between the ruins of An My and the village of Tan Phu Khan.

I was still on edge, and scared, patrolling at night. We moved quickly, but so smoothly and quietly that I was astounded. I kept feeling clumsy, as though I was making more noise than the rest of the patrol. I tripped over something and despite myself, muttered "Goddamn!" I felt an elbow or a fist slam into me, and somebody, probably Donaghue, whispered in a hoarse voice, "Shut the hell up, asshole, bite your fuckin' lip or something. I don't want to get greased 'cause of you!" I felt the hot flush of embarrassment rush to my face. I was sweating like a pig now, trying to keep up and keep my safe interval at the same time. The smell of the earth and jungle growth took over. Everybody seemed to know where we were going, the feel of the land, the whole scene, except me. I can't see anybody or anything. I'm feeling like I'm all alone. There were no flares or any light except the stars, prearranged with Division Artillery because of our ambush. Artillery knew how long it would take us to get to our position and exactly where it was, in case we got hit and needed fire-support. We finally reached our spot in a jungle line, covering a large dirt trail near An My, my legs aching and numb.

I was set up in a position next to Earl and Baca. They whispered directions to me quietly, and Earl crawled out with me, helping me set up my claymore mine in the right position and slid back, unrolling the detonator cord. Then we settled down for the night, touching each other. I was in the dirt on my belly, out on the cutting-edge of this war. It was sure comforting to me to feel another guy right next to my shoulder.

For hours there was complete silence; broken only by the artillery firing flares again, now that we were set up, with an occasional blast of H&I shellfire. The flares lit up the jungle trees like bizarre skeletons. The RTO broke squelch every so often on the PRC 25 radio handset, communicating with clicks to our CP back in the camp to let them know that everything was quiet. Just after midnight we heard shuffling noises and murmuring out in front of us. Men started nudging each other quietly all along the line. Earl put his face next to mine, his lips just touching my ear and whispered silently, "Enemy movement, An My." My hair prickled. Bushes rustled, small clanking noises came to us out of the darkness. The tension heightened until it was something you could have grabbed. It seemed almost like quiet, dragging movements out in front of us, but too far to blow the claymores or the ambush.

All the rest of the night I couldn't relax the tension in me. The same thoughts kept running through my head, over and over, "The Viet Cong are out there right in front of me, with only rotten air and a little space between us." The noises stopped just before dawn, and with the first light we rolled up our claymores and broke up the ambush. The sunrise was a great relief, bursting over us and heating up everything like an oven almost immediately. We started a combat patrol towards the An My battlefield right in front of our ambush position. Earl and I walked together, but spread out with our M-16s ready.

"That was V.C. still dragging off their dead from the battle last night, man," he said. "They'll do anything they can to get their bodies back. That's how come we set up the ambush here." I could see the sense of it all now, as we started coming across dead enemy soldiers scattered around. Most of them were in NVA uniforms, blood-stained and shot full of holes, guts or brains coming out. Some were burned black by napalm, shrunken vestiges of human beings, hands still clutching at the ground like claws. In the distance I can see the perimeter bunker I was shooting out of, during the battle on the 1st and 2nd of February. One of the guys yelled out, "Hey! I found a VC still in a spider hole!" He reached down into the little fighting trench or foxhole and started pulling the dead enemy soldier out by the belt. As he reefed him up, the mangled body broke apart at the waist into two pieces. Earl started yelling, "Put him back in there, put him back!"

Some of the dudes, spread out on the patrol, began kicking the bodies over, that were under now-dead bushes and clumps burned by napalm, kind of giggling or laughing and calling them "crispy critters." A couple of them called out, "Where's that new guy? Come on over here, Brown. Ain't this pretty?" They made me take a good long look, and roll one over, kicking with my boot. Part of the burned flesh fell away from the enemy soldier's face and the white bone showed. The NVA looked like he was grinning, though it was really the grimace of death. I felt sick, but tried to hide it.

"Jesus Christ Almighty," I was thinking, "this is disgusting."

Another of the guys, Sergeant Lewis, was standing on a mound of soft dirt, kicking with his feet and staring down. He suddenly started mumbling, "Oh my God, my God. This stink is all bodies, man; this is gooks." A horrible smell rose from the earth. As he moved around, dirt began to crumble away, exposing human arms, legs, and heads. Clouds of flies buzzed up, and maggots seemed to erupt from the earth. Somebody moved forward, grabbed an arm and pulled; a whole human body in a Viet Cong uniform slid out, complete with web-gear. I felt violently sick again, but concealed it. Earl was yelling, "No, no, leave him alone, he's dead. Let's call in what we found and get outta here." The RTO reported into headquarters that we'd found a mass grave of seventy-five to a hundred VC/NVA, and we got in line and left. We'd all had more than enough of this place of death.

Later in the afternoon, after a long cloverleaf beyond the battle zone, as we were moving back in towards Phu Loi, we suddenly came under sniper-fire from enemy troops firing at long range from a jungle wood-line area. They must have been remnants of the VC force at An My. I had a weird feeling they had been watching us all along and were trying to pay us back for abusing their dead comrades' bodies.

The bullets were cracking and ricocheting, *Pop-crack! Beowww!*, sending up spurts of dust, and we opened fire. My stomach knotted up, and I had a flash of ending up looking like one of those dead NVA, face down back there in the paddies. Then I started shooting back, and my fear went away, though one bullet went past my ear so close it "whizzed" loudly, and I jerked around. For a second, Earl thought I was hit. Donaghue opened fire with his M-60 machine-gun and totally hosed down the woodline, leaning forward into the gun's recoil, the shells spewing out. He was screaming out unintelligable curses. Gradually, the enemy fire slackened and then stopped. They retreated, and we didn't follow. As we humped back into the base camp, I was thinking I'd sort of had my cherry busted during the last few days. I felt like I was a real "veteran."

A letter home from this time shows the contrast between what I wrote and what I'd seen in the first ten days of February 1968.

Combat Recon Platoon
H.Q. 2nd Brigade 1st Inf. Div.
Phu Loi, R.V.N.
10 February 1968

Dear Mom and Dad and Family,
Well, I've been in this infantry recon-platoon now for a while. It's not a bad deal, as far as grunts go. We have two hootches near the outer perimeter wire. We're under command of Col. Henry Schroeder, the Phu Loi Commander, through 2nd Brigade G-2 Intelligence, and 1st Infantry Division Artillery (intelligence). We are treated pretty good by the command, like their own little private army of scouts. However, it's not all fun. Out in the field I carry an M-16 automatic rifle with over 300 rounds, two belts of M-60 machine-gun ammo for my squad's gun, four frag grenades, three smoke grenades, two canteens, a claymore mine for ambushes, several pounds of C-4 plastic high-explosive for demolition, plus the other equipment a grunt carries. The guys in this outfit are outstanding, all volunteers. Our sole officer is a first lieutenant named Marano who got wounded about three weeks ago. The platoon sergeant, Carlisle, 16th Infantry, is also good. Southern, cold, and efficient. As I believe I said before, there are only about thirty people in this platoon and I think I already made clear that our mission is patrols and ambushes. There's been heavy fighting around here but I've been lucky. I've already been out several times, it's not very nice.
Yesterday we had another mortar attack and VC shooting into the perimeter. I will take care of myself so don't worry about me here.

Love,
John

Around this time we began hearing reports of the overrunning of the U.S. Army Special Forces Camp at Lang Vei by the NVA using Soviet tanks. Half of the American advisors had been killed, the rest escaping into the jungle before managing to make it to the Marine base at Khe Sanh between encircling enemy units. The word "tanks" rippled uneasily all through Vietnam:

"The gooks are upping the ante, huh?"

Simultaneously, the 2/16th and 2/18th Infantry were operating in the

Phu Loi area. Elements of both units had gotten in a heavy firefight north-west of An My, losing thirty-two American casualties and killing forty Viet Cong. The surrounding area seemed to be infested with enemy units.

Out on combat patrols or inside the wire, we'd run into armored cavalry units or truck drivers waiting for convoys.

"Man, the VC are everywhere up and down Thunder Road. They been attacking all over the place down around Tan San Nhut and Cholon. There's even been a whole bunch of MPs hit."

"The 101st Airborne and 199th Infantry's been runnin' into some bad shit down in that Phu Tho racetrack battle, beaucoup KIAs, man. We're waiting on orders to go out on another road-clearing mission. These truck driver dudes're gonna follow us."

We would lean up against the shady side of the tracks, feeling fortunate. I was talking to one APC gunner:

"Hey, we been skatin', except fer the damn rocket attacks. All we been runnin' into around here is dead bodes an' snipers. There's gooks all over the place around here, headin' down to Cholon, but we been lucky as hell. Good luck to you guys, too."

Just when we were feeling comfortable staying around our own area, Tommy Donaghue came up yelling: "All right you guys, Major Bennett volunteered us to go get a truckload of ammo down by Tan San Nhut. I'm gonna drive, and Rocky's goin' with me. Earl and Brown, yer goin' too, an' I wanna few more guys for firepower."

We climbed up into the deuce and a half; with Donaghue at the wheel, it turned into a crazy ride. We went full speed down the back dirt roads off to the east side of Highway 13 because we figured the gooks would have their new ambushes on Thunder Road.

When we finally got to the ammo dump we were all very nervous and in a hurry to keep moving. One of the REMFs at the dump was looking at our list saying, "You need this, this, and this, huh? O.K., well, that's what all their other trucks need, too. You guys get in the rear of the line and we'll load you up in maybe forty minutes to an hour."

Donaghue said, "O.K., man, sounds good." As soon as the guy disappeared, Tommy says to us, "Bullshit on him, we're goin' now. You guys jump up in that truck at the head of the line. It's already loaded with everything we need an' more. The drivers ain't there, so we'll jus' take their goddamn truck."

We roared out of there laughing and headed north toward Di An. Near the village adjoining the base camp we ran straight through a firefight on both sides of the road with tracer bullets flying out of a big grove of banana trees. In another spot, we roared past an ambushed and burned-out truck between Di An and Phu Loi. After seeing that, Donaghue drove like a maniac and finally got us home safely on that load of ammo.

The trip heightened the contrast between the easier time before the offensive and now, when nobody felt safe anywhere.

The area all around Di An was the scene of scattered fighting between the First Infantry and Viet Cong units at this time, and we must have run right through one of these actions. Korean troops also operated in the area, and several times we ran across them during our operations in the Phu Loi area. They were much feared by the Viet Cong because of their ruthless methods of dealing with prisoners and their bravery during firefights. Several times we saw groups of the ROKs temporarily bivouacked inside Phu Loi, practicing their hand-to-hand combat routines.

Early in the morning of the 9th of February, we came under mortar fire inside the base camp again, followed by incoming small-arms fire on the perimeter at about 6:00 a.m. The bunker guards returned fire, and a few of us went up to bunker 26 to join in. The enemy action never developed into an actual ground probe that day. The night of the 10th saw another attack, this time by 122mm rockets. The 1st Engineer's area and nearby units took most of the incoming rounds.

Our job during Tet was to help protect the base camp and to patrol the surrounding jungles, rice paddies, and villages. Our field-recon mission was to ambush or make artillery targets of any enemy force coming down from Cambodia or moving out of their bases in the surrounding "Iron Triangle" to reinforce their comrades already fighting. We kept humping hard every day—days full of dusty, sweating tension.

At dusk on the 12th of February, we "saddled up" with our gear again for yet another night ambush. We'd already been through a pre-dawn rocket attack. About two-thirds of the platoon were going; the rest remained on bunker guard duty. An intelligence report had come out the night before from Division Artillery that said The 273rd Viet Cong Regiment had orders to attack an American base camp believed to be Phu Loi. We had information on a VC base camp two kilometers east of us, between Tan Phu Khan and Vinh Loi.

I was getting my gear on and checking my weapon when Earl said, "We're going to hit some damned VC one of these nights, man." I just nodded.

"Yeah, I know buddy, we keep hearin' all this trouble going down. It's about time. I hope when we do it turns out O.K. fer us."

All around us the guys were rustling around in the hootch, getting it together. We fell out and lieutenant Marano briefs us a little. There's about twenty of us going out, including him. By now, I'm more familiar with it all and getting a little smoother in the night movements. Sliding along in the darkness can protect you, too. At the bunker line, as the guards eyeball us, we load and lock our weapons. We file out through the dust at the perimeter gate, spread out and competely silent. It's so dark, it's almost like being alone. This time we're moving slowly and carefully. There's been so much enemy activity we're expecting trouble now every time we go anywhere. We're not going out very far, because enemy units are operating in large groups in the surrounding country and it's too dangerous for a small recon patrol. After creeping along for maybe a half hour, we reach a preplanned ambush position in a Buddhist graveyard near some jungle, a thick woodline close to Phu Loi. We set up our weapons and claymores in perfect silence and settle down to wait. I could feel Earl breathing next to me. Gradually, I can see better and better from a little moon and starlight. Weird noises come from the nearby jungle area occasionally, and I feel jittery. The first thing I notice is a sudden stiffening and tenseness rippling down the ambush line towards me from lieutenant Marano's position next to Sergeant Carlisle.

Combat Recon Patrol
Phu Loi R.V.N.
(Tet Offensive)
Mailed: 15 February 1968

Dear Mom and Dad,
I want to say first of all that if I get through this I'll be lucky.
I'm getting quickly acquainted with my new life here, just getting through an ambush of the enemy. I have seen my first live Viet Cong and North Vietnamese Regulars from the ground. This was almost a personal experience for me, even though there were eighteen or nineteen other Americans present at the time. We were set up in an old graveyard near a line of thick jungle somewhere near a village. It was about midnight and we had a semicircle of claymore mines out in front of us. I was half-asleep when the lieutenant whispered loudly into his radio,

"Get those goddamn gunships up!" He had a night vision starlight scope, but it was light enough for me to see the woodline where an enemy point-man was kneeling down, and another with a long Bazooka-type recoi-less rifle or rocket slanting back over his shoulder. We heard shuffling and clanking noises as more and more came in sight. It was a long line of NVA regulars with AK-47 rifles slung, canvas tubes of rice across their shoulders like old Confederate blanket rolls, Bangalore torpedos, packs, RPGs, machine-guns. Close, so many I couldn't count them all. They were moving, marching in column, either to attack Phu Loi or rein-force the enemy attacking around Saigon or Cholon. Meanwhile the lieu-tenant had been calling in our artillery and armor fire right on top of the enemy over our own position. I heard a sudden whispered order in my ear. "Lay down flat, pass it along." The night just erupted with a tremendous blast as Division Artillery, 4.2 mortars, Duster-APCs, and machine-guns opened up around and above us. It burst on the enemy line in front of us like lightning. I didn't feel completely scared until the lieutenant quit whispering and screamed, "Run for the wire! Get out, there's too many of them!" That scared the hell out of me because he'd seen more than I had, and I'd seen plenty. I could see them being blasted apart and falling as we backed away. Some of us turned and fired into them as we moved toward the base camp. Through his starlight scope the lieutenant and Carlisle had made a quick count of over 150 heavily armed soldiers, outnumbering us about 8-1. We attributed his actions to the fact that he knew there were too many for us, and realized that the sole responsibility for our lives was on him. We later learned from dead bodies on patrol that it was the Viet Cong 273rd Regiment rein-forced by new NVA regulars. That was one ambush that really succeeded. Probably the 1st Division Artillery or some (?) armored Cav got all the credit, but it was us that spotted them and sprang the ambush. There were many dead enemy, we figured at least fifty of them killed.

General Westmoreland says we have defeated the enemy but more hard fighting is ahead. We have been experiencing a big attack all over Viet-nam. I guess it is still going on now. I have been out again on the 14th on a small ambush, since our big one.

I am enclosing the newspaper clipping about the fighting from The Stars and Stripes *that you asked for.*

I will keep you informed on what is going on.

Love,
John

When we'd first pulled back from the cemetery with the initial burst of fire into the enemy column, flares were lighting up the whole area, and helicopter gunships were overhead, firing rockets and mini-guns. We'd slid down into a large, white, sandy gully and had set up quickly in a defense circle. Between mortar and shell explosions we could hear the heavy rustling of enemy movement through the vegetation all around us. The sand was also crisscrossed with heavy trails left by enemy troops passing through earlier in the night, as if groups of them had been scouting the perimeter. We were pinned down by heavy fire for long minutes in there. The night was being torn apart by a huge *BRRRRRPPPPPPP!* punctuated by *SSHHH-BOOMS!* and flashes. The enemy was firing back at the perimeter over our heads, and the self-propelled 40mm automatic duster-guns and 4.2 mortars were blasting all around our position, intermingling with the green AK-47 tracers of the Viet Cong. We heard from the RTO that an ARVN and 4.2 mortars were blasting all around our position, intermingling with the green AK-47 tracers of the Vietcong. We heard from the RTO that an ARVN armored cavalry unit had responded to our call and was attacking the flank of the Viet Cong at the same time. During a short lull we got the chance to move out of that sandy gully and raced back inside the Phu Loi wire.

Back inside the perimeter I was soaked in sweat, still gripping my rifle as the artillery, duster tracks, and 4.2 mortars continued to fire. The air was fuzzy with booming cracks and ripping roars.

One of the tracks was gunning its engine and moving forward to get in a better firing position, when its tread got caught in the concertina tangle and started pulling the perimeter apart. Lieutenant Marano clicked on a flashlight, shining it on the wire for the tank commander so he could see what was happening. I heard a snarl amid the roar and rattle of incoming and outgoing fire.

"Sir! Would you mind shutting the damned light out, I don't wanna get hit!"

The light clicked off. The concertina wire continued to be dragged around while the track guns opened fire into the enemy position again. I fired a few magazines on automatic into the killing zone before the uproar finally subsided. In the ensuing silence, I found myself shaking, staring out into the night along with Earl, Donaghue, and the other dudes around me.

"God Almighty! That was a lot of Viet Cong, man. Jesus Christ, we're lucky we got out of there!"

I closed my eyes and took a deep breath. For a second I was back out there in the open—outnumbered, scared, with no wall or wire or fire-power machine between me and them in the dark. I had a panicky urge to burrow into the ground from fear. Then, seeing the sudden destruction of our firepower hitting them was so shocking it dazed me. The huge unending roar, the flashes, and the jerking, twisting human bodies all ran together in my mind. The armored-track dudes were laughing and congratulating themselves now from inside their steel boxes. Flares were still popping and occasional artillery shells exploded over that smoking scene of destruction. I shuffled on back to the hootch with the other men and lay on my back for a while, but couldn't sleep. We had to get ready for another combat patrol of the area. I stared at the faces around me: Tommy Donaghue, our RTO, Cortez, "Rock" Allen, McQuade, Reynaldo Garcia from Los Angeles, Evans, Earl, and Baca, and Joe Miller. They looked like skeletons in the dark, as though I could see right inside them. I knew now how much we had to count on each other, how things could fall apart any minute, any day—no matter how boring a patrol might seem. I was in a tight brotherhood of men who knew where it was at.

The same enemy 273rd Regiment we'd ambushed stayed close to Phu Loi, dug in, and was attacked by the 3rd/1st ARVN Armored Cavalry, who killed eighty VC/NVA two kilometers south of the Phu Loi camp. Many of their dead were killed at the beginning of our own ambush, which was responsible for the success of the South Vietnamese action. This was exactly what our Recon platoon was supposed to do, and it was fast action and luck that got us through untouched. At the same time our ARVN allies were fighting the 273rd VC, we could hear the rumbling thunder of an "arc-light raid" of B-52 bombers dumping tons of explosives to the south of Phu Loi and Tan Phu Kan. This is the only thing that tied us to the overall campaign against the enemy all around Saigon.

We're really into weapons. We're not part of a regular line-infantry battalion, so we've got lots of leeway. In the field we mostly carried M-16s and M-79 grenade launchers, and M-60s, but we're always experimenting with this or that exotic piece. I tried M-2 automatic carbines, M-3 grease guns, a submachine-gun, and a Soviet AK-47, but I ended up liking the new M-16 AI improved. One of our guys always carried a 12-gauge pump shotgun loaded with buckshot. The enemy weapons were excellent, but their popping noise was so distinctive that using one could be dangerous; if you got separated, your weapon could draw fire from your own guys. We were working patrols and ambushes with LRRP teams off and on, and one dude on a team we saw a lot, always carried a Soviet RPD light machine-gun he'd captured during the offensive. In their little five-man group he could afford to do that and get away with it.

The Phu Loi Long Range Recon Patrol lived in a hootch next to ours and often worked in conjunction with us. When we were not out in the bush we'd often visit together telling stories and swapping informaiton about the surrounding area. They were reportedly part of F Company of the 52nd Ranger Infantry. The one I remember was the team leader named Siegal. He was pointed out to me by Tommy Donaghue, who said, "That's Sergeant Siegal from the LRRPs. He's fuckin' crazy." Coming from Donaghue, who I had decided was crazy, that was quite a compliment. Everyone had a high opinion of this squad because of their success in pinpointing enemy units and calling in fire on them. They also kept the base camp commander informed of enemy movements. Our recon missions and night ambushes were often coordinated with Sergeant Siegal's squad, and his team's expertise raised our own standards of operation, camouflage, concealment, and noise discipline. We became more adept at these things also by going out with his squad individually or in small groups and being forced to match their conduct. Gradually, we learned the art of using camouflage paint and jungle leaves to blend in perfectly at night. The skills they had learned at the MACV Recondo School were acquired by us and made our platoon more effective. Occasionally we saw other LRRP squads for a few days, because while in Phu Loi, they were bivouacked in our hootch. One squad had the distinction of being all black, with one white "mascot." I believe he was their RTO, and when they'd go out on a mission and take some fire or get hit badly, somebody in my hootch would always ask, "Did their mascot make it, man?"

Weird, strange 'Nam—after a while you could say you'd seen everything. In addition to the LRRPs and our own CRP platoon, our hootch area neighbors included the 35th Scout Dog Platoon, the 61st Combat Trackers, and the 4.2 (or "four-deuce") Mortar Platoon for base camp security.

The four-deuce mortar guys fired missions in support of our operations alone, or with the LRRPs, and returned fire on enemy rocket and mortar positions shelling Phu Loi. They mostly humped ammo and stayed constantly ready for fire missions. They had helped us out a lot that night of the 13th of February and at several other times later when we spotted enemy movement and called in their fire.

The Scout Dog Platoon and the Trackers were constantly in and out of the field on missions supporting recon and infantry units. Their specialty was finding enemy tunnel complexes and underground base camps, using the dogs' keen sense of smell. When they were in from the field and we were wandering around in the dark, we were damned careful not to trip over their dogs. Whenever that happened, the clumsy fool got a quick education in what a man can train a dog to do. Out of the field, on a stand-down, we'd get mellow from the dew we'd get from a mama-san in Phu Cuong. Earl and I, and Baca and Monty, Joe Miller and Olly, and other dudes would get in kind of a circle and pass it around, telling stories and getting close. It made the nights when we were inside the wire or the time off really pleasant.

"All yer doin' is trying to survive, anyway."

We'd sit and stare out through the humid dark tropical nights and get really off watching the flares put on a light show for us.

One night the lifers were showing the movie "Dr. Zhivago" at Division Artillery in a makeshift theater set-up. A bunch of us wandered over to see the show. Right in the middle of one of the best parts, a barrage of rockets came screaming down on Phu Loi, and one hit and blew up the entire movie-screen end of the building. We'd had some smoke and we'd had some booze, we were all messed-up, anyway—so far gone it took us a few seconds to realize it was not part of the movie. It was for real. Jerked back into reality, we staggered and scrambled into the nearest bunker.

Out in the field, we're straight and real careful. "Recon" is supposed to mean "go out and scout around, find targets, report enemy moves, but be cool." GIs were being killed and wounded all around us, but we kept being slick and careful in our patrols and ambushes, and stayed lucky.

On the night of the 14th of February I went out with the LRRPs of Sergeant Siegal's squad for the first time. He came into the hootch and said, "We got room for two of you guys if ya wanna go."

Siegal was a grim and fearless-looking guy in his jungle camouflage. Art McQuade and I were the first two that stepped up. He looked us over, saying, "O.K., I want you two guys camouflaged and quiet, an' on yer best behavior. Come on over to our hootch when yer ready; we're not going out by chopper, we're walkin'."

About seven of us went out through the wire into the pitch darkness, so well-camouflaged we could hardly see one another. I felt competent by now, and meshed with the tight little squad without trouble; so did McQuade. We moved silently about three clicks north to a position between Phu Loi and Dog Leg, with the ruins of An My to the west and the northern–most hamlet of Tan Phu Khan to the east. All communication between us was done with hand signals; radio communication back to Phu Loi was in click signals on the PRC-25, so talking would be unnecessary. After getting set up in a circular ambush position that enabled us to cover each other, we waited in total silence. If a bug bites or a leech starts sucking when you're set up, you can only move your hand ever so slowly to the spot and squeeze. Any fast motion can be seen or felt or heard, and endangers all the rest. The silence becomes almost deafening, and in that silence enemy movement can seem as loud as cannon fire.

Just before midnight that night of the 14th, we heard our first movement; a short time later we spotted the enemy. We'd counted eight Viet Cong moving along a trail to our front when Siegal popped his claymore with a *Whoomp!* and opened fire. The rest of us opened up instantly, and while we did, Siegal was calling in artillery fire that began exploding in the killing zone within seconds. When the artillery fire was over we began backing up in silence, formed into a file again, and moved our position about a click back towards Phu Loi. We then waited out the dawn in tense silence and after the sun came out retraced our steps to the ambush site. Here and there were blood trails, pieces of NVA web gear and several Chi Comm grenades. The bodies had been dragged off. Siegal was grinning anyway. "The sonsabitches're gonna walk pretty light around here fer awhile, huh?"

We humped our way back into Phu Loi on the morning of the 15th of February, and when McQuade and I entered our hootch everyone started questioning us about our night. We told them what we'd seen and lay down to sleep for awhile. We felt like we'd earned a day's rest.

Next we're sitting around on stand-down reading the *"Stars and Stripes."* The headline proclaims: "Brace for Red Push, Speed 10,500 Troops to Viet." The news story reveals that additional Army and Marine combat troops (later identified as a brigade of the Army 82nd Airborne Division and the 27th Marines) are being shipped over rapidly as reinforcements to prepare for an expected second wave of attacks by the enemy. Some are identified as men who had already served their year in combat. This news starts an uneasy rumor circulating around our area that the one-year combat tour of duty may be terminated. I'm in talking with Earl, Art McQuade, Donaghue, and a few other guys:

"Kind of strange ain't it man? They're givin' millions of students draft deferments at home, an' at the same time sendin' GIs back over here that already made it through a year in combat."

"Yeah, I know what ya mean. They talk about freedom and justice and equality fer all, an' that don't sound much like it. The same people gettin' outta serving over here with student deferments are the ones doin' all the protesting about us fightin' the Communists. Crazy ain't it?"

An inside paragraph tells about a top-ranking VC general being killed in the streets of Saigon on the 13th of February, the same time as our ambush of the 273rd VC Regiment.

Somebody's laughing: "Maybe we jus' blew up all his troops that was goin' down to meet him, an' he was runnin' around lookin' for 'em."

There's a report also of the "108th MG shot down over Hanoi by U.S. aircraft" and the comparison that forty American planes had been downed by Migs in dogfights. It's a different part of the war that we can't even picture. In the stateside news, an article describing how the widow of a U.S. soldier killed in action was harrassed by an anti-war group "sending her bitter propaganda through the mail." This is the first time I'd heard of this cruelty, but in the future it became so common that many surviving family members asked for unlisted numbers to avoid hearing obscenities like, "We're glad your man was killed in Vietnam; he was a war criminal." It seems utterly evil to us here. We pass the paper around to each other.

Somebody snarls, "Slimey hippie bastards. When we get home we oughta kick the shit outta the first one we see!"

Then from behind us comes a sudden loud yell, "All right, you guys, get your gear and saddle up! We're goin' out again, headin' for Dog Leg."

Before this patrol we were briefed that "Bandit" had found tunnels up at Chanh Long (or Dog Leg), and the tunnel rats had taken heavy fire after throwing grenades in and crawling inside, with one guy hit bad. This had taken place on the 13th, the same day that the 1st ARVN Cavalry was still fighting the 273rd after our big ambush. McQuade and I were tired from being out all night on the LRRP ambush. During the patrol north, we were spread out on either side of the dirt road known as 1A that went out of Phu Loi village up through An My and into Dog

Leg. I was so sleepy my feet were dragging. All along the way were thousands of leaflets dropped by the 1st Division PSY-ops helicopters in their fruitless attempts to get the VC to surrender willingly. It was laughable to see the ground covered as if it had snowed paper, while everyone on both sides of the war ignored them. Every so often we would get a little lecture by a lifer to remind us that dropping these leaflets was "hard work," and we should respect the soldiers assigned this duty. We passed the big gulleys off to our right near the site of McQuade's and my previous night's ambush with Sergeant Siegal's LRRPs. It seemed like ancient history already. The same dusty brush and bamboo, deserted looking, as if nothing had ever lived there or passed through. I was daydreaming to myself that the flies had already sucked up the blood trails. Sometimes Vietnam seemed like a huge alien emptiness that could swallow up every American soldier there. The patrol turned into a long hump with nothing to show for it but sweat and dust.

It seemed that whenever we'd get back from a long, tense patrol, grateful to have made it back without running into something bad, we'd come under fire inside Phu Loi. We were hit with hundreds of 122mm Soviet rockets, along with Chinese 82mm mortars. The rockets had a range of about seven miles or farther with a booster charge, and stood about 6½ feet tall. With their long range and short (less than a second) duration of launching flash, they were extremely hard to pinpoint, as were Chi-Comm 82mm mortar-firing positions. Locating these was something we were constantly trying to do out in the bush.

The enemy had moved into the Binh Duong Province–Lam Son area from two directions at the beginning of the offensive, hauling large supplies of rockets with them. From the west they came out of their sanctuary in the Parrot's Beak of Cambodia through Hau Nghia Province, and from the north out of the Fish Hook and base camps along the Song Be River. They joined up with locally mobilized Viet Cong units from the villages around the "Iron Triangle"; these acted as guides and go-betweens with the people. Every day we'd hear reports of the seige of Khe Sanh and the fighting for Hue going on now between the NVA and the Marines, and 1st Cav and part of the 101st Division. Maybe it was a lot worse than in our area, but we were still getting a pretty good taste of war. There were enough incoming shells now to cause real fear in Phu Loi. They could explode around us anytime, any place, whether one was a combat soldier or in a support job at the rear. A split-second of panic with the rushing *Whoosh-Crack-Boom!* when it was almost on top of you, and showers of shrapnel were tearing up the air or ripping into another GI in front of your eyes. Fifteen or twenty heavy-shelling attacks make the stories of other barrages long ago come alive. Almost every American soldier in an exposed position in Vietnam that February of 1968 now has his own little view of the closeness of death.

Buildings and aircraft hangars were blown up, and the fireballs at night from the exploding rockets were awesome, especially when they detonated in fuel, ammunition, or aircraft. One time after a recon patrol, on a stand down, I crossed the shell-pocked airstrip to visit a friend in the 11th Combat Aviation unit called the "Black Cats." An enemy rocket hit a nearby unit's outside wooden shower full of GIs. It was an awful bloody scene of screaming wounded and rescuers dragging out the bodies of dead GIs. Another time, a dude from Division Artillery, real short (ready to go home), was hit right near our hootch by a rocket explosion that blew off both his legs. I was on the scene trying to tie off the stump of one leg with a belt as a tourniquet, while shells continued to explode around us. He later died anyway. I still remember his moaning and crying, and the rush of feelings: "Jesus, I'm sorry, man, but I'm glad it wasn't me."

Later in the evening I remember seeing his large puddle of blood there in the dust with one of our GI belts laying in it and a cloud of flies buzzing around.

Combat Recon Platoon
Phu Loi
(Tet Offensive)
Mailed 18 February 1968

Dear Family,

Well, we had another bad attack at midnight last night, and it's still been going on sporadically all day. They're hitting us in the base camp with Russian or Chinese 122mm and 107mm rockets. These things sound like a jet coming in close, they're so powerful. Last night I was guarding the post defense after several days of patrols and ambushes. I was about half-asleep when they came whooshing in again. They make big orange fireballs with white streaks shooting out at night. They hit our POL (petrol) dump, and blew it all to hell, and destroyed a lot of aircraft, buildings, etc. There were at least (thirty-one) U.S. casualties here. Seven killed and twenty-four wounded, that I heard about myself. They didn't stop with dawn, but are still sending an occasional rocket salvo in now to keep us on full alert. They know it keeps us in bunkers and from getting anything accomplished here. They destroyed our own shower this morning, killing and wounding two GIs, and also blew up our little club-hootch. There was another guy killed and several wounded near me from B Troop of the 1/4 Cav, and several more hit in my old unit, the 1st Aviation Battalion. On a combat patrol out in that direction later today we could find nothing. If our artillery or armor fire hit any of them, they dragged them off. We ran into a few snipers near the village of Tan Phu Khan and over near another place called An My, but none of us got hit. There was also a big ambush on Thunder Road today, close to our position.

Just in this part of the country today they hit over forty towns and forts causing several hundred U.S. killed and wounded. We've heard reports of a thousand American casualties in the last two days. There is a large enemy offensive in progress. I want to say that if you do not wish for me to write what is happening here you should let me know. What did you write about in your war? Remember you could point with pride at your homeland, and the great job they did of supporting you. A lot of time, our country makes us feel like a cross between a band of criminals and a far-off novelty. This place does make you live only in the present. There is no past except mistakes lived through, and no future. I can't live on dreams of future adventures in this environment.

As for your monologue on "not killing VC in tunnels," if I get the chance anytime, I will kill them, knowing that's one less. Try and understand this is a real war going on and anything beyond this place and time is, to me, fantasyland.

Love,
John

This big rocket attack on the 18th of February signaled the beginning of the second wave of the Tet offensive.

While the camp was under fire at about 1:00 in the morning, the LRRPs from our hootch area sprang an ambush on a Viet Cong squad halfway between An My and Tan Phu Khan. One enemy soldier was killed and eight others retreated into Tan Phu Khan village in the darkness and disappeared. The LRRPs got safely back into Phu Loi as we were preparing to go out on a patrol.

This time, everyone carried an extra amount of ammo. We headed northeast out through the gate at Bunker 26. Lieutenant Marano, Ser-

geant Carlisle and Donaghue are on the hump, along with Earl, Art
McQuade, Joe Miller, Monty, Garcia, Evans, Clarke, Baca, and most
of the rest. We start moving in a long spread-out file in the bush to the
side of the dirt road on our way towards Tan Phu Khan first. When we're
almost to the outskirts of the village, we run into a huge roadblock of
cut-down trees, earth, and brush. There's a red, blue, and gold Viet Cong
flag stuck in the top of it. When I saw that the hair prickled on the back
of my neck.

I turned to Earl and said, "Guess what man, there's Cong around.
We better be real cool today!"

Earl was nervous too, shifting his eyes around, M-79 ready. The whole
file was tense as the lieutenant called in what we'd found and got the
word back that we were to skirt the village and move west towards An
My: "Be ready for sniper fire an' stay spread out."

Bravo Co. of the 2nd/16th was operating just north of Tan Phu Khan
in the Vinh Truong hamlet area, and they'd spotted another squad of
Viet Cong moving into the village area—a different unit than the LRRPs'
sighting.

We got the word over the radio that the village chief was hiding inside the ARVN militia outpost of Play Boy, and the VC were all through
the village. We were supposed to stay clear of the area because we didn't
have enough strength to go in, and we also had to avoid running into
the 2/16th by accident.

When we were out a short distance we started receiving sniper fire.
Pop-Craaack! Pop-Crack! Pop! Pop! Pop! Bzzzz! Dust was flying and
men were jumping. Lieutenant Marano yelled:

"Don't fire into that village! Stay spread out, keep movin'!"

We double-timed until we put some cover between us and them and
finally slowed down panting and sweating. Monty Montieth is snarling,
"Mother fucker ain't it? What 'cha gonna do? The gooks're laughin'
at us, man."

I said, "Hey, there it is, there's VC in there an' nobody here's strong
enough to take 'em outta there. It's kinda funny if ya think about all the
grunts out humpin' the bush right now lookin' for 'em."

Whoever was humping the radio, Joe Miller or Reynaldo Garcia, was
monitoring the Division Artillery net and told us: "Bravo 2/16th is calling
in from Vinh Truong. They're findin' tunnels and a bunker complex
about two kilometers from here, you guys. They're sayin' they found
beaucoup VC flags, and they're callin' for the 35th Scout Dog Platoon

and tunnel rats.''

Lieutenant Marano spoke up now. "Hold up a minute, break in place.''

We slumped down in position, leaning against a brush-covered berm for cover. He went on, "We're supposed to be lookin' fer rocket and mortar firing positions. The rockets last night and this morning came from two locations. One was over past Tan Phu Khan in the Vinh Truong area or near the ceramic factory where the 2nd/16th is right now. The other firing point was probably those big gulley ravines north of An My. We're going straight over there now, check it out and then swing all the way around An My, past that little road they call 1A on the map, and come back in on the west side of Phu Loi. Any questions?''

Somebody muttered, "Yeah, whatta we do the next time a sniper opens up on us, Lieutenant?'' Marano looked off towards where we were headed, "Look you guys, I know it's bullshit. We're here, we get shot at, an' we can't fire back into these villages. If it gets bad enough where they're hittin' us, we'll do it, but up 'til then we're gonna hold fire. We're supposed to be on a recon patrol right now. There isn't enough of us to search and clear that village, and if we even tried we might hit those guys in the 2/16th. Where we're going now, most of the people are gone or in the refugee camp, so we're in the clear for civilians. All right, let's go.''

Carlisle took over: "All right, you heard the lieutenant, on yer feet. Donaghue's got point. I want Baca and Okumura right behind him with the 79s. Keep your interval, spread it out.''

We were halfway to An My when Garcia or Miller called on the radio: "Bravo 2nd/16th's callin' in a dust-off. They got two guys hit by a booby trap in that bunker complex, one of 'em bad.''

This caused the entire file of us to start inspecting the ground instinctively for wires, even though we were a couple of miles away. Our attention was constantly shifting—scanning distant woodlines and bushes for enemy ambushes or bunkers one moment, and the ground around our feet the next. The tension was endless and wearing.

We were swinging around the north end of An My towards the suspected area when we heard the medevac chopper far behind us going in to pick up Bravo's casualties.

Way out ahead of us in the direction of Thunder Road we suddenly heard thudding and booming. There was a far-off crackle of small arms and machine-gun fire that quickly swelled to a distant roar.

We continued to move forward into the thick dry brush that separated some old dry rice paddies from the beginning of the gulley area. *Pop-Craaack!* Leaves falling. Sniper! *BBBBBRRRPPPPP!* Donaghue's firing. *BBBBRRRPPP! Thump-Crack-Boom! Thump-Whoomp!* Earl and Baca's pigs. I ran forward a few steps, flopped down and fired a burst into the wall of bush. *"Pop-Craack Pop! Pop! Pop!"* AK-47s, two of them. Rocky rushed forward, ready to help if anyone's hit. He pulled out a .45 automatic in the meantime and started to bang away with it. The lieutenant was yelling something unintelligible. Carlisle was yelling, too: "Spread it out! Spread it out! Keep your fire low!"

On either side of me the staccato cracking bursts of M-16s were drowning out and suppressing the enemy AK fire. Then there's a lull.

Lieutenant Marano called out, "Anyone hit? Everybody O.K.?" The answers came back from all around, "Yeah, lieutenant I'm O.K. don't see nobody hit. Sounds like the gooks pulled out."

We wait in long, tense silence, every sound magnified. Off in the distance we could still hear heavy firing towards Thunder Road.

"All right you guys, they must've pulled out. Let's go ahead real careful." After a short and fruitless search for enemy bodies in the area, we moved forward in a file again and broke through the brush for another twenty minutes until we crossed the dirt road that ran north of An My. Here the tank guns and firefight roar ahead of us was even clearer The day had given us the feeling that we were surrounded by VC but were incredibly lucky.

As we moved down the road towards Phu Loi, the RTO finally discovered what was going on a couple of miles to the west of us. There had been an ambush over there on the road. The Viet Cong had set it up near one of their roadblocks and sprang it when the road-clearing convoy stopped. It turned out to be a platoon of the 1st Engineers, a platoon of the 2nd/2nd Infantry and two tanks from the 2nd/34th Armored Cavalry. While we were listening to the roar, thankful not to be in the middle of it, helicopter gunships came clattering over our heads towards the fight, and soon came the scream of jets. The attempted ambush turned into a slaughter of about fifty Viet Cong with one American killed, sixteen wounded, and several vehicles hit. We slid along on our patrol in tense silence, eyeing every clump and patch of jungle bush.

Once we were back in Phu Loi, we were continually under 122mm rocket fire. There'd also been another attack on the ARVN Quang Tung training center in our area, by our old adversaries, the 273rd VC Regiment, and jet fighter-bombers were receiving anti-aircraft fire near the east side of our perimeter from the same VC who had shot at us near Tan Phu Khan earlier in the morning.

Lieutenant Marano told us we wouldn't be going out on an ambush that night because we were going to occupy a blocking position for Bravo 2/16th tomorrow afternoon, and stay out on ambush all the next night. Bravo was moving towards the northern edge of An My, near where we'd run into the second set up of snipers, in the hope of catching the Viet Cong who had retreated from the big ambush on Thunder Road.

After we finished the blocking mission, we were to change our position and pull back towards Tan Phu Khan to set up an ambush near the site of Bravo's booby trap and the two sightings of Viet Cong squads by the LRRPs and Bravo 2/16th. This was the same area in which the first sniper had fired at us today.

The rocket attack finally stopped, and we spent that night writing letters home, cleaning our weapons, and visiting with each other. In our corner of the hootch, Earl and I always had soft folk music going from his little machine, and other guys would come to visit. We'd tell each other stories about what we did when we were kids and what our plans were when we got home. Monty, Baca, Miller, and McQuade were always around, and sometimes Donaghue would come join the group with Rocky, Garcia, and other guys from the first hootch. When it got dark, we'd drift out behind the hootch and pass a few bowls around listening to the night sounds of artillery fire and staring at flares until we got high enough to forget everything and sleep.

The morning of the 19th was quiet and laid-back for us; we weren't going out 'til the afternoon.

About 1:00 p.m. we saddled up with our gear and fell out waiting for the word. About twenty of us were going, the rest having other details or guard duty. Half of us wore bush hats and the other half steel-pot helmets. A lot of us had camouflage fatigues by then.

At the An My gate we locked and loaded our weapons and got a short briefing about the mission, which was the same as we'd heard the night before.

After about three or four clicks of humping, we'd reached the gulley areas to the north of the ruined village and set up in a long spread-out line facing the direction that Bravo/2/16th was working, about a kilometer northwest of us. It was hot and still. Nests of biting fire ants were all over the place and kept us jumping and moving until everyone found a secure spot.

We couldn't see any sign of the grunt company, but about 2:00 p.m. we suddenly heard firing break out to our front. The news came over the PRC-25 that Bravo had spotted VC and had opened fire, and now were under fire themselves.

They had two guys hit—one in the arms and leg and another in the arm and rear, the R.T.O said.

We waited in tense silence watching for any movement in front of us. The firing broke out and then fell off in front of us for the next two hours. I was almost asleep when somebody near me—Montieth or McQuade—yelled, "I see one!" and opened fire. *RRRRPPPP! Crack! Crack! Crack! Crack!* Earl started thumping out 79 rounds and whoever was in charge screamed, "Recon by fire! Mad minute!" At this, we all opened fire with a blast into the bush in front of us. Somebody called, "Aim low, grazing fire!" I fired two or three magazines on automatic with nothing in sight.

After our firing stopped, we could still hear shooting way out beyond us, M-16s mixed in with AK-47s.

One of the dudes near me was saying, "I saw one, I'm tellin' you. We turned 'em back."

We lay flat and waited. Bravo 2/16th was calling in on the radio; they had three Viet Cong bodies now and seven or eight prisoners, several of them wounded. At about 4:00 we heard they had one GI killed and six wounded and were calling a dust-off for their casualties. Two or three of their wounded were hit badly; they asked for an urgent dust-off. A little later they called in again about the time we heard the chopper coming and said they had a total of six dead Viet Cong and ten or twelve prisoners.

We were told to saddle up and get ready to pull back towards Tan Phu Khan in time to set up an ambush.

We humped back the way we'd come, but on a different trail in case the VC were watching us. When we were about one kilometer north of Phu Loi and a little west of Tan Phu Khan, we called in our position at XT874161 and set up an ambush just about dusk.

Division Artillery told us they'd had more reports on a squad or platoon—ten to twenty Viet Cong in black pajamas carrying AK-47s—spotted again in our area by ARVNs from Play Boy outpost.

We were tired from the humping during the day. I set out my claymore with Earl and after we'd rolled out the wire we took turns sleeping, not paying much attention to anyone else. The ants and mosquitos were so bad we couldn't sleep long on the hard, dry ground. About 9:30 we got a radio message that Sergeant Siegel's LRRPs, who were set up three clicks east of us on the other side of Tan Phu Khan, had spotted another group of VC carrying rockets and mortar tubes, but they were too far away for them to blow their ambush. They had starlight night-scopes as we did, and were probably using them now. About midnight of the 19th, we saw mortar and rocket flashes to the north and east of us. About a click behind us, rockets started exploding inside the Phu Loi base camp. We were all wide awake by now, watching and listening.

The rockets quit after a few minutes, and the only noise was counter-mortar fire from the four-deuce platoon inside the base camp. Division Artillery called us to double check our position so we wouldn't get hit by friendly fire.

At about 3:00 in the morning of February 20th, the Viet Cong fired another barrage of rockets into the base camp. This time, their firing position was obviously and definitely inside the village of Tan Phu Khan, at the northern end. There was no way for our artillery to return fire without hitting so-called "friendly" villagers.

Early that morning, just as we were beginning to think we'd wasted our time, we started hearing shuffling and rattling noises. They were too far away to blow our claymores, but the word was passed in a whisper to "get ready."

The noises grew louder and clearer, sounding like about twenty people. Someone in our line couldn't stand it anymore and pulled the trigger. We all opened fire at once, M-16s, M-79s and an M-60 machine-guns. The VC fired back and held their position, but they were firing high. For me, it was shooting at enemy green tracers and muzzles; I couldn't see any figures. We put out a wall of bullets until their fire stopped. We waited in place for some long minutes sweating and straining our eyes and ears for sound or movement. Then somebody—Marano, Carlisle or Rock—called out, "O.K., let's move up and see what we got!"

After some searching in front of us, we found one dead Viet Cong in black pajamas with a khaki uniform shirt, NVA web gear, and a new Chinese Communist AK-47. His body was a sieve of bullet holes. A few minutes later we found another one, badly wounded, with the same gear. He'd gotten rid of his weapon. There were two or three other blood trails, but we had no desire to follow them that day.

We called in the action and the coordinates to the 1st Aviation Battalion and asked for a gunship to come up and scout the area. They logged the report and sent over a light fire team from the Rebels, but the rest of the VC had disappeared.

We were told by Division Artillery headquarters that we'd probably shot up one of the VC rocket platoons that had been hitting Phu Loi.

The prisoner lived, and intelligence worked him over until they found out he was from the 3rd Platoon of the 3rd Company of the VC Phu Loi Battalion. Our location was close to the spot where the 2/16th had hit the booby trap and probably near one of the VC firing positions or rocket caches.

When we got back into Phu Loi, we discovered that LRRPs had been in contact the same night and called in artillery on another VC unit two or three kilometers from our position.

The Phu Loi Recon Patrol was slowly becoming a more professional unit, despite the sneers we often got about being a bastard unit that no one wanted to acknowledge.

As a group, we were accumulating detailed information on the villages and bush surrounding Phu Loi because of continually operating in the same area.

Another incident occurred around this time in the nearby area of large, dry gullies north of An My. We were searching for mortar–and rocket-launching areas again, and when we came up out of one of the gullies with Sergeant Carlisle at the point, he suddenly yelled, "Down!" At that instant a *Boom!* went off, with shrapnel and pellets zinging through the air around us. It was a command-detonated claymore mine backed up against an old tombstone. He'd spotted it just as the VC detonated it, probably saving some of our lives. We moved up on line and opened fire into the bush. Carlisle was yelling, "Recon by fire! Recon by fire! Do it!" Tommy Donaghue and Sergeant Rhiener (Rock) were on my right as we started shooting. Rocky Allen and Earl were both carrying M-79s and moved up to shell an angle of the woodline with grenades where it reached out close to us. We were taking some light automatic fire from there, but with all of us shooting at once and the '79 grenades exploding, we silenced it and moved on out without any casualties. I had shot off five magazines totaling a hundred rounds of ammunition.

We continued the patrol in a big circular cloverleaf out around this jungle, and on the return came back near the same area through a large bombed-out area of craters.

As we came up over one rise, we got the drop on three Viet Cong in uniform wandering around in a daze. Their eardrums had been blown out and blood was dripping from their noses as a result of shell or bomb concussion. We took them prisoner without any trouble because they were in shock. That same day we captured three or four more we had caught digging in the bombed-out area. We figured later they were trying to excavate buried comrades or weapons.

There were just a few tense seconds after we came up over the rim of a gulley and spotting them digging. In our miserable Vietnamese, we ordered them to come forward and surrender.

"Lau Di, Lau Di, mother fuckers. *Lau Di* or *chieu hoi,* but don't do nothing fast, gooks!"

The sight of our grim faces, pointing weapons, and gestures were enough. They could see they had no escape, no chance to run. One of them grunted, "Chieu hoi, chieu hoi," and stepped slowly towards us, hands over his head. The others followed. One of them was wounded. Their brown Viet Cong uniform shirts were torn and ragged. They wore shorts and Ho Chi Minh sandals, made of American rubber tires.

Years afterward, I would remember incidents like this while listening to harangues by American radicals about "ruthless, murdering GIs who shot anything that moved in Vietnam." It was a tribute to our discipline and regard for human life that these helpless enemy soldiers caught without weapons in their hands were not shot down in cold blood. That day in February marked the largest capture of prisoners we had ever made in the Recon platoon. It must have been the result of a successful U.S. airstrike. We were picked up by trucks on the dirt road 1A near the ruins of An My village along with our prisoners, and returned to the base camp. I'm sure the Colonel and the intelligence people were happy that day because they didn't get many chances to interrogate live Viet Cong prisoners.

Every long day or night in the field was marked by some small ordeal. One day, it would be a shaft with a side tunnel off of it. We'd lower Steve Hustler on a long rope with a pistol. Sweating and straining, nerves on edge, he checked it out. "Not a damned thing," he called. Or another day, when we're moving along, tired out, sick of the same old jungle sights or stupid gooks saying to us, "No VCs," and a sniper opens fire when we're least expecting it—bullets cracking out of hiding. You hit the dirt, open fire, shoot up the jungle, move forward and find a little spider-hole or fighting position, no bodies, nobody hit on our side either, but shook up again, sharpened up a little more. Or Earl and I stumbling on a huge king cobra, coiled up, hood spread, ugly, ready to strike. We stared at this thing in disbelief for a moment, then noticed it was right near a well-shaft. We clicked off our safeties in unison, shot it into the hole with bursts of automatic fire, and threw a couple of frag grenades down on top of it, blowing it to pieces.

One morning, around this time in February, we came back from an all-night ambush through the gate between Bunkers 51 and 53 facing An My. We were tired and irritable, after almost a month of tension, shooting, rocket attacks, and casualties in Phu Loi. We filed towards the base camp dump in our camouflaged fatigues, hearing erratic gunfire that sounded like pistols. We came upon a strange sight. A line of military police were shooting at something down in the dump with .45 automatic pistols, some laughing and yelling, some looking upset or sad.

Tommy Dongahue, taking the lead as usual, with his M-60 machinegun balanced over his shoulder yelled out, "Whatcha doin', guys?" A few of them turned as we walked up.

"We're shootin' these dogs, man, mostly puppies."

We saw them, a writhing, crying, yipping, squirming mess down below. Puppies with half their heads shot off, bullet holes dripping blood, guts hanging out, jaws blown half off... Donaghue suddenly shouted, "You stupid REMF pigs, what's the mattah wit' you? Ya can't even hitta buncha dogs!"

"Colonel Schroeder ordered us to do it man, he said they found some dogs with rabies an' we gotta kill 'em, puppies an' all, every dog we can catch! All we had on us was these .45s."

One dog was directly down below us staring right up at Donaghue, McQuade, Earl and I. One of his legs blown off, but it was a clean amputation. You could see immediately he might even make it if they left him alone, but it was obvious we couldn't stop the slaughter. The dog moaned piteously and stared up at us with big round eyes as if to say, "Save me, can't you? I haven't done anything." Suddenly Tommy Donaghue exploded, "Fuck you incompetent fools." He swung the M-60 around and down leveling it.

"Ya do it like this, assholes!"

The gun erupted in a long ripping burst with the tracers richocheting straight through and beyond the howling dogs and puppies. I stared for a split second, yanked out a frag grenade, pulled the pin and threw it in yelling, "Fire in the hole!" Everybody jumped back and down, the grenade exploded and three or four more guys ran up spraying the dump with M-16s.

Then there was silence. The MPs stared at us, looked down at the pistols still in their hands, and holstered them. We shuffled off cursing and muttering at them, "Screw you, and your goddam pistols, too, assholes."

First Division Artillery was sending us out constantly to look for enemy firing positions after the mortar and rocket attacks, and sometimes we found them, little empty pits or open bunkers and range cards, complete with calculations to hit different parts of our base camp. We'd destroy the bunkers by demolition with C-4 explosive and move out again. Another day of incoming shells and we were rushed out towards the firing positions.

"This time we're right on top of the bastards!"

We moved forward on line, trading fire with enemy snipers trying to cover the gooks' retreat, but this time we were quicker than they were. As I was moving and firing, Earl was on one side of me and Bernie Bernard on the other. We overran a firing position and captured a new Red Chinese 82mm mortar with high-explosive shells, baseplate, sights, plus other enemy gear. The gooks retreated now from the position, we didn't know whether we had killed some and their bodies had been dragged off or not. We were happy anyway. Bernie, who ended up here by way of the Haight-Ashbury hippie scene, was nodding and laughing,

"Hey, man, far out. We got one of those sons-of-bitches!"

"I bet this thing's blown up a few GIs in Phu Loi."

We stand around admiring our prize. It's beautifully made, a quality weapon, the huge round base plate made of bronze with fitted shoulder straps. Somebody else said, "Those dudes humped this thing from Hanoi, man, or China. You know that?"

Everybody was mulling that over and Earl observed, "This war's gonna go on a long, long, long time."

We humped the captured mortar back into Phu Loi and set it up as a trophy near our hootch. REMFs came straggling in to look at it as though it's a tourist attraction.

"That's good, you dudes, yer cool, yer doin' yer thing the way yer s'pposed to," they told us.

We nodded, pretty mellow. "Yeah, we like it too. We like foolin' with the gooks."

I took a picture of Bernie Bernard posing for the REMFs in an undershirt, trying to stuff a football down into the Chi-Comm mortar and we got a few laughs.

Enemy ground action continued in the area, but other outfits were not as lucky as we were. On the 22nd of February, a company of the 1st/16th infantry lost four GIs killed and four wounded in a firefight south of us near Di An, killing twelve Viet Cong. The 1st/16th had been operating out of Di An up towards Phu Loi and over towards Thu Duc and Lai Thieu, and gotten in a whole series of firefights.

On the night of the 23rd we went out on another night ambush in a combined operation with the Phu Loi LRRP squad. We moved into two positions slightly to the east of An My, set up, and waited.

After midnight, both our ambush and the LRRP squad had large-scale movement of fifty to a hundred VC in front of our positions. We called in the 1st Division Artillery on the coordinates at XT850187. The night erupted with volcano-like displays of 4-deuce mortars, 105s, and 155 howitzers. In the morning, we moved into the area and found numerous blood trails but only one dead body. Papers we stripped out of the dead VC's pockets turned out to be letters to his family that identified him as a member of the Reconnaissance Company of the 273rd VC Regiment. Later on, inside the base camp, we had a good laugh with the LRRPs.

"It takes a Recon dude to kill another Recon dude. There it is."

We learned a little of what was going on in the rest of Vietnam from the military newspaper, *The Stars and Stripes*. We'd always grab fresh copies that showed up and sit around behind a bunker between patrols, reading and commenting. One that seemed interesting enough to send home later was dated the 26th of February. Reports in it told of mopping up after the battle for Hue. Sometime later, when the existence of mass graves of thousands of Vietnamese anti-Communists murdered by the NVA were publicized, these deaths were attributed by the Viet Cong and American anti-war radicals to "American bombing." A few kilometers to the northeast of us, the 3rd Brigade of the 101st Airborne Division was reported to be in contact with the enemy along the Song Be River in the Catcher's Mitt area beyond Tan Uyen. Fifteen miles to the southwest of us, the 3/4 Cav of the 25th Infantry Division was said to be fighting with a Viet Cong regiment seven miles west of Tan San Nhut airbase. This enemy force was believed to be shielding the rocket gunners who had been firing shells into the big base since the "second wave" began on the 18th of February. On Saturday the 24th, four Americans were killed and thirty-four wounded inside Tan San Nhut, and eleven Vietnamese civilians were killed. Shelling of the Khe Sanh Marine base continued.

The most interesting article to me though, and the reason I saved that copy of the *Stars and Stripes*, was about the Tonkin Gulf incident. The headline said:

"Certain Reds Struck First, McNamara says."

The incident referred to was one that I first heard about while living in the outback of Australia, and served as the excuse for authorizing the commitment of half a million U.S. combat troops to Vietnam. There had been two reported attacks by North Vietnamese patrol boats on U.S. destroyers. At the time, South Vietnamese raiders were attacking positions along the coast of North Vietnam in the same locality as our destroyers. Whether our ships were providing protection for this operation and thereby inciting attack was a good question. In 1964, the reelection campaign of Johnson was on, along with promises by him not to expand the war and accusations of war-mongering against Goldwater, the Republican candidate. During the first action in the Tonkin Gulf, one single bullet had struck the U.S.S. Maddox. During the second reported "attack" which may never have occurred at all, no damage whatever was done, no enemy sighted or firing heard. But it provided a convenient reason for the President and his civilian advisors to seek the passage of the Tonkin Gulf Resolution. Out of this came the bombing of North Vietnam, the escalation of the war, and my reason for returning from Australia. I was possibly more interested in it than some of the other GIs around me because of my self-education in history, but to several of us discussing it at the time it seemed a pretty flimsy reason to go to all out war. In 1964, McNamara had in fact lied to a joint Congressional Committee including Senator Wayne Morse of Oregon, the first opponent of the U.S. action in Vietnam, who was seconded by Senator Earnest Gruening of Alaska. McNamara had testified categorically back then:

"Our Navy played absolutely no part in, was not associated with, was not aware of any South Vietnamese actions if there were any. . . .I say this flatly. This is a fact."

This part of his testimony led to the Congress of the United States authorizing the deployment of American power to "repel attacks." A resolution passed by our representatives as a result of careful planning, manuevering, and deception by the Executive branch of government. It was voted against by only two members in the entire Senate and House: Wayne Morse and Earnest Gruening; the latter said that all Vietnam was "not worth the life of a single American boy."

Now in 1968, after some 20,000 American boys had been killed in Vietnam, McNamara was saying something quite different. The captain of the U.S.S. Maddox "was aware of secret South Vietnamese combat operations occurring simultaneously in his area along the coast, but not aware of the details." Also during the same 1968 hearings, McNamara claimed he "could not remember" when secret plans had been drawn up to bomb North Vietnam. Actually, declassified documents later revealed that the bombing plans had been drawn up by McNamara, Rostow, and Bundy well before the Tonkin Gulf incident even occurred.

We were taking turns pulling a little guard duty inside the perimeter. The brass was uptight about enemy sappers sneaking in with RPGs or satchel charges and blowing them up in their comfortable quarters. In fact, we got word that they actually did happen on the 25th of January at Lai Khe, with ten killed and twenty-two wounded. Reportedly, they "blew up the officers' club full of majors, colonels, and generals drinking whiskey, and hit the colonel's villa, too." I watched some of our old grunts from Lai Khe smirk at the news. One night I was on guard near the 1st Division Artillery HQs looking out for sappers when we came under another heavy 122mm rocket attack. The shells were blowing up around me pretty close, and everybody was in bunkers—but I was not supposed to "leave my post unless relieved." I was crouched down next to the sandbags with my rifle near the 234th Radar's machine used to pinpoint enemy rocket-and morter-launching positions for the Division Artillery cannons to shoot at. In the light of flares and exploding rockets, I saw a Vietnamese running for the generator that powered the machine. I moved up fast with my piece ready just as he scuttled out of there and bumped right into me. For a split second, I considered shooting him, but instead I dragged him by the hair to the officer of the day, holding my rifle one-handed on him, with the safety-off.

He turned out to be one of the teen-age Vietnamese working in the Division Artillery messhall—"just another kind of sneakin' Viet Cong." He was handed over to a CID agent or military intelligence. He'd been pulling out a few wires during each attack.

I wondered: "What are we going to do in this kind of guerilla war? Totally segregate ourselves from the population we're supposed to be helping and defending? How do we ever separate the friends and the enemies?" We never did figure that out in 'Nam. I found myself thinking about the lessons I'd learned from Smitty and Simmons when I'd first hit the country.

On the 26th of February we were alerted that the 35th Scout Dog Platoon and tunnel rats were going into a tunnel and bunker complex that the 2/16th had found in the "ceramics" hamlet of Vinh Truong, north of Tan Phu Khan. They wanted our Phu Loi Recon Platoon as security for their operation. We filed on out of the perimeter on foot and headed north again between An My and Tan Phu Khan to link up with them. Once there, we spread out in a wide circle, while they were going in and out. The Phu Loi LRRP Squad was there too. During the underground search, guys like Steve Hustler, who enjoyed tunnels, were going in with them using pistols and flashlights. It was a good find of Russian anti-tank mines, VC flags, grenades, and gas masks. At the end of the day, we humped back into Phu Loi, but the LRRPs moved three clicks north and set up an ambush. In the middle of the night of the 26th, they ambushed a platoon of twenty VC moving north out of Vinh Truong, killing one. He turned out to be the Viet Cong village chief of Vinh Truong, part of the Communist "shadow government" in all the villages around us. The base camp came under another rocket attack early in the morning of the 27th.

During late February and early March back home in the states, the perception of the war was changing much faster than before the Tet Offensive. With lurid television coverage of the increased fighting and publicity about 3,000 American casualties per week, the reality of war struck home. I received long letters from my father asking if we were in danger of being overrun or captured, and giving his homefront view of the war. His letters showed that Vietnam had finally become real to him and his friends. In every letter he sent me clippings from newspapers, and repeated things he'd heard on television. Almost everything I saw or heard from the U.S. news media was negative or anti-war. Hundreds of New York–area editors, writers, teachers, and professors announced their refusal to pay taxes used for the war effort.

James Reston, an influential writer for *The New York Times*, claimed that "the Saigon government and the Americans together could not defeat the Communists." *The Washington Post* had also run a front-page story headed "Ho (Chi Minh) Cheers Viet Cong Victory." In another article, their writer Joseph Kraft flatly said "the war in Vietnam is unwinnable." Walter Cronkite, one of the most prominent and respected TV commentators, offered the opinion that "the South Vietnamese government might salvage a measure of victory from defeat, but that such a thing was unlikely.'' Later, newsman Frank McGee of NBC observed that "the war is being lost.'' Such statements shocked my father and other Americans. My father's response was that since we were already committed to the war, the best answer to an enemy offensive would be an even more powerful counterattack by us.

This is natural and intelligent reasoning in men who know war. But the people in Washington D.C. who had initiated our deployment in Vietnam, who called on the patriotic feelings within us, were getting cold feet.

While thousands of GIs humped, sweated, searched for and fought the enemy, the specialists in the Defense Department and State Department watched the television war. They saw film of people being shot in Saigon, and close up scenes of blood on the streets. They heard panicky reports from reporters and perhaps for the first time it actually sunk in. . .when you send men to war, somebody gets hurt. Those bureaucrats and technicians who had worked so carefully to arrive at this point could not face the results of their actions. Maybe it was because some of them had made their little token trips to the ''field'' in Saigon. Perhaps Dak To or Con Thien of Loc Ninh had seemed so remote from the plump life of Washington and Saigon that the fact of war hitting the capitol was too much of a shock. An offensive that started as a temporary surprise and setback for us was now being seen as a defeat by many important people.

The slaughter of the Viet Cong main force units at An My, all around Phu Loi, Bien Hoa, Saigon, the Delta, and throughout Vietnam was not to be in vain. The turning point of the war was happening now, in February and March of 1968, but those of us on the scene didn't know it yet. We thought from what we'd seen that the enemy had been defeated, but in reality our own leaders at home had been. In March of 1968, Americans all over Vietnam hunkered behind cover from 122mm Soviet rockets that seemed to be flowing into Vietnam in an uninterrupted stream. At the same time, important meetings were occurring in Washington D.C. Robert McNamara, the strategist, the manipulator of defense, was resigning in favor of Mr. Clifford, a high class Washington lawyer. Mr. McNamara, the author of so much, had seen the light and decided that victory was unattainable, so he stepped aside. Untouched, unbloodied, he left half a million boys in the positions prepared for us, and went on to become president of the World Bank. For many years to come, he could now apply his techniques to siphoning billions of dollars of American money into the hands of Third World "progressives." Eventually, his pet projects were to become the "world population explosion" and defeat of a necessary strategic defense initiative.

An official named Paul Warnke, who was destined someday to be one of our prime arms negotiators with the Soviets, was busily converting the new Secretary of Defense, Clark Clifford, to his own defeatist views on Vietnam. Mr. Warnke was also put in charge of developing Vietnam policy proposals to alter the President's ideas.

The representatives of the American people, the U.S. Congress, were beginning to find their voices and assert authority, but it was now somewhat late. The antiwar sentiment was growing in the Capitol at a time when our forces were committed on the field of battle. From now on through the next four years the question became: how to disengage. These changes in attitudes by influential news media figures, bureaucrats, and politicians set the stage for an ever intensifying growth of the antiwar movement throughout the country. However, even with the public proclamations of the impossibility of a U.S. victory, polls showed that a majority of Americans favored, as my father did, stronger military action against the enemy. When it gradually became apparent that the President and his men were not going to do this, public support for the war fell off even more rapidly.

The spreading, academia-based antiwar movement was being greatly broadened and encouraged by all these developments. The war in Vietnam had never been declared by the Congress. The people had never mobilized or were told that this fight was for the survival of America. The Gulf of Tonkin resolution had been passed because of a perceived enemy threat, by Johnson, McNamara, and the rest, to our "freedom to operate on the seas." The Congress had not specifically authorized commitment of a massive U.S. force in a mainland Asian war when it permitted the defensive use of American power. Johnson's own rhetorical promises of "not widening the war" or "using American boys" before his 1964 election had contributed to the misconceptions.

The families of the United States Congress did not suffer unduly from the consequences of the war, however. Out of several hundred sons who came of service age throughout the period of American involvement, not a single one was killed, and very few ever served in Vietnam, because of deferments or "alternative service."

Here, in the meantime, we were dug into the dirt of Indochina at Phu Loi and a hundred other bases and camps. Deeply, fully, and totally enmeshed in the Vietnamese Civil War, confronting the weapons and supplies of Russia and China in the hands of dedicated Communist soldiers.

Sometime in late February we pulled security patrols around U.S. engineer units engaged in jungle-clearing operations. Some of the units I recall were the 1st Engineers of the Big Red One, and Op-Con companies of the 34th and 168th Engineers. The idea was to deny the Viet Cong sanctuary under the heavy jungle cover within striking distance of U.S. bases like Phu Loi.

Usually we rode out to the east towards Check Point 84 and the Dong Nai River on armored tracks that guarded the Rome plows of the engineers. When we reached the work area, the APCs and tanks would deploy out in a defense circle surrounding the huge, jungle-clearing machines and we, along with any other infantry platoons there, would dismount and spread out beyond the armor to pull security for them.

The first jungle-clearing operation the patrol had been on was before I came into the platoon, in December or January. This one in late February was mostly dull work, sitting out in small OP groups in the surrounding jungle with rifles and machine-guns ready, alternately watching the bush in front or the engineers working behind. Every so often one of the Rome plows or tracks would trigger a booby trap or mine explosion that usually resulted in a flurry of activity and occasional American casualties.

We spent most of our time slapping biting insects and spiders, watching for stirred up snakes, and staring into the foliage wondering where the enemy was.

On several of the clearing days, we humped security behind the 35th Scout Dog Platoon. One day the scout dogs discovered a large underground tunnel complex we had missed in one of the few remaining areas of standing jungle where we were working. The dog suddenly disappeared underground snarling, and we knew we'd found the entrance.

One incident etched vividly in my mind was an engineer-operator screaming out over the roar of his big machine, "I got one! I got one!" His Rome plow was pitched as he throttled forward full speed. A Viet Cong guerrilla frantically pushing himself halfway out of a spider hole was ripped in half by the blade before our eyes.

The worst area we entered was the remains of the Ong Dong Jungle to the east between the Phu Loi-Dog Leg-Tan Phu Khan area and on the Dong Nai River. This was a staging area for the enemy moving south from the Catcher's Mitt-Binh My-Song Be River area towards their targets around Saigon. It had been undergoing clearing operations since late 1967, but the VC and NVA still kept using it.

When we weren't on jungle-clearing operations, we continued our long patrols and ambushes day after day. One landmark in our humping was south of the base camp—a pink church with a cross on it beyond Vinh Loi village. Whenever we were in this area, we'd always be followed by a large crowd of Vietnamese orphans and children of refugees. They'd scream at us the usual tirade: "GI No. 1, souvenir me cigarette, you gib me chop-chop, GI wanna buy good smoke?" If we didn't want them around, we would tell them, "You VC, GI no like, *Di Di Mau.*" They'd give us obscene Vietnamese elbow gestures and screaming taunts. The only person in the platoon who could ever handle them was Rocky Allen. He spoke more Vietnamese than anyone else, and in one long guttaral phrase I saw him reduce the little rats to tears on several occasions. What he said I don't know, but he had learned it up the Song Be River in Phuoc Vinh on a previous tour with an assault helicopter company stationed there.

Another landmark was the ceramics factory near Vinh Truong in one of the outlying hamlets of Tan Phu Khan village, northeast of Phu Loi. Tommy Donaghue was convinced the VC used a large brick tower here as an aiming and connection OP for their rocket and mortar attacks on the base camp.

On a search and seal patrol of the ceramics hamlet in early March, we were operating in conjunction with the 7th of the 1st Cav, an independent unit freshly arrived in Vietnam about the middle of February as part of reinforcements for Westmoreland. It had been a good day because we found some gook booze while searching houses and stores in the village. Rocky Allen was drunk out of his mind, and collapsed while crossing a small bridge. Donaghue was our patrol leader for the day, and was worried that his best buddy wouldn't be able to make it, for Rocky couldn't walk. Tommy Donaghue stopped one Vietnamese on a Lambretta who was selling cold bottled Cokes and gave him a dollar MPC.

The Viet handed Tommy one Coke intended to sober up Rock. All of a sudden Tommy shouted at the startled Viet, "Bullshit one Coke, here we are hot as hell, savin' yer rotten country; we want 'em all!" The Vietnamese babbled incoherantly as we surged in around him, his bird-like voice raising to a screech as he saw his wares disappearing.

The M-60 leveled at his chest convinced him who was in the right, however, and he finally rattled away luckier than he knew.

Because Rocky was temporarily incapacitated, Donaghue decided it was time to prove his theory about the ceramics factory. He pointed at the kilns.

"Those ugly silo-lookin' things are full of rockets. I've known it fer a long time. Over there's where we found those mortar baseplates the other day, an' that damn gulley over there is a perfect firing pit. Nobody could see the flash. This's gotta be the place."

The Chinese-looking owner or manager was meanwhile hovering nearby nervously eyeing us in our raggedy camouflage jungle uniforms, with our loud accompanying shouts of agreement to Tommy's revelations. He knew something bad was in the air when Donaghue turned on him.

"You No. 10 VC, son-of-a-bitch. Beaucoup rockets here, kill GI!" The skinny little man shrieked, "I no VC! I no VC! VC No. 10. I like GI. No kill GI." He grabbed at Tommy's arm and dragged him into a doorway where a portrait of the Nationalist Chinese leader Chang Kai-Shek hung.

"I No. 1, No. 1, no Communist. I make cups, I like GI!"

Pushing my way forward, rifle in hand, I stood beside Donaghue and shouted, "Bullshit, gook, everytime the VC come through here you know goddamn well, you whip that picture down an' hang ol' Ho Chi Minh up there!"

Donaghue hadn't even waited for a reply. He was pulling C-4 plastic high explosive out of a claymore bag and packing charges against the nearest silo-kiln. As he was hooking up the det-cord, the Chinese Vietnamese became almost hysterical.

"No! No! GI No. 10, go 'way. I go tell MP you No. 10!"

I snarled at him, "MP, my ass Luke, you better get yer little skinny dink ass outta here!"

The other dudes in the patrol were giggling and backing up as Donaghue howled, "Fire in the hole!"

I dragged the protesting Sino-Vietnamese backwards just before the charge exploded with a muffled boom! Chunks of mud brick and clouds of dust erupted and we surged forward to the gaping, blasted hole in the wall. Peering inside all we saw were stacks of new baked cups, saucers, plates, bowls, and pitchers.

Donaghue was still sure of himself.

"Gotta be rockets in the nex' one guys. I'm sure of it." He quickly and expertly packed and wired another charge and blew it with the same results. No rockets in there. This time some of us crawled inside, dumping and scattering the contents to search underneath. We had all been so sure this was a launching area for weeks; finding nothing was only making us angrier. Over and over we repeated the procedure until the ceramics factory was a shambles, and still hadn't found anything Viet Cong.

Finally, dusty, sweating and tired, we formed up for the return hump.

"Goddamn VC are jus' packin' the rockets over here outta the jungle, an' usin' crossed aimin' sticks down in that pit. This tower's still the place. It's the only goddamn thing fer miles around high enough to correct their aim when they see the explosions inside the camp. There ain't nothin' we can do though; we don't even have enough C-4 left to blow that big son-of-a-bitch down."

Rocky had gradually sobered up from all the explosions and excitement and was ready to move out with the other eight or ten of us on the patrol.

"Hey, what the hell you guys been doin'? This place looks like shit around here. Besides I gotta damned headache. Let's get outta here."

As we were moving out, we heard a sudden, tremendous outburst of automatic fire break out where the tracks of the 7th/1st Cav were positioned. Tracers and shell explosions were ricocheting and bursting through part of the hamlet, and when we moved over and made contact, they shouted, "We been takin' fire outta there, AK-47 and SKS. We got one guy hit! Watch yerselves, dudes."

The local people, including the ceramics maker, scattered in panic at the first volleys down into their mud bomb shelters under the hootches. The shooting died down quickly. We never knew what happened, or if there had been more casualties. It was just part of the memory of a bad day in 'Nam, a synthesis of the craziness ever present here, never knowing how to locate an enemy that was continually hurting us. Without taking and permanently holding the ground in and around every village, we could never know who, where, or what the enemy was until they rocketed or ambushed us.

The long recon-patrols and night ambushes went on and on, day after day. Gradually, I got as worn down and raggedy as everybody else. The most wearing part of war for a grunt is the interminable humping, marching, sweating—not the occasional burst of shooting which was almost a relief from the endless tension. The constant dependence of us all on one other made us as close as brothers in a big family, arguing, fighting, and squabbling as brothers will do, but always pulling together when outsiders threatened the group.

One day around this time we were ordered by the Colonel to dig out and build an underground bunker for the "Donut Dollies." We hardly ever set eyes on these Red Cross girls, as they were considered officers' property, the only round-eyed women for miles around. On the appointed day we straggled over near their hootch and started digging. Tommy Donaghue, as our squad leader, was in a foul mood over his men doing shovel work.

"We're combat soldiers, we ain't REMF laborers. Let 'em dig their own goddamn holes. We don't even have decent bunkers ourselves!"

We tried to ignore his railings and kept chopping away at the rock-hard IndoChinese laterite, hour after hour. Times like this would frustrate Donaghue until he almost vibrated.

"Fuck this, we're supposed to be out on patrols in the bush huntin' gooks. I'll show ya how it's done."

He hustled back over to our hootch and returned with a claymore bag full of C-4 high explosive. We started grinning to each other, looking the other way and backing up as he packed the charges, muttering to himself, "Goddamn lifer assholes and REMFs always fuckin' with my men. I'll show'm how we dig a hole in Recon."

He backed up, unrolling the det cord without bothering to inform the unseen Red Cross girls still lounging in their hootch at midday.

"Fire in the hole!" "Ka-Boooom!"

The huge charge he'd detonated made a giant explosion that shook the ground and blew out a large crater in the laterite. Piercing screams and crashes rose from the nearby Donut Dollie hootch, as chunks of rock smashed into their walls and roof. Two of them ran out half-dressed, wailing, "Incoming! Incoming! We're hit!" Their hootch was shaken into a shambles inside and out, and the whole area was lost in a giant cloud of red dust.

Donaghue was laughing insanely as the rest of us disappeared. Later that afternoon we were relieved from the detail by some engineers and sent out on another ambush patrol that night. Our reputation in Phu Loi was growing.

About the time in early March when we worked the ceramic factory hamlet with the 7th/1st Cavalry, the "Blue Spaders" of 1st/26th Infantry of our Division, were working the area north of Dog Leg, between

Phu Loi and Lai Khe. They got in a heavy firefight on the 2nd, nine miles north of our base camp, losing eight U.S. casualties and killing thirty-two enemy soldiers. On most of our own patrols around this time, we stayed in close, making sweeps around the perimeter about one or two kilometers out. We kept passing through the same old gullys, patches of jungle, hamlets, and villages that we all knew by heart.

We alternated squads on patrols and night ambushes so that we all got a chance to sleep. The 2/16th still had platoons operating very close to Phu Loi, and we had to communicate our positions to them and the LRRPs constantly to avoid friendly fire.

On the night of the 4th of March, I was out on an ambush with half the platoon to the southeast of the camp between Tan Phu Khan and the "pink church hamlet" of Vinh Loi (or Xon Noi). There were at least three ambushes out in the area when the VC or NVA opened fire into Phu Loi at about 1:00 in the morning of the 5th.

We could see the flashes of rockets arching up and long streaks of 75mm recoiless rifle shells shooting out flat and exploding inside the perimeter. Both our ambush and a platoon of Charlie 2/16th called in the coordinates to Division Artillery so they could return fire. The word came back fast:

"We can't bring it in there, guys; that location is inside a friendly village. We can't get clearance on a fire mission, just sit tight and wait it out."

The sixty or seventy rounds of 107, 122, and 75mm shells caused casualties and damage inside the base camp, yet no effective response was possible. None of the three ambush patrols could have safely moved their positions in the darkness, entered the village, and engaged the enemy in time to stop the attack or catch them at all. They had the perfect strategy if the ARVNs couldn't act in their own villages. Intelligence was building up that an NVA unit was in our area. The newer Chinese Communist 107mm rockets and 75mm recoiless rifles were one indication. Another came on the 6th of March, when the government chief of Tan Phu Khan reported that 50 NVA soldiers of the 165th Regiment had moved into his village among the people, surrounded Play Boy Outpost, and set up road blocks again between there and Phu Loi. Division Artillery had other intelligence reports that the same NVA unit had left their base camp in the Catcher's Mitt-Song Be River area north of Tan Uyen and Binh My, crossing the half-cleared remains of the Ong Dong Jungle east of us and the Suoi Ca Stream between Phu Loi and the Dong Nai River.

On the 7th of March an ARVN Company from their 5th Division base camp adjoining us got in a firefight with part of the 165th NVA, killing nine of them and capturing several AK-47s and a Chi Comm .51 cal. anti-aircraft machine-gun. The location of the action was only a click southeast of the enemy rocket-firing position in the "pink church hamlet" on the 5th.

For the next few days we were kept in very close to the base camp as a ready-reaction force unit. The indications were growing of the possibility of another Tet-style attack. We almost had a vacation for three or four days, barely going outside the gate, pulling guard duty in the perimeter bunkers and around the Division Artillery headquarters. There was an announcement to the troops on the 8th of March that Major-General Keith L. Ware was taking command of the 1st Division from General John Hay. There was a vague stir of interest among the GIs when the news filtered down that General Ware was originally a draftee in World War II who had won the Congressional Medal of Honor. The word was passed that he was a "mellow dude." It made little difference to us; we never saw major-generals where we were, anyway.

We lay around in the hot sun on the sandbags close to the hootch or up by the perimeter wire waiting for something to change. It was dusty, dry, and incredibly hot in these lowlands during the dry season. When we got time off like this, it was easy to fall asleep in the middle of the day, wondering how the hell we had ever managed to hump for weeks through the bush without complaining or quitting. About this time, we got a few new guys. One of them was a big, heavy-set dude from Buffalo, New York, named Banko, whom we soon knew as "Bear." He'd come to us as a volunteer from the Graves-Registration Unit of the 1st S & T Battalion, where dead bodies were handled. He had an Infantry MOS and nobody, including him, could figure out why he'd ended up in such a strange job. The Phu Loi Recon Platoon was his only way out, so we gained another rifleman. He was also the only grunt I ever knew in the Infantry who had a college degree.

6 Operation "Quyet Thang"

*"The greater the indifference of the
masses and the less serious the tensions
which exist on the grounds between the
states, the more dominant and decisive
will the political object be. There are cases
in which it is, almost by itself, the deciding factor."*
—Karl Von Clausewitz

On the 10th of March action began to pick up again in our area. The 2/16th killed eight enemy soldiers in a firefight six kilometers southeast of us, and Sergeant Siegal's LRRPs were reporting sightings of larger enemy groups at night. On the 11th we got more intelligence information from Col. Schroeder at Division Artillery that the 165th NVA Regiment had been reported in and around the Tan Phu Khan area by the ARVN RF/PF militia of Play Boy Outpost. At 10 o'clock that night, 150 NVA were spotted at XT8713 only 2000 meters from Play Boy. That same day the 1st Infantry Division had initiated a new operation called Quyet Thang, or "certain victory." This was supposed to be a counter-offensive following the Tet operation called "Lam Son." The operations of the 1st/26th to the north of us were near the center of a mass of U.S. troops at XT8720, four kilometers north of the Phu Loi base camp. The idea was to try and stir up hidden enemy units so they could be pinpointed and destroyed. On the 12th of March, we were put on alert in the base camp because of renewed sightings of two hundred or more NVA in and around Tan Phu Khan village. The regional force ARVN militia in Play Boy Outpost were reportedly "under siege" and receiving incoming mortar fire.

The 13th of March, 1968, just before dawn. We were already up, getting our weapons and gear ready for a patrol, when the tracks and self-propelled 40mm automatic duster-guns opened fire on the outer perimeter, a few yards away. Mortar fire from Play Boy Outpost also exploded out beyond the camp. We ran towards the shooting with our weapons and equipment, some of us grabbing steel pot helmets. The enemy was moving in towards the wire in a ground attack. It felt eerie, actually seeing them advancing on us, firing. The first five or six of us to reach the scene opened up on them with our rifles and machine-guns, adding our fire-power to the armored-tracks and dusters, who were firing cannister and HE. Incoming bullets, *Tang, Tang, Tang, Beowww!*, ricocheting off the tracks around us. The attack was shot to pieces; we could see enemy soldiers spinning around and falling. Enemy fire fell off. It was proba-bly a frontal assault wave to see if they could take us by surprise and overrun the perimeter and make way for others in the rear. The rest of our guys came up at a run, ready to go.

We of the Recon Platoon were ordered out on-line, through the wire, as the enemy was retreating. We spread out wide and advanced towards a jungle woodline, near the village of Tan Phu Khan. The first two freshly-killed NVA were just outside the wire, lying next to a long Ban-galore torpedo they were carrying, to blow up the gate. They looked bad, full of bullet holes still oozing blood, with the weird, pasty dead-look. We continued to move forward slowly. Among the bodies, we spotted the first live enemy soldier. He was crouched down with an AK-47 across his knees like he was wounded, but he shouted, "Chieu hoi" at us, meaning he wanted to surrender. Those of us in front turned to relay this to Lieutenant Marano, and the son-of-a-bitch saw his chance. He suddenly jerked his rifle up and fired a burst at us on full-automatic, just a few feet away. A series of loud *Crack-Pops!*, with green tracers flying. One bullet hit Joe Miller beside me, just to my left. He was shot through his helmet, wounded in the head, and flew over backwards. Somebody screamed "Medic!" as Donaghue and I opened fire on the NVA immediately from either side of Joe, shooting him to pieces. I fired a whole magazine into him on full-automatic at point-blank range, as Donaghue, enraged, ran through a whole belt with the M-60 machine-gun. Even as I was firing into his body, I could see Donaghue's burst skipping off the ground into his face. I had no hesitation; the training just took over again, like shooting into a jumping, raggedy target. Rocky Allen, with his medic bag, ran to Joe as we kept moving forward under fire.

The NVA were shooting at us from the woodline they were retreat-ing into. Those way out in front of us were popping up out of the bush firing bursts; others still armed, wounded in the attack, were real close.

The morning sun, just rising in the east, was shining straight into our eyes, half-blinding us. We were shooting into moving forms a few feet from us, ducking at the same time, as bullets *Crack!* and *Whizz!* going by close. Art McQuade appeared, yelling, "Watch out for that son of a bitch! Get him! There's another one over there! Get'm! Shoot 'im!" I was next to Don Gould as he blasted shot after shot into a crawling, shuddering, NVA fifteen feet in front of us. For a split second I stared astounded at him, like I'd never really known he had it in him. An explosion suddenly went off nearby.

"KaBoom!"

I figured it was a grenade rolled out by one of the wounded NVA. Baca, my good buddy, was knocked down, wounded in the back and arm by shrapnel. Another yell of "Medic!" Rocky ran to him. Enemy resistance was more than expected, so Sergeant Siegal's LRRP Squad was called out of Phu Loi to support us. They moved quickly up behind us and around to our side towards a woodline, hoping to hit the NVA from the flank. A big berm in front of us rose above the scrub brush and I saw at least one NVA scrambling over it to cover as I fired a burst at him. I wondered how many more were behind that thing.

Combat is always on sort of a higherplane, as if in a little bit of a daze. While the close-up shooting was going on we could see a number of enemy soldiers out in front of us, running towards the jungle and Tan Phu Khan, actually throwing off their NVA uniforms as they went. Now, we could see they're pulling on black shirts, like we find later in all the NVA packs lying around. We couldn't tell how many of them were in the attack and had already gone. As they retreated into the jungle, we fired our rifles at them. We could see some of them jerking with hits. Bell and Alexander were standing close to me firing fast. Now was our chance, a damn good payback for all the Americans killed and wounded in Phu Loi by rockets during the last month and a half. We were lucky to be the ones who got to do it. I slammed a fresh magazine into my hot, smoking rifle. In the distance, their comrades were helping to support or drag the wounded. It's one of the most incredible sights I've seen in 'Nam. They will mix and hide with the villagers, and if those people don't play along, they will damn-sure pay for it later, in blood.

Donaghue moved over near me again and fired his M-60 in long bursts into the woodline. "The Kid" Evans was there too, along with Gould and "Smiley" Clarke. While we were all firing we got a sudden call from our RTO.

"Cease fire, yer pinnin' the LRRPs down! They're comin' in on the flank over there. Cease fire! The LRRPS are comin' in from the side!" The enemy fire coming from the bush near the village was slacking off now, and we moved forward, killing several wounded ones, not taking any more chances. I shot a burst into one more wounded one who was trying to raise an AK-47. Donaghue yelled, "Don't shoot 'em all, you guys, let's capture some for Intelligence!" We took at least one prisoner, because we could see that he was an NVA officer. While Steve Hustler was taking him, the gook tells him, *"Du Mau, Du Mau"* (to fuck his mother, in Vietnamese). His voice is high–pitched, death is staring him in the eye. At that, Steve slugged the gook hard in the head. Blood and little bits of brain flew out of the wound on the other side. Incredibly, he still lived.

Tommy Donaghue yelled again, "Leave him alone, you assholes, he's a live NVA colonel!" We called in a dust-off for him. When the bird landed, some of the guys lifted him up and heaved him in. He hit the firewall so hard that his brains splashed out and he finally died.

Out of the corner of my eye, I saw a dude in our platoon cutting a scalp from one of the dead NVA. Next, I watched a couple of other buddies cut off ears to make necklaces. Looking over to the LRRPS I saw one of them waving some other dripping thing . . . Blood was running down his arm. I didn't really care about that myself; I just couldn't get into it. It didn't seem as though it really meant anything anyway. Dead's dead.

I got a 7.65mm Chinese automatic pistol from an NVA officer I'd shot. I had to argue with another dude about it later, but I'd shot him and I got it. It was a slim, black piece with Communist stars on the grips. The enemy used them as public-execution guns in the villages—on people that didn't cooperate with the Communists. I carried it on my belt the rest of the time in the war. While I was jerking out papers and pictures of Ho Chi Minh from the dead bodies, another chopper landed. Somebody said that it was Col. Schroeder, the commander of Phu Loi. He surveyed the scene quickly, nodded a "well done," and lifted off.

Another sudden outburst of shooting erupted about 1000 meters away, near the north end of Tan Phu Khan. Automatic weapons popped and cracked and grenade explosions went off. We found out later it was a platoon from Delta 2/16th who were set up in the area and who had just killed two more NVA retreating from us. One of Delta's GIs had been seriously wounded in the head and shoulders.

We reported in through our RTO to whomever we were supposed to: 1st Division Artillery, G-2, or S-2. After we gave the figure for how many bodies and weapons we had, a REMF came back at us, accusing us of "exaggerating"! We figured twenty NVA had been killed during the firefight. We had seen them dragging off some of their dead, but the reaction to our report was "just too damned much." Somebody got the bright idea of giving the REMF pig a body-count in person. One of the guys went back through the perimeter and got a ¾ ton GI truck out into that mess. We had maybe fifteen dead bodies, besides other blood trails, and ones we'd seen being dragged off or wounded along the wood-line near the village. So, we gathered up a good bunch of them, drag-ging them by their still-warm arms. I kept noticing that each of them had a neat, military type white-sidewall haircut. We set about ten of them upright on the benches of that truck, threw in eight or ten AK-47s, the Bangalore torpedo, and Chi-Comm grenades. We straightened those gooks up, shoved them in so tight they were sitting up pretty tall and squared away. We even lit some cigarettes and stuck them, smoking, in their dead mouths.

Then we took that truck, blood dripping out the back, into Phu Loi. The rest of the platoon was marching behind, our weapons at ready. The MPs and REMFs around the wire and the buildings didn't say nothin', but the track-duster dudes were laughing, getting off on it. They thought it was a trip. We went up to that REMF lifer major or colonel's air-conditioned Quonset hut and just started yelling, "Hey, REMFs, here's yer bodies!" All kinds of shiney officers and EMs came running, and when we had us a good audience, we just started heaving dead enemy soldiers, weapons, NVA packs, everything else, down in the doorway in a bloody pile. Nobody said nothin' to us; we were standing around with our weapons, enraged.

Finally, a real brave REMF officer went and got his camera and had some private take his picture, in a pose. Then they all came out of the woodwork, snapping pictures. The minute was gone, the cards were on the table. Some of us just shuffled over near the perimeter and shared a smoke in the sun, staring out at the bush—enemy territory. We were never accused of exaggerating our kills again; I don't know to this day who cleaned up that mess.

Baca never came back to us as part of the unit. Joe's bullet wound just ripped up his scalp pretty bad, and blew a hole through his helmet— real close call. He came back to us after being in the hospital for a while.

A long time after, I saw him on a street in Philadelphia, and recognized him by the big part down the middle of his Afro. I don't remember if some of the LRRPs or armored dudes were hit. I was then only paying attention to our own little group; our scout dog, "Heinrich," was hit and wounded, too.

Earl and I became tighter—closer—when Baca was hit. It shook me up a little because he'd been so careful and smooth in all his actions. Of course, he could have been killed by shrapnel from any random explosion in a firefight. So could any of the rest of us, anytime. Joe getting shot in the head taught me to never take my eyes off the enemy for a second or my finger off the trigger. I never forgot that either.

After that firefight and the clean-up and the cooling off, we lay back, tired out. Earl was next to me, drowsy, saying, "They're crazy, man. They just keep doing it, and doing it, and then coming back for more." I'm saying, "I know, Earl, and where's it all going to end when they just run into these villages we're supposed to be saving and hide out with the people. Man, it's happening all over 'Nam in a hundred places like this, and it just keeps going on and on."

All around us, the other men are muttering the same kind of stuff, some still cleaning their weapons or checking their gear. It's sort of weird to look at Baca's and Miller's empty racks, a reminder to be sharp, be cool, or your turn may be next. I was also thinking how these two guys who were just hit while advancing into enemy fire, would be called greasers or niggers by a lot of their countrymen back in the United States right now, living high. Baca, whose ancestors had been settlers in New Mexico long before the first Anglo fur-traders pushed through from St. Louis to Santa Fe; and Miller, brave as the Black Lion that he'd been.

Combat Recon Patrol
Phu Loi R.V.N.
13 March 1968

Dear Mom and Dad and family,
  Today we had another firefight. I guess I'll tell you about it. The rear gate and outer perimeter wire of the camp were attacked before dawn, by NVA regulars fresh from the border. We cut them to pieces, and about 6:00 am advanced into them with some LRRPS, out in front of the armored-tracks to follow out our work. As we approached the slaughter zone, we came upon the enemy, some dead, some still fighting. They

were perfectly equipped and armed, as well or better than us, but our superior firepower and armor defeated them. We were in a shoot-out and took casualties. I shot into several enemy soldiers that were shooting at my buddies. One man we must have shot over a hundred rounds into before he quit dying. It was the closest–up and most terrible thing I've seen with one brave man, an enemy. We called him a fanatic, but on our side, he would be a hero. We continued running into heavier fire and shooting at them, and they finally broke and ran dragging some of their dead, and throwing off their uniforms, right in front of us. They retreated into Tan Phu Khan village and the jungle. We brought a truck load of dead bodies and weapons into the Phu Loi base camp. I took some things from one I shot into—a pistol, and a picture of him in his wallet, and some stamps from North Vietnam. I enclose them; take care of them.

They are so incredibly brave, and put up with more terror and privation than we do. The thousands of Viets who only profit from this war and escape all punishment, I hate. But a brave enemy soldier I respect. I'm afraid as long as there is a foreign face in this land, there will always be others to take their places when they die. These kind of things happen with many other people all the time here, but usually we shoot at distance, that prohibit such personal feelings.

I have gotten to the point where I don't always think I'm going to get hit when the shooting breaks out, but I'm extremely careful with all my movements, and will continue to be so. I guess I'm not one of those people who do brave and brilliant deeds, but maybe I'll make it home for that. Try not to worry too much. I am taking good care of myself. Thank you for your recent letters. Mom's of the 29th February was one of the nicest I have ever gotten.

Love,
Johnny

The failed assault on Phu Loi's perimeter and our resulting firefight developed into four days of enemy actions in a wide circle around Phu Loi, causing at least fifty-two American casualties. After losing about twenty killed in our action, including those they'd dragged off, the enemy apparently decided to split up. Some moved south to a position between Phu Loi and Phu Cuong in preparation for an attack on the ARNVs there. At the same time, we heard intelligence of the enemy retreating through Tan Phu Khan towards a NVA base camp north of Dog Leg. While we were patroling later on the 13th of March, searching slowly through the bush for enemy sign, the first of the 16th Infantry made contact three miles southwest of us and killed one, capturing an AK-47. Almost simultaneous with our action on the morning of the 13th, the 1st/26th operating south of Chanh Luu towards Dog Leg village had also made contact. This firefight developed into a hot action, with the grunts being reinforced by the 1/4 Cav firing cannister from tank guns. Twenty-three NVA were killed, while one American was killed and three wounded. The next day, while our platoon was on a long patrol near Dog Leg, the 1/26th and 1/4 Cav continued hitting the NVA. Sixteen more American soldiers were killed or wounded; thirty-four more enemy dead were counted, along with twenty weapons captured. We could see the helicopter gunships and F-4 Phantoms flying north over our heads to "bring smoke" down on the NVA at the battle zone.

The disparity in numbers between American and enemy casualties was often doubled back in the States or questioned by civilian correspondents here in Vietnam. It stemmed from not being on the fighting scene and being able to see the result of armored track or air support after an enemy position had been located by ground troops. In a one-to-one shootout, the figures would be close, but as soon as U.S. fire support was introduced, the enemy had either to go underground or retreat, losing heavily in the process.

That same day on the 14th, the 1st/16th had also gotten into renewed fighting "with an unknown-sized enemy force," losing twelve Americans killed and wounded to small arms, RPG fire, and a booby trap four miles southeast of Phu Loi. Only one body was found after the enemy retreated. They had probably dragged off some of their dead, as we had seen them do in our firefight. In that exchange, the higher American casualties may have reflected the lack of immediate effective mobile fire support. Action continued on the 16th of March in our area. The enemy attacked the ARVN Engineer School near Phu Cuong with RPGs and automatic weapons, inflicting losses on our allies; they also fired a barrage of rockets on us inside the Phu Loi Base camp. We had at least two more Americans killed and fifteen wounded. The casualties I was aware of were in Bravo Company of my old unit, the 1st Aviation, the 340th Aviation detachment, and the 610th. This attack was the last attempt by the enemy at vengence for their loss throughout our area of some seventy-five to a hundred killed in four days.

Those days could be called the end of the Tet Offensive (or counter-offensive) in our area. It had been our luck as a platoon to inflict heavy losses on the enemy, while suffering light casualties ourselves. Many other units were not so lucky. In the Tet Offensive up to this time, the 1st Infantry Division had lost about a thousand killed and wounded, and this did not include several hundred more American casualties in units within the Big Red One's geographical AO, but not part of the outfit. The level of the war had risen for all of us in the last six weeks. At this time, out of a field force of more than 500,000 Americans in Vietnam, about 10½ percent, or roughly 55,000 hunted the enemy in infantry, recon or cavalry units, another 15 percent of 75,000 men served in artillery, engineer, or aviation units. The remaining 75 percent were primarily in rear support jobs, usually well-protected.

During Tet and the seven weeks following into late March of 1968, approximately 4,000 Americans were killed, 19,000 wounded, and 604 missing in action. The ARVNs lost about 5,000 killed, and contrary to newsmedia expectations, didn't collapse or "go over to the Viet Cong" (as had been loudly predicted by the prominent professor John Kenneth Galbraith of Harvard University on February 16th). In fact, the 1st ARVN Division, one of the "important units in the 1st Corp area" that Galbraith had publicly proclaimed as "having a close working relationship with the Viet Cong," had fought heroically in the battle for Hue. Man for man, this division had suffered heavier casualties than most American units throughout Vietnam. Like the performance of the 1st ARVN Cavalry on February 13th near Phu Loi, it was an indication for a possibility of success if the South Vietnamese would ever have seriously addressed the causes of revolution in the countryside. Even when we soldiers were disgusted by the performance of many ARVN units, we knew that tough and aggressive ARVN units existed. As our military and political leaders had said, "They need time." The problem with this, however, was two-fold: first, the anti-war movement in the United States was rapidly growing more vocal and influential, and most of the news media were negative. Second, in retrospect, the South Vietnamese government was not doing enough to counter the reasons for which the Viet Cong continued to fight. Practically no progress was made towards the mass distribution of private farmland to millions of peasants or to truly protect them from the Viet Cong. So thousands of hamlets allowed the enemy, including infiltrating NVA regulars, to move about or to hide freely. The weakness of the South Vietnamese government led to isolation of many local Vietnamese militia units in outposts in the most critical areas. A village like Tan Phu Khan in the populated areas was a good example. In places like this, the winning of the war by our side or theirs would ultimately be decided. The locating and defeat of main-force Viet Cong or NVA units could continue almost indefinitely if the enemy were willing to pay the price in manpower in the hope of eventual victory. This could also be continued indefinitely by main-force ARVN units if they were willing to pay the price, and we were able to buy time with American blood. Had genuine support been gained by the non-Communist government in the populated countryside, such battles could eventually be fought on the country's borders in wild jungle country, the only possible remaining hiding places for the Communist forces. But without widespread anti-Viet Cong feeling in the villages, the war would only continue to cause more suffering, subjecting the South Vietnamese to constant VC terrorism, and would eventually wear out the patience of America.

At home in the United States, millions of television sets brought the war home daily. The brutal suddenness of death and young GIs wounded by bullets and rocket shrapnel was continually contrasted against scenes of mangled Vietnamese bodies, aerial bombing by U.S. jets, and burning, napalmed villages. The constant repetition of this theme in news media coverage had the same effect on many Americans, who felt an involvement and complicity in the war that could never be transmitted through written accounts of earlier conflicts. The young students in the generation actually involved in the fighting were most strongly affected. It was they who were destined either to go fight the war or escape service through student deferments. Women students were as heavily affected as the boys in feeling a necessity to take a stand against the war. Millions of students and hundreds of universities and colleges across the country were being trained in liberal theory about history, reasoning, judicial process, traditions, of peaceful change or coexistence, while being daily subjected to the reality of Vietnam war news. By 1968, news media coverage was becoming more consistently biased against the cause, and this was the only readily available information on the war effort. Kids their same age were fighting, killing, and dying every day for a cause made obscure by liberal thought and teaching. The contradictions were too great, both in relating the reality of war to their own education, and in the actual day to day tactical conduct of an anti-Communist, counter-guerilla war. Protest was inevitable in a society that prided itself in freedom of speech and press. But as the peaceful protect and rallies went on unanswered or ignored, frustration grew and spread. Cynicism tempered idealism in many, and a feeling of confrontation rose.

At Columbia University in New York on February 28, 1968, a small group of students among a university population of several thousand had protested the presence of Recruiters for Dow Chemical Company on the campus ''because they made napalm for the war.'' Among the picketers was an eighteen-year-old girl named Josephine Duke. She had come to Barnard College at Columbia as a freshman from her mother's home in Florida in September of 1967, just about the same time I was shipped to Vietnam.

The education she had received in high school and continued to receive at Columbia had little or no bearing on what she perceived as the burning issues of her own time. As the daughter of Anthony Duke, a former U.S. Naval Officer and Commander of LST at Normandy, and great-granddaughter of a famous Marine colonel, Anthony Biddle, a veteran of the First World War, she was aware of the traditions of service. She was a descendant of an old, established American family, often stereotyped or sneered at by radicals. She was, however, from a line of descendants who had served the Republic in many capacities in every war since the Revolution, including both sides of the Civil War.

For her to take part in the beginning of a protest movement against an ongoing battle involving other young Americans was a major step, particularly with her father living nearby in New York, and her uncle serving in President Johnson's administration.

It was difficult for her to keep her mind on English literature and mathematics when the TV screen daily flashed pictures of baby-faced U.S. casualties and American napalm exploding among grass thatched huts of peasants on the other side of the world. Her first conscious disagreement with the government's Vietnam policy was the fact that the Congress had never declared war. The official reasons and explanation of the war seemed so obscure and contrived that she had found herself listening more frequently to the explanations of her own classmates at Columbia.

The only people who seemed to be consistently discussing Vietnam and holding strong opinions about it were members of a nationwide radical organization known ambiguously as SDS, or Students for a Democratic Society. As her perception and understanding of what was occurring in Indochina grew through the only exposure available to her, TV and SDS, so did her disagreement with American policy there. As with most American citizens at the time, there was no real understanding of the complexities of the war, and no impartial basic knowledge of its history, or why we were fighting there. After reaching the conclusion that it was wrong for our country to be fighting in Vietnam, it was a natural step to protest the presence on her campus of representatatives for a corporation making napalm that, according to the news media, burned villages containing helpless peasants.

It was an example of what was occurring across the United States at the time. Columbia SDS in March of 1968 was a relatively small group of two-hundred students under a newly elected president, Mark Rudd. This college sophomore had just returned from a journey to Communist Cuba, where he had been reinforced in his Marxist beliefs by dedicated revolutionaries. This ultimate example of the freedom and tolerance in our society that allowed him to visit and plan with the Communist enemy we were fighting, including representatives of the Viet Cong, was lost on Mark Rudd in his radicalism. Other leaders of Columbia SDS at the time such as Teddy Gold, Nick Freudenburg, and John Jacobs were just as publicly dedicated to Communist principles supported world revolutionaries, including the Viet Cong.

They had reached their state of belief primarily through intellectual groping, study, and exposure to the persons and writings of older self-proclaimed radicals like Tom Hayden and Herbert Marcuse. To the leaders of SDS the strongest gut issue was to obstruct the American War in Vietnam against the Viet Cong and North Vietnamese Communists. The object of the leadership was to organize newer, more pliable students around any issues that were locally popular, and then steer them into an ever more radical stand against the war effort itself. To the SDS leadership, action and confrontation were more valuable to organizing than peaceful protest. Frustration of the rank and file membership was good for the objectives of the leaders.

Josephine Duke and hundreds of other idealistic students like her at Columbia, attracted to the movement by the moral questions raised by the war, were moved deliberately towards violence themselves, by their own leaders.

On the 12/13th of March while we were in Combat at Phu Loi, anti-war Senator Eugene McCarthy had astonished the political arena by nearly defeating President Johnson in the New Hampshire primary. Also on March 12th, *The New York Times* ran a headline including words to the effect that the U.S. was losing the war in Vietnam. On March

16th, Robert Kennedy announced his candidacy for President after being unable to get Johnson to change his tactics on Vietnam.

At Columbia University the SDS leadership and antiwar students simmered, protested the presence of IDA (Institute for Defense Analysis) on the campus, and cast about for additional issues with which to organize many more students.

In Vietnam, in Binh Duong Province, the war went on.

I couldn't have been too hard a dude yet, because I remember getting shook up by my first experience with MI around this time. Military Intelligence lived and operated in a comfortable hootch complex in Phu Loi, and had the enemy prisoners brought to them out of the bush by grunts like us. I never saw one of these dudes out in the field with us the whole time I was in 'Nam. Anyway, it was after this last firefight or one of the previous actions, when we had captured another NVA prisoner in uniform. His arm had been almost shot off by our bullets, he was in bad pain, and had lost a lot of blood. It drenched the whole side of his uniform and dripped on the ground. For some reason no one had killed him, and one of the guys of the patrol and I had been ordered to take him into the base camp. After humping in to the perimeter wire from the firefight zone where we had captured him, we got a ride in a jeep. He had been bleeding so badly, we put one of our compresses on him, and I tried to keep him cool. As soon as we got to MI, the jeep driver went in, while me and my buddy covered him with our rifles.

The MI REMFs came scrambling out of their office, just grinning, with their shiny boots and green suits. It was as though they were some clean little kids, I was thinking, whom we had brought a real neat toy to play with. This NVA soldier with his white-sidewall haircut was maybe seventeen or eighteen years old and he knows what's about to happen and he's putting on a tough face but he's scared. I can feel him shaking, trembling next to me. The MI dudes get to us, and I see it all like it's slow motion. The first thing they grab is his wounded arm that I just bandaged and twist it right around, just about tearing the mangled thing off. Kind of like introducing themselves. The prisoner screams like I've never heard before. They drag him along into their clean, little office, getting ready for some real fun.

By now I had been around awhile. I had seen GIs killed and wounded, been under plenty of fire, shot into the enemy, and all of it, but I was a little shook up. The driver and my buddy had left, but I just couldn't. For maybe twenty minutes I sat in the dust out there like some Vietnamese peasant, listening to the terrible screams coming from that fine little all-American hootch. I could feel the pain that enemy dude was going through. I felt like I was responsible for it, like he was mine or I could be him or something. I didn't like the enemy, but I kept having urges to kick in that door and waste those MI sons-of-bitches with my M-16. Finally, I couldn't stand it anymore, and shuffled away through the dust out towards the perimeter wire. For a long time, I remember just sitting and staring out at the silent jungle and thinking about the "Lord God who created us all in his own image."

Years and years later, sitting and drinking with my man Dennis in Kodiak, we were into a long, bitter rap about our prisoners-of-war, and the thousands of missing Americans who had never come home or showed up again. Dennis, who had gone through Khe Sanh in the Marines, suddenly jerked his head up with memories and pain in his eyes, and said, "Yeah, man, that's too true, but remember what we did to their prisoners: Do you remember, man?" And yeah, I remembered.

Earl and I were pretty close by now, always into long raps. For some reason we had this thing in common. We were both really into Vietnam. We both liked the village life, the farming culture, the livestock work, the open market places, the crowds of children. One day after a long patrol out past Tahn Phu Khan to Chanh Long or Dog Leg Village—always kind of a mean sniper-type area—were back safe, worn out. We were mellow and laid-back, and he turned to me and said, "Hey, John, you wanna extend with me? We could transfer together and get into civic-action, some kind of advisor trip. We could live in a village all the time, just stay there."

Now, I was just letting my mind flow with him, thinking about having our own little hootch, and maybe a sweet little mama-san each, and doing something like setting up new schools or building hootches for refugees. Something besides hunting to kill. I said, "Yeah, I can see it. Sounds good, real fine. Earl, let's do it, man."

He was laying back, feeling good that I didn't think he was crazy. "Fire up another Kool, man. I want to dream about this," he's saying. I'm fumbling around, looking for my deck. We got our weed, our dew, all stuffed into American cigarettes, sometimes in Phu Cuong by mama-san and her kids. It was all sealed back up on the bottom of the cellophane. You couldn't even tell, looking at the deck, that it's grass. I fired one up and it barely pops, it's so clean. Coupla' good tokes each, and I was really dreaming with him, now. I liked the draft buffalo, that's what really impressed me. I was always thinking about what a power-ful, quiet machine they are. For the Viets, they're like a Ford tractor, except better, because they make new little tractors every year.

When I'm out on patrols and ambushes in the villages and rice pad-dies and jungle, my mind's often drifting to how much we're disrupt-ing this slow country with our endless number of huge machines, caterpillars, loaders, trucks, tanks, power-driven generators, and on and on—roaring and spitting, grinding down and overpowering the old way of doing everything, just negating their whole way of life.

Well, Earl's lying there, thinking and dreaming, too. I know his family came to the Hawaiian Islands to labor in the canefields for the big plan-tations. They're into better things now, but he's already told me about the internments in World War II, and his father fighting in the all Hawaiian-Japanese Infantry Battalion of the U.S. Army. I know he wants his father to be proud of him, but Earl's seen enough fighting to want to move beyond that. He's one of those guys who are gentle and have a good heart, but he can't see being back in the rear, staying all the time with a bunch of REMFs who never do anything. His eyes are so bad he's almost blind; on night ambushes he always hangs some blocks of white C-4 explosive on his back so the guy behind him will notice if he starts to wander off. It seems crazy, but it only makes me admire him more.

Out on patrols, we hump together, him with his M-79 pig, and me with my '16. We got into one weird thing together that really got us to knowing each other. We were just finishing up this surround-and-search operation in a little bush hamlet, way out beyond Tan Phu Khan, and everybody was already in motion, straggling out for the long march back; it was real hot and damp. Donaghue's yelling at the other guys, "All right! Let's saddle up! You guys keep it spread out now!" Earl and I were drag that day, supposed to cover the rear. We were standing around this little thatched hootch, with a brush fence surrounding a few pigs and chickens, rooting and scratching around. We were watching the rest of the patrol filing out in the hot dusty trail, waiting for a good, wide interval between us.

There's this old, raggedy papa-san eyeballing us with our weapons, and behind him this real pretty, no, beautiful young girl, maybe seven-teen, standing behind him in the yard. We were both staring at her and thinking the same thing. Neither goes in for whores, and it's been a long time. The girl was kind of blushing and trying to hide, and the old man saw that look in our eyes. We were muttering to each other now, "Man, it's been a long time, you know what I mean?" "Yeah, there it is. God, she's a beautiful thing. Maybe we ought to get a little of that!" We kept rapping with each other, staring at her, not paying any attention to the rest of the platoon already disappearing. We both moved forward in unison towards the girl and she backs up, really scared now. The old man let out a kind of groan or moan, like he knew what was happening, and moved up between her and us. Just that quick we jerked up our weapons and snapped off the safeties. Earl's '79 was loaded with a buckshot-cannister round and I had my '16. The old man groaned again, he was brave and terrified, but we grabbed him and shoved him out of the way. One of us says, "I'll hold the old fool, you go first."

The girl had run into the hootch, crying. The old man was begging, terrified. Now, he was wringing his hands, moaning, groveling. We took one long look at each other, Earl and me, and we grinned, shitty-like, and looked down at the ground and the old man. Then we said to each other, "Hell, man, I can't do this kind of deal. It just ain't in me," and, "Yeah, I know, man. I don't want it that bad either. These poor sorry people, they're gettin' it every day, fourteen different ways. Let's just leave 'em alone."

We patted the old man on the head and shoulders, telling him in pidgin, "It was just a joke, It's all right now." We started to give him things: everything we had, all our C-rations, a pocket knife, stuff like that. With gestures, we made him call the girl out, and when she peeked around the corner of the door, we tried to smile at her and tell her its O.K.. Then we turned red and embarrassed, and trotted off down that trail, trying to catch up with the platoon, and looking back over our shoulders every so often, in case some gook decided to shoot us in the back.

And after that, we knew what was in each other's hearts, where we were both really at, and we liked each other more. To this day, despite all the war stories, atrocity tales, and horrible press reports, I think most American soldiers were like us. In almost fourteen months of Vietnam— in an aviation company, a recon platoon, and a line infantry battalion— I didn't witness rape or even hear of one actually happening. Others can say what they want, but I know what I saw and heard. There were some weird, off-the-wall things, maybe, but GIs were a pretty good bunch of men.

I read the letters that I mailed home those years ago, that my mother saved. They seem kind of factual, concise, yet leave so much unsaid.

Combat Recon Patrol
Phu Loi, R.V.N.
23/24 March 1968

Dear Family,
   Please send my apologies to sisters Joan and Priscilla, and brother
Bob for not writing yet, though I appreciated their letters. I just can't
write anymore except to the family as a whole. It's so repetitive, and
I have little time to write anymore. Lieutenant Marano has left us— trans-
ferred to the First Cavalry Division up near Hue. We have no officer now.
   We have had several small clashes with the enemy out in the Iron Tri-
angle, since I wrote you last. Today we found an enemy base camp, a
small one, probably of the so-called "Phu Loi Battalion," the local Viet
Cong. It is nothing but an incredible number of tunnels, caves, bunkers,
galleries, etc., dug in and camouflaged on a hill in the middle of the
bush. As is pretty usual, they got some advance word of our coming and
mostly retreated, leaving only a machine-gun nest, dug into a bluff, to
slow us down. This, we ran right into and got pinned down, but laid
out a heavy fire and killed probably two VC, called in a tank of the 1st
Squadron/4th Cavalry to blast the machine-gun for us. It kept right on
firing anyway, through the shelling, so we pulled back and an airstrike
blasted it to hell, burying it. I took some pictures of the shooting, which
I am sending to Honolulu to get developed, and will send them to you
when I get them back.
   I need $100, and an extra pair of glasses. The army is so slow.
                    Pray for Peace,
                    John

   Yeah, so I read over this letter now, and it comes back to me, little
by little. We were getting intelligence reports of enemy units using the
Iron Triangle again as a rest center for VC/NVA troops retreating from
the Saigon-Lam Son area. When we headed out the Phu Cuong gate to
start the patrol, Donaghue and Rocky Allen dropped out at the bar in
Phu Loi Village to get some slack time because none of us thought we
were going to find anything. Sergeant Rock took over the patrol. Going into the thick, jungle area around Vinh Loi, after a long march, approaching it from a rice paddy area, it was easier going 'cause of the
dry season. Earl is just ahead of me carrying the '79. He's also got my
Chinese pistol I lent him, because we know we're going into a real thick
area, probably full of tunnels and spider holes. I remember after long,

hard humping, sweating, towels around our necks, we're just about there when off in the distance we see a black pajama gook way out in the fields who's fooling around with a hoe or something.

Suddenly he drops it, and starts running into the jungle to our left. It's real long-range, but a few of us start firing slow, single shots, leading him like a bird, seeing if we can knock him over.

"The shy dude's running like that, he's an enemy!" At every shot, he jumps or hops. We can even see dust flying around his feet from close hits. Just before he streaks into the jungle, he finally jerks like he's taken a hit, and scrabbles into the bush like a crab. Moving in towards the hill, thick rippling bamboo, and jungle all around, point-man cutting and slashing a little with a machete, sweating, cursing, real quiet-like, advancing towards another target. "Bear" Banko took over the point at the bottom of a steep bluff. He and "Frenchy" Fournier started scrambling their way up it with the rest of us close behind. Just as they reached the top I heard Frenchy yell, "Two VC! Shoot the fuckers!" He and Banko opened fire at the same instant as the rest of us close behind jumped on either flank.

Brrrrppppp!

Banko's first five round burst hit a Viet Cong smack in the body, and he pitched over to the ground. They're both in web gear and uniform beside a long black machine-gun and a small smoky fire. A total surprise for everyone!

In that split second, I opened fire along with five or six other guys. Banko's M-16 jammed after his first burst, and he ducked down behind the berm, frantically working on it. The other gook lunged to the machine-gun and jerked it back into the bushes with our bullets cracking all around him. Hit by several of our bullets, he still kept going.

Pop! Pop! Pop! Pop! Crack! Crack! Crack! Crack!

He fired a burst right across our front, dust flying from ricochets. We all flattened down behind the rise for cover.

"Pull back!" Sergeant Rock yelled behind us. "We'll get some support. There might be a whole platoon of them."

He didn't have to say it too many times. The VC machine-gun was going again, *BRRRRPPPP!,* branches and twigs flying, leaves falling. As we back out firing, Earl's thumping out 79 HE beside me in an arc, his shells exploding around the enemy position, *Whump! Whump!,* he's muttering at me now.

"Must've been a couple of guards, man. There's more of 'em in there." Reynaldo Garcia was behind us calling in the coordinates to our CP, "Custer flats 6, this is 2, we got contact at XT872134, we got one Victor Charlie Kilo India Alpha, one more hit, we are under fire at this time, gonna pull back an' get some support." When we were away from the gulley-bluff area and crossing a small open spot, the gook machine-gun opened up on us again:

Pop! Pop! Pop! Pop! Pop! Pop! Pop! Pop! Brrppp!

We hit the ground again, firing.

Don Dunce, our machine-gunner for today, remained standing up for a second longer than the rest of us, bold dude, firing from the hip, leaning forward into the recoil, running through a whole belt fast, empty cases spewing out. Bell, our hillbilly, was kneeling down on one knee to my left, calmly blasting out aimed shots with his M-14, "like he's on a fuckin' rifle range." Our scout dog, Tom Hine's pet "Heinrich," was barking, yipping, all excited. "Little mutt's already been hit one time, and not scared of nothin.'" Good, good little dog. Down flat—enemy round snapping by overhead—it's impossible to get that son-of-a-bitch without a plain old frontal assault, and we don't know if there's a whole hidden ambush waiting out there, keeping quiet, hoping we'll do it.

Rock called up the ¼ Cav on the PRC-25. They were operating around here, too, and could help us out and get a little themselves. A tank came clanking and screeching along after a long little wait—a nice sight. Turret swiveling around, big 90mm gun easing down point-blank, *Ka-Pow!!* *Ka-Boom!* Shell blows up, dirt and debris flying.

Pop! Pop! Pop! Pop! Pop! Pop! Crack! Crack Craaaaack!

Gook machine-gun doesn't give a damn, he's dug in real good.

Ka Pow! — Boom!

No good; the machine-gun was still going, but more inaccurate by now. We sat up looking on the edge of a high berm now, we advanced a little behind the tank, into the open, looking over to the jungle-covered hill he's dug into.

Off to my left "Pancho Villa," Reynaldo Garcia, was standing up behind Rock with the PRC-25 radio on his back. He's got his weird-looking earphones on, and his sunglasses and he's had an AM transistor radio blasting out at the same time. It was tuned to AFVN radio in Saigon, where some fat-ass REMF announcer in an air-conditioned room was spinning discs and babbling out over the jungle airwaves at us:

"I'm gonna play one now for Smokey Joe from California with the ¾ Cav of the tropic Lightning."

Garcia said, "Hey! Hey! Sounds good you guys," and he turned his radio up higher, as high as it'll go. Amid the popping of bullets and explosion of 90mm tank shells, a wailing song blared out over the jungle: "I've got sunshine on a cloudy day. When it's cold outside, I got the month of May."

I looked over at Garcia in awe. He was snapping his fingers in time with the music and nodding his head to the beat, his shades flashing in the sun.

"This dude is definitely cool, Pancho Villa knows how to fight a war."

Sergeant Rock turned around and grabbed the hand mike of the PRC-25 in the middle of the song saying, "Hey Garcia, would ya' mind turnin' the music down just a little? I'm gonna call in an airstrike on the VC."

Garcia nodded in time to the music, and cut it down a little, Rock made his call. From my time with the 1st Aviation battalion I knew what was going on at the other end. Soon the gunships came clattering in over our heads firing rockets past the smoke we've thrown to mark our line.

SSSSSHH! — Wham! Wham! Wham BRRRRRRRRRPPPPP! The mini-guns ripped into the jungle ahead of us.

Garcia turned the music back up and it wailed out over the mayhem. Finally there was silence and Garcia snapped his radio off at the same moment. He turned to the rest of us. "Now you tell me, man, wasn't that the way to handle it? Ain't that the way to go? Hey, that dude's had it, man. He's been totaled, buried, gone." The tank didn't seem to give a damn, and went rattling off, swiveling around like some weird armored toad. Clouds of color billowed from the smoke grenades we'd thrown for the airstrike. We advanced again. Ground and trees were blown-up, jumbled mess, blood trails but no bodies, like they'd disappeared underground. We went over the little jungled hill and broke through into a hidden, small, open patch. Suddenly another Viet Cong was running. He took us by surprise, heading for a huge thatched-hootch, like a barn. Earl was swiveling around beside me, quicker, '79 angled up a little, *Bloop!,* his grenade perfect, *Crack-boom!* Pieces of the hootch flew just as the VC skated inside.

"He's hit!"

I fired a burst from my '16. We ran forward crazy, stupid, covering each other. Earl slammed a cannister round into his "pig." He blasted, and I fired a burst through the straw walls, and we crashed in. Blood spatters were here and there. "Son-of-a-bitch's gone! Hole out the back, another gook in there dragged him off.'' Off to our left a sudden *Shhh-Wham!* Banko fired a LAW rocket at another hootch with a sniper in it. Again, no bodies. It was an eerie day. We knew we killed some, but they keep disappearing.

On and on, we humped all the rest of the day, around and around the area: tunnels, underground rooms, spider holes, some enemy gear here and there, but really, mostly clean. They knew we were coming, back in the beginning that bastard out in the paddies probably got through to them, wounded. We were hot, sweating, dirty, exhausted, with a long hump back still ahead of us.

"Another stupid day, in the stinkin' 'Nam."

The patrols and ambushes went on and on, sometimes hot, sometimes dull. I can't remember most of them anymore. We just kept humping and getting our little pleasures when we could, from our own company and from our little friend, "excise," the dew of Vietnam.

Around the end of March, we heard that Lyndon Johnson, whose war it had become, had cut back the bombing of all of North Vietnam except the southernmost panhandle north of the DMZ. To us in the field that seemed like a sorry thing to do when we were still out there humping and fighting and all. If you're in a shoot-'em-up-war, do you cut the enemy some slack when he's killing your boys?

"Is this a war we're fighting, or not! If we're not gonna bomb 'em when they're ambushing and rocketing us, what're we doin' here?''

In any case, I know the enemy was glad. They'd been getting chased and hit hard, south and north of the seventeenth parallel, and now they had an opportunity to move lots of supplies, ammunition, and troops farther south to the beginning of the Ho Chi Minh Trail. It ran right down the whole border inside Laos and Cambodia to their target areas all the way to Saigon and the Mekong. They had just started getting ready for another offensive. Looking back on it now, this was the turning point of the war, the time when the enemy became convinced we would quit.

In our hootch, which was separate from the CP, we got pretty relaxed when we got the chance. If we were in at night and sure we were not going to get sent out on an ambush, we'd start getting stoned at dusk. There was nothing else to think about or do after our weapons were clean and we were ready to go out on a patrol the next morning.

One evening we were very high indeed, and Joe Miller was in control of the group. Everybody from our hootch who smoked was there and Donaghue, Allen, and a few others from the CP, too. Miller was telling stories and talking his cool, low street jive. We were nodding and going with the flow. There's one low light burning and the cheekbones of his lean, bronze face are highlighted. Everybody was quiet, eyes riveted on the man of the hour, when he slowly shifted his gaze to the open door at the perimeter end of the hootch. Two snakes, side by side had entered and were sliding along together, working their way down the warm cement. Miller stopped his dialogue and stared at the reptiles.

"They're slidin' on through to the other side, dudes, jus' like we're gonna do here in the 'Nam."

All of us were staring now in stoned wonder at this apparition. As the snakes reached Miller's end he uncoiled his body in a single, smooth motion, stretched out an arm and gently opened the door. The snakes never flinched, but kept on sliding out into the warm dust, and the humid tropical night. A wise, knowing grin was spreading over Joe's face.

"Tha's the way we gotta be out in the dark, dudes, steady an' smooth. There it is."

I guess it was around late March that Sergeant Carlisle left the platoon to go back to his original unit, the 1st/16th Infantry. He'd been a good dude and we missed him. We still didn't have a lieutenant, but we got a new platoon sergeant as Carlisle's replacement. This one hardly ever went out in the field with us, and his style couldn't be compared to that of Carlisle. He was an old veteran of much service, but he told us he was too tired to hump anymore. He did his job by staying in our CP hootch monitoring the command radio when we were out on ambushes or patrols. During time off, he visited his old lifer drinking buddies in the ¼ Cav.

Steve Hustler had gone home, back to the world, and I don't remember seeing Bernie Bernard anymore, either. We'd gotten a new rifleman named Carson Cheek to replace one of these guys. He was another stocky, tough dude we called "Cheeko," from Washington state. He became the AG for Joe Miller, who had taken over my squad's machinegun.

Bear Banko and I were both self-proclaimed historians and among the "intellectuals" of the platoon. We often debated the history of the Indochina War under the French and then under the Americans. I maintained that we were going down the wrong road with our methods and he maintained our strategy was correct and we were winning.

One day when a group of us were supposed to be on a combat patrol, we sneaked out and got drunk instead in a muggy, hot bar-whorehouse on the road to Phu Cuong, near the base camp of the ARVNs. Banko and I began to talk politics amid the drunken din. Our tempers were already short from the constant tension and dusty heat. All of a sudden we were swinging at each other and then jumping for our M-16s in a face-off. Donaghue, Allen, Gould, Miller, and the rest jumped in and grabbed us from behind, separating us before a shot was fired. It was a close call because of the gook booze and our inclination to solve all problems by flipping a selector switch to full-automatic and pulling a trigger. Donaghue cooled us out. "It's O.K. guys, save yer fightin' for the Cong. They're out there waitin' fer us somewhere. They'd love it if we all killed one another."

We broke up the party and shuffled back up the road to the wire. We were wearing rubber thong sandals, non-regulation uniforms, carrying strange weapons that must have presented the MPs at the gate with a very weird sight.

"Where you guys been? Jesus Christ, you look like a bunch of gooks." They glared at us accusingly.

We looked at one another. Camouflage fatigues, North Vietnamese bush hats; Don Gould was weaving around with a shotgun, another guy had an SKS Chinese carbine, some had M-16s. Most of us were wearing shower slippers, but one guy had on a pair of tennis sneakers.

"We went out on a patrol man, but we decided to take a holiday instead. O.K.? We're Hell's Rangers, ya know, Phu Loi Recon Patrol; we deserved a break, 'cause we're so bad."

In their clean-pressed jungle fatigues, the MPs glared at us as we swayed together in a raggedy drunken column through the concertina. Our reputation was spreading.

The next day we straightened up our act, got equipped and outfitted properly, and went out on a real patrol. Our platoon Sergeant had been mad at us.

"You sloppy guys are the sorriest set of soldiers I ever saw. You better get yer shit together or I'm gonna ride yer young asses into the ground. Now you go on out there like yer part a' the Big Red One and find me some gooks!"

We straightened up and slung our weapons and lined out for the perimeter wire. It was about the 1st of April and we were not too far out from the base camp heading towards a bamboo and jungle bush area we always searched.

We were sliding along slow and careful, weapons ready, with Bear

Banko on point. He'd only been with us for two or three weeks but he liked being up front. This was how he killed his first VC at the machine-gun-nest on the 23rd.

We were working our way down a trail into a steep washout gulley when I had a sudden premonition. I looked again quickly. It was the only way down through here and we'd been on this trail twice before recently. Those sons-of-bitches were always watching us. It was too narrow, and I didn't like the look of it. I yelled out, "Hold up!", but it was too late.

Ka-Boom! Dirt and dust went flying. Bear's knocked over, screaming. It's a booby-trapped Chi-Comm grenade. He'd run into a little leafy branch across the trail that concealed the trip wire and brushed through it, triggering the explosion. Now he lay moaning on the ground, legs and back bleeding from shrapnel, a wounded but living lesson to all of us. We got him out of there and he was gone for two weeks in a field hospital, coming back to us with one leg in a cast to convalesce for a long time.

When a dude in the platoon gets hit, no matter whether you've had a fight with him or not, it's like your own brother's been hurt. He's still one of us, and you feel it just as bad. We're all more careful than ever, knowing Banko is lucky to be alive, and that it could have been any of us. Another letter home:

> *Combat Recon Platoon*
> *Phu Loi, R.V.N.*
> *15 April 1968*

Dear Mom and Dad and Family,

Well, the Recon Platoon is being converted to more night operations —not just stationary ambushes, but moving around in the dark, after enemy night patrols and marches. This is being ordered by 1st Division Artillery, HQs because the VC and NVA in our area are doing any of their moves now at night. We are now practicing more operations in platoon strength, in the jungle and village areas in the dark. We are still using two night-vision starlight scopes to help out. It is more danger-ous and intricate, continuously moving in the dark, instead of sitting still in ambush, but they hope to force the enemy to operate in bigger groups like during the Tet Offensive, to make us find better targets for 1st Divi-sion Artillery and Armor fire. We're supposed to use our intelligence reports to search them out and attack them. This job is also covered in our area by LRRPs, but their squads are spread out real thin in the Iron Triangle. One of their teams, working together with some of our platoon, got ambushed north of An My taking KIA and WIA. I missed that one, I was on bunker guard. A buddy of mine, Don Dunce, from our platoon, was with them in the firefight, and made it through to tell us about it later. We were recently told again that we are directed in our operations by the Commander of Phu Loi, and 1st Infantry Division Intelligence. One of our guys was wounded by a booby trap explosion about two weeks ago, but otherwise we've been real lucky.

I have gotten some nice letters recently from you and Ma and Joannie, also some cookies that Joan made. Please thank Aunt Mary for her note and her prayers.

> *148 days left,*
> *Love,*
> *John*

Rereading this letter brings back memories of other incidents in early April after Bear Banko was wounded. On the 2nd of April, Tan Uyen Village was attacked by the Viet Cong over to the east of us again; on the 3rd, while on the perimeter lines. I watched a Birdog, an Artillery spotter plane, coming under enemy anti-aircraft fire as it headed into the strip. Pieces of metal flew off it as the bullets hit, but it managed to land. The VC disappeared. On the 4th, we heard that Lai Khe was under a bad attack by rockets, RPGs, and then sappers with satchel charges. Our turn came again on the 5th with a heavy rocket attack on Phu Loi with more casualties, and followed by small arms and automatic weapons fire into our airstrip.

The same day in our area, the ARVN Engineer School adjacent to Phu Cuong, and Di An came under attack. Intelligence sources reported all the attacks were the work of the Viet Cong Phu Loi Battalion again. The ambush referred to in the letter home took place on the night of the 13th of April when a combined patrol of our combat recon platoon and Sergeant Siegal's LRRPS got in a bad nighttime firefight out beyond An My and Chanh Long (Dog Leg Village), near Chanh Luu. It was the same area the 1st/26th and ¼ Cav had defeated the NVA in, after our March 13th firefight. I don't remember now who went from our platoon besides Dunce, but I knew from his face the next morning that it had been a bad night. One big dude from the LRRP patrol whose face I remember was killed, and several others were wounded. Gunships were scrambled to bail them out, and at least five of the enemy were killed.

This letter home reminds me again of those days, moving around at night, camouflaged and painted, practicing total-silence, noise-discipline, unreal tenseness, and exhilaration. A couple of times in early April we spotted small groups of the enemy and called in artillery fire on them. That's what we were supposed to be doing. Another time some VC sneaked up on us, turned Donaghue's claymore around, and disappeared without a shot. Sometimes we'd exchange rifle fire with them at night, our two snipers using starlight scopes for accuracy. They always seemed to retreat, avoiding contact with us. We were operating at this time in conjunction with ambush patrols of the 2nd/28th Infantry who were then in our area.

I remember one night in particular when I was out on point with Earl as my slack behind me, carrying his pig grenade launcher. We spotted enemy movement ahead of us near Tan Phu Khan village as usual. We never did find out whether it was merely a patrol or if they were setting up a position to mortar or rocket Phu Loi.

It was cool in the tropical dark—nice compared to those sweltering, burning days. We were laying there side by side, me and Earl, out in front of the rest of the patrol, strung out behind us in a file, down flat and still in position, where we'd motioned to them to stop. I was getting a little crazy by then. We were watching an enemy point-man clear as can be, way out in front of the other Viet Cong, almost pouring himself over a berm. I thought: "I'd like to knife the bastard." I put my lips to Earl's ear and soundlessly whispered, "I'm going." He nodded, covering me with his weapon angled at the other enemies behind. I started to crawl forward, gently dragging my rifle through the soft dust with my left hand over the muzzle, my sharp bayonet in my right. As I moved toward him, sliding like a snake, I felt that I was never so turned on in all my life.

"The gook's well out in front of the other VC, I got a good chance." The only thing I could think about was getting close enough to hump him and stab him. Then, halfway to him, the son-of-a-bitch catches my slinking movement. I see him stop, then he's making low, flicking motions with his hand out behind him, to his dudes, and skinning backwards. I'm so goddamn mad and let down that I whipped my rifle up and opened fire on him.

Pow! Pow! Pow!

Well, that started a little shooting. I was pretty sure I hit him, but I was backing up quickly and they were retreating now. I couldn't see anything because of the flashing of muzzles and grenades. I get back to Earl as he's firing the '79 over me and told him quick how close I got and all. The other dudes behind us didn't even know what went on. I no longer cared enough to tell anybody else.

So there it is, you just got weirder and more into your own head; maybe sharing with one or two other close dudes. About this time Earl went home on leave, anyway. He never said why or anything about whether he'd extended his time or not, and I didn't ask.

On the 4th of April in the United States, a violent incident occurred which had far-reaching consequences.

Martin Luther King, black leader of nonviolent protest against racial discrimination, was murdered in Tennessee.

So, at the height of the war in Vietnam, black GIs throughout the services suddenly went cold as stone and drew together. It was as if the assassination was a symbolic act that left the blacks with no choice but to turn from non-violence to militant confrontation.

In the Phu Loi Recon Platoon, one of our main brothers, Joe Miller, became sullen and cold to whites. For several days he spent most of his time walking around alone or glowering with a small group of blacks, including MacQueston. When we asked him, "Hey Joe, you O.K., man?" he snapped at us, glaring.

"What the fuck you white chuck dudes care? Ain't yer people's leaders bein' shot down back there while we over here fightin' colored people fer white masters. You dudes don' know nothin'. The brothers are gonna burn and destroy in the ghettos now. Shit's gonna hit whitey's fan."

Joe was talking and acting as he never had in all the months we'd known him. We'd been as close as brothers in the face of danger and death. The truth of his predictions was quickly evident. News reached us in Vietnam of outbreaks of rioting, burning, looting, and killing.

After a few days, Joe Miller came back into our group again, stopped talking about the things that were eating at him, and continued to do his time as a soldier. He was always one of the best. But his anguish over the event radicalized all of us in some small way because of our affection and respect for him. It was another part of the learning process we were all going through within the microcosm of a combat platoon.

Back in New York City, the King assassination helped set the stage for another momentous event. Up until now almost all the college anti-war protests, with the exception of the Berkeley free speech movement, had been peaceful. The demonstrations were mostly low-key and the dissent tolerated by the authorities in power. After the death of Martin Luther King and the widespread rioting that followed, the tempo at Columbia University picked up.

The protest by radical antiwar students against IDA was one of the starting points. The Institute for Defense Analysis on the Columbia campus did military research studies for the U.S. government to the tune of $15 million a year. The students weren't quite sure what the secret studies entailed, but as a link to the Vietnam War effort, IDA became the target. Over one hundred students of SDS had gathered 1,500 signatures on a petition to remove the institution from Columbia, and marched into the Low Library on March 27th to present it to President Kirk and the administration with chants and screams of, "No help to the fascist war in Vietnam!" and "Columbia belongs to the people, we are the people!" "One, two, three, four, we don't want your racist war!" The slogans had been dreamed up by the leaders.

The radical leaders, Mark Rudd, John Jacobs, Teddy Gold, and Nick Freudenburg played the crowd, urging them to trespass into the building, leading the chants and slogans and raising the level of confrontation when they ran into opposition at the doors of the library by one of the university vice presidents.

For Josie Duke, a young woman student marching with the crowd of demonstrators, the trespassing was a giant step. To intrude into the inner/giant sanctums of the authority figures she'd been taught to respect all her life was dangerous. She was one of a freshmen class of hundreds who had been chosen out of thousands of applicants all over the United States. Being at Barnard-Columbia was the result of years of intensive study, preparation, and good grades. The IDA confrontation at Low Library fizzled out after a few shouted insults, and eventually resulted in six of the student leaders, including Rudd, being put on probation. The petition was totally ignored by the administration of the University.

King's assassination had resulted in an intensifying confrontation between the students and university administration. The question of whether Columbia should build a new gymnasium on university-owned land presently occupied by Harlem's black residents had already become another SDS issue that King's death forced into greater prominence. SDS and Mark Rudd took the lead again by disrupting a memorial service for Martin Luther King at St. Paul's Chapel on the campus next to Low Library. Amid a large hymn singing crowd of students, faculty, and distinguished visitors, Rudd disrupted the service by seizing a microphone and shouting out charges of Columbia's racism in relation to the gym and other matters, backed by forty chanting SDS supporters. This action had the effect of further radicalizing the SDS participants, including the young woman student, Josephine Duke. To be seen and recognized by the university authorities present, in such a manner, caused her further alienation from the sanctity of the institution.

Through these radical actions the SDS leadership was following a "line" laid out by Carl Davidson, an SDS strategist on a national level who'd taught that universities could not be "liberated" without radically changing (Capitalist) society itself. He proposed that society be attacked through the universities by radicalizing young students through various popular issues, never accepting any liberal reform, and desanctifying the institutions through militant confrontation.

The SDS leadership carefully swayed students towards insulting, mocking, or assaulting student participation in University decisions by any staff or faculty member unsympathetic to radical causes. This theory and its practice was to dominate Columbia in the coming weeks and eventually spread throughout institutions of higher learning across America in the next few years.

To Josie Duke, the assassination of Martin Luther King was as much a symbol of what was wrong in America as the Vietnam War. Her growing radicalism was an outgrowth of frustration in a family tradition of liberalism. Her great-grandfather, a reluctant Confederate veteran named Washington Duke, was one of the earliest supporters of black independence and dignity in North Carolina following the Civil War. He had opposed the Ku Klux Klan when it was unpopular to do so and passed his strong beliefs on to his sons and their descendants. The family had supported black educational institutions in the South, and her own father was a lifelong champion of civil rights.

Anthony D. Duke had founded Boys Harbor in 1937. It was a multiracial educational institution dedicated to extending economically underprivileged youth of all races an opportunity to grow up with better prospects in America. On the night of the King assassination he had been called by Mayor Lindsay of New York to ride around in a squad car at the risk of his life, through an explosive Harlem, and attempt to defray violence through meeting with his many contacts in the black community. This was the family heritage of Josie Duke, student, in April, 1968.

America was going through great changes in that year of 1968, as far as dealing with individual rights and racism, but not changing fast enough for the idealistic youth of the universities. Additionally, there was the strange, frustrating, and bloody war in Indochina dragging on day after day. The educated youth, privileged enough to be in college and exempt from service, still dealt with their rising social conscience every day. They saw the war as immoral and senseless for their America, and the assassination of King as a vindication of their belief that America was a sick society, with grievous problems close to home needing to be solved. The stage was set for a confrontation between the authorities and the Josie Dukes of upper-middle class America, growing up at Columbia University. How the authorities would deal with the confrontation would determine the level of radicalism attained by student activists in the coming critical year of the Vietnam War, following the Tet Offensive.

By April, SDS was the leading protest organization on the Columbia campus, forming the catalyst for other groups that were to evolve. Its leadership was dedicated to Communist principles of revolution and was attempting to organize students' widening disenchantment with the war and other issues like the "racist gym." Mark Rudd, as the newly elected President of the Columbia SDS, was setting the tone of confrontation. He had returned in the late winter of '68 from Castro's Cuba where he had met with representatives of its government and the Vietcong, and had absorbed the latest international Communist dogma. In renewing his efforts at organizing against IDA and the Harlem Gym, he was assisted by Nick Freudenburg, John Jacobs, Teddy Gold, and Tony Papert.

Josie Duke was greatly impressed by the five radical student leaders. She admired their action-responses to issues that concerned her, and found herself accepting a more radical line than she really believed, in order to remain part of the group.

At the urging of several SDS members she read Herbert Marcuse's book, *One Dimensional Man*. This seemed to point out to her the absurdity of accepting the peaceful production of the means of destruction by our own society, and how it followed that our society was thereby irrational. Peace was to be maintained by the constant threat of war (or the practice of limited wars like Vietnam).

Another piece of required reading was the *Vietnam Reader* by Marcus Raskin of the Institute for Policy Studies, published by Random House. This book promoting a Communist solution became a bible for antiwar students across the country throughout the war.

She was also influenced by Oglesby's *Containment and Change,* which was a criticism of "American Imperialistic Capitalism" around the Third World, and our policy of enforcing it through the use of military power. The SDS line was that the "Domino Theory" (in which one country falling under Communist domination would thereby cause a chain-reaction) had to be attacked as "anti-progressive" and "anti-self determination." The world Communist powers' actions were to be discounted or applauded. An additional influence was and writings of Tom Hayden, another Communist sympathizer and SDS leader from the Midwest area, who had already been to North Vietnam twice.

There was no countering ideological study made available or popularly presented which detailed the constant failures in practice around the world of Communist regimes to provide guarantees of personal freedom or initiative to people. Our battle in Vietnam was not given even the slightest benefit of legitimacy or moral rightness and the continual antiwar bias of the news media promoted this view. The line was that America was constantly wrong and evil, the enemy of the world. What SDS was concentrating on in mid-April was to organize students around their sympathy for the plight of black America and to stop construction of the gym on black-occupied land. But the ultimate object of the leadership was a more general and ideological attack on the whole American system and the Vietnam war-machine represented by the Institute for Defense Analysis. The demands for removal of IDA continued to be pushed on an equal footing with the gym issue by the Marxist leadership.

The majority of SDS followers were beginning to adapt the long hair and ragged dress that later characterized both the mass of protestors and the generation as a whole. It seemed the easiest way to announce one's rejection of the traditional society that was condoning the war and continued racial injustice.

The use of cursing, threats, and confrontations was steadily increasing in April, which gradually had the intended effect of stifling dialogue between the administration and the radical leadership.

On April 23rd the radical leadership of SDS led a group of 100 student supporters into Hamilton Hall and confronted and detained Dean Young, who ended up confined in a barred office. The students then occupied and held the building in defiance of authority, until their demands of the ouster of IDA from campus and no gym on Harlem land were met.

By April 24th the white radicals had been driven from Hamilton by a more militant group of black students supplemented by Harlem blacks from off-campus claiming to be carrying guns. The white radicals then broke through locked glass doors and occupied the Low Library building at the urging of Rudd and other leaders. Upon the threat of a police raid Mark Rudd fled through a window, followed by others, while some twenty-five dedicated followers under Tony Papert remained to face the music. The police entered, secured some valuable property and, ignoring the students after a short confrontation, left. After this the Low Commune grew rapidly in numbers as word of the action spread around the campus among hundreds of other students who could identify with the demands. Rudd then reentered the "Commune," reassumed leadership, and attempted to further raise the level of rhetoric and confrontation. Meanwhile, more students not radical enough to join the SDS members in Low, occupied other buildings to show support for the basic demands. The blacks had released Dean Coleman by then, on threats of being charged with kidnapping, but continued to hold Hamilton.

By April 26th and 27th the architecture students held Avery Hall, moderate students held Fayerweather, and more still occupied the Mathematics Hall. The uprising had grown to over one thousand students and there had already been a militant march of Harlem blacks showing support who had entered the campus. National protest leaders such as Rap Brown and Stokely Carmichael had arrived to hold press conferences and add their weight to the tense situation.

Inside the Low Commune Josie Duke sat on the floor with over a hundred comrades, girls and boys. The walls were colored with posters of Ho Chi Minh, Che Guevara, Mao Tse Tung, and Malcolm X. Red flags and armbands were everywhere and the furniture from the upstairs offices had been piled against the doors, barring entry. Tom Hayden had arrived from the national office of SDS, and was lecturing the younger students seated on the floor below him from a dominant position on President Kirk's desk. Rudd and other leaders took over whenever he tired. Their purpose was to raise the level of consciousness in the newly radical rank and file to the correct Communist line on the "internationalism of the struggle . . ." They were educated on the heroics of the Viet Cong fighting the American Imperialists for the "liberation" of Indochina, and the solidarity with the French students rebelling at the Nanterre Campus of the University of Paris. The important task of the leadership was to relate the local issues of the IDA protest and the Harlem Gym to overall radical ideology.

By the 29th of April all dialogue between the student protestors and the University administration had failed. The radical leadership had seen to it that the demands were non-negotiable and that discussions with the faculty or administration ended in threats and foul language. The time had come for the inevitable confrontation with the final authorities.

The faculty and administration turned to the Mayor of New York, John Lindsay, and his appointed Police Comissioner, Leary, who ordered the police to clear the occupied buildings. The object of all SDS plans and organizing had come to fruit around grievances that over a thousand other students felt were legitimate.

Inside the Low the mood was one of tension, exhilaration, and danger. Josie Duke waited fearfully for the reigning authorities' answers to her disagreements with them. Looking out a window, she caught a glimpse of one of Columbia's radical professors elevated to guru-status by the students he counselled in revolutionary action, standing safely beyond the occupied buildings. Tom Hayden had disappeared also.

In the middle of the night of the 29th/30th of April, 1968, police floodlights lit up the common in front of Low. Crowds of conservative students still shouting and heckling the radicals within, encouraged the approaching squads of the elite Tactical Patrol Force, regular patrolmen and plainclothes cops. The demonstrators challenged police, screaming curses and their now familiar slogans of defiance. Police trucks and paddy wagons appeared rapidly with more reinforcements, and hundreds of police now advanced into the area of occupied buildings. Cordons of faculty members sympathetic to the students stretched out to protect their campus were violently pushed aside.

Hamilton was cleared first, the police removing the blacks gingerly, in their fear of igniting a black riot throughout Harlem. When the operation to clear the white student occupied buildings began, violence erupted. Inside the second floor executive offices of Low Library the striking students huddled in a circle on the floor singing the civil rights hymn, *We Shall Overcome.*

Squads of police rammed the barricaded doorway and forced their way inside. The first thing the young student Josephine Duke remembered upon looking up from her place in the embracing circle was the face of Dr. Thomas Harper. The older, balding physician had been the volunteer "medic" to the rebel students. Now his face was distorted in agony as burly police spun him around and around, beating him on the face and head with blackjacks and nightsticks. Even after he fell to the floor the bludgeoning continued, as blood spattered sideways and ran down the side of the doctor's head. He rolled on the floor groaning and writhing in pain. The young girl who disagreed with so much shuddered as the police dragged the doctor out through the door, his head bumping and banging.

Her group reacted to the naked violence by rising from their places. Police surged in around them, grabbing at students, beating some, merely dragging others. Josie Duke was seized in the melee, her arms twisted and bent until she cried, and handcuffed as she tried to back away. The group was dragged, pushed, kicked and shoved down the steps into a waiting gauntlet of more police outside. In the floodlight illuminated predawn night of April 30th, 1968, the plaza was an uproar of screaming and scuffling and beatings. The students were dragged down the front steps by their feet with their heads slamming against the concrete. Police on either side of the gauntlet rained down blows with lead-weighted billy clubs or blackjacks, screaming, "Fuckin' Commie kids!" The officers of the law, supposedly trained to be disciplined and impartial were going berserk by now. Plain-clothesmen beyond control, without names or identification, were viciously beating both girls and boys bloody.

The violence spread rapidly as the other buildings, starting with Fayerweather, were cleared. Students were picked up or thrown through the air. Groups of three or four police beat others until blood ran on the pavement, and bones broke. Screams and cries were rising all around as Josephine Duke was rammed into a paddy wagon for the trip to jail. Faculty members trying to restrain the police were attacked with metal handcuffs held in one fist and swung as maces. Reporters from newspapers were dealt with the same way, though they showed their credentials and screamed, "Press!" For Josie Duke, one of the last sights was the vicious beating of two more friends, one a white civil rights activist student, Ron Carver, who had marched in the South under Martin Luther King, and another, an architecture graduate student whom she had gotten to know while babysitting his children so he and his wife could work late.

As the police wagon door slammed shut on the pile of injured students she heard chants of "Fuck you cops," and "Up against the wall, mother fuckers!"

Out of perhaps one thousand protesting students, approximately one hundred had suffered wounds and injuries ranging from cuts, lacerations, and bruises to broken bones and fractured skulls. The percentage of ten percent casualties was about the same as an average military combat operation at the time.

7   The May Offensive

*"Confusion concerning the
character of the opposition,
especially its intransigence
and will to power, leads regularly
to downplaying the amount of
force required to counteract
its violence."*
— *Jeane Kirkpatrick*

Towards the end of April we realized in Phu Loi from
intelligence information and an increase in enemy activity that the Communists were building up for a new offensive. Before dawn on the 25th
of April, enemy small-arms fire came in over the perimeter wire, hitting buildings and aircraft hangars. This was a sure sign something was
up. The Phu Loi base camp was put on high alert because of an enemy
force in the area.

The 1st Engineer Battalion began the clearing of several thousand acres
around our perimeter to make sure there was a clear field of fire. Sometimes we'd pull security for them or run into them on patrols, big Rome
plows roaring, the engineers sweating and cursing, watching out for
booby traps and mines; their M-16s hanging on the machines. Watching them was enough to make any grunt feel pretty light-footed. I
wouldn't have liked crashing around Vietnam in such a big, noisy target.

On April 26th Quan Loi and Lai Khe were attacked with rockets, and
Lai Khe also had a Viet Cong sapper-satchel charge attack. That same
day we received another intelligence warning through Drumfire Zulu
(Division Artillery) and Colonel Schroeder: A VC document captured
that day by troops of the 199th Light Infantry Brigade indicated that our
area in Third Corps Tactical Zone would have a series of attacks beginning on the 28th or 29th of April. On the 28th another intelligence
report confirmed a sighting of a hundred or more NVA Regulars believed to be the 165th NVA Regiment, equipped with mortars, RPGs,

and automatic weapons at XT9116, only 3 kilometers east of Tan Phu Khan village. Charlie Company of the 2nd/28th Infantry next got in a firefight in an ambush position immediately adjacent to the northern edge of Tan Phu Khan village. They saw some thirty enemy troops retreat into the village and their CO decided nothing could be done about it because of the presence of a large civilian population.

All these events later proved to be the starting point of the May offensive in our Brigade area. The enemy began with coordinated attacks on ARVN and RF-PF Outposts on the 29th of April. The assaults spread to include over a hundred military camps, villages, and towns, including Saigon, causing American casualties in the thousands.

The loudly proclaimed bombing halt by President Johnson and the recently appointed Secretary of Defense Clark Clifford had just helped the enemy rebuild their commitment, courage, and strength.

On the 29th of April, the same night as the violent end of the Columbia uprising in New York, we received orders for another night-movement and ambush. We were supposed to start out in the middle of Tan Phu Khan village and move in the darkness through it to the edge of a jungle "no-man's land," and then to set up an ambush in a combined operation with South Vietnamese militia. First Infantry Division Intelligence had received information from a village chief of a large-sized enemy movement of the 165th NVA Regiment into the village, and possibly a follow-up attack on Phu Loi about May 1st. Combined with the 2nd/28th sighting the night before, this should have been warning enough to intelligence of treachery. At this point in the war, most remaining village chiefs were either corrupted by fear of Viet Cong terrorism or by the privileges of being mini-dictators supported by the Saigon regime and the U.S. Army. Intelligence information like this should have been treated as a distortion of the truth to either appease intelligence or possibly set up a trap. We were in for our own share of the May offensive.

Combat Recon Patrol
Phu Loi, R.V.N.
May 1, 1968 Late p.m.

Dear Mom and Dad and Family,
I would like to say everything is still quiet, but it isn't. I just came out of forty-eight hours of straight contact with the enemy without a scratch,

so you know "Lady Luck" is still with me.
On the night of the 29th of April, as we were setting up an ambush,
the Viet Cong and NVA sprung one on us. We took 50 percent casual-
ties of our small force. Two of my buddies killed, six more wounded,
seven ARVNs and one U.S. advisor with us also hit, and thirty or forty
enemy and civilians killed and wounded. It's a long story of what strange
things happened to Don Gould and me, like something out of a book.

Love,
John

It had started, as usual, in the late afternoon, with about half the platoon or a little more, maybe sixteen guys, going out on patrol. We saddled up with our gear and camouflaged each other's faces with the sticky,
waxy colors that kind of puckered-up your skin, but keep your face from
shining in the darkness. Soft, camouflaged bush hats were pulled down
low over our heads. All loose or noisy gear was taped or tied down over
our camouflaged-colored jungle fatigues. We carried extra ammunition,
claymores, grenades, PRC-25 radio, one machine-gun team, and one
dude even had a 12-gauge pump shotgun.

We were ready now. We'd finally gotten a new Lieutenant named
Donald Becker, from Missouri. He's going with us. Most of us hardly
knew him yet. The old lifer platoon Sergeant stayed in the CP monitoring the command radio. My nominal squad leader was a dude named
Bryson, but the guy we listened to was still Tommy Donaghue, humping an M-79 grenade launcher tonight. Joe Miller was carrying the
machine-gun because he'd been humping it while Donaghue was on R
& R for the past week. Cheek was his AG, packing extra ammo for Joe
and his own M-16 rifle. Cortez was carrying the radio; our medic was
a new guy on his first patrol named Speez. Richie Evans, "the Kid,"
was with us along with "Smiley" Clarke and Art McQuade, carrying
M-16s. Rocky Allen stayed behind in the CP because he was about to
rotate home. Banko did not go out tonight, either, because he still had
to take it easy with his booby-trap wound.

In a rare change of operations, we were loaded in GI trucks and transported by road to the ARVN militia fort in the middle of Tan Phu Khan
village. It looked like a raggedy, beat up, sandbagged version of the
Alamo, with a big old gate. Inside the fort, we lay in the dust with all
our gear on, returning the chatter and grins of the RR/PF, "Ruff-Puff"

ARVNs with blank stares, waiting for pitch blackness. Finally, it became late enough, and dark enough to move. I was partnering with Don
Gould tonight, because my regular field-partner, Earl, was home on leave
in Hawaii. Don and I have been together a good while now since Tet.
He's a careful, sharp dude, really alert, and we're into philosophical
and historical raps occasionally, and get mellow together, when we're
on stand-down. He looked thin, with all his gear on tonight. Another
Hawaiian dude named Stone was near us, also waiting. One U.S. Advisor to the "Ruff-Puffs" is by the wire, as we head out. I watched these
half-assed ARVNs pretty closely. They acted like they don't want to
go out there at all. We were supposed to be totally quiet, and those little rats were kind of whining and rattling around. One of them is trying
not to go, period, and an American Advisor is so enraged about it, he's
kicking the son-of-a-bitch out through the gate, literally with his boot.
The crooked little traitor sure must have known something.

We file on out carefully, completely quiet. I can barely make out the
faces of some of our other riflemen like Montieth, Bell, and Don Dunce.
The ARVNs were rattling, rustling, stupid. Through the village we
moved over trail-like roads of velvet dust in the dark, past silent hootches,
a Buddhist temple, out past the village now and into a graveyard.

"Another graveyard," I'm thinking. "I remember the last time we
set up an ambush in a damn graveyard, all right, back in the Tet Offensive." Around us, everybody's just setting up, I'm sliding my claymore
out with Don. It isn't even done yet, when all of a sudden a temple bell
starts ringing.

CLANG! CLANG! CLANG!

"My God!," I'm thinking, "that's gotta be a signal!"

The night exploded right then, first a single grenade—*Ka-Boom!*, then
RPGs—blowing up blue-white against the tombs, heavy automatic rifle
fire! *Whooosh - Wham! Whooosh - Wham - BBBRRRRRPPPPP!* I hear
"the Kid," Evans, get hit—screaming as two more grenades go off to
my right. I recognized his voice. He was off to our right flank. Gould
and I are on the extreme end of the left flank. This whole barrage was
hitting us, and I could see a wide crescent of flashing muzzles moving
towards us like the jungle is turned to spitting fire, and coming right
over our position fast. I heard Clarke and some other guys cry out, "I'm
hit!! Jesus Christ, I'm hit! Medic! Medic!" In the light of explosions
I could see enemy soldiers coming over a berm in front of me.

I started to fire my rifle into the oncoming enemy line. There were shadowy forms out there, jerking and falling from our first volleys. Donaghue was firing his M-79 and one of his grenades blew up in front of us, silhouetting the advancing NVA, including one flung back by the blast. I could hear and see the tracers from our machine-gun team, Joe Miller and Cheek, firing in long low bursts into the rushing enemy line. I can't even see Don Gould. He was down flat somewhere right near me, when all of a sudden Lieutenant Becker ran shouting along the line right in front of my rifle sights. I realized in horror that I had almost shot him. I grimaced at him. He's screaming, "Fall back, fall back! Run for Play Boy Outpost!"

"Orders, fuckin' orders."

I didn't want to move. The shooting was intense, tracers flying everywhere, orange-blue-white explosions; shrapnel whizzing around. In a glance to my right, I could see Art MacQuade, a half-crouched form firing long bursts full-automatic in the middle of our line. Further to our right more of our dudes were screaming, shooting. There were maybe 150 heavily armed enemy soldiers against our thirty or so. Almost half our number were worthless Ruff-Puffs, some of whom were obviously traitors who signaled their comrades with the bell. One of them had thrown the first grenade near Donaghue, badly wounding Evans. Now the lieutenant was screaming "Fall back!" again. The booming, cracking, popping bullets and shells were like a ripping roar. The enemy line was getting extremely close now, but with the eerie, erratic light, I can't tell for sure how many I've been hitting. About that moment Art MacQuade was hit by several bullets in the chest refusing to retreat, dying or dead already. A few seconds later, I hear terrible screams from our medic, Speez, hit in the guts by a point-blank RPG explosion. He'd been trying to reach Art MacQuade when the missile blew up in front of him. Cortez has been hit by an RPG too; he was badly wounded in the shoulder and back; later he would lose one of his arms.

Gould and I found each other, and started to pull back together as we had been ordered. We didn't know where to go; it was so dark behind us; in front it was flashing, lit up, and crazy. In the light of exploding shells I could see some of the guys on my right dragging our own worst-hit casualties one-handed, including Art MacQuade's body. Tommy Donaghue, already wounded by grenade shrapnel in two places, had Evans thrown right up over his shoulder, and was dragging Clarke under his arm (Clarke had been hit by two bullets and wounded in twenty-one places by shrapnel). We were trying to move towards this right flank of our ambush where we can still hear Miller's long bursts with the M-60 into the enemy line. He was putting out an almost continuous wall of fire. I was thinking "he's gonna burn the barrel outta that thing." It sounded a lot farther away though now, as though they all pulled back. Well, he's helped save all our asses already tonight with that machine-gun; a soul brother, a hero. Carson Cheek had been throwing him belts and firing his own M-16 in support, though already wounded himself. More flares popping revealed, to our front and right flank, a horde of enemy troops charging over dead bodies toward us, muzzles flashing.

Everytime we tried to move towards the rest of our patrol, we were pinned down by heavy bursts of fire. We were with one other GI, who was an advisor to the ARVNs and two worthless Ruff-Puffs. We tried to withdraw straight back, but came under enemy fire from the "friendly" Tan Phu Khan village itself. Green AK-47 tracers were cracking from front and rear both. We pulled back further to the left, separated now by the enemy from everybody else. We crouched by the first outlying hootch of the village, whispering quickly, hoarsely, "We're overrun! What the hell are we gonna' do? The other dudes are gone, man. They found some hole over there, way off to the right. They're getting back to Play Boy!"

The ARVN's advisor whispered back, "I know exactly where I am, I know this whole goddamn village!" We knew the American position had been overrun now. The rest of the patrol had retreated and the ene-my were all around us. We couldn't break through this many VC with-out all getting hit. The Advisor led us quickly along the edge of the village with the shooting and crashing still going on, bullets cracked and whizzed by. We felt totally naked and exposed, as though every Vietnamese and Communist soldier in the world could see us.

Finally we pushed our way into a small hootch, taking it over from a woman and kids, at gunpoint. We must have looked like monsters to them, bursting in with our weapons; painted up and camouflaged, dirty, sweating, and raggedy, fear in our faces. We were still at the outermost edge of the village, overlooking rice paddies and jungle that we can barely see. We were overrun and surrounded, nothing to do but hide and hold out 'til friendlies retook the village. We were a hundred meters behind the advancing enemy line, that was now shooting into the outpost—in the part of the ville that remained in their hands until the next day. We spread out quickly on the floor, setting up our weapons. The Advisor is jumping down into the little, foxhole-like bomb shelter muttering, "I'm too goddamn short for this shit!'' The two ARVNs were cowering in a corner, shaking their heads and moaning; they were in total terror. We heard the enemy clanking and rattling in the next hootch, setting up a machine-gun, and then they started firing towards the ambush retreat and the outpost from fifteen or twenty feet away, right through our hootch. The bullets came crashing all through the walls, ricocheting across the floor, keeping Gould and me rolling and dodging, terrified. They are probing everywhere for return fire, looking for us or any cut-off dudes. Off in the distance near Play Boy Outpost we can hear a chopper descending.

Whack! Whack! Whack! Whack!

Anti-aircraft fire is going off around us.

Pop! Pop! Pop! Pop! PPRRRRRPPPPPP!

"Must be a dust-off comin' in to medevac the guys," I thought.

"They must've got back O.K. Oh, God, I wish we could be there with them!'' The medevac took off again, jet-turbine engine screaming at high pitch. More shooting. Grenades started going off, *Boom! Boom!* everywhere; and one rolled up against the wall of our hootch and exploded with a *Whooom!* The first foot of the hootch wall was mud-bricks, and absorbed most of the blast. Shrapnel whizzed through the air and roof. They were searching and shooting all through the village, looking for missing Americans and killing Vietnamese anti-Communists.

We could hear them talking and searching right around us, and I held my cocked Chi-Comm pistol against the head of the shaking woman with my left hand, while she cowered under the wooden rack with her kids. I had my rifle set up, facing the door, with my right finger on the trigger. Don Gould and I whispered, together, and agreed not to fire and give our position away, unless they assaulted us right through the opening. It seemed like a long time went by when a U.S. Psy-Ops chopper clatters overhead, blaring our names on a loudspeaker and saying, "If you're cut off down there, we'll come looking for you tomorrow." They started to draw enemy anti-aircraft fire from all around us and thumped away.

About 2 a.m. a squad or platoon of heavily-armed enemy troops in uniform marches up and stopped by the hootch, talking and drinking from a well. My scalp was prickling, and my hair stood on end. An enemy soldier with an AK-47 slung and belts of squad machine-gun ammo wound over his shoulders came right up near the doorway, covered only by a loose, leaning piece of tin. He started to wash his face in a bowl on an outside table, not four feet from where we lay watching him through a wide crack, not breathing and ready to fire.

We could see all the others behind him, fifteen or twenty of them. I was so close to instant death I just prayed, "Yea, though I walk through the valley of the shadow of death, I will fear no evil, for Thou art with me." Their faces were lit up every so often by flares popping over the militia fort. They were lean and evil-looking, laughing and talking together in short, terse sentences about their good night's work. The smell of their stale sweat and the nuoc-mam rotten fish sauce they ate with their rice permeated the air already laden with burnt cordite. They had on NVA regulation uniforms and web gear, magazine pouches, and bush hats. One had a Soviet RPD machine-gun, another an RPG, and the rest AK-47 assault rifles. I decided they were NVA Regulars from the 165th Regiment or Main Force Viet Cong, or both working together. I was covered with sweat from head to foot when they finally marched off with all their weapons and gear. We found out much later from the village chief that the reason they didn't search our hootch was that the woman I was holding was a VC officer's wife.

We waited in complete, utter silence the rest of the night, small arms rounds still popping, some artillery flares and shells going off in the distance. After dawn, the shooting finally stopped, and the enemy started to melt away. From our position on the edge of the village, Don and I got a perfect view of a large group of them in a file, marching into a jungle area beyond, with their AK-47s, machine-guns, and RPGs, and mostly disappearing. We saw maybe seventy-five heavily armed enemy-in this group. I was feeling crazy and started to aim my rifle at the line, when Don grabbed my arm, whispering hoarsely, "Are you going fuckin' crazy, man? We just made it. They'll come kill us, sure as hell!" I got a hold of myself, and nodded, muttering. The tension had almost pushed me around the bend. A few moments later a handful of them came out dressed like peasants and slipped into the village.

About 6:30 a.m. we sneaked out of our hootch-haven and linked up with a Vietnamese Army patrol gingerly advancing through the village towards the battlefield. What happened during that long night put some years on Don and me, and on the others who made it back safely, each with his own memories and stories to tell.

Patrolling with the ARVNs, we crossed the firefight zone, and picked up Art MacQuade's rifle where he'd been killed. There was a big pool of blood where our new medic got hit (we were told later he died of his wounds) and signs of our other casualties, like ripped-open, dropped, bloody compresses. Out in front close to our position, we found a large number of blood and gore spots, where enemy soldiers had been killed and wounded and dragged away, maybe 30 or more. Eventually we worked our way through the scattered firefight-junk of unblown claymores, empty magazines, dud grenades, scattered pieces of uniforms and equipment, and back through the silent, hateful (to me at the time) enemy village. I walked behind the ARVNs as I was now afraid to turn my back to them.

We passed a number of Vietnamese civilian houses damaged or blown apart by the Soviet RPG anti-tank rockets or hand grenades. Groups of Vietnamese were standing or squatting around dead bodies of family members caught in the crossfire, crying and moaning. Several of the males had also been shot and executed by the Communists as collaborators. I guessed at least fifteen or twenty civilians had been killed or seriously wounded.

At the militia outpost was a restrained and quiet group, the remnants of our ambush patrol. They told us about the dust-off of our other casualties. We had lost eight killed and wounded out of the sixteen who started out, besides about seven casualties among the ARVNs and advisors; a total of about fifteen killed and wounded, 50 percent of the ambush force. There were also the uncounted or recorded civilian casualties. The other men were surprised to see us; they figured we were dead. Even the usual chatter and giggles of the Ruff-Puff ARVN militia was stilled. They squatted around staring at us in our dirty camouflage uniforms, as if waiting to see our emotions at the evidence of traitors among them.

Back in the Phu Loi camp later, the other guys of the platoon who hadn't gone out, who'd been on stand-down or guard, and our lifer platoon sergeant, wanted to hear the story of Tan Phu Khan, but Don Gould and I were ordered to report to a headquarters hootch, where we were interviewed by the Assistant Division Commander of the Red One, a brigadier-general named Emil Eschenburg, I believe. He was a clean-looking, abrupt lifer, second in command under Major-General Keith L. Ware. He listened to exactly what we'd seen and where, and ordered a helicopter air-assault into the spot. We were requested to "volunteer" to go out with Delta Company of the Black Lions of the 2nd/28th Infantry as scouts. We were supposed to show them the lay of the land and the jungle hide-out. The idea was to assault quickly with choppers, march into the hide-out and heavy-weapons position, in the hope of stirring them up, then later to set up a night ambush. The next day we were to surround and search the central area of the village of Tan Phu Khan.

By now, Don and I had been up for twenty-four hours straight. We were worn and tired, but the lifers gave us a bottle of dexedrine tabs, stuff the hippies back home were calling "speed." Pretty damn soon we were buzzing along again, among the tired and ragged looking company of grunt rifleman. The assault helicopters came roaring into the strip to pick us up for the CA.

So we just kept moving and going with the flow. I think the air assault turned a little hot; there was an exchange of shots after jumping out, but I hardly remember or paid attention. We marched a good ways quickly, and set up a fast, smooth position. It was a tense night ambush, especially for Don and me, lying together, ready for anything. All night there were noises and movement out in the dark jungle ahead of us. It was raining and cold. In the pre-dawn drizzle and darkness we broke up the ambush and started slogging through the jungle bush towards the objective.

It was May 1st, the Communists' favorite, "May Day." A *Time* magazine correspondent was with us, right next to me, and he was babbling with excitement. We kept him in the file of men, whispering to him, "Shut the hell up, man, there's gooks around!" Man followed man in the drizzling darkness. There was tangible fear in the air. Suddenly, a violent explosion erupted twenty or thirty feet in front of Don and me. A goddamn booby-trap mine! Three GIs are blasted up in the air like rag dolls, with the *KA-BOOM!*, while a fourth screams and falls over backwards. They absorbed the blast and shrapnel, while we others were untouched. The air stank of burnt-explosives, blood, and blown-up earth. We rushed forward to help drag back the bodies when, to add to horror, bullets and M-79 grenades started cracking and exploding around us. Two more guys are hit making a total of six. The wounded were screaming, crying, moaning, somebody was yelling "Medic!" Blood was literally spraying from one of them, and splattered all across my face. We're down flat, rifles out, taking rounds from front and rear in a crossfire. We knew out in front was another ARVN outpost. Just as we start returning fire on our "allies," the platoon leader we're with gets the ARVN's Advisor on the PRC-25 and the shooting from the front stopped. Shortly after, the sniper fire from the rear flank ended; it was the enemy, but they didn't want to take on a whole company of "Black Lions" of the 28th Infantry.

The author in "The Iron Triangle," July 1968.

Earl Okumura, March 1968.

Phu Loi Combat Recon Patrol in contact with the enemy, March 1968.

Phu Loi Combat Recon Platoon, 10 March 1968
Front Row, left to right: Steve Hustler, Rocky Allen, Tom Hines, Lt. Mike Marano, Ritchie "The Kid" Evans, Ernesto Baca, Earl Okumura, Sergeant Bryson. Second row, left to right: Sergeant "Rock" Rhiener, Tommy Donaghue, "Smiley" Clarke, Don Dunse, "Frenchy" Fournier. Standing, left to right: "Bear" Banko, Joe Miller, "Monty" Monthieth, Don Gould, Ernest Abner Bell, Emil Krone, Arthur McQuade, Reynaldo Garcia, John M.G. Brown. The dog is "Heinrich".

The author in NVA webgear, Tet Offensive, 1968.

Don Gould of Chicago, March, 1968.

Joe Miller, the "Black Lion," with his M60 machinegun, April, 1968.

Company A, 5th Battalion/60th Infantry moving out of firebase Moore on 22 October 1968. Photo taken by author on point. Welch on right, Winters on left in front. Also included are Bergy, Gaddy, Sergeant Wilbur Gordon, Lt. James Brown, Sellman, Shaeffer, Novak, Bartel, Robby, Cannady, and Troutman.

Company A on tracks of 11th Armored Cavalry, "Iron Triangle," July, 1968.

Left to right: Gaddy, Troutman, and Owens at 1st/16th NDP, July, 1968.

Robby Robinson at firebase Moore, Mekong Delta, October, 1968.

The lieutenant's calling in the dust-off now. "We got six WIAs. Three critical-severe, and three moderate. I need a priority dust-off now or some of these people are gonna die."

The medevac chopper came thumping towards us through the rain to take away the casualties. We half-carried and dragged them towards the chopper, blood and wounds all over, intestines coming out of one guy's belly. They were moaning, "Ohhh. Oh, Jesus. No, no. I'm gonna die! Christ, oh, Jesus my belly!" The medics were still frantically working on them. They had some bags of plasma going and were shooting morphine, while we helped them and held the guys. I was feeling sick. Two of them are bad off, with that gray look. I shove a lit cigarette in a third dude's mouth, and with my arm holding his head up a little, tell him to be cool, "Yer gonna make it, buddy, you don' look too bad at all. It's all right, man." When you're hit and down, there's a lot of comfort in just having a brother GI stay close to you.

The dust-off chopper down, we carried them over, and the *Time* magazine correspondent jumps in with them with his "big story." "A little too real, huh, man?" He was stone silent now. And this was the combat action that would be reported in the news bulletins—a half-story really, compared to what happened and what was going to happen here shortly afterward. This was the only time I ever saw a "war correspondent" in the field with a grunt unit.

A lieutenant was shouting through the rain now, "Battalion's calling fer their names, who got hit, who were they?" A wet, muddy sergeant pushes past me up towards the lieutenant, the medic still yelling names behind him.

"All PFC's sir, all six of 'em. Deloa, severe; Schultz, severe; Chadd, severe; Murphy, moderate; Heard, moderate; Hammond, moderate; the machine-gunner tripped the booby trap wire, sir."

The chopper was up with a roar and we were off marching again, around and around in the rain, through this wet, stinking jungle, looking for the enemy or weapons caches we know are here, but can't find anywhere. By now, Don Gould and I were becoming exhausted. We were mighty glad when we finally got back to the base camp.

Sitting in my cabin on Kodiak Island, I can remember that nonstop forty-eight hour ordeal as though it was yesterday, and I know Don Gould does too, if he's still alive. The RF-PF ARVNs later claimed that firing on us after the booby trap explosion was a mistake, thinking we were VC. We shit-laughed in mirthless rage at the official line, remembering the betrayal by members of the same group in our ambush.

Lying on the rack after sleeping a long stretch, I stared at Art Mac-Quade's empty rack and the other empty places: Speez, Cheek, Cortez, Donaghue, Clarke, Evans, and the rest, and wondered why I was the lucky one. MacQuade was so young, so good looking and brave and tough. He had put his life on the line with our new medic and the rest of us, while back in the world mobs were chanting, "Hell, No! We won't go." I wondered what it all meant?

"Nothin'," I thought, "just drive on, just keep trying to make it. Why I'm here, what I'm doing, I don't know. I just know it's my place, my job, I belong. We're all here in it together."

Don Gould and I were told that we had been recommended for the Bronze Star Medal for our conduct in going through the ambush, surviving being overrun, gaining valuable intelligence on the size of the enemy force in the area to enable the 1st Division to react, and voluntarily going on the scouting mission again with the 28th Infantry. The recommendation went through Colonel Henry Schroeder, along with recommendations for Joe Miller and Tommy Donaghue for heroism.

Of our award citations, none of us was to hear another word.

After a long, long sleep I woke up in a filthy rage over the ambush, our casualties, and my own several close calls with death. A strange feeling of mixed luck and guilt pervaded my mind, because I was personally unharmed while some fifteen other American soldiers had just been killed or wounded close by me, aside from the twenty-five or so ARVNs and civilians and twenty-five or thirty enemy troops. The next day, I wandered from our CP radio hootch to Division Artillery listening for news. Quan Loi and Ben Cat had come under rocket and mortar attacks on the night of the 29th, and Cu Chi on the 1st of May. A helicopter lightfire team of the 7th/1st Cav had spotted and killed three Viet Cong somewhere beyond Chanh Long, or "Dog Leg Village," as we called it. There was a lot of talk about our ambush "tearing the top off a hornet's nest." The next few days showed how true that was, in the Phu Loi area.

On the 3rd of May, the unit Gould and I had scouted for—Delta Company of the 2nd/28th, "Black Lions"—blew an ambush on part of a large enemy force of over a hundred about 2000 meters north of the jungle hideout where we'd seen them disappear. They killed nine VC/NVA, captured four AK-47s and two wounded prisoners. That same day, with Phu Loi on yellow alert for an enemy attack, the following order came down from the 1st Division Commander, Major-General Keith L. Ware:

"Commanders will insure that sufficient ammunition is on hand, all aircraft will be in revetments, all clubs will close, no movies will be shown, no large group of troops. Effective 2130 hrs. until further notice."

(Signed) Ware

Also, an intelligence estimate stated, "Viet Cong forces appear to be moving into the Lam Son-Saigon areas to launch a 2nd all out offensive." Our ambush had evidentally circumvented a bigger enemy attack, probably on Phu Loi itself. The 165th NVA Regiment had moved into our area in late April, along with the Viet Cong/Phu Loi Battalion, and other units. Part of the Phu Loi Battalion kept moving south and later took part in heavy fighting around the Y Bridge and Cholon in the "Battle of South Saigon" with the U.S. 9th Infantry Division. The 165th NVA Regiment that had overrun our ambush stayed very close to Phu Loi, and on the morning of the 5th of May we came under a heavy barrage of incoming rockets and mortars that caused casualties and damage. One of the ARVN compounds southwest of Phu Loi took mortar and automatic weapons fire, too. In this rocket attack I got hit by two small pieces of shrapnel in the leg while running for a bunker. The steel slivers didn't go in very deep and I pulled them out myself and bandaged the holes.

Major battle had been going on three miles southeast of Phu Loi and north of Di An between the 1st/18th, 1st Division, and the VC Dong Ngai Regiment since the day before. We heard platoon leaders were being hit and the grunts were taking heavy casualties; it ended up being called the "Battle of Tan Hiep," and more than two hundred VC were killed.

On May 5th, after the fighting at Tan Hiep ended, part of our Recon Platoon was helping to guard the base camp; our casualties—except for Tom Donaghue—were still in hospitals. I was on the perimeter in a bunker again when we came under small-arms fire and bursts of automatic weapons. We returned fire at the enemy tracers. Out beyond the concertina wire of the camp a short while later, the whole country seemed to explode. About a thousand meters away, B Troop of the 1st/4th Cavalry went into heavy combat. The 165th NVA Regiment, which had started the offensive by attacking our Recon Platoon, was out there and fighting hard. It reminded me of An My again. Helicopter gunships were clattering in toward the battle over our heads, coming under anti-aircraft fire. Some were taking hits. A Troop of the ¼ Cav was rushed in to reinforce their brothers, the tanks firing 90mm cannister and with A-Cavs mounting '50s and flame throwers. Pretty soon the Tac Air came—the Phantom fighter bombers—throwing in napalm and bombs. The ground shook as I stared out at the bursts of green tracers arching up at our aircraft. I couldn't help but admire the deadly enemy for their guts at taking on our enormous firepower.

The VC/NVA began scattering in all directions, including toward our perimeter at Phu Loi. Any time we saw movement or running forms, we opened fire. The enemy probes against our perimeter went on past midnight and into the early morning. We had spotted several with bangalore torpedos and AK-47s and had taken them under close fire when Donaghue and Banko spotted another NVA out near a rice paddy dike. Banko grabbed a LAW rocket launcher, took careful aim and fired with a *Woosh!* It was long range but a perfect hit. As the rocket explosion splashed, the enemy soldier was flung like a limp rag.

Banko screamed, "Did ya see it? Did ya see it?'

Donaghue shouted back, "Whadda shot!''

We were hearing reports of 40 U.S. killed and wounded in this battle of Vinh Loi (or Xon Noi) and 137 enemy KIA. When I left that bunker I felt like there'd been a good "payback'' on some gooks out there for Tan Phu Khan.

The next day, we heard that Quan Loi, Lai Kai, and Bien Hoa had been or were then under attack. At the same time, reports were coming in about Viet Cong attacks in the Saigon area. They had captured part of Cholon, and heavy fighting was occurring around the Phu Tho race track and the Y Bridge. My buddy Earl had just gotten back from leave in Hawaii, and we had climbed up on the hot tin roof of the hootch together to visit and share a mellow smoke. I'd already told him about the ambush at Tan Phu Khan and our casualties. I was real glad he'd missed it, because I figured he'd already seen his share. We were on stand-down and he was talking about his home visit. He kind of flicked his head sideways a little to shake his long black hair out of his face, the way he always used to.

"Man, people back in the world, in Hawaii, they don't know nothin; about the war goin' on over here. They're jus' skatin' along havin' a good time. It's like it ain't even happenin'.''

I looked over at my main man. I didn't know why he'd come back, whether he'd extended his time or what. All I knew was he was my brother and I was glad for his company.

I said to him, "It's O.K., man. It's cool, we're just doin' our time for those people."

"I know watcha mean, we coulda got out of it with a college deferment or a medical deferment, we coulda shammed a bad back or bedwetting or suicidal tendencies, but we didn't. We're the ones here in this insanity. I guess for us it's just what was supposed to happen."

Right about then, yesterday's firefight beyond the perimeter blew up again. The roar of battle came to us, of the 7th Battalion/1st Cavalry (Op Con) armor assaulting, RPGs and rockets exploding, mixed in with tank guns and automatic weapons. We were mesmerized by the sound, living through every second of it because of our own experiences. I felt somehow privileged to witness the valor of our grunt brothers out there advancing into heavy enemy fire of bullets and shells, amidst the screams of "Medic!", the overwhelming noise, and confusion of combat. For an instant I felt what it must be like to be a war correspondent or general viewing troops engaged in battle, and wondering how they were going to do. We stared out at it all, as gunships swooped in again firing mini-guns and dodging anti-aircraft fire. Every so often a whole burst of green tracers would erupt up and out of the enemy position. We could see choppers taking hits and clattering back into the Phu Loi airstrip, some just barely making it. Now the sting of CS gas started coming through the air on the wind all around us. They were smoking the NVA out. The artillery was going off behind and over us in a continuous barrage of *Crack! Boom! - ZZZs*. The air was vibrating and the ground shaking when suddenly a burst of AK-47 fire came cracking in over the perimeter, pinging and clanging through the roof all around us. We slid down and jumped fast, chagrined and shit-laughing a little, running for a bunker.

"Goddamn, man! That's a little too close," Earl yelled.

The enemy out there, crawling around through the bombs, artillery, tank guns, automatic weapons fire, and gas, suddenly let loose another huge burst of fire, highlighted by green tracers, almost like one last big volley. We stood at the entrance of the bunker with our rifles in our hands, wondering if it was going to turn into a call-out for us. But it didn't, and finally the show was over. We heard later that on May 6th there'd been twenty-six more GIs killed and wounded, four more tracks hit, and a huge body count of VC/NVA. At about nine that same night on the perimeter, we came under another volley of small arms and automatic fire. Some 800 yards to the south we saw a burst of heavy anti-aircraft fire hit a chopper, shooting it down in front of our eyes. The sight of the tracers slamming into it sent a chill down my spine. Within the next hour, another bad rocket attack of about 150 shells came whooshing and booming down on Phu Loi. There were KIAs and WIAs in the base camp around us and buildings on fire. I stayed in a bunker all that night with Earl, singing him the old American folk songs and ballads that he loved so much. Right then I didn't know or care what was going on except I had about four more months to go in this crazy place, and a few good friends I could count on. Tommy Donaghue was going home now. He'd been living in a bunker his last few days because of all the rockets. When he'd come back from the hospital after having been wounded, he'd told us of running into our old platoon sergeant, Robert Carlisle, in a wheelchair there with both his legs blown off. He'd been hit in April after he'd gone back to the 16th Infantry. It must have been the final straw to Donaghue, and it shook all the rest of us up, too. Nobody was so tough he couldn't get it.

This was the May Offensive of 1968 around Phu Loi, Binh Duong Province, from the end of April at Tan Phu Khan, 'til the middle of May. The significance of the final battle of the offensive in our area was to be revealed in the three days after it had ended. Units engaged in the battle uncovered a large tunnel complex and hospital of the 165th NVA Regiment a mile and a half from our own "secure American base camp." This was in an area that our platoon and other units had patrolled intensively for months. The grid coordinate location of their base camp was the exact site of our small firefight with the machine-gun nest on the 23rd of March, where the VC kept disappearing. Only one other thing happened that I want to record, and I won't give the date, except to say that it was in early May after our ambush, while the offensive was raging over our part of Vietnam and enemy action was occuring at Phu Loi. After all the trouble from Tan Phu Khan and the hamlets around it for months and months, we were beyond reason about the place. The area had been a haven for Communist troops since the days of the Viet Minh, and the enemy Phu Loi Battalion dated back to the French Indochina War. The constant rocket and mortar attacks, snipers, ambushes, mines, and booby traps had finally put some of the guys in the Recon Platoon in the mood for revenge.

One night while all this fighting was going on, a couple of men from the Recon Platoon drifted over to the closest part of the perimeter that faced the nearest hamlet village at long range. There were some bullet-scarred APCs with .50s, and self-propelled 40mm duster guns of the 5th/2nd on line between the bunkers. These dudes were just in from the field and had caught some shit out there, too. Because of occasional incoming shells and sniper rounds coming from that direction, it was easy. After half an hour of rapping with the armored dudes, about a dozen more Recon guys drifted out and moved into the bunkers, with the REMF guards. All I saw was a dude running towards the wire, Cav or Recon, I don't know. He was back even quicker and then came a *Flash! Boom!* We assumed we were under attack from Tan Phu Khan and opened fire in front of us. At that instant somebody called the lifer-brass and told them we were taking fire. I was on an M-60 machine-gun, already firing.

Before they could be heard or even answer our radio, thousands of rounds ripped into that place. Even at such long range we could see hootches shot to pieces, explosions from the 40mm automatic guns, tracers from the machine-guns, both M-60s and .50 cals., setting fires. The shooting spread to all the men on the bunker line of that side of the perimeter. It was a true Vietnam "Mad Minute," with a damned good target. I put out over 500 rounds myself through my machine-gun. The barrel was sizzling hot. I was shooting for my buddies and all the other American casualties in and around Phu Loi the last few months.

I was shooting into every gook with a smirk, sneer, or blank look in the whole area who ever said, "No VC, no VC here."

Then there were REMF officers running up and down the perimeter screaming, "Cease fire! Cease fire, you assholes!"

I leaned back against the sandbags, hundreds of empty brass shells around me, exhausted from emotion. And to this day I still remember that I didn't feel any remorse. All I saw was Art MacQuade's laughing Irish face, our tall, new, serious young medic, Speez, Cortez, Evans, Clarke, Donaghue, Carlisle, Baca, Cheek, and the crying, shrapnel-hit rocket casualties in Phu Loi. To us the whole damned place was full of enemies. They had sent us over here to do a job, "defeat the Communists," win the war—and then made it impossible with their methods. Their ideas of "limited war" dreamed up in clean White House and Pentagon offices didn't work. It was becoming more obvious all the time that the Vietnamese we were supposed to be defending detested us. They fought us openly or secretly, or preyed on us, doing whatever the enemy said to do. When an organized Communist force fights a war, they don't fool around. They involve everyone in it at all levels. The people do what they are told to do or they pay in blood.

Many American leaders are remote from reality. Concepts of legality, fairness, and morality work against us in the guerilla wars that continue to this day. If America chooses a place in which to engage an ideological enemy dedicated to conquering us and our way of life, it doesn't make sense to stop bombing them in the middle of the war, thinking that will buy peace. It can only be seen as weakness. You don't take ground with American blood and then abandon it, only to fight for it again. And if the enemy has a rigid hold over the people because of terrorism or respect or both, you must get their attention. They must be made to see that it is worse for them to go against you than the enemy you're fighting. If we learn the lessons of Vietnam, we may defeat our enemies in the next war of this kind. Otherwise write it off, stay out, forget it.

Binh Duong Province of Cochin China in Vietnam absorbed the blood of thousands of American soldiers during the war. What happened to the myths? The traditions of service that we who had gone were raised with? On our return home to jeers and stares and shrugs, they crumbled away like childrens' sand castles on an ocean beach to be replaced with a hard core of bitterness.

By mid-May we were out on our endless patrols and ambushes again, introducing the new guys into operations, new riflemen to replace Art MacQuade, Clarke, Evans, and Cortez and another replacement medic for Speez. I can hardly remember now who they were. Carson Cheek is back from the hospital, too, recuperating from his wounds at Tan Phu Khan.

I was feeling tired and disillusioned, and so were some of my closest buddies. I'd catch myself wondering if I was actually going to live through the war. The first ten days of the Communist May Offensive of 1968 had cost the lives of about a thousand American soldiers killed in action, with about six thousand wounded. The first week of the May offensive reportedly caused the heaviest American combat deaths of the entire war. We heard the news on AFVN radio or read in the *Stars and Stripes* about the student uprising, barricades, and molotov cocktails in Paris; the large antiwar demonstrations by our own American students at home are multiplying since the Columbia uprising. The home front news media continued to escalate their stand against the cause we were fighting for. Their encouragement of the antiwar movement added to the weakness in our political leaders. We have discussions about the captured crew of the USS *Pueblo*, taken by North Koreans immediately before the Tet Offensive started. Some of us still think this was part of a plan to divert attention from the coming enemy attack here.

Another battle northeast of Phu Loi, beyond Dog Leg Village, took place between the 2nd/28th and 11th Armored Cav with the 141st NVA Regiment. About twenty more GIs were killed and wounded, one tank destroyed, and thirty-nine NVA killed. On our patrols nearby we're working very carefully, ready for anything. The day before, we'd had another rocket attack on Phu Loi that caused casualties, and two more on the 12th and 14th with more GIs hit. The number of killed and wounded around us was small but constant; and we were always trying to catch them launching or to ambush their rocket crews.

The incoming rounds from the surrounding villages had gotten so bad that Colonel Schroeder decided to act unconventionally. He called in the three village chiefs of the area and complained to them about how we couldn't return fire on their people, but something had to be done. The chiefs of Tan Phu Khan, Vinh Truong, and Vinh Loi were put on the spot because they were supposed to be in control of things in their villages. One of them asked the Colonel for half a dozen claymore mines and said he'd be able to help out with them. He took them back that night and an old retired AFVN soldier set up an MA. He caught the Viet Cong ammo bearers with the first string, the guerillas carrying the mortar tubes with the second, and their reaction force with the third set of mines. Incoming rounds from that area stopped for a while, but the rocket attacks continued from elsewhere.

We're staying in pretty close to the base camp and only made a few contacts with snipers. We shuffled along the dusty trails or slashed our way through wet, dripping jungle thickets. The Main Force Viet Cong seemed to have pulled back into their bush hideouts and base camps away from our own immediate patrol areas. For my part, I couldn't understand why our government would not allow our forces to go on the offensive and pursue the main enemy units to their remote base camps, no matter whether they retreated into Cambodia. The entire time I was in the field I expected a change in tactics that never came. The rocket attacks had become so common and damaging that the whole Phu Loi base camp dug in deeper and increased its defense capabilities. In our platoon area we're building a huge half-underground rocket bunker. Sergeant Rock blows the hole with a shaped charge, shaking up the whole area and cracking the floors of several hootches. He was using Donaghue's technique for digging holes.

> *Combat Recon Patrol*
> *Phu Loi, R.V.N.*
> *15 May 1968*

Dear Family,
Well, things have gotten quiet for us since the last offensive. About a thousand enemy were killed in our area of Vietnam alone.
I'm starting to get "short," and more careful all the time. The enemy rocket attacks continue on us, but you learn to live with them, and they aren't bad, compared to a close-range firefight when you're outnumbered. We in the Recon Patrol are building four powerful bunkers on the perimeter and going on short-range patrols and ambushes.
Anyway, things are sort of peaceful in a noisy kind of way, and I've started reading again about our Civil War. You are forgetting after so many years of peace what the good feeling of not worrying about just living is like. That's why I'm glad the war is over here, and I wish people would get along at home. Here especially in combat troops, everybody forgets the racism, and it's not in evidence where I am. I know one black guy, Joe Miller, in my unit, who has probably saved several of our lives with his bravery. It's unexplainable, that feeling.

> Well, love to you,
> John

The day after I wrote that letter, NVA Regulars attacked Firebase Coral of the 1st Australian task force, fifteen miles northeast of us, in what was called "AO Surfer," along the Song Be River north of Tan Uyen (in the area of the 1st Division called the "Catcher's Mitt"). This country was the beginning of the heavy, virgin jungle where enemy units that fought in our AO like the Dong Nai Regiment, the 273rd Regiment, and the 165th NVA Regulars had their base camps for refitting and reinforcement by infiltrators coming down across the border. The Australians took heavy casualties and forty-seven more NVA killed. When I heard about it, I was reminded of the times the Aussies in their bush hats visited Phu Loi since the Tet Offensive. They always seemed to be able to get their hands on good booze somehow. Whenever I was with them I ended up drunk and singing "Waltzing Matilda" to them. The year I'd spent in Australia in 1964 and '65 had made me feel close to them ever since.

We had more rocket attacks on Phu Loi, on the 16th and 24th at least, probably more. I was feeling tired of it all and not paying too much attention to much except Earl, Don Gould, Monty, and a few other buddies, and ended up getting taken by surprise and shaken up pretty good.

It's somewhere around the end of May and after an all-night ambush, I'm asleep in my rack with my camouflage fatigues on and my rifle next to me. I feel someone roughly shaking me, and I wake up suddenly. MPs are standing all around the hootch with their plastic helmets and .45s in their hands, loaded and cocked. They tell me to get to my feet and "move out." I know it's some kind of bust. I've got a little bit of dew in my jungle pants. I'm moving along between them in the hot dusty sunshine thinking, "I'd better drop this stuff somewhere!" I move my hand to do it, and one of them snarls, "Keep your hands still or I'll shoot." Now, I was thinking they could cut me a little slack, but oh, no, they are going to get their points, make sure to keep that nice job.

Well, I'm pretty tired from the last four months of Recon service, I just say to myself, "Ahhh, drive on..." But for a long time later I sure hated MPs for their comfortable quarters and skating jobs, sitting around gates or driving jeeps.

They march me up to the REMF office housing the CID. The smooth and clean-looking agent takes me in charge. He even knows me because of the time in Feburary I caught the VC saboteur, and another time when I ran off a dude robbing the PX hootch, at gunpoint. He says, in an oily, friendly voice, "John, I hate to see you like this. I've got to hang charges on you." He's already made me empty my pockets and there's a few joints worth of weed. I say, "No, you don't, you could just throw it out the window, and say you didn't find nothin', man."

He says, like they all do, "I'm just doing my job. You've been had, and that's it." Next he says, "Who else is doing grass?" I tell him, "Everybody, man, the whole U.S. Army, don't you know that?" He looks at me like he's actually astounded or something, and says next, "You've been reported by one of your own buddies, and the Platoon Sergeant in the Recon Patrol, and we're going to bust a whole bunch of you." I'm just thinking, "Buddy, my ass, you guys will do anything, say anything, to kiss ass and make a little rank. MPs and CID pigs preying off combat soldiers, looking for a chance to prove how bad they are... Yer a lying bastard..." I'm thinking, "Nah, it don't mean nothin'. What are they gonna do, send me to 'Nam?"

He couldn't resist one little rear echelon remark about grunts.

"You guys think you're special because you go out in the bush and do a little fighting. Well you're not, you're not any different than any of the troops that stay in this base camp all the time." I looked at him and grinned, "Wanna bet?"

I went through a long ordeal; chopper flight to Lai Khe, endless jobs for some days back at my old helicopter company welding steel plates on reinforced bunkers for rocket attacks. Finally I got a little court martial and I was sentenced to three months confinement at hard labor in LBJ. It was suspended on the condition that I volunteer for transfer to a line-infantry battalion and identify the Vietnamese in Phu Cuong I got my dew from. I was immediately transferred to the 1st Battalion/16th Infantry operating out of Lai Khe. I never saw Earl alive again. I missed him for a long time.

> *Phu Loi. R.V.N.*
> *1 June 1968*

Dear Dad and Mom,

I have received your latest letters. I don't understand for what reason you made public a letter which I wrote under great stress to my family, who I thought would keep it in confidence. I have no desire to have all the various uncles, aunts, cousins, "friends," etc. read things I wrote personally to you. Also, if you feel as you said "embarrassed" about me and my mistakes, do not ask them for any help on my behalf, as I am perfectly willing to take my punishment.

The funny part of all this is that the military is aware that a very noisy person, who has the ability to communicate with the people in writing, could make the issue of pot into one of the biggest scandals in the history of the army. Since you probably didn't believe what I wrote you before, I will tell you again that hundreds of thousands of troops over here are using it to cool off. Of all the troops I have met in this country, three-quarters have used it or are using it.

My counsel is in agreement with me on this. At any rate, I'll try to get as light a sentence as I can and volunteer for a line-infantry battalion, as they always want grunts.

You might be interested to know that there is a huge black market and smuggling operation over here. Viets, American generals, admirals, higher officers, air transport companies, Filipinos, the CIA, Koreans, Chinese, and Aussies are all mixed up in a huge dope smuggling racket back to the States, which the news magazines refuse to recognize. The corruption of our army and civilian hangers-on is magnified a hundred times over here. The hundreds of thousands of rear echelon troops live easy and comfortable, while a few men are out in the bush doing the fighting.

The whole system of our lying, cajoling government and army brass has become more evident to me since I've been here, though I've had little time to reflect on it, being so damned busy defending it, and killing other human beings it says to destroy. What this war seems to be doing, despite what you might think, is creating disgusted young men and hippies by the thousands, more than the young left and universities, and it is being done and learned in the furnace of war, rather than the safe, secluded campus. Almost all the soldiers I have met anywhere in this war are aware of the painful fact that the nation they sweat, bleed, and die for is less than half in support of what we're doing. Do you realize what that makes you think when you see your buddies die or blown to hell for a cause hard to explain, which most of their generation and a great deal of the rest don't believe in, riot against by the thousands, etc.?

If I come out of this reasonably well and go back into combat, it will only be for my own personal sense of honor and the duty I feel to you and my immediate family to come home as a soldier who has done as ordered in the ancient tradition, for better or worse, and I can't shake the feeling loose.

John

After four months in the helicopter company getting something of an overview of Vietnam and four months in ground combat with an Infantry Recon Platoon, I was beginning to see the future. By the middle of 1968, after two enemy offensives and the first bombing halt, many of us in the field could sense that America was giving up on the war. It was being lost at home by many of our politicians and people. General Westmoreland was replaced by General Abrams after the Tet Offensive when he asked for 200,000 more troops; he was sent only one brigade of the 82nd Airborne, a Marine regiment, and some support troops.

The war was gradually turning into a stalemate. Communist troops, heavily supplied and armed by the Soviets and Chinese, hid out in largely underground base camps in remote areas accesible to the ''neutral'' border sanctuaries. From these strongpoints they could rapidly deploy troops into populated areas to attack when they thought it possible to overrun an American or ARVN position. Our troops were forced to hold onto numerous defensive positions to protect the towns and roads. We also had to keep enough recon, mobile-infantry battalions and armor to locate the hidden enemy and to protect the thousands of miles of borders.

By this time I'd begun to lose interest in the progress of the war. A similar deterioration of feelings and attitudes gradually affected most of the other soldiers around me. The casualty reports and assurances of success by our leaders merged into an unending obscene stream. After fighting and dying in the same areas, over and over, "progress" seemed to be a bad joke. Perhaps harder to reconcile though, was the effect of the growing antiwar movement at home. Public burning of draft cards, refusals to serve, and mass demonstrations had an increasing effect on many soldiers. When more and more U.S. senators, congressmen and other leaders vehemently opposed what we were doing, it made our being here seem pointless. We soldiers were all products of a tradition of service and therefore inherently respectful of our political leaders. The more we heard about protests and dissension by political leaders, the more our trust and belief in America's purpose was eroded. Slowly and surely, many serving soldiers were pushed toward the same antiwar position by the influence of the activists thanks to mass media coverage, and our knowledge of what was taking place here.

Although I could vaguely see what the future held, I and thousands of other soldiers had to find a reason to keep fighting. After all, we were there and we had to "do our time." With all the contradictions of the "no-win" war policy in Vietnam, those reasons gradually boiled down to one thing: brotherhood of grunts trying to stay alive.

8   The Line Infantry

*"Democracy can defend itself
only very feebly; its internal
enemy has an easy time of it
because he exploits the right
to disagree that is inherent
in democracy."*
—*Jean-Francois Revel*

The guarded truck convoy of ammo and supplies was hot and dusty in the June sun as we roared into Lai Khe. What always impressed me about the place was the thousands of rubber trees, carefully planted years before under the French, and now shielding most of the huge base camp. A Vietnamese village surrounded by barbed wire lay in the middle, along with some impressive arched and columned French colonial stone buildings with deep, cool verandas. These housed the higher-up commanders of the division, the big-brass, the REMFs, and the CID. But brooding among all of them was a tall, round, stone watchtower with firing slits all around, bullet-scarred and shell-chipped. It brought to mind the violent collapse of French Indochina after the Battle of Dien Bien Phu only fourteen years before.

With these thoughts, I humped through the red dust and found my new unit's base camp area. This was a group of semi-permanent hootches, bunkers, and tents similar to and just about as raggedy as those of the Phu Loi Recon Platoon. The company areas here though, were now virtually empty. Most of the battalion was out in the field except for a few rear-echelon support dudes, and a few really short-timers, ready to go home any day. I shuffled and scouted around the whole place in a wide circle before I went on in, to completely familiarize myself with the layout and get my bearings. Artillery batteries and armored cavalry or mechanized track units were not far away. The whole scene looked and smelled familiar to me, and I was satisfied. I walked into my new company's orderly room.

There I met this clerk named McNeilly. McNeilly was definitely a trip. He was our company clerk, a REMF, of course, but he was more. He was stoned, he was light, he stayed cool, he was a pleasure to know. I never thought of him as a REMF; maybe he'd been a grunt or hadn't, I don't know or care. He was "our clerk." He did our paper work, dealt with lifers, and got mellow with us when, on rare occasions, we were in from the field. My man McNeilly eased me through the base camp paperwork, and I soon got my new M-16, A-1 "improved," my rucksack, ammunition, and all the other paraphernalia. I still had my Chinese pistol and NVA belt on and felt ready to go. I was informed by the first Sergeant that I was going out to the line in the field the next morning by a resupply chopper. I was now in Alpha Co., 1st Battalion, 16th Infantry, "Rangers." The battalion commander since March was Colonel Richard Eaton who had taken over from Colonel Benedict after the Tet Offensive. Colonel Eaton was a "mustang," an officer who had risen from the rank of Private, having served in an airborne regiment during WWII.

McNeilly said, "Yeah, well you've been in a recon platoon a while, huh? Okay, you know where it's at. I don't need to say nothin.' I sure wish you good luck an' all that."

I smirked and said, "Okay, dude, there it is. I'll be seein' you around as long as yer here."

I shuffled on over to my new empty platoon hootch and found a rack, dropping my gear in a pile. The first thing I did was to go through every single twenty-round magazine, loading them and packing them into my captured NVA ammo vest (which I wore because it was better than U.S. web gear) after checking the spring tension. I took my new '16 apart, cleaned it, checked all the pieces, and put it back together. My dog tags were already taped up, quiet. I went through my rucksack and packed everything carefully, making sure I had my towel, poncho liner, extra canteens, and all the rest. My little Chinese automatic pistol was already squared away; I always packed it.

I now felt that I was completely ready, self-contained, and comfortable. I could go anywhere, do anything they told me to do. "I got all I need." I was cool, collected, and glad to be here—real glad I wasn't down breaking rocks in LBJ stockade. That thought put me in the mood to get mellow and I drifted on out the back of the hootch where there was a half dug in sandbag bunker for rocket and mortar attacks. Lo and behold, there's a circle of beat-up, twenty-year-old grunts getting high. They're done, finished, "short-timers," heading "back to the world."

I ease down an' say, "Hey, what's happenin', man? I just transferred in from a recon platoon down in Phu Loi, got about 100 days left to do."

They're grinning now, "You goddam cherry, I'm S.H.O.R.T.! I got two sorry days!" or "Keep your head down, dude."

I feel a little small, but just snatch their pipe politely as it passes, thinking, "These dudes are old—363 days in the line. I hope I make it."

Pretty soon we're cruising, telling stories to each other, war stories, people stories, back-in-the-world stories. I'm just enjoying the hell out of it, thinking how glad I am not to be in the pound. I knew by instinct I wouldn't have stayed sane or alive in that stinking LBJ with its infamous pig-guards.

So the stories went on, late into that hot June night. I listened mostly and rapped a little. I could feel that I was still on my own strange journey in this weird Asian place to a destination I didn't know and that my life and soul was being changed in a permanent way.

About midnight, all of a sudden came the *SSSShhhhh Boom!* *SSSSShhhh Boom!* again. Flashes and shrapnel streaks. Somebody in the distance was running, shouting, "Incoming." Another gook mortar and rocket attack exploding around us. The short-short timers I'm with are already rolling smoothly down into the bunker, reacting instantly out of habit. Me, I'm not really too excited. I've got too much time to do still. I slide down last, a little respectful, thinking that this is maybe their last one. We continue our rap under the dark sandbags as our artillery opens fire.

Early the next morning at the airstrip with my loaded rucksack, web gear and ammunition, grenades, canteens, and weapons, I was helping to fill a chopper with supplies and ammunition. There were a few wounded returning from hospitals, too. The air is full of the smells of jet fuel and earth damp after a rain. Pretty soon we jumped in, even though there was hardly room for us. With our feet dangling out the open doors, weapons in our hands, we rose out of Lai Khe and headed back out to the war.

Somewhere near the Michelin plantation, beyond the northern Iron Triangle, we slanted down towards an open hillside rising above the jungle near a large river. Then we're down, gunner and crew chief nodding, five-foot-high elephant grass billowing, and the strained, dirty faces all around peering at us as we jump out. We pass out the ammo and supplies, as the chopper lifts off again in a thumping cloud of dust.

I look around me at the sweaty, worn-out faces, the raw torn-up ground, getting my bearings, all my gear on, my rifle in my hand. I was thinking, "Okay. This is it, I guess this is my place here, where I belong. Gotta do my prime time."

I sniffed my way around until I found the company commander in his little shelter tent. He looked tired, his face lined. He turned me over to my platoon leader and sergeant quickly and went to resting. This is resupply day. New C-rations, plenty more malaria pills, some clean jungle uniforms, and mail. Everybody's sitting in the dirt reading letters from home. They're yelling news and funny, "back-in-the-world" stories to each other. The Sarge showed me to my new residence, a series of deep holes in the ground in the process of being sandbagged all around and over the top by the grunts around me. Machine-guns are set-up, and a 90mm recoiless rifle mounted, pointing towards the silent jungle, fifty meters away.

My new outfit was the 2nd Squad, 2nd platoon of Alpha Company. My squad leader was a tall, thin, nervous-looking dude from Oregon, named "Cleve." He's a buck sergeant. Within the first five minutes of meeting him, he let me know he was real tired of the war and the army. I told him short-like how long I'd been in country and where I'd been. I spent the whole rest of the day digging in with the other dudes, as this was a new NDP, and needed beaucoup work, if the gooks came at us. During the day I started to meet the other guys who were to be as close as brothers to me for months to come.

To me it was almost like I'd defeated the lifers busting me and bothering with me. My new dudes around me just took on the same faces and personalities I'd left in my last platoon. The area was different, hardly any villages, the operational style different, bigger, heavier duty, but really the same, except that we hardly ever left the bush, the jungle. We just stayed out there nearly all the time, moving around constantly, instead of operating in and out of a base camp. After a long time of it, and some deep thinking, it occurred to me later that a small infantry-recon type unit, staying in one area, really learning and knowing it, was more effective in a guerilla war.

But the guys were the same, almost to the point of each one being a twin brother to someone in my former platoon. So it was an easy, fast, smooth transition for me—as though I'd been there all along. I was glad to be back out in the bush, in the company of grunts, away from the

REMFs and lifers. At least these were real combat soldiers.

The 16th U.S. Infantry, 1st Division, is an old and famous Regular Army outfit. Its regimental flag has streamers recalling many famous battles of the Civil War, Indian fights on the frontier, the Spanish-American War, the Phillipine Insurrection, and World Wars I and II. In the Vietnam War since late 1965, the 16th had participated in many operations and battles, inflicted and suffered many casualties. Our general AO was war zones C and D in the III Corps zone from the Lai Khe, Iron Triangle, Ho Bo Woods area through the Michelin rubber plantation and up to the Song Be-An Loc-Loc Ninh area along the Cambodian border. Down through the middle of it ran our old friend, Thunder Road, also known as Highway 13. The whole area had been blown up, shot up, and fought over since the days of the French and had been sprayed with Agent Orange defoliant in places for years. Most of the area we spent the next three months in was jungle or overgrown new bush; in the northern corner, the plateaus and hills of the highlands began, surronded by heavy virgin canopy-jungle. It was one of several "bad AOs" in 'Nam—a main line of assault from the NVA sanctuary in Cambodia and the Ho Chi Minh Trail. A scene of constant fighting throughout the entire war, it was to be a corridor for the final North Vietnamese Army attack on Saigon in 1975.

That was our home, physically at least. Your platoon, company, or battalion is really home, though—not where you dig your hole. It's an alive thing, made up of many parts that work, function, and fight together. We were digging in for defense. I looked around as I worked, shoveled, heaved, and sweated. Short, tall, thin, heavy guys; Anglos, Hispanics, black dudes, American Indians, Hawaiian pineapples, city boys, farm boys, cowboys, hoods, and characters. Shoveling dirt, digging trench-bunkers, their weapons close at hand, watching the hostile jungle territory out of the corner of their eyes. I've been reading about our Civil War, "A Stillness at Appomatox," and I'm watching the dudes around me, thinking, "Yeah, they're the same." The same boys who dug and fought in the Petersburg trenches in 1864 and 1865, when that war, too, was most unpopular, the same men that always do their time whether they volunteer, or submit to a draft.

I am one with them at this instant, our own little burning time, this war that our country's leaders have put us into and called on us to back up their words. We're here in the fighting line, and most of the country could care less or is sick of it or actually hates and detests us, cheering the enemy, waving his flags in Harvard Yard.

"So be it, we're here anyway, you backstabbers; we're the same dumb sons-of-bitches that didn't leave that winter at Valley Forge."

Back then, most of us didn't think about much except doing one day at a time. I was shoveling and working with this short blond dude who introduced himself: "I'm Mike Sellman from Arizona, man."

We were working and grunting and he told me his old man's in some kind of cattle business back in the states. I liked the guy right away. He was quick, smooth, and steady and I soon came to find out he was the main point man for my platoon, scouting the trail for everybody, like the "old Cowboy." As we worked away, bantering back and forth, I filled him in on where I'd been and how many days I had left and he told me what's been happening with them lately. Not too bad, hardly any action in the May Offensive.

"The last time we hit anything real bad was in April when we tried to take an NVA base camp near the Song Be River, about twenty miles northeast of Lai Khe. We lost about twenty guys, hit, and killed a bunch of VC and NVA. We had a black lieutenant back then in Alpha Co. named Fabian Franklin, an' one of the guys killed an' some of the wounded was in his platoon. It's kind of weird 'cause he jus' went down to that same Tan Phu Khan area you came from to be an advisor to those Ruff Puffs yer tellin' me about."

I thought about the strange twists of fate in the army, how in April, Carlisle had come on back to the 1st/16th from our platoon too, in time to lose his legs at Song Be.

Finally the burning tropical sun set again, it was evening, the holes were dug deep, the ambush patrols and the LPs snuck out quietly into the jungle and the NDP settled down. It seemed like a real mellow piece of Vietnam, so a little dew was going in the new bunker without a coal or a spark showing. A small crowd of dudes is in where I'm at, saying howdy, checking me out a little. Besides Cleve and Sellman, I meet Phil with the drooping mustache and steel-rimmed glasses. He leaned back against the sandbags, exhaling a long toke.

"Say, my good men, that's a buzz! I can be anywhere I wanta be right now."

He spoke for all of us. The grunts around nodded their heads, muttering to themselves. His voice echoed in the heavy, humus-smelling air.

The dudes felt me out a little to see where I've been. Some of them have come in-country since Tet, and it's obvious I'm not a cherry, everything's cool. I feel good, like I'm home. Ramos was a Mexican-American dude like my old buddy Baca. He was field partners with Phil and they roamed together in the bush physically and intellectually. Owens, this gangly, laughing, happy black dude was like a fresh breeze. He never let his mind dwell on the bad times or worried, and anyone who couldn't be that way drew from him. Now Brown was another brother, a blood from Chicago, but opposite from Owens. Always sensitive, thinking deep thoughts. We gradually became close friends, and were together 'til I left the 'Nam for good. John Shaeffer, a tight partner of Sellman, was blond, baby-faced, and good-looking, a strong, steady dude, solid and intelligent. He humped our PRC 25 radio. Robby, our huge black gunner, was from Georgia, and a finer soul I never did know. He was like a rock to lean against and always did his share. Truby Gaddy was a North Carolina Tarheel, a reincarnated Johnny Reb, one of those dudes who hardly ever said much, but you listened when he talked, always ready and uncomplaining. Troutman from Missouri was so young-looking to me I wondered if he was eighteen. When I think of his face I can't picture it without the smile that was always on it. Joe, our Polack rifleman, was always serious, often outraged, did his time well, and ended up humping an M-60 machine gun. Welch, a dour young Appalachian dude, was from the coal mining country. I remember him to the last day I was in 'Nam, still right up front, putting out the rounds.

So I met all my partners, the ones I was going to be closest to for months, and after the long day we split up the guardtime and got a little rest that night.

I'm immediately back in the combat patrol rhythm. Working at night our platoon ambushed a group of enemy on a trail out of this NDP, killing three of them on the 27th of June. Robby, our gunner, blew a claymore on the first one as he was bending over it to see what it was and pick it up, and two others were shot down right after. For that first Viet Cong it was like finding or winning the ultimate "booby prize." Before we crawled out at dawn, the bodies had disappeared, another reminder that in 'Nam, nothing works right. Even the dead won't stay put. Truby Gaddy got hit that night, a light shrapnel wound, and was back with us a little while later from the hospital. We eventually became tight.

Every morning after dawn we march and hump, hour after hour, all day long, in the suffocating heat and sudden downpours. Most of the time we grunts don't know where we're going, why we're going there and we never know what we're going to find around the next bush. We've got to always be ready, hunched under our load of gear, GI towel around our neck or under the rucksack straps, our rifles carried by a long-extended sling, one end looped around the butt, hung under the right arm, pointing straight out, parallel to the ground. It was locked and loaded, ready for instant fire, one-handed or two, thumb always on the safety and finger laying beside the trigger. If a place smelled funny or got very quiet or a sniper bullet cracked out, the safety was snapped off. We were always careful, always trusting each other. Day after day, night after night, week after week, month after month, and you'd love that M-16. You kept it clean, you babied it, you were never without it, twenty-four hours a day. It was your best friend. Every so often it would spring into life and repay you just by spurting out a wall of bullets between you and them.

So we sweated and humped and searched for the enemy. The front line was ahead of you, behind you, above you rigged to a tree, under your feet ready to blow you to bits, it was nowhere, anywhere, everywhere. We searched the bush in this area constantly, finding small enemy trails, spider-hole fighting positions, log and earth bunkers, the enemy always disappearing or retreating.

One day we were lying down exhausted, taking a break in place when I saw this weird, white shining thing off in the distance. I was just as tired as everybody else but kept getting more and more curious. I tried to get somebody to go with me and check it out so I won't be alone but nobody wants to move. Finally I got one guy to go and Cleve said, "It's all right," bitchin' a little and mumbling to himself about "crazy dudes who'd want to hump one extra meter in this fuckin' shit hole." I agreed with him but I can't stay away this time, and we headed out. It was a building, all right, in a beautiful grove of tall trees, probably planted long ago. Now, we get up closer.

"Man, it's a palace!" Massive white stone walls, courtyards, wide windows and everywhere signs of the endless war. Bullet and shell holes, gouges, streaks, and pock marks covered the once beautiful French plantation home. I pushed in through the rubble with my rifle ready, safety off. Smooth, fine tile floors covered with litter, old broken water-stained pictures of the Alps, green oxidizing empty cartridge cases, rusty pieces of steel shrapnel. Out through another door into the sun I ran into a huge square stone reservoir, high in the air on massive columns. It's all shot up, too, as though it had been used as an emergency fort or watchtower in some long-forgotten firefight. I walked around, tripping and mumbling to myself. My buddy was sitting staring towards the bush, and I felt like some Saxon barbarian after the fall of Roman Britain, picking through the ruins of Hadrian's palace.

"God, it's been a long war, and they fought that French Foreign Legion and their paratroopers to a standstill, and fought each other and are fighting a half a million of us now, and I know it's Communism, and I understand the strategy of the world conflict, but why, here, now in this god-forsaken, alien, strange part of the Asian mainland?"

We went in and out of deep rubber, some of the big, straight trees still being tapped, and other stands abandoned, reverting back to jungle. We could feel the enemy is around with the abandoned positions and the trail ambush and the occasional sniper shots, but we didn't hit them solidly anywhere again and they didn't hit us. A little to the northeast of us Charlie Company of our Battalion wasn't so lucky and got in a firefight on 29 June, losing one killed, and five wounded.

One day some of our battalion and company officers visited the main plantation headquarters of Michelin Rubber, but we didn't know or care much about it—just heard vague rumors of round-eyed French men and women being there—and kind of muttered bitterly among ourselves about how they must have managed to pay off the NVA and Viet Cong to leave them alone. The chain of grunt information that's passed on from man to man, company to company for years here, tells of the endless enemy ambushes and firefights in the Michelin plantations, and all the GIs who were blown away around here. I still hate the sight of the name everytime I see it on a car tire.

On the 1st of July our company was on a small operation separately from the rest of the battalion and, during a patrol in the afternoon, got in a fast shootout and killed a single VC. We also captured a Ford truck being used to transport supplies for the enemy.

A Co. 1st Bn./16th Inf.
Rangers
In the field
3 July 1968

Dear Mom, Dad and Family,
Well, I'm still out in the bush with the 1st/16th Infantry. We stay out in the jungle for longer periods of time than Recon. We had some shooting but things are fairly quiet now. I may be lucky and go back without any more fighting. I believe I have about eighty more days in the line in

Vietnam.

It's the rainy season again now, and we're living like pigs out here, but it's a real fine unit and they try to send us extras like more cigarettes.

I'm still in my favorite position as flank rifleman, off to the side of the point-man or slack behind the point. They are talking about making me the point-man, but my buddy Sellman is a real good one. The next letter you write me, tell me of brother Bobby's status. If they draft him, he will probably get put in the grunts like me, and that's not good for him.

At this point I could extend my service here for six months, get a thirty day leave, get out of the Army early and keep Bobby out of here all at once. Since I've been here so long, I've gotten to understand it. An extra six months won't hurt me, while they may allow Bobby to go to Germany since both brothers don't have to be in combat at once. However if he wants to come over here, that's his business.

If you want to do me a favor, send me about ten small cans of peaches and some small books on history. Nothing else, unless it's more peaches or pears in small cans so I can carry them.

I'm still in good physical condition. All I've gotten is two small pieces of rocket shrapnel in the leg since I've been over here. I've been real damn lucky.

I'll write again when I get a chance.

Love,

John

Well, it turned out later that my brother got himself into some college and got a deferment so none of that mattered. And it turned out also that most of my relatives weren't thinking about the war or the mud and rain, or the snipers, but just about "pot." It was all right, though, because I and the rest of the men were only thinking of each next day.

The monsoon rain came down in pouring, drenching sheets on us wherever we were, whatever we were doing, so that we became so sick of it we thought we couldn't stand it anymore. We lived in the slimy mud, in the bush—bamboo, rubber or jungle—day and night. Our only salvation was the nylon camouflage-pattern poncho liner we each carried rolled up. It was a tent or a blanket or a pillow, and a hell of a friend. When the hot, burning sun came out, the jungle would steam and so would we as we marched.

With the rains came more jungle sores and open ulcers. Things that suppurated and pussed and would send a person "back in the world" rushing to a doctor, worried that he had leprosy. Here, we hardly paid attention to them. What could you do? You washed a little occasionally, in a muddy creek or a shell- or bomb-crater. We had all long since quit wearing underwear. It just rotted out your whole crotch; the only way to go was with only the plain, baggy cotton jungle pants with the big hip pockets to hold your little junk. Our jungle shirts have no rank or names or badges, just a Big Red One on the shoulder, which blended in with the olive green background.

All of a sudden we snapped out of our exhaustion and solitude. Enemy troops were found by the 1st Infantry Division in the Ho Bo Woods, a jungle area in the northern Iron Triangle between Ben Cat and Ben Suc. There were rumors of fighting and casualties. We got rushed to an open elephant grass area for an LZ. We were spread out around a perimeter to secure it, but lifted off by platoons and squads in the Hueys. Now they were in our sight, thumping in on line. Everybody's talking and grumbling, hustling their gear together, checking their weapons, glad for a change, nervous about what's next. We hear the whole battalion's going in but we don't know.

We climbed in under the rotor wash, dust and debris flying, nodded at the gunners, and were up and off. The wind rushing in cooled our sweaty bodies through the open doors. Going in for the CA, we locked and loaded our rifles, ready in case it was a hot LZ. Then we were suddenly down again, leaping out full speed for the jungle edge, the thundering noise drowning out everything. Spreading out and down, rifles out in a defense perimeter, with the choppers lifting off as fast as they'd come, the gunners tense with their '60s aimed, touching off a burst or two of machine-gun fire into the surrounding jungle to make any gooks there keep their heads down.

After the sudden, quick change of AOs, we were right back in the field where we were a few minutes before. Instantly, we became plain old infantry with many a mile of marching ahead of us again. The Ho Bo Wood was another old Viet Cong and NVA stronghold since the days of the Viet Minh. Many a body there, the jungle fertilized by blood. We began our long, hard humping again. Strung out in platoon files we hardly even knew what was happening to the rest of the company, let alone the whole battalion out around us. Parts of the area had been heavily sprayed with Agent Orange defoliant, and other stretches appeared near virgin. The defoliated area is like a weird, stick forest, everything dead. The bare ground showing clouds rising in the air as we shuffle through. As usual, the grunts don't know where we're going—we're not important enough to be told. Occasionally we hear shooting and artillery fire around us in the distance. We had to thread our way or hack out a trail as we went. The point-man, Sellman, took a few slashes to squeeze through; the slack (me) sliced out a little more; the next dude, a little more, and by God, it's not bad for the lieutenant, CP, and the medic group. We were searching constantly for signs of enemy troops, under hair-trigger tension every second of every minute of every hour because we're fresh in this country. Sometimes we cut across deep-worn six-to-twelve-inch-wide foot trails; at other times we stumbled into spider holes, and deeply dug-in bunkers. The enemy had retreated again, waiting for their chance, waiting 'til they were ready to hit someone hard.

Sweating, grunting, and tiring, we cut and slashed with machetes through vines, bamboo, and jungle bush. Often the second growth is worse—thicker than under the canopy of virgin trees. Humping for hour after hour each day, until we're dripping with sweat and exhausted.

We finally stopped for a few minutes, sipped some canteen water, and maybe quick-smoked a cigarette. For chow, we wolfed down the best parts of the C-rations, trading around with others for our favorite stuff. There's always one dude crying, "Jesus Christ, I got ham and mother fuckers again! What do you want fer that can of fruit cocktail, man?"

This part of the Iron Triangle had been reported as the Communist command center for years. There have been uncounted firefights and a seemingly endless supply of Viet Cong guerillas in this region. We were somewhere near the Ben Suc village area that Division had tried to clean the enemy out of the year before in Operation Cedar Falls. We're only twenty kilometers northwest of Phu Loi, feeling lost on another planet in this bush, but officially we're at XT6635 on 6 July.

We sat in the mud and debris of our trail amid the smells of fresh-cut jungle, bush, and mud, weapons pointing out and ready, picking at our sores and scabs, talking low about meaningless grunt things.

"Where the hell we goin', man. You hear anything?"

"I heard there's definitely gooks, man. I heard recon's in contact."

"We're gonna hit those dudes one of these times."

"Shaefer (RTO) said he heard recon's had one guy hit by RPG's we better be cool."

We never get much of a break because the battalion commander up there cruising around in his chopper is contantly encouraging our platoon leader or CO, forcing us on.

"Keep movin', find somethin'!"

"Saddle up and move out!"

We heaved to our feet, legs and backs aching, started marching again, loosening up, humping the whole afternoon again, and constantly waiting for the jungle to explode. At nights we usually spread out in a wide circle and down, roll out the claymores, set up in an ambush position at some likely-looking stop by a trail or a stream ford. We're almost never invited into the dirt-dug NDP where we heard the battalion CP and armored cavalry was operating out of. Sometimes we could hear mortars or shellfire in the dark.

Distant *Whoomp-Whoomp-Whoomps,* ground trembling; closer *Shhh-Wham! Shhh Wham!,* trees shaking, snapped awake from exhausted sleep, eyes jerking around, ears listening, not incoming, not on top of us anyway, thank God. Another sudden tropical dawn in the jungle, then the sun slanting lances of heat down through the trees. We quick-wolfed our Cs, waiting for the dreaded call of "Saddle up!" It came just when I was beginning to think we might get to skate a little this morning. We humped, cut, slashed, and humped some more.

As we were coming down a slope through patches of jungle and nice open elephant grass, all of a sudden we ran smack into a blown-up American tank, the whole underside and tracks blasted apart, probably by a big Chi Comm mine. The hatch is wide open and the turret covered with bullet streaks, dents and scratches from shrapnel of RPGs. You could clearly see the last seconds of the crew. We didn't look too long or hard at it as we file by. One quick look shows it's old.

Down this slope and out into another open patch, and small-arms fire suddenly blasted out to our right front. Automatic weapons open up, machine-guns cracking and popping, grenades exploding.

The Lieutenant shouted, "Recon's getting hit bad! Move!"

We were trotting forward now, safeties snapping off, the firing roars, we hear shouts and screams on the jungle slope above us. We were running now, ready for it and our own 1st/16th Battalion Recon under Sergeant Tom Sisk is now in sight, backing towards us, shooting fast and hard. I see some of the GIs dragging shot-up, wounded buddies by their arms. Then we were on-line with them, opening fire into the enemy position. I saw tracers from AK-47s to aim at. I'm firing short, three- or four-round accurate bursts, *BRRRRP! BRRRRP!* Lots of bullets are going through this air, but the firefight's almost over already. I heard wounded GIs again.

"God, Oh, God! I'm hit bad!"

There were dead ones, too. Then, there's artillery and armor fire, *SShhhhhhing* in overhead, *BOOM- BOOM! Ka-boom!* The gun fire seems smaller now, and suddenly the shooting has stopped. The NVA retreated again, but there were two more American boys dead in Vietnam and four or five more wounded, and our recon platoon has been shot-up, with only one dead VC and a carbine found.

The telegrams and letters will go home to parents and wives or girlfriends this 8th of July, 1968, and more brothers and sisters will cry. And the filthy Ho Bo Woods will have gotten a little more blood to feed its roots.

We pulled back to a defense perimeter and the medevacs are clattering in, taking out the casualties, and I'm staring out at the jungle, talking and muttering to myself, still alert. The gooks had pulled the old ambush trick again like the Apache and the Sioux, showing a few of themselves as bait, drawing us in to a hidden, dug-in, main-force, and hitting us suddenly and hard.

"Uh, huh, another rotten day in Vietnam." And this sentiment was probably repeated one hundred times all over this country. We know there's been other fighting by our division, out around us, but don't know what or where.

All of a sudden the Armored Cav came roaring and clanking and screeching in. We heard orders yelled to us.

"Mount up, get up on those sons-of-bitches!" Now we were riding. "Jesus Christ, we're sitting on our asses and riding!" Like it was a holiday or something. A little crude maybe, big, fat-tracked tanks and APCs with M-60s on the sides and Browning .50 cals for the TC. The gunners are ready, weapons pointing out and down a little, long shining belts of machine-gun ammo feeding in.

I think it was the 11th Armored Cavalry that time, the "Black Horse Troop," commanded by a "super lifer," Colonel George Patton, son of the famous Patton himself. "Well, that's O.K. anyway, this war's good enough for all of us right now." The big boy tanks bust the jungle, smashing down the little stuff and bouncing around the thick. We lay back in the sun, swigging water by the gallon, hanging with one hand, stuffing ourselves with the good parts of Cs. These armored dudes had tons of everything, even water coolers down in there. But, by God, they shared every bit of it with us. If there's anything a line-dog in the infantry learns, it's how to get along on little, and how to make a pig out of himself when the chance comes. I smelled that funny smell in the air now, somebody was getting ripped. It was a little risky around here but it had been a long time.

I'd lost track of time. We were swaying and crashing through some really thick stuff, all kinds of jungle garbage raining down on us, leaves, vines, spiders—huge fat ones, little snakes, nests and cascades of horrible, biting fire-ants that cover you all over in seconds, and every other imaginable kind of crap. The track gunners were yelling over the horrendous racket, "Watch out for damned booby-traps and grenades rigged to vines in the trees! They'll blow us all away in an air burst."

All of a sudden up ahead, firing broke out and we heard the *Pop! Pop! Popping!* of enemy AKs. We were moving forward fast now, and the grunts were getting ready to jump off. Quick-tightening our belts and web gear, double checking our rifles, crouching, ready to spring. A roar around us.

A Co. 1st/16th Infantry
In the field - Ho Bo Woods
10 (?) July 1968

Dear Mom, Dad and Family,

We're still out in the bush in the "famous" Ho Bo Woods, somewhere near Ben Suc in the Iron Triangle. We have been in contact with the enemy. Yesterday riding on tanks and APCs we overran one of their base camps under fire. One of the tracks struck a mine and had a guy wounded bad. The day before that on the 8th after our Recon Platoon was ambushed, the tracks we're on from the 1st/11th Cav got hit by RPGs and automatic fire. There was one guy from the Cav killed and five more wounded near me.

I just got your letter that urged me "to follow orders and do a job." I have nothing to say about that, other than what do you think I'm doing? As for what you said about the colonel and his letter and the "big chance" he gave me, you should know there was a pre-court martial deal between my army "lawyer" and him and the JAG office: that if I volunteered for the line and told them the Vietnamese source I would be given another chance to get my ass blown off in the infantry, which took little magnanimity on the lifer's part.

I've been sitting here in the mud and rain thinking about what to write next, but I am almost at a loss for words. This is a war, those lifers do sit in air-conditioned offices while we fight, and you speak their language, and I speak mine. There is, at present, a hell of a gap between us, and

I feel less and less like writing.

I wonder if what I'm fighting for is wrong morally; most of us do now, here. We all feel sort of isolated from the needs of America. I guess I deserve to die because I have killed people here for something I don't know whether I believe in anymore. But I would rather have the danger than be back in the rear somewhere. I am more mixed up now than usual because my mind is nothing but contradictions. I know what I'm doing may be wrong but I am doing it anyway. I even sort of like it. Yesterday we blew up four tons of rice and the enemy didn't get any dinner. That gave us all a laugh.

Your son,
John

Round and round, this rotten area we marched and sweated and dug in constantly. The enemy appeared and disappeared. We kept being lucky, but the 1st/11th Cav, with whom we were operating lost thirteen more casualties, three killed, and ten wounded close to us between the 8th and 10th of July. It must have been like fighting the Japanese on the Pacific Islands, except this enemy had a thousand miles of jungled mountains, swamps, and plains to move around in. Maybe it was impossible from the very beginning, I don't know. And now there were no more bombing raids on the heartland of North Vietnam, and the enemy laughed and moved thousands of tons of weapons and ammunition off the Russian ships in Haiphong, and the trucks from Red China, and hauled them in an unending stream down the Ho Chi Minh Trail along the Laotian and Cambodian borders. And they hit the Marines, the Americal, the 5th Mech, the 101st, the 4th and the 1st Cav, the Big Red One, the 11th Cav, the 82nd the 25th, the 9th, the ARVNs, and the lonely Special Forces camps, and then they pulled back and down into their thousands of miles of underground tunnels and came out somewhere else and blasted a few more GIs.

We dug in and built bunkers each night, filling sandbags that we humped empty everywhere we went. We shoveled and sweated and bitched, but we were damn glad to have those holes if Chinese mortars or Russian rockets exploded around us.

9   Song Bé

Every war inevitably is a matter
of national interest and must
be conducted in that spirit, with
the intensity of effort which the
strength of the national character
allows and the government demands.
— *Karl Von Clausewitz*

I guess it was somewhere around the 12th of July when we humped our exhausted way out of the dripping, steamy jungle into another elephant-grass clearing. The pace suddenly quickened when the lieutenants tell us we're going into Lai Khe for a couple of days on our way to a new CA. The rumor was that we were going into the Catcher's Mitt—Song Bé River area, where the Dong Nai Regiment and the 165th NVA Regiment had their base camp.

We were out in a circle with our weapons ready and went to work with machetes, slashing out a wider perimeter so choppers can LZ in and extract us. Chainsaws were dropped in by an LOH, and the usually silent bush echoed with their piercing whines and the crash of big, falling jungle trees. Finally whoever mattered was satisfied, and we slumped down, facing outwards, waiting.

Sellman said, "Man, I'm gettin' ready for a cold bottle of beer, know what I mean?"

I was lying there dreaming about it now, too. All we can barely manage to think about is some little, short break in this endless humping. I've gotten to admire this guy, though, the last few weeks. He's really had a sense of direction in the jungle, like the whole scene was always a map in his mind or something. I was mostly working along with him, usually off to the flank, parallel, or slightly in back of him, but always using him as my guide. A rifleman out on each flank of the point made it harder to ambush a whole file of men from the side, for the enemy could hear the noise of 25 or 30 men in column, no matter how quiet they were trying to be. We lay there, resting and mumbling to each other about how lucky we'd been. We kept hearing rumors and reports of other units being shot up and wasted around us.

Then the choppers were thumping towards us and as they start the lift, Whoosh! Kaboom!—ZZZZZ. RPGs! The LZ was hot. The gooks were giving us a goodbye party. The choppers came in, one or two at a time, the others circling and we backed off the shrinking perimeter by squads, shooting. What a relief it was to sit and ride in the cool wind, after that suffocating jungle. We're up and out and gone, the bush and jungle looked almost inviting from the air.

Rivers and creeks wind and sparkle in the sun. Off in the distance to the west, we could see the 3,000-foot peak of Nui Ba Den, the "Black Virgin" Mountain jutting up alone. We knew that it marked the border of our neighbors the 25th Infantry, the "Tropic Lightning Division." We lost interest in the scenery quickly, and dreamt about a day or two of real food, and maybe some gook beer in the village. We clattered into the Lai Khe Airstrip, a perfect view below us of the rubber, roads, buildings, hootches, artillery batteries, bivouacs of mechanized or armored cavalry tracks: such a concentration of supplies and power.

Once down, we jumped out, lugging our rucksacks and weapons, dirty-filthy, raggedy half-bearded, boots caked with jungle mud, standing in the sun; and staring at these clean, tittering Red Cross girls from "back in the world," tripping towards us. They had trays or something in their hands, with little paper cups half-full of cherry Kool-Aid. They stuck them out at arms-length, trying not to get too close to us, because we smelled. I guess they meant well, but we all knew they spent most of their time chasing fat-assed REMF officers. They stared at us now like we're a tribe of savages, and we knew they were thinking "God, what dirty grunts!"

Jeeps wheeled up from battalion HQs, to pick up our platoon and company officers and give them a ride. We can see them being handed cold bottles of beer. Most of us don't mind or gripe too much about that though. We're pretty close to our lieutenants in the bush, they spent more time out there worrying and planning about us than we did. The higher-ups whom we hardly ever have seen, nobody liked or had a good word for.

We straggle-marched through the base camp towards our hootches, passing the Quonset huts, supply depots, and hootch offices of REMFs who made up 80 percent of the service in Vietnam. They stared out at us, but avoided our eyes. We didn't give a damn—made a few catcalls or half-hearted insults, maybe. In our platoon-hootch, it seemed like paradise: the empty spring-racks, without mattresses felt strangely soft. The temporary plywood walls and corrugated tin roofs, were so straight and smooth after a world of formless mazes. We cleaned our weapons, gear, and magazines and repacked our rucksacks. We got an issue of new ammunition and clean, faded worn jungle fatigues. We took our first shower in weeks, and got to an honest-to-God mess hall to eat a hot meal. The line-ups, trays, and normality of it seemed strange, but it felt nice. The rear-area cooks of our battalion were fairly decent and respectful in a cook's-kind-of-way. McNeilly was in there too, saying hello to everybody, mellow as usual, telling us every tidbit of rumor or battalion-clerk gossip he heard lately. He shares everything he knows we're interested in, and that's what makes him a good clerk-dude. He said we were heading into a bad area pretty soon. ''Yer goin' into the same place along the Song Bé as that operation in April.'' Over the next few days the battalion was kept busy with short patrols and air assaults, but no real action.

We finally got time off, and headed out through barbed wire perimeter of the Lai Khe Vietnamese Village. Its people were the workers on the original plantation, who now work in and out of the American base camp. It was off limits and locked off at night, but up 'til a certain hour we drank and got stoned in the bars and whorehouses, telling stories, speculating on what's next, and mixing with the Vietnamese. They clustered around us, little kids grabbing things from us, shrieking about dew or having their ''big sisters'' for a few piasters, or some MPC, the army funny-money. Most of us were blanked out on Viets, period, by now anyway. But, it was like going to a sorry little circus or something for a few hours—mildly entertaining.

Gradually we drifted out of there and back to our own battalion's home area, and to our little EM Club. It was a shack-like hootch, too, with a homemade bar and a maybe-former-grunt bartender from our outfit. We got 'em set up and started in to get seriously drunk. We stopped only to alternate dew, and so got completely wasted. Forget it all, the bush, the gooks, the screams, the tracers, the ''back-in-the-world'' family troubles, all of it. Into a staggering, foggy oblivion.

At one or two in the morning, passed out on the racks and floor of our hootch, we were blasted awake by Whooosssh-CRAAAAKKK! Whooossh-CRAAAKKK! BOOM! Ka-Boom! Those chilling orange-white flashes!

"Goddamn Russian 122mm rockets incoming again!" We were so exhausted, or hungover, most of us just barely rolled across the floor against the solid lower portion of the walls for cover, instead of running for our bunkers. The flashes and explosions lit up the night, the artillery batteries opened fire, and Lai Khe lived up to its nickname again of "Rocket City".

"Jesus Christ! Them things are coming down somewhere, somebody's gettin' hit!"

And out there around us, somewhere there were more names to add to the weekly casualty lists.

In a day or two, about the middle of July, we loaded up and lined out for another air-assault, heading for the bush again. I think we were flown first to Phuoc Vinh in Chinook double rotors. I remember us all spread out on some other airstrip in the dirt; lying in our gear with our weapons mixed in, visiting with the "Black Scarves," the 1st Battalion of the 2nd Infantry of our division who were on their way to Loc Ninh.

The headquarters guys told us we were going into the "Catcher's Mitt." it was near the boundary dividing Phuoc Long and Binh Long Provinces—the same area the battalion had fought in during late April. I'd heard of this place before when I was in the Recon Platoon, an area of wild jungle around the Song Bé River, northeast of Tan Uyen and Binh My. The Viet Cong and NVA had used it as a sanctuary to hide in for years. It was about twenty kilometers east of Lai Khe and the same distance northeast of Phu Loi. Constantly bombed by arc-light raids of B-52 bombers, the enemy stay there because it's the closest wilderness country in which they can keep base camps to assault ARVN and American positions in the populated area.

We went in near the location of the fighting by the 101st Airborne during the Tet Counter-offensive and also close to the spot the Australians fought for in the May Offensive, when they defeated the 141st and 165th NVA Regiments. The 2nd of the 28th and 2nd of the 16th had been operating in there in June and early July, too, losing casualties. It was also the location of base camps for the main-force Dong Nai Regiment that had also fought at An My and Tan Uyen in the Tet Offensive. According to intelligence reports, this regiment was now heavily NVA in composition.

The Song Bé River winds from the Cambodian border, out of the southwestern foothills of the highlands—the "Mnong Plateau," the beginning of the Montagnard area. In the heavy canopy jungle along and around this river, the main NVA base camps and depots were hidden, dug in deep and connected by a network of miles of underground tunnels. One of the main staging areas for the enemy, it crossed from the sanctuary of the "Fish Hook" area of Cambodia, and was so well protected they felt safe from American bombers. From there they could attack nearby northern district army camps and towns like Quan Loi, An Loc, Loc Ninh, Phuoc Binh, Song Bé, or Bu Dop. Or they could move straight south, towards Michelin, Lai Khe, Phu Loi, Bien Hoa, or Saigon-Cholon. It was a constant battle area from the beginning of the war until Saigon fell in 1975 in an assault that came out of here. The entire area was drenched with the blood of thousands of soldiers.

We're lying on that lonely dirt airstrip, and we heard the rumbling of the assault choppers coming, the UH-LS, the Hueys, the ones I had sat in or worked on ages ago. We clambered to our feet, adjusted our straps and loaded and locked our rifles as the choppers clattered in on line.

We "Rangers" loaded in as many as they'd pack, our feet hanging out the open doors again, and then it was up and away. We said goodbye to the "Black Scarves," a few waves and thumbs up for luck. Wild-looking, wilderness jungle was below us, hills rising over there, low jungled mountains out far beyond, nothing else; then we were down, leaping out again. I don't remember the CA much beyond that, whether there were snipers or whatever. It doesn't matter now anyhow—we were humping again back to what we are: eleven Bravos.

This time we've been supplied with LRRP rations instead of Cs; it was light and freeze-dried. We heated some water in our tin canteen cups by burning a little C-4 plastic-high explosive, poured it in, mixed them up, and had a good meal. We can carry beaucoup days of grub now. We love them, steal them if we get the chance back in the camps and NDPs.

At this LZ we moved out on the operation now into heavy canopy jungle. No more sandbag filling, never an NDP or firebase. Just marching and marching, setting up where we crash every night in a defensive circle.

A Co. 1st/16th Inf
In the Field
Song Bé River
18 July 1968

Dear Family,
We've been on the Song Bé River in a bad operation now; it flows

from Cambodia, somewhere. It is rough country, bad jungle; there is enemy around. We are humping in canopy jungle.

I got your letter saying you were going on some vacation trip. I definitely don't want to go anywhere but to sleep when I get back to the world.

I will most probably be in Pennsylvania about 20 September. I don't have much to write about except I'm tired of all this and I'm ready for a rest. I should see you in a little over two months.

Your son,

John

Early in this operation, maybe on the first day, our company had run into a small enemy base camp of about thirty bunkers on which we had called in an airstrike and destroyed. Our battalion was now under the operational control of the 11th Armored Cavalry, and the next day, the 16th of July, one of their APC tracks was hit by RPGs; a tank was blown up by a mine a few clicks from our Battalion. They had lost one GI killed and five wounded. On the 17th we moved in this direction, and late that night our Recon Platoon under Sergeant Sisk made enemy contact, killing two Viet Cong with one GI hit.

Sometime in the next day or two our company hit another enemy base camp. This time the Viet Cong or NVA opened fire on us with a few 60mm mortar shells. They were hitting and exploding right on our position, but we had hit the dirt fast and I don't remember anyone being wounded. We called in artillery fire on the enemy position, wiping it out or silencing it. The howitzer shells had hit so close to us I thought we were going to take a short-round and get blown away by our own dudes.

Our new company commander, First Lieutenant Gerry Harr was trying to tighten us, sharpen us—and he was the man to do it. He had previously commanded our Recon Platoon, and was a huge white dude from Tiffin, Iowa. I believe he told us that he had gone to college in Washington State. He had the kind of penetrating eyes that could bore right through you, was about six feet four inches tall and weighed 250 pounds. Yet he moved through the jungle easily and with speed, dragging his CP group of RTOs, FOs, medic and all in a trotting, straggling, wire-linked chain. We used to get some of our few laughs watching him. It seemed to me that whenever one of us felt ready to fall down exhausted from humping our gear in the jungle heat, or it was pouring rain and we were cold and shivering, he'd get you. There'd be a sudden little kick in the ass, not too hard; you'd jerk around, and he'd be there looking fresh as a flower.

He'd boom out, "Come on, men, grab ahold of yer balls and move out!" It was his favorite expression, and he knew just how to say it. Unlike a lot of officers I knew, he was the leader of his men by example. The rare kind, the best kind, the one you'll follow even though Americans aren't followers. Guys would mutter about his past deeds to the new cherries: "Ya oughtta see him in contact man, he's good. Like at Ap Bang and Song Bé in April and May. I saw him charge a goddamn bunker with the gooks inside still shootin'. . .blew 'em away with a LAW rocket. He's crazy." There have been few people in my life I looked up to, but "Ell Tee" Harr, U.S. Army, was one of them. All around us, fighting would be going on, other companies of our battalion got hit badly or ran into ambushes and we had to race to help them, but we kept making it through in good shape. Looking back on it years later, I think a lot of it was due to his leadership and careful planning of our movements by day and set-ups in position at night.

My next clear memory of the Song Bé operation was of the 20th of July. There was a sudden interruption of our long, driving-sweating, marching, and searching for the elusive enemy. A far-off roar of battle exploded and an urgent call came for help from Captain Stephan Farris' Charlie (C) Company of our own 1st/16th Battalion, and the 11th Armored Cav. Lieutenant Harr was in fast motion. He started us out at a slow run. We always stayed off trails as a common practice to avoid ambush, but now we hit a wide-dirt NVA trail, almost a road, sometimes called a "Red Ball"; it's heading right towards the sound of fighting. He doesn't hesitate and is yelling at the company point-man to "take it!" on the run. The dude on point, from another platoon, not my man Sellman, is getting scared, trotting towards that machine-gun, RPG and tank gun fire, and he slows way down, barely moving.

Lieutenant Harr was yelling again, his voice booming, "Gimme a point-man, I wanta volunteer!" Something makes me yell out and run to the point towards the firing. I'm moving along fast, dog-trotting, safety off and my rifle on full automatic. The entire company's strung out behind me.

The jungle loomed on either side, the cracking, booming and popping ahead was swelling in volume. Suddenly I ran right smack into some wounded American GIs. They were crawling back from the battle on the ground, screaming or crying.

"God, I'm hit bad! Jesus, oh Jesus!"

"The lieutenant's been killed!"

I had an instant stark vision of ending up like that myself, and a feeling of fear spread over me. I slowed down quickly, scared, my rifle out and ready, enemy rounds were snapping by through the air. Just then, Lieutenant Harr came running right up beside me, looking over calm and smiling!

"Let's go on in!" he said.

We came next to another lieutenant almost in a panic, stumbling back from the firing, screaming, "I lost my maps!" (with our positions on them). Then we were running between the bodies of dead GIs and came up to the line under enemy fire. I opened fire back in long bursts at the green tracers and dived down amid the weapons, equipment, and bodies scattered around. There was always something much more fearsome about seeing shot-up Americans as compared to enemy dead. The 11th Cav had been fighting along with our infantry battalion, trying to break into this big VC/NVA base camp. We were deployed to the right.

Off to my left was a smoking, blown-out American flame-throwing track hit by RPGs. On the perimeter berm and off to the right a disabled APC. The enemy had dug in to fight here instead of retreating. Sergeant "Little John" Eickendorf's squad of Charlie company was over on our left flank and had borne the brunt of fighting with the rest of their platoon. Lieutenant Hugh Brown of C company had just been killed leading his platoon forward in support of one of the disabled APCs. Casualties ties were screaming or crying all around. Our battalion commander, Colonel Eaton, was at the scene having ridden into the fight on the back of the track hit by the RPGs. He was attempting to provide fire support following first contact, and was slightly wounded.

The shooting went on until night with the Americans stalled at the perimeter bunkers of the enemy. Artillery and airstrikes exploded out ahead, and behind us medevacs were coming in under fire, taking out casualties. In addition to the bullet-and shrapnel-hit dudes, I remember seeing GIs horribly burned all over. There were maybe 25 GIs killed and wounded around my area of sight to the rear, three killed and seventeen wounded from our own battalion, besides more from the 11th Cav mixed in with us. One of their tracks had been blown up by a Russian anti-tank mine and eight more guys had been hit. Just before nightfall, while we were deployed on the right flank, the Colonel went forward with part of Charlie Company to retrieve the Lieutenant's body. At dusk the sky was lit-up by the flash of "Spooky" or "Puff, the Magic Dragon"—Airforce gunship planes firing ripping roars of bullets with a column of lit-up tracers from mini-guns. The flares and exploding shells kept the night lit-up. The enemy retreated, dragging off as many of their dead as they could. At first there were only nine VC/NVA bodies found on the field, but eleven more were found later, making a total of twenty. That night we heard from our RTO that Bravo Company of our battalion had been fighting all day long for the Song Bé Airstrip, losing an additional two killed and six wounded, with twenty more VC killed.

In the morning we pushed in through the blown-up bunkers and NVA junk strewn around. We began to explore the huge complex. Lieutenant Harr told us later that it extended over sixteen grid squares of the map, sixteen square kilometers of bunkers, spider hole fighting positions, underground rooms and storage areas all connected by thousands of feet of tunnels. In retrospect, the amount of digging we saw was incredible and to try to describe it to people later was to invite disbelief.

As tunnel rats for the company, Sellman and I went to work with our flashlights. I was in the tunnel business mostly because of my Chi-Comm 7.65 pistol still on my belt, one of the few men in the company packing a side-arm. Besides, I liked being "a super explorer scout." We approached the first cavern-like entrance past the perimeter defense bunkers, threw in some grenades and, when the smoke cleared, crawled in from opposite ends. I hold the pistol out in front of me, locked and loaded, the light close and behind the sights, so I can shoot straight if I have to.

The air smelled of rich humus, the tunnel is huge, it seems to go on and on. I don't know where Sellman is. "Christ knows what direction he's off into." I hit wooden and metal boxes and crates filled with Chi-Comm grenades, AK–47 ammunition, medical supplies, and more. I kept moving ahead, slowly and carefully on my elbows. My light picked up a lumpy form ahead, an NVA soldier in uniform, blood glistening. I fired on shot into him to see if he was dead or not; I couldn't tell for sure by the twitch from the impact if he's alive when I pulled the trigger. I don't give a damn anyway, "He ain't gonna bother me now." I continued to crawl right over him, finding more and more munitions and supplies, on and on, side tunnels, small rooms shored up with logs, stacks of NVA uniforms. It was like an eerie, underground village. I pushed up through an airhole, back into the light and noise, and milling, yelling GIs. Sellman was way over to the side, at another entrance. I started to yell to the nearest dudes about what I'd found, and everybody got excited. It was like Christmas: we were heaving up crates, boxes, tins, bales, and piling them up on the ground. They kept rushing me and Sellman, telling us, "We have to go, move out, pursue the enemy." We begged for more time. We were on to something real here, something solid that we could grab and feel.

Working like madmen, we rushed through separate tunnels that went for hundreds of feet in every direction underground. We found large rooms with beds in rows, racks for equipment and weapons, side rooms, connected defense bunkers, mortar and rocket firing positions, and tunnels straight down to other tunnels underneath. Everything was beautifully dug and built, shored up with logs, with slits and airholes to prevent concussion of bombs from killing the occupants. There were even tight-stretched tarpaulins for ceiling covers, to prevent dust sifting down during airstrikes. Every room was filled with abandoned equipment and munitions by the ton.

I crawled along again in yet another direction, sticking my bayonet in the walls as I went, sometimes uncovering the best stuff that way. This time, digging, I hit more wooden crates with Chinese characters stenciled on them. Working them out of the dirt, my fingers suddenly closed on an oval metal object jammed between them. Grenade! The pin had been pulled, booby-trapping the whole pile of Chi-Comm 82mm mortar shells—set to go if they're moved. Grasping it and holding the spoon down, and my pistol, I scuttled back in the dark to the last airhole, pulled myself out, yelled "Fire in the hole!" and rolled the son-of-a bitch in, letting it explode.

A little later, moving over nearer Sellman to a series of fighting positions from the previous day's battle, prodding with my bayonet, I hit heavy, grey metal cases again, and started to heave out one after another loaded with thousands of rounds of .51 cal. machine-gun cartridges. From the adjoining connected room-bunker came crates of long, wicked rockets and RPG shells. This was real paydirt, the stuff that blew out tanks and killed GIs. Next there were hundreds of Chinese potato masher grenades. Everything I found was marked with Chinese characters or Russian letters.

Finally they screamed at us, "We gotta' go!," ordering us. But I'll always remember the look of pure joy on the faces of those armored cavalry dudes above us at the sight of all those armor-piercing shells safely out of enemy hands. We heard later that the Division Commander, General Ware, who had observed the fighting from his chopper the day before, along with General Orwin Talbot and Colonel George Patton of the 11th Cavalry had come in to see the captured supplies.

As we moved out, we could hear somebody blowing the NVA ammo in place with huge *BOOMS!* The full amount of captured equipment was probably never recorded. Behind us a couple of thousand meters to the south, three more A-Cav tracks of the 2/11th Cav struck anti-tank mines, with more U.S. casualties.

We continued probing forward the rest of that day, but with every azimuth of the compass we took, we ran into more bunkers, more camps, and sometimes enemy sniper rounds. We could hear roaring behind us— they were bombing out the base camps as we moved. We heard that a troop of the ¼ Cav was operating with us, in a blocking position, across from the 11th Cav, and had been in contact nearby.

While waiting in an elephant grass clearing we had surrounded and turned into an LZ for resupply, we were spread out thin—too thin, it turned out. Enemy soldiers were sneaking up along trails we later found, watching us, and guessing our intentions. They set up between and beyond our outposts and waited, hidden and silent. According to our RTO we were "in the vicinity of XT9435" and it was the 21st of July. We kept our eyes open and rested, talking and bullshitting about everything we'd seen. As the big, double-rotor "Hillclimber" Chinook helicopter came roaring down, the clearing suddenly turned into a hot LZ, with long, stuttering bursts of automatic AK-47 fire raking the chopper. The helicopter machine-gunners were firing over our heads as we started to shoot into the NVA positions. Tracers were flying in every direction. I clearly saw the crew chief or a gunner jerking as AK bullets slammed into him and he fell forward in his harness, hanging half-way out. The big chopper shuddered noisily trying to pull out as the enemy fire raked it. We were all firing fast as the chopper almost hit the ground. I think maybe one of our grunts was hit in the shooting and thrown on the Chinook at this moment. Then, it just barely gained enough altitude to clear the trees and peeled out. If we had hit any of the enemy, they had already dragged their casualties off or we couldn't find them in the jungle. We didn't learn whether the chopper made it. The NVA had done their work well; we were really low on ammunition and rations, almost out of food.

It's funny to think now, that during the next twenty-four hours we destroyed tons of enemy rice and supplies, never thinking of eating any of it. We ripped open countless sacks, dumping them out and strewing the rice with CS gas or burning stuff. Hundreds of sacks were marked with a "Alliance for Progress" handshake, the names of U.S. manufacturers, and large "gift of the American people—not to be sold." We concluded that more fine people—both Americans and Vietnamese—were getting rich on the docks of Saigon. The grunt mutters continued, "Jus' keep on keepin' on. Keep on humpin', do yer time."

After the Chinook was shot-up at the LZ and a long tense march, rifles ready every instant, we were set up again in yet another NVA base camp. Sellman and I, with Newall from another platoon of our company went tunnel-ratting again. We were moving around underground, exploring, finding "treasure", and yelling to each other. The rest of the guys are standing or sitting around, resting, cleaning their weapons or watching us moving in or out. In one long tunnel with several entrances, we threw down grenades as usual, waited a few minutes, and crawled in from different directions, calling out to one another.

This time we cornered a live prisoner—grenade-shocked and wounded—in an NVA uniform between us. When we dragged him out, Newall wanted to kill him with his bowie knife but the dudes stopped him. Newall's been in the grunts in 'Nam for "fuckin' years," longer than anyone else here. He was a little "dinky-dau," but real good in the field. This prisoner was strange, anyhow, he's worth saving. He had Mongolian features and hair on his body and legs unlike the Viets, and he claimed in sort of garbled Vietnamese to our interpreter that he was a "Russian advisor to the NVA."

A small chopper came in around then with some ammo, but no rations, and we sent him out on it. The lifer-brass were very happy: "better than bodies."

Under interrogation later, our prisoner revealed that he "was part of a 300-man reinforcement of NVA regulars who had just infiltrated in from the Fish Hook area of the Cambodian border to reinforce the Viet Cong Dong Ngai Regiment in this area."

Meanwhile Sellman and I have gone back underground again, and this time we found an entire underground armory full of enemy weapons being repaired, with benches, lathes, and tools. Next we found hundreds of pounds of high-explosives and grenades, and a whole new series of unexplored tunnels and bunkers full of supplies and NVA uniforms. It just went on and on and on.

We were getting tired of the constant tension, marching, and digging, but there was no end in sight. We didn't know what's going on out around

us in the overall battle-plan or operation. "Nobody tells us nothin'."
That night we set up in an ambush-perimeter near this last tunnel complex; out beyond it was the retreating enemy. We didn't have much to
eat, we're worn out, and they were still pushing us hard. We divided
up LP and guard time and took turns sleeping with our weapons on the
bare dirt and jungle leaf mold. Several times that night I woke up quick
hearing noises, but nothing blows. I had another of my premonitions
during that long night, though—one that the enemy is around. I could
feel them out there in the dark watching us.

Our little 2nd platoon of about twenty men is up at the crack of dawn,
eating the last of our rations. We're still in our ambush position, tired,
filthy and bearded—but alert. My squad was in a little group; we were
talking low, finishing our grub, and checking our weapons. Suddenly
Robby shouted a warning, "Gooks!" and jumped for his machine-gun.
It was a point-element of uniformed NVA, AK-47s at ready, advancing towards us through the trees. There was a split-second of shock at
seeing them so close. Then three or four of us open fire at once, including me, ducking at the same time for cover. *POW! POW! POW! POW!*
BRRRRRRPPPPPP! We shot down two enemy soldiers point-blank in
front of us, killing them, my bullets blending with Robby's, Sellman's,
and Gaddy's in a stream of death. The NVA soldiers jerked and twisted
under the impact, faces in shock, dropping their weapons. The gunfire
spread. Robby fired his gun in long bursts beyond the crumpled bodies
as we came under fire ourselves from more of them behind, and we kept
on shooting. Out along the line of the company, four more are killed
up close.

A third VC/NVA goes down hit, in front of us. He scrabbles over,
wounded, to a nearby tunnel or bunker and disappears. The other enemy
retreats or pulls back from our heavy fire and Lieutenant Harr shouts
for someone to crawl out in front of the line.

"Throw a grenade in that hole!" I was the closest so I felt that he was
directly ordering me. I moved ahead, crawling with my rifle, grenade
ready, pin pulled, sweating like hell, my buddies covering me. I thought,
"other gooks behind are gonna have me dead-to-rights." I got to the
entrance after what seemed like forever, and rolled the grenade in from
one side. It blew up with a hollow, *Boom!* and when the smoke cleared,
I slid down in. It was dark as hell, with just a little light from somewhere far-off. I see a small movement and fire into it with my pistol,
three shots quick, but I can't find that gook, and I'm getting really scared

and feeling alone. I backed out quick. If he got away in there, he was so shot-up from bullets and shrapnel, he was going to die anyway, and I didn't give a damn anymore. I crawled up out of that maze of darkness and scrambled over to the rest of the dudes, telling them, "I've had enough of tunnels fer today, man!"

Adrenalin was coursing through me like speed. We dragged the dead NVA into our line by their warm, bloody-wet arms and hands, stripping them of their weapons and web gear. Company A had a confirmed body count of six enemy soldiers killed that 22nd day of July, 1968. I looked down at the ones I helped kill. They were regulars in brown khaki uniforms, grunts just like us. These didn't look like skinny little kids. Their legs and arms were heavily muscled, men who've humped many a mile—the same as us.

Some FNG took an Instamatic picture but I'm shit-laughing as he did it, thinking to myself, "You stupid fool, you gotta ways to go!" Some other guys were arguing over an AK-47 and a Soviet SKS carbine. I thought it was funny. "What are they gonna' do with the damned things, carry 'em around for extra weight?"

Sellman and I and Gaddy and Robby hunched together muttering, "Glad nobody got shot that time, man. There must be stinkin' gooks all over this goddamn jungle, huh?" The tension had been building the last few days. "God, we're lucky we ain't been ambushed ourselves," we agreed.

They must have still been bombing out the base camps all around us, we kept hearing rumbling and booming in the distance. We didn't know where the main Viet Cong/NVA force was hiding around here or retreating towards Cambodia or what. Nobody thinks to tell us anything. We know it's a big operation around us but we can only guess at enemy strength or American casualties.

We saddled-up and left the dead NVA where they lay. We were marching forward again now, and behind us could still hear the Phantoms screaming in, dropping bombs in the distance. Sometimes the ground trembled. Far in the distance we heard the rumbling thunder of heavy bombers, B-52s from Guam or Thailand.

In a front-line platoon of a war, you can be in a big campaign or battle and hardly even know it. There may be fighting going on all around you, movement of troops, casualties, shooting, or noise in the distance, and yet all you care about is your own little platoon. You know and hear reports of other companies of the battalion fighting, the division as a whole, suffering hundreds of killed and wounded, but you're just try-ing to look sharp, and survive with your own little band of buddies.

We marched through huge, endless bomb craters from B-52 heavies, many yards wide and deep. They seem to follow each other in succes-sion as far as the eye can see. This is what we're supposed to be doing on this operation, a "BDA," or bomb-damage assessment. Infantry bat-talions humped through the endless jungle to B-52 airstrike locations, looking for signs of bombed-out enemy base camps or casualties. They've been dropping millions of tons of bombs every year in this war, and most of them exploded on empty jungle. By now more bombs had been dropped on Vietnam than during all of World War II, but 90 per-cent of the enemy homeland in North Vietman, the source of weapons, ammo, reinforcements, and political leadership, was going untouched since the bombing halt.

Up and down, in and out, and around the rims, it was like being lost on some weird moon desert. Burned and twisted remains of trees and vines tear at us, and our legs sink up to the knees in the soft, spongy dirt that has been blown in the air and sifted down by the huge blasts. Sometimes we found pieces of enemy bodies and uniforms, or "Ho Chi Minh" sandals made from old rubber tires.

In this place we were getting Agent Orange defoliant dusted all over us from aircraft spraying and airstrikes stirring up clouds of it in the barren remnant of a jungle beyond the craters. I use my lucky-towel again now, my all-purpose baby blanket; I wet it down and wrapped it over my nose and mouth to keep from breathing so much in. Something told me that if this stuff is killing 120-foot-high trees, "It ain't good to in-hale too much of it."

We were still humping forward, collectively worn out, but still on edge when we heard firing break out way in front of us. First comes the individual popping and cracking of AK-47s and U.S. M-16s, then the machine-guns join in, and it quickly swells to a roar. The RTO was yelling to Lieutenant Harr that Delta Company (of our own 1st/16th Bat-talion) is in heavy contact and taking casualties. We quick-glance at each other, tighten up our gear and double-check our weapons. Sure enough he yelled, "All right, Alpha Company, move out! Double time! Move! Move!" We started taking chances right away, coming to another NVA trail, jumping into it on the run, knowing our buddies are in trouble up there and needing help fast. Our own artillery was exploding around us in the jungle, dangerously close. Pieces of shrapnel, debris and dirt flew through the air with each *SSSSHHHH-Boom!* What we didn't know at that moment was that Colonel Eaton was in his chopper calling in the battalion Recon platoon for an ambush of any enemy that might retreat from our onslaught. We came up to the firefight and went on line with Captain Sonny Smith's Delta Company, and started moving forward mixed in with them, opening fire into the enemy position. All we saw was AK-47 tracers coming at us and a little smoke and movement. The smell of burnt powder and shot-up dirt hung heavy in the air.

I was shooting my rifle steady and accurately, moving forward, noticing that the NVA were firing too high. I kept my bursts low, just grazing the ground out in front. Casualties, shot-up GIs, were being dragged to better cover behind us. Suddenly I heard some weird screeching noises, quavering wails out in front of us. For a minute I didn't know what the hell it was, then I picked out a clear voice.

"GI, you die!"

"It's the damned gooks." I screamed back, "Stinkin' gooks, yer gonna die!" I was shit-laughing, even though the sound of enemy voices chilled me.

I shot up that position with my grunt buddies on either side. We advanced again when their fire lulled, hugging the ground low when they opened up. I'd already shot off a number of twenty-round magazines of my ammunition in the reinforcement of Charlie Company, the Chinook LZ and in our ambush this morning. I had a moment of panic when I actually ran out of rifle ammunition. The first thing I did was unsling the LAW rocket off my shoulders, telescope it open and zero it in on a low, dark hump in the bush ahead that looks like the bunker they're firing from. Sometimes the LAWs fire and sometimes they don't. This one did. *Whooosh-crack boom!* The 66mm shell exploded into the hump with a huge flash. The LAW has only the one shot and isn't reloadable. For a few seconds I started shooting my pistol at them, and then I crawled back and got a bandolier from one of the wounded. Out in front of me I could clearly see one of the Viet Cong low-crawling across our front with an AK-47. At least five of us fired at once into him on full automatic, ripping his body to shreds with bullets. A chopper swooped in low overhead now, firing machine-guns into the enemy position, under anti-aircraft fire itself.

Another smaller chopper seemed to be hovering almost over our heads. I glanced up. So close, it was in the treetops. It turned out to be a 3rd Brigade Aviation C & C ship piloted by Warrant Officer Harry Loersch.

He was flying our Battalion Commmander, Col. Richard Eaton, an officer who went in where his men were getting hit. The chopper was under fire from two ChiComm .51 cals tied up in the trees with their gunners. The little aircraft suddenly took some hits point blank, jerked off sideways and veered away just off the ground behind.

Somebody yelled out, "The Battalion Commander's been hit!" He'd been trying to lower a stretcher and medevac a wounded lieutenant of Delta Company. The deep, heavy popping of a ChiComm .51 cal anti-aircraft gun was going again, and the other chopper, a Huey 1-C gunship, was hit by the same anti-aircraft fire.

The RTC was yelling at Lieutenant Harr and his big voice boomed out at us, "Pull back now! Airstrikes coming in! Tac-Air! Pull back on line! Make a perimeter!" I guess whatever brass was in charge figured on not wasting anymore grunts, but to "use bombs." I saw nine GIs who were hit near me besides our battalion's CO, severely wounded. Two of the grunts were dead.

The Phantom jets came screaming in very low, sounding so loud it would petrify anyone. This noise, combined with the bombs exploding practically on top of us, blocked out the rest of the world like a thousand storms. Hundreds of trees and tons of earth were blasted in the air right in front of our position, pieces falling all around. We lay petrified at the thought of the slightest miscalculation by a pilot. With blast after blast our bodies were shaken. We bounced right up off the ground and went fuzzy all over. My ears were ringing-clanging even with my hands covering them, and the right one had blood on it when I felt wetness and looked at it. For minutes after each bombing run, we couldn't move. They were hitting awful close to us. When they ran out of bombs, they used napalm, the exploding cannisters bursting into a sea of fire, some of it spattering and burning all around us. Then came the awful ripping-roar of automatic cannons and machine-guns, completely tearing up the blown-up, burning, smoking enemy line all over again.

We didn't even advance and look for those gooks after that. There was at least the one shredded dead body of an NVA in sight in front of me, half-buried by tree branches; several other guys and I had shot him. There were more dead ones in there both from our shooting and the bombing. Let someone else get a "body count" if they wanted one; we didn't care anymore.

We started to pull back in case the Air Force decided to do it again. All around us was the smell of blown-up earth and smoking, shattered trees. We began hauling the casualties up out of a bomb crater where they'd been stashed for safety. Slinging my rifle and lending a hand, the first GI I half-carried and dragged up had been shot in the face with a bullet. I could hardly make out the shape of his features. As I pulled him over the rim, I saw him look up at our own Lieutenant Harr. He was standing there looking down, speaking something low, to comfort my dude. Our grunt brother was trying to smile through the mess of shot-up protruding bones and teeth; he was trying to lift up his hand, and give us a "V" sign. I hugged him a little and whispered kind of hoarsely to him that he looked O.K..

"Yer gonna make it all right, man. Yer goin' back to the world, an' get better."

Down in the bottom of the bomb crater with the other shot-up GIs, I saw one of the medics standing, his wide-eyes shocked and his hands half-raised in a hopeless or helpless gesture, staring blankly at his charges. I guessed he'd already done what he could. There were some IVs going from blood-bags, and red, dripping compresses; we were helping anyway we could. Dudes were in bad pain, needing morphine. Another medic was down there crawling around wounded, yet dragging his bag, still trying to help patch up other guys. When we pulled him up and laid him out at the top, I saw he had some bloody compresses tied on. He couldn't move his legs.

I asked him, "You all right man? What happened?" He kept looking around like he'd lost somebody.

"I'm the Doc from Delta, man. Buddy Roche. I can't move my legs. I think my back got paralyzed." Doc Roche told me quickly how it started. "We left outta' our NDP and went across a big swamp; we had a new guy on point named Schneider, an' he saw movement across a creek where we saw some big bunkers. We went on in there an' them big bunkers were real old, but right behind 'em, past a bomb crater, was some new ones. The NVA was in there. They hit Schneider with a ChiComm .51 cal just as he came outta the crater, whacked him right down in there again. I run in there an' Ross followed me. He's a black dude—Luther Ross. He had the sixty and they caught him with a burst next an' killed him, too, right behind me. Then they blew a claymore on us an' I got hit. The gooks with AKs were firin' from all around. I seen Oleck get hit next."

Somebody started yelling at me, "All right, Brown, quit talkin', keep movin' 'em up." The booming and cracking were still going on, and officers were yelling, "Let's go, we've gotta move out! Take 'em with us. There's gooks all around us here; medevacs won't come in—the whole area's too hot!"

So we used our trusty poncho-liners again, this time as stretchers. The casualties, both killed and wounded, were rolled on, and suspended between sweating, straining GIs of both companies, and we moved out. The jungle was so heavy and thick we had to cut and slash our way to make a trail. The wounded are groaning and crying. "Oh, God! My God! Oh, Jesus, oh-somebody. I want my mother!" On and on. I was on the left flank as we moved. I looked down at other guys' blood on my fatigues, and then NVA snipers opened fire on us from the sides. I fired bursts back at them only when they hit too close. "Bastards!" "Slimey sons-of-bitches!"

It had taken a long time but I was finally starting to hate them. We marched and humped, crawling like a long wounded snake and finally got out of the range of the enemy and reached a clearing called "safe." We huddled in a round perimeter circle in the wet, muddy grass waiting for the dust-off choppers. Lying there exhausted, with my rifle pointing out towards the enemy, I listened to a couple of Delta Company guys saying they'd just killed another NVA at close range. I heard voices behind me in the middle of the perimeter above the noise of the RTOs and lieutenants on their radios.

"I got his canteens, man, an' some peaches and pound cake outta' his Cs; he ain't gonna need 'em no more."

"Yeah, well, O.K.. I'll take this dude's poncho liner. At least it ain't all ripped to hell like mine was."

Another voice joined in, "Is there any ammo on those guys? I'm damn near out of '16 magazines."

My buddies behind me were dividing up the belongings of the killed and wounded. All I could think of then was what shape my own gear and ammo were in, and whether I was missing out on anything myself. I decided my stuff was O.K.; besides it felt so good to just lie still for a while.

The medevacs finally came in, a bubble LOH and a Huey, and took out the casualties and one medic. In a cold, pouring rain we continued to march, hearing from our RTO that Charlie Company had spotted fifty more enemy nearby and had killed three of them. Lt. Landgraf's recon platoon ambush position on the other side paid off. They attacked a retreating column of about 40 VC, killing five and capturing several weapons. We hit yet another enemy bunker and tunnel complex ourselves, capturing four AK-47s and over a thousand more shells, mines, and grenades. The gooks had retreated from it, thank God. We moved later in that long, dark night, setting up a different ambush position to fool the enemy, probably another good idea by Lieutenant Harr.

All around us and from one end of Vietnam to the other, the same thing was going on; that week there were thousands more casualties. And our country's leaders, without the slightest understanding of our Communist enemy's strength and determination, prattled on about a "negotiated settlement" or a "mutual withdrawal" or some other weak-kneed crap. We, in the field, knew what the North Vietnamese thought. They were dug in under this jungle ground forever. We knew that instinctively in our guts. We mumbled about it a little to one another in a front-line grunt kind of way once in a while, but mostly it's so obvious nothing needed to be said.

And the politicians chattered on, "Stop the bombing!" or talked about "resuming the bombing again," or talked about a "peace conference." All the while, the enemy gloated and laughed, hugging each other. To them, it was as good as victory already. And it was all as old as the world, written in blood on the pages of history. You want to fight a war? You want to transport your armies across the ocean and take on a continent? Well, you'd better not blink your eyes from a little blood. You'd better not let this enemy know what you're thinking all the time. You'd better be tough and mean and destroy his will to resist, and do it quickly, thoroughly, and resolutely, or stay out in the first place. If not, if you know you're not going to make it, then get out now, before your losses hurt too much, destroy patriotic spirit at home, divide your people, and inspire your enemies.

For me, it had been a long learning process these last ten months as I had grown and had come to understand the nature of this war. I hated the enemy for killing my brothers, but sometimes late at night, alone with my thoughts on an LP, I knew I would be fighting foreign invaders in my country, too. I'd sit and think for hours about the villages around Phu Loi I'd seen so much of, and how the war was being lost to the Communists there by practically every action we took. Our presence alone was enough reason for at least half the people to fight us. If we were to defeat the Viet Cong in the villages, how could it be done with this "limited war" concept? If they had unending quantities of weapons, ammunition, supplies and NVA reinforcements coming in from safe "neutral" Cambodia and Laos, how could it ever be stopped in the villages? Even to a rifleman in an infantry platoon, there was something wrong with our strategy, and what I believed then and believe now was that it was a civilian leadership's mistaken fear of attacking the cross-border sanctuaries and the North Vietnamese homeland early in the war. This would have immediately taken pressure off South Vietnam and most of the fighting in village areas, and these nearby jungle base areas could have then been left to ARVN units. The enemy would never have been able to build up so much strength, and the negative American effect on both the civilian population and ARVN morale would have been minimal.

10   Gettin' Short

Take the war out of the TVs and
put it in the complacent streets
Kick America awake
Before it dies in its sleep.
—Charles M. Purcell
(from Winning Hearts and Minds)

We continued our humping-marching in the jungle, still operating with D-Company. The next day, in the rain our battalion had three more GIs wounded in small enemy contacts. The operation between July 20th and 23rd already has cost about sixty U.S. casualties between us and the 11th Cav. Perhaps we were pursuing a retreating enemy force, but nobody told us anything. I remember going up and down small steep jungle hills, across rushing creeks, cutting and slashing trails in the pouring rain and the sweltering heat. I remember the whole company crossing a roaring river, probably the Song Bé, on the old blown-up twisted remains of a French steel bridge. No signs of civilization could be seen in any direction, and there we were balancing our way over on these lone twisted girders. We heard animals moving at night, monkeys and deer; one time a tiger screamed. Out on the flank on the ground, I saw tracks of wild buffalo and elephants.

Just about then, during a resupply by choppers, we got some new guys, including two "instant NCOs" who had become sergeants by going to a "shake 'n bake" school back in the world. I remember Sergeants Brackett and Barnett. Herman Brackett was a short, strong-looking white dude with glasses; he listened and learned fast and became my good squad leader. Roger Barnett was just a nice mellow-fellow who later took over a squad and remained partners with Brackett. Also around this time we got another Mexican-American dude, "Pancho" Reuben Carrera. He also became a smart soldier and good brother. Pancho developed a weird phobia about being hit in the chest, and wore a homemade armored vest made of claymore bags full of junk tied across his front. Funny thing, when he did get shot up in a firefight, it was everywhere but there. We also got a new little Polack to keep big Joe company, "Shot" Shotkowsky from Colorado. When I first met him, we'd gotten to sit around in the dirt somewhere together on a break, and I told him some good war stories, full of advice about how to make it here. He was small, blond, and good-looking, and turned into a number-one dude. Bergy was another I remember from this time at Song Bé, solidly built white dude with close-cut, black hair, squared away and businesslike. He was a good soldier, and he, too, was destined to get hit. A new platoon sergeant who came to us was an E-7 lifer named Garza; he tried to do his job but I wasn't ever close to him. I stayed with my buddies Sellman, Gaddy, Robby, Shaefer, Brown, and Owens, who were all still making it. Out of about 450 grunts actually out humping, fifty-three men of our battalion had been killed or wounded by enemy action during the month of July. During that same month, we had killed fifty-five enemy soldiers by confirmed body count, and captured two NVA prisoners. Our sister battalion, the 2nd/16th Infantry, had been operating within a few kilometers to the east and south of us, and after our operation moved to the area we'd been fighting in. During the last days of July, they found ten more dead NVA soldiers in the exact location of our firefight reinforcing Delta Company on the 22nd and 23rd of July, when Colonel Eaton was hit.

I don't remember when we left Song Bé nor do I have any memory of the LZ extraction. We were relieved by the 2nd/28th Infantry, the Black Lions. In the months and years to come, First Division soldiers, our successors, would continue to fight the same Communist forces, bleeding and dying for the same Song Bé River jungle as our grunt predecessors had from 1965-68.

We were on our way to the Michelin Plantation again, just hitting Lai Khe long enough for resupplying and reorganizing and another rocket attack.

At dawn on the first of August, I was sent on a quick courier chopper ride to Phu Loi to straighten out my pay records that were still disorganized from the recon-patrol and the helicopter company. That same morning when I hit the Phu Loi base camp, I had another premonition and headed straight for the recon platoon CP hootch. The radio was going full-blast when I walked in like a ghost out of the past with my NVA webgear across my chest, my Chinese pistol and M-16 slung, uniform and boots still filthy with the mud of Song Bé. Sure enough, the platoon was in a firefight with the enemy at that instant and taking casualties. It may have been the same old E-7 lifer monitoring the transmission. I screamed at him, ''Who's hit? Who is it?'' The radio was crackling again. It was Earl, Earl, my old best buddy, my main man, shot dead. I felt tears rush to my eyes.

''Earl Okumura killed in action in fuckin' 'Nam.'' I kept thinking, ''He's too good to get it; it can't be true.'' My ears were buzzing, I could even hear the shooting going on from here, it was only a click south of the wire. I turned away feeling the urge to rush out through the wire to help, to be with him, but then I knew, ''He's dead, I can't do nothin' now.''

I hear a little later he was shot by a VC in the bush at point blank range, the Green tracers blasting straight through his chest and out his back. One of the dudes, I hear it was Bear Banko, killed the gook. It made me feel almost like I owed him. Emil Krone was in the first shootout, too, and in the ensuing firefight two more VC were killed.

I headed on out, still crying a little and mumbling to myself about ''this stinking place an' the politicians.'' I remained an extra day to go to Earl's memorial service at his original unit's hootch in the 701st Maintenance Battalion area. His bayonetted rifle was stuck upside down in the dirt with his muddy old grunt boots in front. A clean, pasty-looking chaplain was chattering away to deaf ears. None of us believed what he was saying about ''helping preserve the valiant Republic of Vietnam'' anymore. We were just in it 'cause we're here to help out our buddies. An old buddy from the Recon platoon, Stone, who's also from Hawaii was to escort Earl's body home to his family, stood next to me, crying quietly.

I was standing there in a row of men at parade rest, and those damned memories kept coming back to me and the plans to go around New England together, something he always wanted to see. He was an American as much as I ever was. He was my brother and I missed him; years later I named one of my sons after him, and everyday I say his name now, I remember him and all of the others. After that I turned away and never wanted to go back and mix with that old recon platoon again. I went back to Lai Khe, fast as I could and on the new CA into the Michelin with my 1st/16th brothers.

On the 5th of August our battalion was air-assaulted into an LZ in the ''Trapezoid Area,'' approximately 160 square miles of bush and jungle south of the Michelin Plantation and west of Lai Khe. It was a joint operation with the 2nd/2nd mechanized infantry, a few kilometers east of Dau Tieng. My company was working in conjunction with Delta Company again, when they came under small arms and RPG fire and had three men hit. We found several base camps that day and the next, and had occasional contact with the enemy. The monsoon rains were still pouring down on us day after day, making our short hours of night rest in ambush positions into restless ordeals of slimey rotting. On the 7th of August, as we were humping our way through the bush, our recon platoon suddenly hit the enemy and Delta Company was sent on the double to reinforce. Several NVA regulars were killed and enemy automatic weapons captured. There were also more American casualties.

An hour later as were moving forward, tense and ready, dripping with sweat, came the sudden popping and cracking again. Then we dived down, firing bursts at sudden-moving forms. Tracers streaking, men yelling, I was shooting low bursts, skipping the rounds into the enemy position. The firing dies down, we move ahead a little and three dead Viet Cong ate on the ground. The RTO was calling in our action and the coordinates of the body count, "in the vicinity of XT604352." We win, they lose. This time again, we shot straighter and faster than they did.

On that same 7th of August, the NDP of the 2nd/2nd Infantry we were operating out of was attacked by the enemy, causing American casualties. It's like an endless repetition of an old song you're tired of. The next few days, the 1st/16th and the 2nd/2nd kept making light enemy contacts. There were a few more VC/NVA killed by body count, more of their food and equipment captured. I hardly cared. I was sick and tired of it all; I felt completely cool and professional, but my mind was still on Earl's death, even though there have been five more GIs killed, nineteen more wounded in the last week, and at least ten more enemy bodies to "count" during our little operation.

Back-in-the-world news keeps drifting into our lives about the "long hot summer-in-the-cities." We were hearing and reading news of black uprisings in the ghettos. At the end of July, riots erupted in Ohio, Michigan, and Indiana simultaneously; sniper fire, the National Guard called out, ten people killed in Cleveland alone.

The antiwar movement was growing and spreading in colleges and universities, in the Congress, Defense and State Departments, in the editorial offices of newspapers and TV stations. It even became incorporated into the dialogue of the civil rights movement, "Racism in American and the Vietnam genocide are part of the same oppression. Some radical members of the black leadership such as Stokely Carmichael had already begun calling for the "defeat of U.S. forces by the Viet Cong."

The continuing bombing halt north of the 20th parallel had been both a propaganda and a psychological victory for the North Vietnamese Communists, while those American leaders, whose weakened resolve about the war after the Tet offensive had pushed the President into a tactical retreat, now took credit for "bringing the enemy to the negotiating table"; and the NVA grinned.

Vietnamese Communist propaganda at the time captured by us in base camps and translated or aired over Radio Hanoi rejoiced in the American anitwar movement. They saw it more and more as an important ally in their battle to win against the strongest power in the world. The bombing halt greatly assisted the enemy as a psychological turning point in the war. They could afford to "negotiate" in Paris for years while more GIs died, and so they did. What our liberal, intellectual, civilian masters didn't realize was that, in war, one is not appreciated for gestures demonstrating a weakening resolve by an enemy that is killing one's young men.

For the "doves" in the White House, State, and Defense Departments who had involved us in the war and now turned against it, the bombing halt did not have the desired result. It did not appease the antiwar movement people, many of whom hardly believed anything the government said it was doing anyway. This feeling was an extension of what was called the "credibility gap." For movement activists, the continuation of the war on the ground was enough reason for them to continue to demonstrate.

In New York City, Barnard college student Josephine Duke reacted angrily to the violence of the Columbia uprising. After getting out of jail in early May she had joined the SDS antiwar movement full time. With the gym issue settled, the leadership had steered the members into full time work against the "imperialist American War" in Vietnam, and began to move towards a position of "supporting the NLF." Josie had quit going to classes and devoted all her time to the movement. In the summer of '68 she was working at the "Liberation School," an alternative study program conceived by the radical leadership for spreading their message after the violent confrontation of April. Some of the courses offered included "Imperialism" (and how that theory related to the U.S. war in Vietnam), Marxist economics and the Capitalist media. The idea was to build rapidly on the emotions generated by the April uprising and organize more massive numbers to take a stand against society. Four hundred became involved in this "Liberation School," and underground press interpretations of Vietnam and "imperialism" flourished. Liberals like the author Norman Mailer, who had thrown their influence behind the antiwar movement, contributed money for the cause.

In August, Josephine Duke was made Press Secretary for SDS, partly because her famous family name caused media attention to focus on Columbia SDS. She became more deeply involved with the interminably long radical meetings at which strategy and "politics" were discussed and planned. The level of dialogue since April had risen from non-violent confrontation to how a Molotov cocktail is made, and when it would become "correct politics" to begin using them. The careful planning and coaching of the leadership during the building occupation towards confrontation and the undisciplined, violent overreaction of the police had achieved the desired effect. Violence entered discussions and meetings naturally, it was no longer something strange or imaginary.

For us soldiers actually meeting the enemy in battle with rifles in our hands, the effect of the continued bombing halt, home-front antiwar feeling and "Peace Talks" was powerful and detrimental.

"Lookit this, you guys, it says here, in Paris, Averell Harriman and Cyrus Vance are reporting absolutely no progress in the peace talks because of the stubbornness of the Communists." The American negotiators complained about VC rocket attacks, saying, "There is no excuse for the shelling of Saigon by the enemy."

I looked at at that line about four times before I began to laugh so hard I almost vomited into the mud I was sitting in.

"No progress, stubbornness, no excuse for shelling."

These then were our leaders? These were the people who sent us into war here? These were the spokesmen for our brothers killed by the thousands from Ia Drang to Dak To to An My and Hue, in the May Offensive, and at that miserable Song Bé River? These were the men who brought out the utmost in Earl? He who was sacrificed on the altar of "limited objectives, not requiring the total destruction of the enemy's cities and people," while our "losses in United States troops killed-in-action are kept to an acceptable level."

During the Trapezoid operation I wrote my last letter home to people who didn't understand anything about any of it.

A Co. 1st/16th Infantry
Michelin - in the field
11 August 1968 (approx.)

Dear Family,
We've left the Song Bé, we're still in the field on an operation south of this huge old French plantation. A lot of GIs have died in this damned place. We made contact with the gooks on the 7th but it was light. We have been staying deep in the jungles for weeks. We hardly ever get resupplied, just live on dried LRRP (Long Range Recon Patrol) rations.

My best friend in the recon patrol I used to be in, Earl Okumura, is dead, shot by a Viet Cong. On my way from Song Bé to here, I was in Phu Loi two days and got mixed up in Earl's funeral.

On the last operation in Song Be, we had to carry out our dead and our screaming wounded in poncho liners, cutting our way through the jungle under fire because there was too much enemy-fire for the medevacs to come in.

I hope you realize now I'm only a very average guy, because I am. I'm no great leader or hero. I'm just like the majority of grunts here. When I finish my army time, I will just follow my dreams for the rest of my life. Don't expect anything great out of me ever. Maybe I'll find happiness somewhere, even if you're not satisfied with what I am.
                    Love,
                    John

After that, for the rest of my time in the field in Vietnam, I never wrote to anybody again, parents, family, or even girlfriend. There didn't seem to be any point from then on. I had come to the conclusion that the people back home had no understanding or feeling for the war or the soldiers fighting it. For my part I felt completely caught up in it, and my 1st/16th Battalion of infantry had become my world. All the previous experiences had led up to this place. There was no turning back ever again in my life from what I'd become. Even in the mud, rain, and jungle heat, working with my fellow-soldiers for survival, the intellectual corner of my mind said, "This is it, this is the point, the place, you were meant to reach. A oneness with all the soldiers of all the millennia of history. Whatever else life has in store for me and us, we will never be what we were before."

And looking around me, all I saw were those brave, haunted faces, and I knew the strength of our mixed American people. The ability to adapt to any circumstance or challenge, but also take command in a moment, to question bad decisions, but also to follow orders. For years, through a period of decline in our national purpose and prestige, the memories of my grunt brothers of every American division in that impossible quagmire of Vietnam gave me hope and assurance for our future as a nation.

The marching-humping went on and on. The enemy retreating or hiding from our constant probing. We had, of course, gotten a new battalion CO to replace Colonel Eaton, shot by the NVA at Song Bé. He was a short, clean, shiny-looking lifer, and the rumor was passed that he'd come from the Berlin Brigade of the U.S. Army in Germany. It seemed to me that the atmosphere of the battalion had changed with his taking command. First of all, he made sure everyone knew he was from the "South"—Texas, I think. I remember sometime later seeing a Confederate flag flying over our NDP. I hated what it stood for, but the black dudes in our battalion—fighting for their country over here—hated it worse. It was exactly the kind of exacerbation that we didn't need at the time.

In that summer of '68, the first racial troubles in the 1st/16th took place that I remember. Up until then, we had all worked together and nothing like that had occurred. But, we got another new guy named Cannady, a follower of the Black Power movement growing back in the world. "White man's war, black ain't gonna do it no mo'." He came in fresh and tough among all these tired dudes, and immediately struck sparks with southern white dudes like Mallet who'd been around a while. The tension had been building up ever since Martin Luther King's killing, and it hadn't even existed before. The new colonel's weird southern hangups didn't help things but also it took very little in the summer of 1968 to perhaps unknowingly aggravate a tense situation. Guys like Robby and Brown and Owens who had been tight as brothers with us, drew off a little and reappraised the situation. The war was so strange, with its constant gook-racial undertones, that it provided a logical extension of the white man vs. colored Third World philosophy. It seemed to make sense, and the rest of us of other races or in-betweens had no defense against it because none of us gave a damn about the "cause" or "reasons" either anymore, just our brotherhood-survival.

The assassination of Robert Kennedy in June by an Arab fanatic and of Martin Luther King by a Klan-type back in April added tension and restlessness to the uneasy feelings already felt by the grunts, both black and white, all over the 'Nam. The murder of King didn't fade for a long time. The feelings of Joe Miller in the recon platoon at Phu Loi in April were reinforced by King's death.

"They kill the King, man, they killin' us mother fuckers!" I heard the black GIs for months and months later talking about it, rehashing it, using it as the ultimate expression for our society towards them and their leader of peaceful, non-violent protest. It was a further justification for the animosity and radicalism of the Black Panthers that was spreading through all the services.

The Army officially tried not to care, not to notice the unravelling going on. Unit cohesiveness was disappearing, with constant hair-trigger racial tension, especially in the rear echelons.

Out in the field where we were in the jungle and swamps with the enemy-of-the-moment always nearby, there really wasn't much time or chance for trouble. Back in the rear, with more leisure time and the skating jobs being squabbled over, the race-scene was getting bad. On the few times we were out of the bush for a day or two, we had brushes with it or our own ranks divided up as the brothers sought their own blood. To me, it was a sadness because I loved Robby and Owens and Brown, but there it was, it was real: "They gotta find themselves." And most of those dudes never crossed us or turned on us or let us down. One or two other new men did, but that's to be expected, no matter what their skin color.

So Robby and Owens and Brown and the other black brothers of the company got more into each other and their "daps" and their color, and it became a new dimension of 'Nam. Cannady was a vehicle for it, not right or wrong or evil or good. He was an extension of Huey Newton and Eldridge Cleaver, the radical black leadership of the time. In a sense, he was fulfilling his historical role, and thousands of others all over 'Nam were doing the same thing; in a way, it was all right, even though many fights developed and GIs even killed one another. It was one of the outgrowths and part of the growing pains of the Vietnam War for the American people. The ultimate acceptance of the black man as an American, a whole man, an equal warrior.

All the military services went through an upheaval over it during the next few years. And it further derailed the war effort, disorganized the fighting units, and was exploited by the Communist enemy through propaganda and encouragement. Looking back years later, I see the greatness of our country that it could handle it, absorb it, adapt to it, and still maintain a field army, a continuing offensive or defensive force, without the bloodbaths that our enemies inflict upon themselves because of race or ideology.

We were humping combat patrols and ambushes out of Lai Khe, Ben Cat, Ben Cui, and Ap Ben Chua, sometimes trading shots with snipers or coming under enemy RPG fire. We were working with Bravo, Charlie, and Delta Companies, and sometimes the 2nd/2nd Mechanized, in searching and sealing villages. There are about seven more guys hit in the battalion between the 13th and 15th of August. No end is in sight besides a dead body or two here and there and more "VC/NVA equipment captured." It was junk and trash to us. The rainy season was still drenching down, we were constantly exhausted, wet, steaming, sored and ulcered and tense. On the 11th of August part of our sister battalion, the 2nd/16th, had been attacked and mauled badly, losing twenty-four casualties. We'd gone on an alert, but the enemy retreated before we took part. During one shootout, I remember killing a water buffalo that went mad from the uproar and charged at me as I fired at him full automatic.

We were set up near a river. There was to be a big event. After something like fifty days in the field on rations, they were going to bring out the cooks and mess tents, and serve us a hot meal in the boonies. We grunts were out around the perimeter; we're securing, rifles and machine-guns pointing out, skeptical and ready. It was warm and pleasant and around me are spread out Gaddy, Brown, Sellman, Owens, Robby, Shaeffer, and the others—new and old. We'd vastly enjoying the break and the rest, anticipating the hot, normal meal. The choppers had already brought it to us, the cooks were banging around back behind us, cursing and bragging—to each other and any of us who'll listen—about being "out in the field." To us it was sort of funny, in the ironical way that anything was funny then.

There were a lot of grunts around, maybe from another unit, I don't remember. I was half-asleep by a big old tree leaning out over the river bank, with my rifle set in a crotch and pointing across. My boots were off—I was trying to dry my rotting feet in the sun. Then *SSSShhh! Thump! SHHH-SSH! Thump!* Shouts of "Incoming!" Enemy mortars, shrapnel whizzing through the air, cooks screaming, pots and pans clattering, feet running, tents shaking and ripping with explosions. *Pop! Pop! Pop! Craaack! Craaack! Craaack!* AK-47s shooting in. I was down next to my startled buddies again, safety off, searching out a target. Tracers were coming in; short squeeze-burst, firing back felt so good. The shooting on both sides turned into another ripping-roar around me.

Bark flew off the tree above from enemy bullets, somewhere behind I heard that scream, "Medic!" again. "Dudes're being hit." Then, the mortars stop coming as our back-up artillery sends shells blowing up into the enemy firing position. Our heavy output of rifle and machine-gun fire drowned out and suppressed the incoming.

"Just leave us alone, you bastards," we're thinking. "We won't bother you if you don't bother us." The cooks behind us are down and scrabbling around in the dirt, terrified. I don't know how many casualties there were; I heard that one of the two German immigrant brothers serving in our outfit was killed in action. I could see wounded being patched up again, look for my close buddy faces. They're still all there.

Out in the field the news of the outside world occasionally broke through our cocoon of indifference. Some guys always had a little pocket transistor to listen to; AFVN radio, which came on early with some high-pitched REMF announcer, "Good morning, Vietnam!" From homefront magazines we heard that there was news of more antiwar demonstrations back in the United States and of commissions studying "violence in America." We heard that in the third week of August, 1968, there had been 308 more Americans killed in action and 2,000 more wounded in Vietnam.

Meanwhile, we had gotten another young sergeant in the platoon, a white guy named Otis Norris, from Champaign, Illinois, nicknamed "Pete." He was one of those nice, mellow dudes, tall, good-looking, and easy going. He'd been sent through the instant-NCO-school with another guy named Bennett, and they came to us all ready to be squad leaders. And here we were months and months in the line, broken in, tested, tired, and all our illusions gone. Next we were quick-teaching our new sergeant how to get by; it's strange, the ways of the Army. He's got one of those fair-skinned open faces, with smiling eyes. I had been in 'Nam a long time, so I spent quite a bit of time with him, educating him by actions or stories with a moral. I was getting to like him as a friend and I shouldn't have. I should have known, but I didn't—he only had a month and a half to go before he would stop an enemy bullet in the head. But I didn't know that then, and the days went on.

We marched along, humping our loads of gear and ammo through the jungle again. Cutting trail hour after hour 'cause it was real thick stuff, searching for the enemy, finding nothing, finally we "take a break, break in place." We had all started to sink down, worn out. I was behind Pancho Carrera in the file. I could see him settling down, almost ready to hit the ground in front of me, and there was a goddamn snake there, right under him, a nasty little coiled bamboo viper—one of the most deadly snakes. He didn't even notice as he went down; my old bolo knife came out, arced up and sliced down; the head of the filthy thing flew right off. Pancho settled down on the little body, hardly noticing. Wiggled around, looked back, down, under. I said, "Damned snake." He mumbled, "Thanks, man," already half-asleep.

We were in heavy, wet, sweltering jungle outside of the huge Bien Hoa Air Force/Army base, on a low rise overlooking the enormous camp-city. Sweating, dirty, and worn-out from humping, patrols, and ambushes, we rested, taking turns looking through a pair of field glasses at REMFs, MPs, and fat-assed officers sitting around; some of them actually were sunbathing in lounge chairs, sipping cold sodas, surrounded by their comfortable barracks and hootches. There was a secret unspoken urge among us to "give the sons–of–bitches a little shock," but it slipped away with the sweat. "Ahhh, everybody's just doing their time, anyway. It's the luck of the draw or you're own karma or whatever. Just drive on, you are what you are."

We were humping again, somewhere, thick, huge bamboo, like giant grass, horrible to go through. We'd just been LZed into the jungle north of Bien Hoa, Saigon-Di An. Our company was off from the rest of the battalion by ourselves. We had a fresh, but old, lifer platoon sergeant. Back in the NDP, when he first hit the battalion, he would tell us war stories of some other war. We were numb, we didn't care; actions speak better than words. It was this old dude we were under, we were out humping, searching, following a grid, following instructions; all of a sudden we old dudes noticed we were crossing the same stream ford again in the same place as we did a couple of hours before. "Oh, oh— no way crazy man, you wanta live?" We stopped still in the jungle by the creek, arguing.

"He's got us lost! Can't read a compass or a map, or shoot an azimuth." We told him, "Look, man, you don't know where yer' going'; ferget it. You don't cross creeks at the same place two or three times in a row in 'Nam." So now this old E-6 or 7 lifer started to yell and

mumble, calling us "faggots," and the whole platoon is at a halt, in re-
bellion. "Hey, we don't need this asshole. He doesn't know where we
are, where we're going, what he's doing." All around us is the vast-
ness of the Indochinese jungle.

We were yelling by then, "Forget it, Sarge! Give the platoon to Brackett. He's only been here a month an' he knows what he's doin'." American democracy in action. It happened; he brought up the rear,
threatening, "You young dudes don't know shit. Yer in deep trouble."
When we finally sorted ourselves out and made it back to whatever forgotten NDP or firebase it was, Lieutenant Harr asked around, figured
out the whole scene, and immediately transferred the lifer-sergeant to
another platoon.

While we were humping, it was common for us to hear, "I'm short!,
I'm gonna' get outta here soon!"

One day Gaddy or Shaeffer yells at me, "How ya' doin', Brown? Ya'
still makin' it?"

I replied without thinking, "Twenty-eight days an' a rosey wake-up,
Cherry. Tha's how I'm doin'. I got 337 days in-country man, I kin smell
my freedom bird an' see them round-eyed ladies waitin'."

I kept on humping but I was thinking, "When I leave, what am I gonna'
do? I got over a year left in the Regular Army. I'll never make it back
there. Besides all I care about anymore is these dudes in my company."

The previous month was a weird jumble to me, anyway, like I wasn't
all here mentally. I was just going through the motions of humping,
scared of getting hit, hardly believing I'd made it so far, but proud of
my serving with the best. All of a sudden, I became afraid of leaving
the now-totally-familiar world of 'Nam, and trading it for more than
a year in the stateside army on some "strack" base full of lifers, REMFs,
and MPs. I asked to see Lieutenant Harr, and when I'm sure nobody
else is around listening, I tell him I want to "extend." "I'll do another
six months in the line, Lieutenant, an' then I'll ETS."

"Brown, yer all right an' I'm glad to have you, but are you sure you
wanta do it?"

"Yes, sir, I'm sure. I made up my mind already, I don't wanta leave
the company."

"All right, we gotta resupply chopper comin' in this afternoon. You
get on it and go back to Lai Khe to battalion headquarters and the company, an' see if they'll give you a 'drop' on yer three-year term."

Without telling any of my buddies what was going on, I headed in on the night of August 22nd. At company and battalion headquarters, it was easy. McNeilly tried to talk me out of it, but I went ahead and signed papers extending my tour in Vietnam for six months. In return, I got a guarantee that I would be discharged half a year early.

That night I got very drunk in Lai Khe, going from bar to bar and unit to unit before finally passing out in a bunker. I started in on my binge again around the middle of the next day; I'd gotten hold of some very fine reefer and mixed it with beer. I was in something of a daze, tripping around the battalion hootch area. All of a sudden there was a lot of shuffling and fast movement around me and I heard the words, "It's a call-out! We gotta' reaction mission!"

Here I was on my own, stoned, self-proclaimed vacation, and the next thing I knew there's a captain or major shouting at me, "Who're you, trooper? What are you doin' standin' there like an idiot? The battalion's goin' out right now. They're bringin' all the companies together, and we're headin' for Chon Thanh and Loc Ninh."

His voice echoed at me.

I responded, "Yes, sir. What should I do?"

"Get your gear an' your weapon, soldier, and make it to the strip. You look kind of odd, boy. What's the matter with you?"

I jerked myself up straight, scared, remembering my court martial and thinking of stockades again. "Nothing, sir. I'm just tired from humping, sir. I'm on my way." I saluted, grabbed my rifle and rucksack and headed for the strip.

The airfield was crowded with 1st/16th grunts, but I couldnt' find anyone from Alpha Company. I kept asking, "Where's Alpha, where the hell is Alpha, anybody know?"

Another officer took me in hand, a captain, I think. "I don't know where Alpha is, trooper, but you can stay with us here in Bravo Company. You just fall in with the 1st Platoon over there and when things get sorted out you can rejoin your company. The whole battalion's going into Loc Ninh."

I shuffled over and sat down with his grunts who nodded a little, then mostly stared off blankly, as we all did then. Their faces looked the same as those in my platoon.

Whether we ended up leaving the Lai Khe airstrip in trucks for another strip farther north or in choppers, I'm not sure. The next thing I remember was loading into Hueys in a different place and being told we were going to form a blocking force for the 11th Cav and the 1st of the 2nd Infantry, who were in heavy contact at Loc Ninh. They'd been fighting since the 20th of August.

On the air assault, I couldn't see the main Loc Ninh airstrip or the Special Forces compound, just rubber trees. When we came in, I could see blown-up dirt and shell craters as though the area had been under artillery fire to prep the LZ. We hit the ground running, and the company I was with took the point for the battalion. The recon platoon went off by itself somewhere.

We'd humped forward for about a mile through pretty clean rubber when the point platoon ahead of us opened fire. There was a hold-up for a while, after which we moved ahead out in the open to near the edge of a village. I saw the new colonel then, gesturing and talking to a lieutenant up ahead; he had some of his staff with him. Inside the village was a shot-up bus. We had been told in the briefing that anything in the area was to be considered hostile if it wouldn't stop. The guys on the point had seen the old bus coming out of the village towards them with fifteen or twenty people on it; when they'd ordered it to stop, the bus had started backing up fast. One guy fired a warning burst behind it, but that started a chain reaction of shooting. The windows and sides were all shot to hell but there was no sign of the casualties, like they'd disappeared. It was kind of eerie, like maybe there had been some NVA on it. We never knew.

We'd been hearing rumors of more fighting by the "Black Scarves" of the 1st/2nd near us and in the distance we could hear artillery fire and airstrikes. We kept moving forward through more rubber, and went into a blocking position around the village. For my company it was pretty laid back and low key, spread out on line, waiting for something to happen. I kept asking if any one had heard where Alpha Company was.

"They must be off on their own, man, same as we are in Bravo a lot of times. You jus' gonna hafta sit tight with us an' we'll run into 'em somewhere."

That night we had a resupply come in near where we set up an NDP. The choppers came in until after dark, and one platoon was left to watch the LZ. As the last chopper took off about 9:00 p.m., the NVA opened fire on it with AK-47s when it was about fifty feet in the air. The platoon at the LZ fired back. That's when we knew for sure the enemy was watching us. When the LZ platoon straggled in later, three men were missing. For the rest of the night around the perimeter, people passed questions to find out if they were mixed up in another company. Several times I was asked who I was again, but by now some of the guys in the platoon I was with said, "We know this dude, he's from Alpha. He jus' got screwed up an' separated from 'em."

Early in the morning the recon platoon was sent out to look for the three missing guys and found them on the way to the LZ. They'd spent all night hiding in the bushes, and said that in the middle of the night the NVA had come out all over the LZ and carried off supplies that had been left there in the dark. They had spent hours hiding within fifty feet of instant death, not daring to move. All three of them were new guys in Bravo Company who had just gotten to 'Nam. We knew for sure now the NVA were watching every move we made.

We kept humping that day through rubber trees that got progessively more overgrown and wild, with second-growth bush between. They had me working in a file as a regular rifleman, but I was humping extra ammo for the squad machine-gun. It was raining and nasty that night in the NDP where we set up so tight and close that guys were muttering, "Hey, if the gooks mortar us, we're gonna get wiped out."

The morning of the 27th of August we were low on water with no resupply coming in. When we finally crossed a creek, a good-sized stream, the whole battalion got slowed down and fouled up as everybody broke ranks and lunged around trying to drink and fill canteens. The colonel appeared again, angry at the confusion.

"All right, move out! Move out! There's NVA around, we don't wanta let 'em locate us. Keep moving! Move out!"

Bravo Company had traded off point by now, and we were drag. Up over a hill and a ways further, the long spread-out line of companies suddenly made a right-angle turn up ahead, out of sight.

Also up ahead, some of recon platoon got a flash sighting of three NVA soldiers on their flank and opened fire. The last platoon of Bravo Company came under small arms and 79 grenade fire and Lieutenant Koelsch and four of his men were hit and wounded. The right turn of the line extended file had put the point element's fire straight through the enemy position into the drag. The enemy was shooting in both directions, too, so there had been a cross-fire.

The medic and RTO were hit, so our medic and several others sprinted back to help, followed a little later by the battalion commander trying to see what was happening. I could hear groaning and shouting but I remained squatting down, staring out into the bush and rubber, listening as the reports rippled up the line.

After the dust-off came in and medevaced the wounded out, we kept on humping. Our position was well-known to the enemy now, and we could hear more artillery and airstrikes in the distance. Late that afternoon we came under enemy fire from both sides, AK-47s and RPGs. I returned fire with everyone around me, flattened out on the ground. I could hear shouts of "Medic!" up ahead. We moved our position several times in the dark that night of the 27th, but still kept taking fire and shooting back at unseen NVA. Our only targets were their muzzle flashes and tracers. It was a long, wet, nasty night. By morning we'd had three more GIs from the 1st/16th killed in action and about thirteen more were wounded. For me, it was the crowning touch of my year in 'Nam— here, I'd just extended. I went into a black and sorry mood.

In the earliest dawn of the 28th of August, after the last dust-off had gone, we moved out again. The rest of the operation was like all the others, abandoned enemy bunkers, frantic, yelling officers from battalion, shuffling, snarling GIs. And this was the blocking operation of the 1st/16th to stop the NVA retreating from the Loc Ninh battle zone of August, 1968. Twenty more casualties to add to the list of 200 already hit in the 2nd/11th Cav and 1st/2nd Infantry. The total was twenty-one killed, and about 200 wounded between the 20th and 27th of August. The 7th NVA Division faded temporarily into the bush back into Cambodia again. They were to reappear for another attack soon enough in early September, in the same area.

When we got back in to Lai Khe, the battalion was spread out on ambushes as far south as Di An. I went to the base camp company headquarters hootch and told them what happened to me. The first sergeant just grunted and nodded.

"I guess it don't matter, Brown," he says. "We're gonna have you for a good long while yet. The company's out in the field, anyway; you can go in on a resupply chopper today."

That afternoon, lifting off out of the base camp, I felt sick about going out in the jungle again. I'm suddenly wondering why the hell I never got an "R & R." Those seven days might have been precious, huh? It was about the 1st of September when I got back to Alpha Company's field NDP. I immediately wangled a pass out of our new platoon leader, Lieutenant James Brown. He was a nice squared-away dude who never made any trouble for us. He agreed with my request because I'd never gone on "R & R." I'm supposed to go home on a thirty-day leave soon—"back to the world." I wanted to ease into it a little.

In a few minutes' flight from the field on another resupply chopper, I came from months and months of primitive and savage life to the well-established, even flashy 1st Division base camp at Di An. Here the clean, spit-shined, easy-living REMFs roar past me in their jeeps and trucks, going about their important business (of supporting us). I walk in their dust with my weapons and seventy-five pounds of ammo, rucksack, and gear, and no one offers me a ride. Some turn their faces, having a good laugh at my futile attempts at hitchhiking.

"That's all right, you guilty-ass, chicken-shit REMFs! I know what yer' thinkin', you don't even wanta look a grunt in th'eye. Okay, no sweat at all; I'm totally used to humpin'; I do it all the time fer a livin'."

I just paced myself, slow and steady, and grunt-marched across the entire camp. "Big deal, nice straight, flat road." At the northern gate, I caught a five-ton GI truck joining a column headed towards Lai Khe. I rode in the back where I didn't have to talk to the driver or even look at him. I wanted to look at the gooks and the villages and the jungle; that's my world, anyway. The convoy, guarded by MPs in jeeps with mounted machine-guns and APCs—and me with my '16—ground north along Thunder Road, past Phu Loi and Phu Cuong, with An My, Tan Phu Khan, and Dog Leg unseen but well remembered. We finally hauled into the Lai Khe rubber. I dismounted, straggled through the red dust to the 1st/16th Battalion area, deposited my M-16 and combat gear, took a shower, changed into clean jungle fatigues, and headed for the airstrip.

The same day, I was on a helicopter courier flight coming into Tan San Nhut Airbase. The scene from the air, after so many months in the jungle, was almost unbelievable. An incredible number, thousands of REMF GIs dressed in clean uniforms, boots shiny, surrounded by hundreds of modern buildings. It was like another world. Thousands of tons of supplies, vehicles, and endless rows of aircraft are spread out in every direction. There are even paved concrete runways and roads. Strange how months can become the equivalent of years.

I made my way to downtown Saigon. Modern boulevards clogged with mobs of people of all races, dressed up clean, looked to me like a dream out of the distant past. Clubs, bars, fancy whorehouses, hotels, apartments, houses with courtyards. I felt like Alice's older brother in Wonderland or the Tin Man in Oz. After so many months in the field, the scene, fast and modern, was mind-boggling. All the American "Saigon Warriors" and Vietnamese "Cowboys" were out in force, strutting their stuff, decked out in civilian clothes, doing what they did every night—living it up.

Americans and Vietnamese, Chinese and Cambodians of all sizes, colors, and shapes. A pandemonium of crowds, tinkling music, honking vehicles, oxcarts, beggars, and prostitutes. It seemed almost like the last days of Rome before the barbarians came from the north. Despite my wonder and astonishment at the pageantry, I couldn't help feeling a bitter resentment at the jolliness of it all and had the crazy urge to throw a grenade into the middle of the whole scene. Although clean, my raggedy uniform and red-stained boots gave me away as a grunt-infantryman, an alien in this place. People of all races gave me "that look" but I let it slide. I wasn't naked with my well-stashed Chi-Comm pistol.

I moved along slowly and carefully with my long-accustomed, measured jungle pace. Watching every move of everyone near me, completely alone in the midst of millions. I lit up a really good "Big O" joint from Lai Khe, painted up one side with black opium, and pretty soon I was floating into this hotel-restaurant. Even in my condition I felt cautious, pausing in the doorway, eyeing the polished, noisy bar and crowded tables, finding a corner seat where I can keep my eye on everyone with my back covered. The place was full of gabbling REMF GIs, slickly dressed civilians, and "war correspondents." Fat, juicy food, clinking glasses, real glasses of booze, Oriental hangers-on and lackeys, Viet, Philippine, Japanese, Chinese, all mixed in, predator eyes on their plump, American cherry prey. "What a disgusting joke the whole thing is." I could see through the haze of it all, every profit-grabbing rear-area of every war in history. And once I put it in its place in my mind, I just mumbled, "Fuck it, don't mean nothin'."

I got a steak dinner, some scotch, and pretty soon ended up with a slim, young Vietnamese girl who had singled me out and moved in as company for the night. It was a really nice night and I needed it badly.

Saigon was good all the next day, too, but by that night I was roaring drunk with a bunch of crazy Australian infantrymen in from the field on a stand-down. We ended up in a barroom brawl that turned into a huge street-riot with a gang of slicked up Vietnamese "Cowboys." Those little draft-dodgers and pimps got me from behind, breaking a heavy whiskey bottle over my head and knocking me cold. I came to lying face-down in the street amidst the broken glass. An MP and the Aussies, who had come to my rescue, were shaking me. The rest of that night continued as a wild drunk in their bivouac area. There my last memory was of the Aussies grabbing one of their officers, "a bloody major, no less," who'd tried to discipline them. They tore off his uniform, sprayed him with shaving cream from head to foot before booting him out. This blew my remaining presence of mind and I passed out.

The next day I decided to go to Vung Tau on the South China Sea coast. I wandered around Tan San Nhut Airbase again, trying to find a ride on a chopper. Lost in the maze of the base, I ended up next to a building full of dead American GIs killed in combat all over Vietnam. A conveyor moved the metal coffins along; the sight of this combined with my hangover made me sick. So here I was, talking to GIs whose job it was to load dead American soldiers onto aircraft day after day for a whole year. They were really matter-of-fact about it, and so my mind was blown again. It's a good thing the families of the dead back in the world couldn't witness that scene.

I shared one of my best Lai Khe "Big O' joints with them, talking about my gig for the last year. I told them, "You dudes are looking at one short-time son of a bitch!" One of them, the main-talker, said, "Hey, man, I'm sure glad I didn't end up a grunt in the jungle." I just looked at the guy and replied, "That's all right, man. You probl'y would've made it O.K.; I'm sure glad I ain't doin' yer job." When we were all mellow, they gave me directions on how to find a ride. I waved good-bye and went shuffling off, mumbling to myself about, "Weird, crazy 'Nam, again! Primitive jungle warfare kills us and twentieth-century American technological marvels picks up the bloody pieces just a few miles away."

Quicker than I can think about it, I'm flying down the snaky-brown rivers to the South China Sea, white sandy beaches, jungled hills and mountains to the north, and the old French town of Cap St. Jacque, or Vung Tau, with colonial-looking villas and courtyards, a fleet of fishing boats and sampans.

I register at the R & R Center, but now that I'm here I don't know what I want. I wander down to the sea wall and the beach. Smoking a pipe of dew, I let the ocean's immensity calm me and reflect on this longest year of my life. Out of the corner of my eye, I see two mean-looking Viet Cowboys, tinhorn-looking hoods, sneaking up behind me. I had already spotted a nice-looking length of rusty metal pipe and was measuring my lean-grab-and-swing time. Suddenly a sharp, authoritative woman's voice came from a pretty young Vietnamese girl on the road behind. The two little dinks slinked away, heads down, like beaten dogs.

"Well, that's kind of far out," I thought. She came over next to me, smiling, looking really fresh and fine. She sat on the seawall, asked me where I'm from, what I've been doing with my time in her country. I tell her, short and simple, and she asked if I'm lonely and need some company. She was soft and kind-looking and asked me if I needed a good place to stay. This was too much, and I asked her, "How much?" She didn't answer but got up and left. I follow her like a puppy. She didn't look back but headed into a nearby nice stone villa surrounded by a walled garden.

Inside, I sat down on a couch with one other American, a young brother who looked tremendously peaceful. I asked him, "What's the catch here, man?" And he looks at me and said, "There ain't one, man. They're jus' nice, an' it's nice to be nice." I said, "How long you been here, Bro?" He stared at me a little while and responded, "A long, long time, man." I still didn't know what was happening, but I decided to go with the flow.

In the other room I sat by my pretty girl as two older men, Chinese-Vietnamese looking, played some kind of Oriental game at a couch-table, discussing business at the same time. "Probably some big-time smuggling deal." I thought to myself, but I didn't really care. The girl brought me some kind of delicious pudding in a bowl and an iced drink. I'm still wary, suspicious, expecting to be poisoned or kidnapped, but "I ain't got nothing to steal and I'd make a lousy prisoner." So I decided again to myself that I don't care about anything—"just ride it out."

Later, when everyone started to go off to sleep in different rooms like some big family, my girl took me to a private room with a big, soft bed. I lay down and she undressed me gently, then went over and locked the door, making sure I saw her do it. This Vietnamese girl looked part-French. She had known war, she knew where I'm coming from, but why was it all so nice, so genuine? She seemed to understand everything, to anticipate my jungle fear and instincts. She shared it all with me and we melted into each other, off to some dream-world, beyond Vietnam to eternity.

For several days and nights I stayed there with her; nobody ever asked me for anything, and she gave me everything they had. It was my nicest experience with the Vietnamese people, and I kept asking myself, "Why?" over and over. I especially remembered the way that nothing was "Americanized" about the household. And the two or three American soldiers staying there had been in country a long time and were completley adaptable to anything.

Then one day I felt my buddies calling to me from somewhere out in the jungle. I was wondering how they were doing, and if they were getting hit. I could have stayed in that house and gone to work at whatever it was they did and deserted, but that was never in me. I was still part of my platoon-company-battalion—a soldier. I said my sad goodbyes and went my way.

Years and years later, after the fall of South Vietnam to the Communist Army in 1975, I found myself wondering what had happened to them. Whenever I heard about "forced labor re-education camps" or "millions of terrified refugees putting to sea" or "marching overland towards the sanctuary of Thailand," I thought of my Vung Tau family. To all the self-righteous antiwar radicals who helped shut down the war, those millions of panicked human beings, escaping any way they could, through every kind of danger, were just another vague statistic. Or maybe "all reactionaries" or "all Catholics" or "all bourgeois class" or some other convenient label. They're real enough to me, and I can still see those huge teeming camps of thousands of refugees lining the roads, living under sheets of tin, pieces of cardboard, or 105mm ammo boxes. They were waiting for the war to end, but they were not fleeing their own country en masse as they did later under the Communists. I decided that my Vung Tau friends must have escaped with "boat people" on the fishing fleet. I pray for her that they did, and that they made it safely through the Communists, pirate ambushes, and refugee camps to a sanctuary in America, where so many others have found a haven.

Then it was back on the magic-carpet ride of choppers across Vietnam, back to the rainy, red dirt of Lai Khe. I picked up my rucksack, web gear, and M-16 and went back out to the field. The torn-up earth of the NDPs and firebases looked the same, our artillery still blasting away into the jungle; the enemy still out there with his rockets and mortars and waiting ambushes.

I went on one more combat patrol with Lieutenant Brown, Sergeant Norris, Garza, Brackett, Barnett, Gaddy, Sellman, Shaeffer, Robby, Bro-Brown, Shot, Owens, Joe, Mallicote, Pancho Carrera, and the rest. I can't remember when and where Lieutenant Harr got shot and wounded, now or before or after? When or where Mallet set off a booby trap that blew off his feet. At about this time, we were told the entire 1st Battalion/16th Infantry was being transferred to the 9th Infantry Division in the Mekong Delta and traded for a track-mechanized infantry unit; our name would be changed to the 5th Battalion/60th Infantry. The idea of leaving the Big Red One and our AO both made me uneasy. I was going through a strange melangé of feelings, fear of death in combat—but at the same time not caring anymore; not wanting to leave my buddies, my company, and battalion home while they were heading into new dangers—but wanting a break. I resigned myself to leaving for a while and coming back.

About this time we heard the uproar over the Soviet tank invasion of Czechoslovakia to end the movement toward autonomy, the brutal repression by our arch-enemy of a glimmer of democracy. It caused barely a stir of interest or conversation. It all seemed so far away and so unreal. The news of frontier fighting between the Russians and Communist Chinese along the Manchurian border is a little more interesting. The approaching presidential election did cause some curiosity because all the politicians were talking about "ending the war." We heard that Richard Nixon was to be the Republican candidate and Hubert Humphrey the Democratic candidate. The news is broadcast to the troops about the demonstrations against the war and rioting by student radicals at the Democratic convention in Chicago. In news reports we see color pictures of them charging police, waving Viet Cong flags. One of the radical leaders at the scene trying to stir up the crowd is Tom Hayden from Students for a Democratic Society. It sounds like the protesters' idea was to disrupt the convention so that no reasonable response is possible from the Democratic politicians. The police of Chicago reportedly went berserk as police had four months before at Columbia University. News media accounts that received the greatest coverage came from columnists consistently critical of the war effort like Tom Wicker of the *New York Times* who wrote that the rioters were kids "that did not threaten law and order" and sermonized about "Mayor Daley's brute policemen clubbing down American youngsters." The reports just make most of us feel even more bitter and cutoff from home. What we GIs didn't know at the time was that Tom Hayden was an old ally of the North Vietnamese. He had first traveled to Hanoi in 1965 to meet with the Communists. Accompanying him was a Marxist professor from Yale University, Staughton Lynd, and a Communist teacher, Herbert Aptheker. It was after their return unprosecuted for dealing with a battlefield enemy, that Harrison Salisbury of the *New York Times* went to Hanoi, joining up with the Australian Communist "journalist" Wilfred Burchett. The combination of their writings, given wide exposure by the U.S. media was to have a profoundly negative influence on the American effort in Vietnam.

Hayden returned to North Vietnam a second time with SDS leader Nick Egleston, and David Dellinger, who was to become head of the "Mobilization" to end the war, and who was also editor of the pro-Communist "Liberation New Service" circulated on American college campuses. These sympathetic pilgrimages to the enemy resulted in further meetings between larger groups of pro-enemy American radicals in Cuba and Yugoslavia during 1967 and 1968. Cadre of the Viet Cong traveled to those locations to discuss coordinating strategy of radical street action to support the Viet Cong in America. The Communists would end up owing a lot to the "Tom Haydens" of the United States.

We tore up our last NDP and LZ, flying into Lai Khe from the field in choppers about the 10th of September. The battalion was packing, up for the move, and I didn't even care that I was going home. Instead, I felt that I was leaving my home. The same day that the company was hauled down to Dong Tam on the Mekong River, I was left at the Lai Khe airstrip with only seven more days in country. There I was put on a detail helping load supplies on choppers heading for Loc Ninh.

There was heavy fighting going on up there, a continuation of the August Third Offensive. The same day the battalion was airlifted south, I heard reports from pilots while working as an extra hand loading ammmo and rations. "The whole area is a madhouse, there's gooks around the Special Forces compound and anti aircraft fire." I worked and lived a few days at the airstrip before I "disappeared-myself." The 1st/2nd and 1st/28th and our sister battalion, the 2nd/16th were all fighting. A hundred and fifty more GIs were killed and wounded, making a total of 400 American casualties in the Loc Ninh battle area since we'd taken part in late August. After unloading three dead GIs in body bags from one chopper, I ran into a dude I'd known in Phu Loi from the Aerial Rifle Platoon of the 1/4 Cav who told me that the 1st Division Commander, Major-General Keith L. Ware, had just been killed in the battle along with seven other men, including the sergeant-major of the Division. The grunts were saying the tail boom of his chopper had been shot off by a burst of heavy machine-gun fire from the NVA position, causing it to crash. I remembered when he'd become the division commander after the Tet Offensive and when he'd come in on our Song Bé operation in July. He was about the only general whose name I ever heard grunts mention without scorn. He wasn't a stiff, strutting type; he'd started out as a private in World War II; the word had spread through the grunt grapevine that he was decent and polite around his fighting men. It figured he'd be the one killed, according to grunt logic. After this, I wandered around Lai Khe and ended up at the memorial service for General Ware and the others in the chopper. At the 1st Division Chapel under the rubber trees, where inside was another symbolic row of helmets and boots. I stood in the crowd, staring at the cluster of high-ranking mourners, including General Creighton Abrams, the Commander of all U.S. Forces in Vietnam, thinking, "Anybody can get it sooner or later around here."

A few more days of chopper details after that one last reminder of the consequences of war, and my 365 days were almost up. Finally, I was on another helicopter, heading south this time.

On the 20th of September my time was up and I was at Bien Hoa again. At the airfield, boarding the big jet, I stared with the other veterans at the big load of new cherries just unloaded for their tour in 'Nam to begin. I remembered so clearly my own arrival such a long time before. Some of the dudes going home were yelling catcalls at them. I didn't feel like it myself, I was thinking that many of them would be killed and wounded over the coming months, and anyway I knew I was coming back.

I noticed the men like myself wearing the Combat Infantry Badge found each other and clustered together. It was a genuine identification, more than medal ribbons which might or might not mean proof of real heroism. It's a sterling silver infantry musket against a blue infantry background surrounded by a silver oak wreath, symbolizing combat. It meant something to most of the grunts who wore it. You had to serve in line infantry in combat a specified time to earn one. In the U.S. Army, one automatically eyes the left chest pocket of a soldier to see if he's wearing one.

I stood among the rest of the surviving grunt infantrymen, eyeballing any Vietnamese I saw, close or far, feeling naked without my M-16. I couldn't keep my eyes still, they jerked around anytime a fast move was made near me. It was the first time in a whole year of tension and war danger that I and the other combat veterans around me were completely unarmed. All our lives were in the hands of REMF guards around us, and I didn't like it.

Finally, on that jet home, hour after hour across the Pacific I kept earphones on, listening to the "Sounds of Silence" over and over and staring at the incredibly lovely round-eyed, blonde stewardess. Because I was a little loaded, she looked to me like a goddess from heaven or a mirage. The REMFs returning home were yelling or jabbering their puppyshit "war stories." The grunts, including me, who had actually seen something of the real thing, were mostly quiet or barely mumbling. Most of the line-dogs could still not believe that the plane would ever get there without falling out of the sky. The strange quiet-relaxation of my nerves was like a forgotten face coming back from long ago. "God, it's been a long year."

The beautiful coast of California came into view to a loud cheer from all the men. The low, grassy mountains and timbered stands of redwoods or the beaches of the Pacific never looked the same to me again after that yearlong war trip across the ocean. Those of us who were there and "saw the elephant" know what America is. We landed at Travis Air Force Base. After the trip to Oakland Army Terminal, we were given new dress uniforms and sent on our way. I don't know what any of us expected as a homecoming welcome, but it certainly wasn't what we did get.

In what felt to us like a space age San Francisco airport, I had my first ugly incident with "long hairs," student radicals.

Coming through the entrance we passed through a chanting crowd of them, with signs and posters. One proclaimed, "Stop the genocide in Vietnam"; another said "The American war machine is slaughtering innocent villagers." We walked stiffly by, burned brown by the tropical sun, hair-trigger taut from surviving so many ambushes and rocket attacks, thin and tight from humping in the jungle for months on light rations. The protestors glared at us and muttered to each other just loud enough for us to hear, "Baby killers, murdering GIs" but avoided our eyes as they spoke and looked up again after each slur, to judge the effect, seeing how far they could go. My blood began to boil, they wanted to insult us, challenge us from the safe position of student deferment in their mob numbers, knowing they had police protection. The same police they were calling pigs would protect them if we moved in and attacked.

One carried a Viet Cong flag with the hated star on it. I thought of all those who had died fighting against that symbol of Communism while these individuals abused the freedom and liberty we had gone to Vietnam to defend.

It was a measure of our self-control and discipline learned in a year of jungle fighting that nothing happened. But it started a "recurring solution dream'' for me. To this day, when I am confronted with unreasonable actions or hatred, I dream of throwing a hand grenade with a fast follow-up burst of automatic rifle fire. I can't shake it even now— fifteen years later. Like a million other veterans, I've kept this temptation under control, and it has subsided a lot.

A returning combat veteran has highly-tuned senses, watches every face, doesn't miss a thing. Out of hundreds and hundreds of people, I passed in streets and airports, the first person I saw to actually look in my eyes and really smile at me was a hungry-looking hippie girl in Dallas, Texas, on a stopover. The rest avoided my eyes or did worse. It was becoming obvious very quickly on my way home across the country that what we had suspected out in the field was only too true. The country as a whole was either ignoring the war, putting it out of their minds, or were violently opposed to it. The emphasis in the news media on the ''overwhelming American technological superiority'' versus the ''poor peasant-revolutionary'' had a wide effect, visible everywhere. The antiwar journalists that constantly reiterated this theme never seemed to consider that using the most power possible in combat saves your own soldiers' lives.

At my parents, house, ''home,'' everything seemed anticlimactic. No one in the neighborhood seemed to notice that I had made it home alive except people in my immediate family. Even with them, I felt like there was an unbridged gap that none of them understood. I knew that I wasn't done anyway; I was going back. At first, I hadn't even told my parents this, but gradually it came out. I was unable to explain why and hardly tried. What is duty? What is commitment to a cause? What is loyalty to buddies that goes beyond fear of death? I didn't know nor had I ever tried to understand those things; yet they had been growing in me over the past year despite my loss of illusions and bitterness.

My father asked me very little about my actual combat experiences. He seemed more concerned with my lowly position.

''Why aren't you interested in leadership, John? You have the brains, you should live up to your family tradition.''

I could hardly answer him in English. ''Leadership, huh, what do you think being in combat over in Vietnam is?'' I'm shit-laughing now, reverting back to being a grunt quickly. ''Out on the point, leading the whole platoon forward into AK-47 automatic fire; leadership, huh? In an undeclared war nobody wants, huh? What for?'' I gave up on my family and almost stopped speaking to them.

I had a feeling that it was going to be up to the soldiers to finish the job the politicians had started. In October of '68 I still expected a change in U.S. strategy that would lead us to a victory in the name of all the GIs sacrificed thus far. Staying away from my parents' house, I gravitated towards the hangouts of my teen years in civilian clothes sometimes, at other times in uniform to invite dialog.

"You've been in Vietnam? Yer crazy ta' go there when ya don't have to. It's easy ta' get outta goin. If ya don't get a student deferment, all ya' have to do is claim you can't control yer bladder or ya got a bad back or pretend you've got mental problems."

"Why the hell go to Vietnam and fight for the big bankers and politicians? You're being used over there and, besides, the Viet Cong are gonna win."

"Man, I heard you guys get some really good dope over there, but that ain't enough for me. I believe in peace and love; I'm against all war."

I gravitated towards that group of old friends that exists in every home neighborhood of every combat soldier in Vietnam. Those who believed in the old tradition of service. I started hearing right away about other guys from my high school getting shot up in 'Nam: Jerry Lyfred, Ricky Gallagher, Jerry Anderson, Harold Baker, and others. A lot of other buddies were overseas in the service. The college boys and preppies, and Ivy Leaguers weren't doing it at all. The record of non service in combat for the privileged of Harvard, Princeton, or Yale speaks for itself. Aside from a few rare and outstanding exceptions this crowd felt that they were too valuable, too important to do their time. It made joining the "antiwar movement" a very convenient and timely thing to do. Taking time off from regular activities for an occasional demonstration perhaps made them feel better about their privileged-class student deferments. Many of those I talked to used their own guilt to condemn soldiers who were doing their time, calling us as a group, "tools of the reactionary-facist rulers." I was astonished at how widespread this radical opinion had become.

As I made the "required" family visits, I felt like a zoo animal. Out of my whole extended family, cousins, etc., most of whom went to private schools or were in colleges somewhere, none served in combat in Vietnam. It opened a gap for me that had been widening all my life. I sat in their hollow houses for long minutes. There was so much inside me bursting to come out; ghosts, screams, rows of enemy and American corpses, and the knowledge that it was still going on; and I wasn't finished, I was going back over. I looked into all their eyes, everyone, and saw nothing.

I sat in my childhood room staring at the walls, mumbling to myself, reliving the past year, day by day. At night came the nightmares of bullets that don't miss, orange-blue-white RPG explosions, screams, bloody human bodies.

At a family meal I stared at the faces, heard the little endless complaints about meaningless crap. I felt so different, so old, the familiar things so empty. It seemed that the only people I cared about were over in the jungle and the real world was over there. It was merely another side of "weird, crazy 'Nam," a feeling completely unexplainable to others. Their many cars, suburban houses, lawnmowers, banks, shopping centers, laundromats, and business as usual, put me in a rage. It seemed as though the whole country or at least everyone I met wanted to forget about the Vietnam War, not hear about it, or were chanting slogans supporting the enemy. Meanwhile, the war was going right on, that day, full-blast. I became convinced that we were going to end up pulling out with nothing gained. The American people weren't sharing in the burden of war at all, just the combat soldiers and their immediate families. It had turned into primarily a working-class war. Many of the more privileged were trying to ignore it or were blatantly rejecting or disregarding the sacrifices of our fighting men.

The politicans and bureaucrats in power, like Johnson, McNamara, Bundy, Clifford, Rusk, and Rostow, who had rammed us into it with their "think tanks" and intellectualized theories about mechanical-electrical barriers through the jungle, were backing off or resigning, now. Double-talking, lying, crying, covering up, not supporting the military leaders on the field of battle. The enemy knew already that they had won, not on the battlefield, but in Washington, D.C., in the quiet, dignified polished offices of "gentlemen"; the same offices Lincoln had sat in unbroken after Fredericksburg and Chancellorsville.

For my part, I got sick of it all so fast, I voluntarily cut my leave short and reported back to Fort Dix early. I wanted to go back to my company. I'd had another premonition; I could feel they were getting hit. I felt a deep dread at returning and an uneasiness that it wasn't going to ever turn into a clear victory. Still it felt natural to be going back to my grunt-buddies, to me the best and toughest of my generation of Americans. I could feel the warm mud, smell the jungle and palm trees, the incense in the temples. In a dreamlike vision, an old Vietnamese man, smiled toothlessly. With his wispy white beard and creased and worn skin, seemed to be beckoning me.

With hundreds of other men going back over, most of them probably as weird and full of contradictions as I was, I waited for available aircraft space. We jumped and stomped in the October-morning cold in our tropical khaki.

Then a fat little lifer-sergeant called out my name from a long roster:
BROWN, JOHN M.G.
RA 11860370   E-4
Co. A 5th Battalion/60th Infantry
9th Infantry Division

11   Back In 'Nam

"Starkly I return to stare
upon the ash of all
I burned."
— *Wilfred Owen*

Flying in the transport loaded with GIs, many of them returning for a second tour, we soon passed through the great time warp of 1968: New Jersey to Vietnam. Cool, crisp fall colors to rich, stinking, after-the-rainy-season jungle smells. "'Nam again."

The noisy, crowded American base at Bien Hoa allowed little or no time for me to reflect on why I was back. I was too soon caught up in the day-to-day events. As soon as my feet hit the dirt of Indochina again, I had a sinking, sick feeling. The sound of jet fighter-bombers taking off snapped my mind into thinking about airstrikes, close-support, fire-fights, the enemy. All around were crowds of REMF GIs and officers—their spit-shined boots and clean, pressed "jungle uniforms" caused my mind to drift to dirty, sweat-stained, mud-covered grunts, out beyond this island of comfort in every direction, protecting these people, unseen.

Loading up and roaring along in a convoy to Long Binh for in-processing triggered flashback memories for me—all the events of the past year rushing by. "The goddamn place looks exactly the same—same little hootch-shacks, same smoky fires, same refugees, same mud." I thought. "Something like 80,000 more U.S. casualties since I first saw this place and nothin' different." After the in-processing was over, I wandered over to the sandbag bunker I had left from a few weeks before. I had a little dew stashed here and I wanted to get with myself, to think about why I was back, and look at the stars. The little bag was all wet and ruined from the monsoon rains running down between the sandbags. Sitting disgustedly on the bunker, I watched the activity, especially the hundreds of new cherries wandering around, talking loudly about how "bad" they were or wondering aloud where they were going. It made me shit-laugh or what you might call an almost smirking-snarl. "The stupid insane futility of it all; well, at least there ain't no incoming mortars."

After a while this brother comes diddy-bopping along with a big, mean-looking German shepherd. I recognized him right away. He was a dude from the 35th Scout Dog Platoon with whom we'd worked on operations up north in the Red One.

"Far out!" He recognized me, too, and slid on over, doing me a dap and "What's happenin'?"

I told him my stash got wet, and he grinned and pulled out a big "O number," lit up, and we got really loaded. He was going home: he'd made it to his date and could hardly believe it. I was thinking to myself, "Yeah, man, I'm sure glad. I hope that the same old black ghetto back there don't bum you out too bad!" But I didn't say it because he was so happy to be going back to the world. We sat together a long time, a little quiet rapping, mostly silent, watching the new dudes, thinking how much some of them were going to learn and see, how some of them were already doomed, destined for a body bag or hospital.

He finally drifted off to a hootch to crash, but his big war dog who'd been through so much with him sat alert for hours afterwards outside the door where his master slept. I finally fell asleep outside on top of the bunker under the stars, wondering what fate had for me. I felt a premonition again that my company was getting hit.

The next day I rode on another convoy to Di An to collect my records from the 1st Infantry Division. There at the airstrip looking for a chopper ride south, I ran into my old Hawaiian friend, Olly Alexandros, from the Phu Loi Recon.

"Hey, hey, my man! How you doin'?" We were glad to see each other alive and had a quick reunion and exchange of news. He was flying as a helicopter gunner to finish up his second tour and was totally sick of the whole thing. He told me about another rifleman in the Phu Loi Recon platoon getting killed in an ambush in August: "His name was Constantine, man, he was a new guy, never hadda chance." We said our quick Vietnam-type "good-byes" and "good lucks," and a word or two each remembering our dead brother Earl. I walked away thinking,

"Yeah, man, you must have been as crazy as me; you came back, too."
It made me feel as though I'd joined some weird, exclusive club.

That same day I was on a chopper myself flying down over the huge, sprawling mess of Saigon and out into the flat, water-covered Mekong Delta to Don Tam, base camp for the 9th Infantry Division on the Mekong River. Circling over the camp, I had a good view of the huge river, or rather one branch of it, with U.S. Navy ships, LSTs, gunboats, and the mass of Army equipment. I thought, "Yeah, this is definitely different," everything in every direction in the distance looked like a gigantic swamp; the Florida Everglades, the lower Mississippi, and the Yukon Delta all put together. They had told us at Lai Khe that we were going "to ride around on Navy boats" for our new operations, but none of us grunts had believed it. It turned to be no longer true after my return there'd been some of it, though, while I was on leave.

After hitting the strip in Dong Tam, I just stood still for awhile, smelling the air deeply and looking around.

"A new AO, huh, the dirty Delta"

I'd heard nothing but bad about it since I'd been in 'Nam. Horrible terrain to hump in, millions of Vietnamese, the densest population in the country, and a lot of Viet Cong—real Viet Cong who came from the villages, hamlets, rice paddy farms, and bush all around, supplied and reinforced by North Vietnamese, but still a lot of mean-ass guerillas who knew their own home country better than just-arrived NVA.

While I had been on leave back in the world, I had done a lot of reading on the history and politics of Vietnam to try to understand it better. How the war had gone on for thirty years, how old a dream the unification of the country was in the minds of many Viets. Why the antiwar movement back home was so opposed to what we were doing. I tried to put it all together with what I'd seen and experienced myself. I had learned that the major uprisings against the French in 1930 and 1940 and the nine years of war from '45 to '54 had taken place in the main population center of the Delta, and that the American presence in this war was small there.

The only U.S. division in the Delta was the 9th and most of the time it usually only covered a few provinces in an arc south of Saigon and was mighty busy with that. My experiences in and around the villages of Binh Duong Province and the Iron Triangle had already showed me what to expect in this area.

"How the hell can they ever deal with the thousands of square miles and millions of people left over?'' I asked myself again. ''If we're over here, fighting the Communists and saving this country and its people, how come they support and hide these Viet Cong in their hamlets and homes?'' It couldn't be explained simply by fear of VC terrorism, although that happened often enough. The combination of American ground-and air-power along with the operations of the South Vietnamese produced more death and destruction than the enemy. Even as a patriotic veteran American soldier, I could see this everywhere I'd been. Our own worst enemy was our frustration at the endlessness of it all because of our attempt at ''limited war.'' It played right into the VC's hands, reinforcing their propoganda everytime we roughed up the people, burned or bombed a hamlet, or shot up a village during or after a firefight. It put our fighting men on almost the same level as theirs, and these same people had seen the French do their damndest and leave in defeat.

It seemed to me that the politicians and bureaucrats who had put us in there and tied our hands strategically had failed us in knowing nothing about the history of the country or the scope and scale of the operations required to control it and win a victory. It wasn't the generals or the soldiers who were to blame for the complexities of the problem. They had only been asked, ''Can you do it?'' and, yes, it could be done with enough men, maybe millions. Defense and State Department officials under President Johnson had never allowed the total destruction of North Vietnam, the source of Communist weapons and ammunition in the south. The millions of tons of ordnance exploded on the enemy homeland had never been permitted to hit the vast dyke system of the Red River Valley to flood the main population center. The cities of an enemy who was killing our soldiers were never saturation-bombed and destroyed as German and Japanese cities had been. The people who had put us there—the politicians, the State Department technicians, bureaucrats and Defense Department planners—were to me the ones responsible for the deaths of thousands of GIs. And to this day they have never shared the burden, championed the cause of, or even acknowledged the victims of their failure.

I humped my way across the muddy dirt of Dong Tam until I found the new hootches of the 5th Battalion/60th Infantry. Searching out Alpha Company, I found the makeshift hootch that passed for an orderly room and went in.

There sat McNeilly, our clerk from Lai Khe. He stared at me a second like I was a ghost, then jumped up saying, ''Hey, Brown, yer back, huh? How ya' doin'?''

"I forgot for a minute whether you'd got hit or gone on leave."

"I been on leave, man. I been up in Bien Hoa, Long Binh, an Di An th' last couple of days. What's happenin'?''

He gave me that weird stare again.

"While you was up there, man, jus' two days ago the Company was gettin' hit bad. It was about fifteen miles up the Mekong an' north into the Plain of Reeds beyond Cai Lay. It started on the 18th an' there was grunt companies from our battalion an' the 6th/31st both. About forty GIs hit total, an' somethin' like 150 VC killed. We captured hundreds of A.K. 47's, too. In Alpha Company we have three more guys killed an' fourteen more wounded''.

I felt a sickness rise in me. My premonition had been right. I felt a huge guilt sweep over me because I hadn't been there. I mumbled, "Who got killed, man?''

"Larry Bennett, Randy Welch, and Pete Norris just got killed on the 19th. You been gone 30 days, man. Sheeit, there's been about thirty killed and wounded in Alpha Company since then. Our good luck finally ran out!''

I sat down a minute, taking it in. "Norris! Otis 'Pete' Norris.'' His smiling face was before me like a ghost. McNeilly was rattling off names now, one after another. Gaddy, Mallicote, Bergy, Brackett, on and on. I kept thinking, "Goddamn, I was right up in Bien Hoa that day, just a few miles away. I guess I'd 'a been hit, too. I guess I'm gonna get it sooner or later now that I'm back."

McNeilly was going on about another firefight two weeks before at My Phuoc Tay on the 4th and 5th of October. Another eight or ten dudes in the company, with a total of twenty-six GIs hit in that one. He was saying, "There's been almost a hundred killed and wounded in the battalion jus' in the last few weeks, man. Why the hell did you come back?''

I'm looking at him, through him, past his clerk-desk, out through the window to the blue Indochinese sky.

"I don't know why I'm back, man. I guess I'm dinky-dau, huh, Mac-Neilly?'' There's been a kind of refrain in my mind with all the names: "Carry it on, carry it on.'' Maybe that's why I'm back, to make sure all these thousands of GI didn't get shot up for nothin', but I know I'm crazy now. Right now I was learning a lesson, but it was very, very late.

"I shoulda' never come back, Jesus Christ! It's gonna go on forever here anyway.''

The old bitterness about the irony and futility of Vietnam came over me again, as I remembered what I'd seen of people back in the States.

"Well, damn it, MacNeilly, I'm back in th' company anyway. Let's go get right."

We blanked out together and almost started crying over the bowl as he told me everything. I suddenly heaved myself into motion and drifted over to draw my weapon, my M-16 rifle. I got my magazines and sat down to check their spring tension and load each one of them. I field-stripped my rifle and checked it out; it looked good. Then I got into a faded and worn jungle fatigue uniform with nothing on it but the "Bloody Asshole" patch of the 9th Division on one shoulder. The "Old Reliable" Division, the Army called it, commanded by General Julian Ewell. I got all the rest of my gear, packed my rucksack carefully, and was ready to go.

MacNeilly showed me where my platoon hootch was, so I went over and dropped my gear in a pile on an empty rack. The place was like any hootch in 'Nam, but right now it was echoing to me. I went out the back to the latrine. Black, oily smoke was drifting up, off behind it where some old papa-sans and mama-sans were burning human excrement with diesel fuel. I looked at these Vietnamese, thinking, "What goes on in yer heads, gooks?? Burning American GI shit?? Do you all hate us, every single one of you, behind those blank looks you always shine on yer faces?" Old papa san just stares up for a second, old, lined face, blank eyes that have seen everything. He's nodding, almost to himself, almost imperceptibly; but it's an answer anyway.

"Yeah, I know, old man, you either do hate us and are gathering VC information today or yer so far-gone you don't give a damn about anything anymore."

I'm now really thinking about Vietnam. I sit down in the shithouse and roll a number, mumbling to myself, "Back in the stinkin', 'Nam again, all right." Duncan came in, tall, handsome black dude. I've humped a many a mile with him.

"What's the score, man?"

Duncan looks at me. He looks old and tired. "I'm through, Brown, my man. It's too true. I'm headin' back t' the world. I've fuckin' had it."

I said, "How is it here, man, in the Delta?"

He looked at me a long minute and said "It's the pits, man. It's worse than the worst, an' there it is."

I was thinking, "An' he'll never be the same dude he was."

Duncan was a guy who hardly ever talked in all the months I'd known him, but we were still all in it together, depending on each other every day. I said my empty-sounding good-byes and he shuffled off, lost in his dreams, but changed forever by this place, like all of us.

Next I saw a few more short-timers doing their last few days in 'Nam out of the field, building new hootches for the company. They were all serious and worn-out looking, with no joking or grunt-talkin' going on at all. That night in the platoon hootch, I was jumped out of my sleep by a tremendous explosion nearby, with shrapnel ripping through the walls. It was a Soviet 122mm rocket, and they were *whooshing* in and *crack-booming* all through the base camp. It was 3:30 in the morning on the 21st of October. I scrabbled around the floor in the dark towards the door and the cover of the nearest bunker, and bumped into a new guy. It was our new platoon medic going out to replace the last one hit on the 19th. I'm thinking to myself, "I'm back alright, GIs out around here gettin' blown up, killed, and wounded. Goddamn, hope I make it, this next while."

The enemy rockets kept exploding, GIs were running, and screaming. U.S. artillery opened fire back at "suspected positions." I spent the next couple of hours filling in our new medic on Vietnam, and what to expect out in the field. He seemed to be really cool and unruffled for his first time under fire.

"Maybe he just don't know enough to be scared yet."

It's sad to think now he was destined to stop a bullet in about four weeks. The rest of that night I slept inside a sandbag bunker, worrying as I nodded off about whether I was going to make it through another tour.

Early that morning the remainder of the company not already back in the field pulled out before I could visit any of my old buddies. I finished my in-processing and got my orders about 9:30.

I climbed up on the second convoy of the day, loaded with ammunition and supplies, heading out to Fire Support Base Moore, where the battalion was headquartered in the field. Riding along in the guarded convoy with other dudes heading back, we broke into the "recombined milk" in cartons stacked up high because it was so cold. I couldn't figure out where it was going, maybe the artillery; I'd never seen it out in the field before. We all shared a nice pipe roaring down those dirt roads through Dinh Tuong Province, not giving a damn.

Passing through larger villages we would slow way down, and the mobs of hundreds of refugee kids and women would run along-side of the convoy trucks, begging their hands out. We'd throw out the unwanted parts of the C-rations to them, watching them fight over the canned "lima beans and mother fuckers." Some of the dudes would wind up a can and let go a real speedball, trying to nail one of them in the head, hard. Some of the little kids had blond hair or black skin, little half-Americans. I'd just stare at them.

Up along the Mekong on those dusty roads, speeding along past endless, swampy rice paddies, lines of jungle, little silent hamlets, not thinking about anything, just "kings for the day." We didn't know nothin' about the Ben Tre uprising by the first Viet Cong in 1960 right near here when a hundred or so old French rifles were captured from the government and passed out to other Viet Cong. The same Ben Tre that had been deliberately distorted in our news media as "destroyed" by Americans to "save it" nine months ago during Tet. We didn't know nothin' about Tran Van Tra, leader of all the military Viet Cong in South Vietnam, who was born in this province of My Tho-Dinh Tuong in 1918. He had been fighting, and leading his fellow Communist and Nationalist rebels since 1939, before any of us were born. His battle was a lifelong fight that he and his comrades would never give up. To us they were just faceless dinks.

None of us had ever heard of Pham Hung, either, head of the Communist Party's Central office for South Vietnam (COSVN) after 1967; born right across the river from Vinh Long on the Mekong; and if we had, we probably would've just said, "Another stinkin' gook. We'll grease his ass, too, one of these days!" How could we know he was a founding-member of the Communist party in 1930 when most of our fathers were young, had taken part in the first uprising against the French in 1930, been arrested in 1931 in My Tho, and imprisoned on Con Son Island until 1945.

What did we know about any of it? Nothin'. Just that our country was fighting here for some reason and we had to do our jobs.

"Put in our years in the service."

Ton Duc Thang, born in Long Xuyen in the Mekong Delta was the man who succeded Ho Chi Minh as president. Nguyen Huu Tho, also born in Vinh Long, became in 1980 acting president of the "United Socialist Republic of Vietnam," after a lifetime of involvement with all the struggles of his country. On and on this list could go, and each of the provinces around here had hundreds of thousands of people, innumerable thousands of hamlets, villages, farms, all with a hatred and distrust of foreigners going back to the Viet Minh and before, back a hundred years or maybe a thousand.

12   Dinh Tuong Province

*If we have to fight we will fight, you
will kill ten of our men and we will
kill one of yours; in the end it will
be you who will tire of it.*
—Ho Chi Minh
(to the French 1946)

The convoy pulled into the sandbag bunkers of Fire
Support Base Moore. Batteries of U.S. artillery were firing H & I as
we stopped in a cloud of dust. It was the 22nd of October, 1968. I shuffled around in my field gear and rucksack with my rifle in hand until
I found my company area. The only man I recognized was Jan Yupcavage from the mortar platoon.

"How you doin', Brown?? I thought maybe you was dead er
wounded."

"Where's everybody at, man?" I asked.

"Oh, they're jus' layin' around here hidin' from the lifers an' sleepin'.
There's supposed to be an' ambush tonight and a patrol tomorrow."

An artillery howitzer let go with a *KA-BOOM* right over our heads.

"Goddamn, I'm outta shape. I gotta ease back inta' this place."

"Come on inta' our bunker, man, they'll get ya' right," Jan said. They
were sandbag shacks really, made out of empty mortar and 105 shell
boxes, covered with a layer of sandbags to protect them from incoming
rockets. A bunch of old buddies were packing a pipe and telling war
stories. Most mortar platoons in 'Nam were salted with ex-grunts who
knew there was a better thing than constant humping. I was getting back
into 'Nam with these brothers of mine. I stared at their sweaty, familiar faces, their dirty, raggedy uniforms, the jungle sores on their hands—
and I felt like I was home.

"Goddamn, I'm glad to be back in the company. It's like my family now."

Everybody was telling me what they knew. All I heard about the Delta in that bunker was water, mud, slime, and more water. Flat, flooded rice paddies with bad cover; rivers, tributaries, canals, streams, and swamp-jungles for the gooks to hide in. The whole area was so full of Viets that you never knew who was the enemy or where. Much more constant contact with the mass of Vietnamese people and, of course, the Viet Cong, reinforced with some NVA out of the "Parrot's Beak," but mostly indigenous to the Delta. Here the enemy was more constantly active, in smaller groups, but hitting all the time. A place of constant fear for American troops, sniping, booby traps, and mines, ambushes coming one after the other, combined with the endlessly wet, swampy, miserable terrain.

It seemed as though the bunker was full to bursting with bad talk and thoughts, and smoke. A feeling of claustrophobia forced me away from the crowd of grunts in there and out into the bright sun and hustling work of the camp. The artillery dudes were busily humping ammo, as they did all the time; some combat engineers were messing around with their heavy equipment. I decided to walk around the circumference of the place. Climbing up on the high berm that had been pushed up all around the bunker line by the engineers, I strolled along from bunker to bunker, surveying my home. All around the defenses was clear land with rice paddies, full from the eight-month-long rainy season, still being tended by farmers despite the endless war going on. In three directions, signs of villages and hootches were evident, partly out of sight. A track led to the main dirt road that wound its way through hamlets and farms to the big town of My Tho, several miles away. The rear of the camp faced wild-looking country to the north, overgrown and marshy all the way to the infamous Plain of Reeds, an old guerilla hideout since the days of the Vietminh and the French. This swamp-jungle led in turn to the Parrot's Beak, an outhrust portion of the Cambodian border and a notorious enemy sanctuary. It was out in this direction around Cay Lay that the battalion had been sent on the 18th and 19th and had run into the Viet Cong.

The camp itself was one of the best I'd seen in 'Nam for a field position. I guess it had been occupied by artillery batteries and armored units a long time; I don't know. The dense population of the Delta called for more static positions than the empty wilderness areas farther north, where the enemy could disappear entirely or move around more. •

There were the usual tracked APCs with mounted .50 caliber machine guns and M-60s of the 2nd/47th Mechanized Infantry to control the roads, besides the artillery and engineers and, of course, leg-infantry grunts like us to hump the boonies. Coming back to the bunkers of the company area, I ran right into a lifer, who caught me.

"You! Yeah, you trooper! Git over here! Who the fuck are you?"

I shuffled to the dude. He was an E-7 or E-8—master sergeant. Probably some REMF from company or Battalion headquarters, I thought.

"I'm Brown, Sarge. I jus' got back off leave. I jus' pulled in onna' convoy. I'm from Alpha since June.

"Yer going out on OP, Brown. Right now. Bravo's out there on a patrol." He pointed to the south. "They're only about two thousand meters out an' they're callin' in gook sign. I gotta 'nother shit-bird like you who needs somethin' to do. I already saddled him with a PRC-25. You go on out through the wire about five hundred meters to that clump of palms, get set up an' call in. There's gooks around and you'll be between the perimeter wire and Bravo, so watch yer asses."

He stared at me with his beady eyes until I said, "Okay, Sarge, no sweat."

He put me together with the other dude who was a new guy I didn't recognize. He told me our call sign and when to communicate, and we headed out through the wire gate.

The dudes on bunker guard were grinning as we passed.

"Messed up, huh? Got caught by that old son-of-a-bitch doin' nothin', huh?"

We moved south of the perimeter about half a kilometer with our rifles loaded and locked. The new guy humping the radio was eyeballing everything I did. He looked scared.

I told him, "It's O.K., man, you'll get used to it, jus' do everything I do an' exactly what I say, an' it's no sweat." He nodded at me, still looking nervous, sweating under the radio-ruck. All I had was about twenty magazines in bandoliers, some frag grenades, and my poncho liner. We got set up where they wanted us and called in a communication check to the CP, "OP Six, all quiet." or something like that.

I rigged up my camouflage poncho liner to make a sun shade hootch with branches. I lay down and stared out across the marshes and paddies towards where Bravo Company was out beyond sight, about fifteen hundred meters away.

The hours went by slowly. The dude with me was telling me that

Charlie Company had been out today already and had come under VC mortar fire, with one guy hit and dusted-off.

Alpha was still sliding because of our losses in the battle on the 18th and 19th.

Vietnamese women and kids started easing up around us, kind of shy at first, then bolder.

"Hey, GI, you wanna fuck my sistah? She numbah one boom-boom. She no got clap."

I motioned them away but they kept pushing. Getting too close. I got that hemmed-in-by-gooks feeling all of a sudden and jerked up my rifle, snapping the safety to full automatic. Every goddamn one of them knew what that was. They backed up quickly, muttering, "Cheap GI, numbah 10." I motioned them with my rifle to keep moving.

The new guy was eyeballing me. "You always do that to 'em, man?" he asked.

"Yeah, yer damn right I do; little bastards might have a frag grenade. An' if they don't, I don't want 'em around me anyway. I don't fuck' em anymore, I don't trust 'em anymore, I don't like 'em anymore. I been here a long goddamn time an' I'm still alive."

So pretty soon this new guy asked me, "What's it like, man? What's it like in a battle or a firefight with the VC?"

I was kind of shit-smiling to myself remembering when I asked that same question about a thousand years ago of Earl and Baca. Then I quit smirking, remembering that Earl had been shot dead and Baca wounded. I looked over at the dude and said, "It ain't nothin', man, it's jus' you an' them. You gotta see 'em first and shoot 'em first, that's the secret."

Late in the afternoon the CP of the company called to our OP.

"You close up yer OP an' come on in, there's VC around. Ambushes goin' out pretty quick."

The new guy was staring at me as I snatched our gear together and told him to "move out!" I kept my rifle pointing out, safety off, 'til we got close to the wire and yelled out, "OP 6 comin' in!"

I headed to our platoon area and finally started running into some of my main men that I'd missed in Dong Tam.

The first person I saw was Robby, our big, black soul-gunner up at Song Be.

He shuffled up to me, not bouncing as he walked, the way he always used to. He acted as though I'd never been gone, didn't ask where I'd been or nothin'. I was mind-tripping on when Earl came back from leave after Tan Phu Khan.

Robby just said, "Brown! Hey, man! Hey, I gotta get outta heah. M'numbah's up." His face, once so full and always smiling, was haggard-looking and marked with a fear that anyone could see. "That las' firefight done did me in, man. I'se had it. It ain't my wah' no moh. It a white man wah! I been learnin' from Cannady. I'm all through, I had enough! Why we ovah heah?" he asked in his soft black Georgia drawl.

We were behind a bunker sharing a smoke now. I passed him a hit and said, "Here ya' go, Robby, my man. I don't know why we're here, an' I don't know why I'm back here. Must be crazy, dinky-dau, I guess. Couldn't do no time back in the world. Now I wish to God I wasn't back, man, but I'll cover yer ass if we get inta some more shit."

He sat down in the dirt in his muddy, sweat-stained jungle fatigues, mumbling, looking around, telling me the last firefight on the 19th was some "baad, baad shit."

"Hey, it's only three days since we got outta that goddamn Cai Lay place with seventeen dudes hit. We was pinned down all night an' we couldn't leave cause Welch's body was layin' out in front a us an' we had ta get' im back. Now they stick us right back out here again an' I'se gettin' scared, man." Here he was a brave dude, too. I knew Robby; I could depend on this dude. He was my bro—I wasn't just "chuck" to him, and he was really shook, which shook me even more.

I started up and dapped his hand and shuffled over to the platoon CP. The artillery was firing again, booming and crashing, probably at nothing. I found Brackett there. Sergeant Herman Brackett, who'd only been in 'Nam about three months but was a No. 1 dude who'd already seen plenty.

"Hey, Brackett, ever since I got back yesterday they been tellin' me about the last battle," I said.

"Yeah, Brown, hey, it was a son-of-a-bitch. I'm glad to have ya back. We're gettin' a whole bunch of cherries to work in. I guess ya heard about the firefight on the 5th, too, huh?"

I said, "Yeah, man, I sure was sorry to hear about Norris, Welch, and Bennett, and all the other dudes. I heard you got hit, too."

"Yeah, well, it wasn't bad, they just patched up an' shipped me right back. Gaddy's gonna be O.K., too. He should be back any day now from the hospital. It wasn't our old Welch, the coal miner, who got killed—

it was a new guy named Randy Welch.

Brackett didn't ask me why I was back, either, just said, "We're goin' out again tonight. I'll let ya' know when we gotta saddle up."

I just smiled and said, "O.K., Brackett. I don't know why I'm back here, but I'll do my time."

I saw some of the CP group and stopped to visit with John Shaeffer to hear the news. Lieutenant Harr was long gone, having been wounded and medevaced to Hawaii. A long time later I saw the name Captain Gerry Harr on the Vietnam Memorial Wall, killed in action 1971. I could only hope he hadn't gone back again. The CO was Lieutenant James Brown who'd given me my in-country R&R back in September. John Shaeffer was now his main RTO. He'd been humping a long time and was tight buddies with Mike Sellman and me. Other guys in the CP group were FOs, RTOs, and a medic; also Bartel, Wilson, Novak, Mackechnie, and Evans, all of whom I'd gotten to know after the Song Be operation.

The next dude I ran into was Joe, our "Polack" machine-gunner. He was as tough as always, shit-laughing a little, cleaning his M-60. "I'm gonna make it, man, no sweat. Jus' keep my fuckin' head down, know what I mean?" He was telling me about how Mallicote was hit and about "Doc," our medic. He told me, "Brackett and Barnett really got their shit together in that firefight on the 19th; they're pretty good dudes fer sergeants."

So I saw the guys who were left, one by one, and some of them asked me about "the world." I told them what I'd seen and felt back there. Several of them told me we'd just gotten a new Ell Tee platoon leader, saying, "He's weird."

Brackett came by and said we were going out on another operation and probably staying out for a while.

"Get yer gear ready!"

Everyone made a mad rush for the ration cases they dumped down and tried to get as many cans of fruit or other good stuff as possible. Since the 9th Division was skimpy with cigarette rations to the grunts, we had to barter and trade the little C-packs of those with the dudes who didn't smoke. I cleaned my rifle and rechecked the ammo loads in all my magazines, my grenades, canteens, and everything else, making sure everything was tight and quiet.

Most of the men were now lying in the dirt in any shade they could find, trying to get some sleep. At about dusk, we were told to "Saddle up! Get it on!'' The new lieutenant gave us a short briefing. It was simple; several days of patrols and nights of ambushes. Then he came over to me to introduce himself, having gotten the word that I was a "madman" who had done a whole tour and come back for more.

I didn't have any trouble relating to the dude; I'd seen a lot of guys come and go in the last year. I had already found out some of the dudes in the platoon didn't like him.

"He ain't nothin' like Lieutenant Harr or even Lieutenant Brown, man. He's kinda belligerent an' he's always sayin' his old man's a general or somethin'."

I figured I'd wait and see about the man, myself.

We walked on out a little later, diddy-bopping along 'til we hit those bottomless marshes and paddies. We headed by the compass for our destination like a boat at sea. The water and muck came up to our knees and thighs alternately, and the deep mud gripped our boots, almost tearing them off. The slowest walking became an extreme effort. No wonder the Vietnamese ran around barefoot half the time. The usual grunt talk disappeared quickly, "Save yer breath." We humped for thousands of meters through this, changing our course occasionally, looking and acting like a long, sinuous snake in a sea of watery mud. We knew full well that every Vietnamese for miles around was charting our course, reporting it to the Viet Cong and laughing over hot rice, in warm, dry hootches as we set out to ambush them.

The lunacy finally stopped near a shot-up abandoned Viet Cong village that still had a few Communist flags with the yellow star nailed on trees. It was in an overgrown bamboo and bush area where we quietly set up our ambush, assigned LPs, and as usual, the old dudes tried to get some sleep, while the new guys stayed up, wide-eyed for hours. I taught a few brand-new cherries how to make a nice bed out of palm fronds and straw, which'll dry you out by morning. I slept, but the tension was back in me now, full-alert even in sleep, weapon ready, tight against my body, ready for the slightest bad sound.

I didn't know where the other platoons were around us that night, but later the next day we were operating in unison, searching for enemy signs. The day for me was a long blur of suffering and dragging my way through the swamps. I was completely out of shape from a month back in the world, and I'd forgotten what the word "hump" meant.

We were still only two clicks from Firebase Moore at six in the late afternooon when suddenly a huge explosion erupted in the midst of our

CP group.

KA-WHOOOM! Mud, laterite, and shrapnel flying. Screams, "Ahhhh. Oh, Jesus, I'm hit. Unnnnggggh!"

Brackett was yelling, "Spread it out! Spread it out, an' get down!"

I ran forward a few feet, flopped down, stuck my rifle out to the flank with the safety off and waited, jerking my eyes back and forth from our casualties to the woodline.

The screaming continued, and medics were running to the scene from the other platoons. I heard the words "Booby trap mine, maybe command-detonated, keep yer eyes open." I could see frantic movement behind me in the area of the explosion. I closed my eyes and tried to shut out the thought that kept surfacing.

"Ya' shoulda jus' stayed back home, man; this is jus' the beginning."

When Brackett came slogging back to our area behind me I shouted at him:

"Who got hit?? Who got hit??"

He told me, "Lieutenant Brown is hit, man—pretty bad. They think it was command-detonated. Shaeffer got hit, too, and Bartel, Novak, Wilson, Evans, and Mackechnie!"

"God almighty," I'm thinking. "Shaeffer! John Shaeffer and Lieutenant James Brown." Their faces came to me, the miles and miles we'd humped together. The sudden blast, the shock. I'd seen it all before.

I could see dudes behind me dragging the bodies towards the dust-off chopper that was coming in now. I kept thinking, "Why them instead of me or any of the rest of us?"

"What about it, man, how bad is Ell Tee Brown and Shaeffer and Bartel an' them other dudes hit?"

Brackett just kind of looked off towards the jungle, with a "thousand yard stare."

"I think Ell Tee Brown's gonna lose his left leg. Shaeffer'll probably be okay. He got hit by shrapnel in the back and legs. Keith Evans, Ben Wilson, and Mackechnie all took shrapnel but I think they'll be okay, too. I don't think Bartel or Novak are going to make it." Norman Bartel, of Berwyn, Illinois, died of wounds on 25 October and Michael Novak, from Grand Blanc, Michigan, died on the 27th of October.

We slogged back into the firebase after the dust-off was complete, but later that night our platoon at least was sent out again on an ambush in the area. As I lay on a bed of palm leaves again in the slimy, muddy dark, I kept thinking, "Twenty-five guys hit in Alpha Company in the las' five days, man, that's like 25 percent casualties. I'm gonna haf' ta be very cool an' very careful ta get outta here alive.''

Early in the morning of the 24th of October, with the hot Delta sun burning off the wet chill, we broke up the ambush and set out on a long "clover leaf" of the area—a patrol. Brackett whispered that he wanted me to be point-man, as we thought there was enemy around. It sounded too quiet, no birds or any kind of noises. I muttered to myself, "Fuck it, gotta do my time anyway." I stepped out quietly through a big hedge-row and instantly came under enemy rifle fire. *Pop! Pop! Pop! Craack! Craack!* I was already down, rolling over and over, continuous movement, bringing my M-16 up on full-automatic, finger on the trigger, squeezing.

Then Brackett hisses, "Don't fire. Don't give our position away!" *Pop! Craack—Ping!*

I mumbled to myself, "I don't need no firefight right now, anyway."

We hugged the ground, weapons out and ready. No more enemy fire. I'm sweating, "Those bullets hit damn close to my face!" We stared out into the silent jungle, completely quiet for maybe ten minutes, then I heard, "Go ahead." I led out again, the silence so loud you could grab it. I could hear my heart thumping, expecting every second those cracking AK bullets to cut loose. Nothing. They were just feeling us out, letting us know we were had or trying to knock off a point-man real easy. I let my breath go. We went out and around about a hundred meters, found nothing; I'm trying to figure out this Mekong Delta area, point-man now.

We kept on marching, humping, sweating, aiming for some objective that none of us were told about. It was the 25th of October. Alpha was down to eighty-four men "paddy strength," grunts actually out fighting, including several new replacements and myself.

At about one in the afternoon we came under enemy fire from AK-47s—automatic and about six RPG rounds blew up around us; I don't think anyone was hit. We were shooting back now, putting out a heavy fire and moving forward again. The RTO called in our location as ''in the vicinity of XS 296485.'' The fighting broke out again at about four in the afternoon. We were in contact with an estimated platoon of Viet Cong who were setting up to ambush our company, but got their surprise party blown apart.

I was competely back in 'Nam again by then, rolling, dodging, and shooting like a machine. By six we had three Vietcong bodies and one prisoner, all in web gear, one or two AK-47s, some Chi-comm grenades, and a couple of heavy blood trails from a gook machine-gun position we'd smoked. We heard from the RTO that the ARVNs just to the south of us were receiving heavy fire from the same retreating enemy force, and one U.S. advisor was shot twice in the side, "severely wounded." Still, it was a little payback for us, a small part of a big score to be settled.

The next day, after humping for about four or five hours, when we're all just about worn out, somebody yelled, "Freeze! Fuckin' booby traps!" We started to look around us real careful, and see them: grenades rigged to wires strung around the ground through the bush about knee high. That afternoon an engineer near us tripped one that blew up, wounding himself.

Humping and splashing through the slime again, eyes alert, rifle ready, my mind keeps wandering back to those last three dead bodies, bullet holes dripping blood, the grimaces and open, staring eyes. How casual we all are to it; except maybe the new guys. To those dead enemy, it's the end of any dreams of future or family or any reason for fighting. To the lifers in the rear who are always demanding them, it's "three confirmed kills and one POW for Alpha Co., 5th/60th." For us, it's almost nothing; just shooting quicker, straighter, and move ahead on towards another nothing.

Days and nights of marching, tense ambushes, wet and slimy, covered with mud, constant sniping by the Viet Cong; harassment by our battalion officers soon put me in the same depression as everyone else. If we were out in the open when they shot at us, we would open fire back, not knowing if we hit them. If we had good cover and figured that they couldn't really see us, but were just shooting at our sound, we'd try to hold our fire and wait it out. The morale was bad anyway, though. Despite our casualties, which should have mitigated their conduct towards petty details, high ranking brass were messing with us all the time, adding harassment to the horrible terrain we had to work in.

We got a new company commander, Captain Alan Anderson, from Florida. The rumor was that he was a "Strak" Airborne Ranger, and we all watched him closely for a while. He turned out good, though; he never bothered us, did his job, and humped the bush with us.

Two of my buddies, Gaddy and little "Shot" Shotkowsky, came back about then, and I was glad to see them. Gaddy had been wounded the second time in the firefight in which my man Otis Norris got killed. "Shot" had been in the hospital, too. Shot had only been in 'Nam a couple of months but he sure was different, old-looking. We all aged quickly out there in the bush. We laughed together about how I had regaled him with war stories when he first hit the country. Bergy was back, too, after being wounded; a solid dude you could depend on. It seems funny now to think how old and strong we all thought we looked; we must've looked like kids to the old lifers, averaging about nineteen.

Truby Gaddy, from North Carolina, was still one of my number-one buddies, sharing a little dew now, which he hadn't done for a while. He was still quiet, tough, and taciturn, as always. Looking at his lean, sunburned and hawk-eyed face, with a stubble of a beard, I thought, "Jesus, we've humped a lot of miles together!" I used to think about how his Rebel ancestors had given us Yankees a hell of a fight. Knowing him, I could see how and why. We sat together cross-legged in the dirt, sharing a smoke and talking after he got back. My new buddy "Pete" Norris had been killed right next to Gaddy in the firefight, shot through the mouth and out the back of the neck.

Gaddy said, "Bravo was already in contact an' takin' casualties when we went into the LZ. We fought all night long on the 18th and 19th, and were trying to reach this shot-down chopper with a dude pinned under it. Welch was KIA out in front of us. We was tryin' to reach his body. Norris was brave. He was jus' doin' what you or me would've wanted done fer us. We overran a VC hospital and a lot of gooks that day, too."

Gaddy introduced me to Milton "Greek" Galimatakis while we were sitting there.

"Hey, Brown, this is one of the guys from 1st Platoon who came in the same time as Norris; we call him th' 'Greek legend' now."

I said, "Hey, how ya' doin', dude?" He was kind of short and dark-haired. He looked up.

"Yeah, I went through AIT with Norris before he became our NCO. He was a good man. He used ta always tell me, "Greek, yer gonna be the proudest PFC in the U.S. Army; you'll get used ta humpin.' ''

Gaddy looked at Greek and told me, "He's kinda small, so instead a' given him a big load, they give him a bag full of a twenty-four grenades. They came in real handy after we overrun that bunker complex aroun' the VC hospital. There was VC inside 'em still hidin' an' shootin an' ol' Greek jus' kept heavin' in grenades an' blowin' 'em ta hell. The only time he fucked up was after a gook threw a grenade back out, Greek got kinda excited an' whipped out a C-ration can a' turkey loaf an' threw it in by mistake th' nex' time." Greek muttered now,

"Goddam VC musta been hungry; they kep' it."

Greek started trailing off in this talking again about "Pete" Norris, and I wanted to quit thinking about it. It reminded me of too many times, from the last mine explosion all the way back to Tet.

It made me sad to talk about Norris, Bennet, Bartel, Novak, Welch, and all the other dudes who were gone. Brought back too many other faces and memories.

Gaddy wanted "to get off the line, get back to my old lady alive." He sounded desperate—like Robby. I was saddened, sorrier than ever that I'd come back to witness more of it all.

"Fuck it," I said to myself. "I'll help out if I can, the next time the heat comes down, do my time, get out of here, be done with it all."

I was telling Gaddy how that mine that blew up the CP group was a "big, bad nasty thing, command-detonated, guys just blown away." I told him how I'd come back to the company the day before it happened. I was remembering other mines now, other times. And Lieutenant Brown and the medic and Shaeffer hit, Bartel and Novak killed, and three other dudes hit; it adds up. Shaeffer had just written to us from Hawaii, saying he was with his girl friend now, messed up, but he was going to make it. Sellman, my old tunnel-ratting, smoking companion, was now the senior RTO carrying the company commander's radio in the bush. I hardly ever saw him anymore except back at the fire support base, where we had some good visits. He was really happy to be getting short, next to go off the line in maybe a month and a half. I stuck with Gaddy, Brown from Chicago, who was still making it, Joe the Polack, Shot, Brackett, Robby, Pancho Carrera, Bergy, Welch, and a few other good dudes. We had a couple of new guys who were turning out all right, Winters and Reising. Winters was a rifleman and Reising had an M-79 "pig" in my fire team.

In the present push we tried to keep up constant pressure on the Viet Cong in the area, making light contact with snipers that sometimes turned into small shootouts. Most of the time we didn't know what casualties we inflicted on them. Every incident, though, made each of us a little better at jumping, dodging, rolling, and returning fire. Day after day in the little 3rd Brigade AO in which our battalion was operating, the casualties of GIs killed and wounded continued to mount.

On a day patrol near an NDP we came under enemy sniper fire again. It was the 29th of October but where I don't know. When the bullets started cracking and whizzing in, I dropped-rolled to cover against a berm, and opened fire at the enemy position in one motion. For another of those moments, there was the sound of everybody shooting a long *RRRPPP*, like someone tearing a giant piece of heavy canvas. When the shooting stopped momentarily, I heard the shout of "Medic!" back in the rear of the column, followed by "Two guys hit!" It's Robby, my Georgia bro and Cannady, who were close together during the shooting. The medic was running to them as a couple of more sniper rounds snapped in over us.

Robby's wound wasn't too bad, but Cannady's leg is all shot up, bones smashed, blood spurting; we have to put on a tourniquet. Cannady, the proud black nationalist, the dude who told us he was a No. 1 "minor league baseball player, heading for the big time when I get outta' this stinkin' place!" We call in a medevac, and two more guys have left our lives: Robby, one of the top dudes of the platoon, one of the best, whether the KKK hiding behind their robes back in the world care to know or not.

Occasionally, instead of the endless marching, we'd ride on APCs or tanks of the 2nd/47th Mech Infantry or the 3rd/5th Armored Cavalry—we never knew which. On one armored road convoy at about the end of October, we got hit by ambush fire from the right flank in the dusk out of some hamlet. Automatic weapons hit us first, followed by heavier machine-guns. When the incoming rounds started cracking and beowing, ricocheting off the tracks around us, we opened fire with such intensity into those hootches and buildings that they finally burst into flames from our concentration of tracer bullets. All enemy fire ceased and the burning lit up the night sky. We kept clanking along on those tracks. Some other grunt next to me was saying, "Goddamn, that's pretty, ain't it, man?" Nobody around me checked the place out for dead gooks; it was just destroyed. We definitely got some. I don't know what American casualties there might have been; I was just shooting and keeping an eye on the guys from my own APC.

We hardly gave a thought that it was probably a hamlet of people that the Viet Cong wanted to teach a lesson to for not cooperating with them by opening fire on us. I can't remember how many of us were moving on those tracks now, but I was thinking, "Well, hell, we just made some more Viet Cong in that place, if any of 'em are still alive there."

Most of the time we just kept humping the bush in the old infantry way. The heat was so bad in this country and with the horrible, flooded terrain, you would think you just couldn't make it. I saw guys in the company, who had never complained before, fall down gasping. We all broke out in running sores and had malarial-type fevers and shakes. We tried to take our malaria pills every day, but if the medic ran out or you missed a day, you might just get it. If we all got worn out at once and collectively decided to take a little break on a long patrol, we'd try and find some little island-type patch of bush or jungle in the middle of all that water to collapse in. Well, like as not when you crashed down it would be in a huge nest of biting piss-ants. They'd spread all over your body under your uniform in a split-second, like a cascade of burning fire. Whoever hit them would put on a hell of a show, rolling around screaming, tearing off the clothes, throwing away weapon and bandoliers, clawing frantically at the insects. Just another added attraction of the country.

And all the time when we were humping the bush, "outside the wire," was the fear and constant hair-trigger tension. It became an endless burden, part of our gear or ammo we humped on our backs. After a long, long time of that wired-out, ready-to-shoot feeling for hundreds of days, thousands of hours, hundreds of thousands of minutes, it just becomes you, part of you forever.

Years and years later, it is still in me, lurking just under the surface. It has caused me to do some rash and violent things later on in life. I've spent fifteen years concealing it, controlling it, trying to channel it into useful forward motion, in living. I see it around me in the other combat veterans with whom I've come in contact. The psychiatrists are calling it by a name now: "post-traumatic stress disorders."

The days went on, but we often marched all night, too, through seas of mud and water to surround villages in the earliest morning hours, when the Viet Cong guerrillas were supposedly there and could be caught visiting family, recruiting new soldiers, collecting rations. There were nights of constant high tension, bullets cracking out of the darkness at us, near battles, with shells exploding around us when we called in barrages of artillery to wipe out the harassers. We became like walking dead men, too tired to care about anything.

I remember one dusk, we were slogging through another rice paddy, afraid to file along the berms and dikes because of booby traps or mines. We came under sniper fire first, then some automatic weapons—AK-47s. They were hitting close, the bullets spurting around us in the water or thudding into the mud banks.

"No way out of it."

I opened fire with my rifle at enemy muzzle flashes; "Aim low, grazing fire, make the sons-of-bitches duck!'' I was crouching behind a dike with the rest of my squad when I suddenly felt so tired and worn out I didn't care anymore. I just slipped down in the muddy water and fell sound asleep, the VC fire still ricocheting around. Gaddy crawled over to see if I'm hit, he shook me and I woke up with a start, still holding my rifle in firing position. We were pulling back to a dirt road and down the other side of it for better defense.

''Damn, I'm sure glad they didn't just forget and leave me!''

We scrabbled over and hid behind the berm, shooting semi-automatic back and forth with the dinks 'til I had a pretty good scattering of shells on my right in the mud ejected out of the rifle, sparkling in the starlight. Goddamned if I didn't fall asleep again, the bullets still *spanging* off the hard surface of the road in front of me. A hell of a shape to be in. And in this manner, the battalion suffered a steady trickle of GI casualties, killed and wounded.

It seemed that with our physical exhaustion we were getting a little more careless about the usual safety precautions, but our luck was holding up pretty good. We constantly had casualties around us, firefights and ambushes, but other than a few wounded, our platoon hadn't hit any really bad time. I remember especially my crazy-bro Owens, who could be anything he wanted to be, getting hit in the arm by a sniper bullet, and going to a hospital for a while, but I don't remember where or when. No-big-thing, he got his ''heart'' and came back O.K.

We suddenly went back to the great glittering American base camp at Dong Tam. Our ''leaders,'' whom we never see in the bush, thought we needed a little rest. A day or two, if we're lucky. We washed off the dirt and some of the memories, getting drunk or stoned or both. Some of us sat and stared at nothing, others stayed high or read a book—each according to his own need. Some old faces came back to cheer us up by still being part of our lives. I sat with my ''intellectual'' friend, MacNeilly, the clerk, getting loaded for a while, then drifted down to play with the pet monkey at 3rd Platoon and the mongoose another housecat dude had. I always loved animals; they aren't as devious and complicated as people.

The nights are so soft and beautiful here; you can get lost in the eternity of the stars for hours. You feel your smallness and weakness, your alliance with death seems not so bad. You know deep in your soul after months of combat that there is a God. He has taken you by His hand here and is leading you ''through the valley of the shadow of Death'' everyday. You know in your heart that if He allows us these Vietnams, this is just a testing ground for something far more beautiful, whether He takes your young soul in death like some of your buddies or leaves you to live as a witness for a while.

I knew then deep inside me that I should never have come back over, but perhaps it was my fate to need to learn more, to go all the way to man's roots.

We roared out of the base on a guarded convoy again. To keep us in the field, there are hundreds and thousands of REMFS in the camp, a ratio of ten of them for every one of us. They would stop along the roads, lean against their comfortable hootches, motor pools, shops, and supply depots. They were all watching us as we went by standing up in the trucks in our wild combination of bristling weapons and ammo bandoliers and belts and strange, raggedy uniforms with loaded equipment. Some of us wear head-bands, scarfs, bush hats, weird token necklaces or peace-sign good-luck medals. We shout obscenities at them that some of us mean and others don't. It doesn't matter, anyway. It's all just a fleeting instant in history; but for a minute we're happy because we're proud. We know our toughness and strength. Each of us has been tested in his own way and has made it through. We are the cream of the crop, "the kings." We are all fiercely individualistic, but to the rest of the U.S. Army we are "them," "the grunts," the infantry.

Out through the wire, past sleepy-looking MPs guarding the gate and checking the day passes of Vietnamese workers. The cops straightened up a little as we rumbled past, nodding with a grudging touch of respect. Down those hot, dirty, dusty roads again, the guarded convoy thundered through the silent, little hamlets. In the bigger villages mobs of kids ran along beside us screaming, "G.I. No. 1, give me chop-chop!" Some of us threw Cs at them, and they leaped all over one another, fighting over our unwanted junk and garbage. For me it's all a bad dream, going back to Phu Loi and Tan Phu Khan.

"Sorry stupid 'Nam again!"

We passed the sandbag forts of the ARVNs and Ruff-Puffs, looking like something out of an old Foreign Legion movie. The Vietnamese soldiers lined the barbed-wire fences they were so afraid of leaving, cheering and waving their newly-issued U.S. M-16 rifles to show us how equal they were, "like brothers to us." The same M-16s that ended up being captured by the Communists a few years later and were shipped to terrorists and revolutionaries all over the world.

At F.S.B. Moore, the drudgery started again; we were right back to being "dirty grunts." The endless marching patrols and night ambushes seemed like they had never broken off for a couple of days.

Eventually I became kind of crazy, as though the past thirteen months were all catching up with me at once. Whenever I wasn't the point-man, I would go way out on the flank alone. Nobody at platoon or company gave me any trouble, because after all, I was serving as a scout. I was performing a useful function—at least I'd draw enemy fire. I'd wander way off sometimes, entering hootches, leaving my rifle in doorways (within arm's reach) as though I trust the Vietnamese, sharing meals with them and sipping tea. I mixed up C-rats with rice, fish and Nuoc-man, making good stews with the mama-sans. The Viets and the dudes in my company both thought I was a little flipped out but I didn't care. I just smoked some smoke and sipped gook booze when I got the chance, and I was always tricky-trotting around somewhere, keeping the company's position fixed in my mind.

We continued the weird night marches, endlessly wet, cold at night, boiling hot in the daytime. We piled up dripping muck and buffalo dung in a mound to lie on when we get a chance to rest. By the time we wake up, we have sunken back down into the watery marshes and leeches up to six inches long have fastened themselves all over our bodies under our uniforms, sucking blood. The biggest, fattest leeches I ever saw were in the Delta. All around, after a slime-sleep, soaking wet, muddy dudes are saying, "Jesus Christ! Look at this huge filthy thing; he's just swollen with my blood!" or "Hey, man, can you get that son-of-a-bitch out of my ass? He's jammed up in there, I can't see 'm." We burn them off with glowing cigarettes because we're out of bug juice again to drop on the bastards. We tell the new guys, "You pull them off like that man, 'yer just gonna' get another big jungle sore from the head ripping off inside ya'."

Everyone had running sores, ulcers, big dripping or scabbing infections, feet swelling or rotting, hair itching or burning, eyes running or ears ringing, or some damn thing. I ended up with amoebic dysentery, hookworms, and malarial-type chills and fevers, too. We drew together closer for comfort and consolation, mumbling to each other, "Grit yer teeth, man, an' do yer fuckin' time."

The colonels and majors, themselves pressured by the Generals, were always pushing us, driving us by radio.

"Move out, get your young asses goin', find those gooks!"

They were clean and fresh back there in the TOC or riding around in choppers way above us in the cool wind. They talked to reporters like they shared it all with us, or cared about us, but it was bullshit. They were just after a name for themselves—more rank and medals—while there's a "war on." Sometimes one of their type might get hit in a chopper or from a gook mortar coming into the camp, but they're clean and rested; and they betrayed us that way. Right about this time, we got the news that the colonel commanding the 5th or the 60th Infantry was awarded the "Silver Star for Heroism." So was the 3rd Brigade commander for the same reason on the same day.

"Well, hmmm."

We shit-laughed and smirked a little to each other, heaved ourselves up out of the slime, moved out again.

In a sudden contrast, we're marching through fine woods, no swamps, vines, or thorns, almost like a park back home. We came to a large clean-looking village. We knew it was there long before we saw it by the burning wood smell of cooking fires and the scent of temple incense, dogs barking, the sound of people. Some of these large villages had stone, brick, or cement buildings, too, besides the usual straw ones. Occasionally we even searched two-story wooden warehouses and stores.

Maybe this one's a Viet Cong village? What the hell is a VC village, aren't they all? We set up in a little overgrown bush area, after searching a few houses and buildings half-heartedly. The lifers aren't watching our company too close today. The dudes were lying around in their gear, eating some C-rations, and I had another one of my urges to wander. I noticed a long, mysterious-looking building in a tall grove of palm trees about a hundred meters away. I slung my rifle and shuffled on over to see it all alone, having a feeling there was something inside to see. As I entered, I immediately found myself surrounded by dozens of beautifully carved and painted statues. It was an especially fine temple, more cared-for than usual. I suddenly felt like putting my rifle down in the presence of such ageless devotion, so I did so by the door.

The altar's beauty was spacing me out and drawing me towards it. The sacred scrolls and documents around and under it looked centuries old. They gave off a feeling of peace and safety by just being intact. In the back was a cluster of monks in colored robes impassively staring at me. As I moved to the side in a dim corner, one statue stopped me. It was a group of four beautifully carved figures of men: one yellow, one white, one black, and one red. They seemed to be getting along pretty well together, too. I studied them for a few long moments in the dim light, and an old monk came foward slowly and stood beside me quietly. We didn't speak each other's langauge well enough to talk, but it didn't matter. Together we stared at it and felt its universal message. Then some dude from my platoon yelled "Brown!" outside. The spell was broken. I backed up, grabbed my rifle, and headed outside to join the file moving out.

On November 1, 1968, we received word that President Johnson had halted any further bombing of the remainder of North Vietnam. There was more talk of "negotiations," and of ending the war. I felt as if I'd been literally kicked in the face. It was the final betrayal to me, and a bitter feeling spread through the infantry around me fighting the war.

"They think that's gonna slow down the VC an' the NVA? Hah! The damn fools."

"What the hell do they think's been goin' on around here since the first bombing halt back in March? They been talkin' in Paris for months an' months an' never said a thing, an' all that time they been killin' GIs. The politicians we got ain't even got the slightest idea what these VC an' NVA are like. The more we back off from 'em and give 'em slack, the longer they're gonna fight."

"Here they are talking about avoidin' 'unnecesary' civilian casualties in North Vietnam, while our own GIs are gettin' killed by the thousands every month. Wonder who the hell it is in Washington that decides that American soldiers are worth less than NVA Communists?"

We had to swallow our bitterness and keep on humping and fighting.

Crucial secret meetings had been held again in the Capitol by the Presidential Advisors group, later known as the "Wise Men." Their final consensus was that the recommendations of Cyrus Vance and Averall Harriman, our "negotiators" in Paris, must be followed through. The North Vietnamese Communists were insisting on the cessation of all bombing in their country before they would "negotiate." Our representatives told President Johnson and his "Wise Men" that they felt the Communists would definitely negotiate and include the South Vietnamese in the talks, as long as the bombing stopped.

The former planners and perpetrators of our war involvement who were now "Doves" like Bundy, Clark Clifford, Hubert Humphrey and others, now urged and approved the action of the President. And so it was done.

For months and years later the enemy procrastinated, stalled and lied, even denying there were NVA in the South. But was it their fault? They had decided to win, that victory was their objective. Their leaders never faltered or whimpered or resigned like ours did.

We GIs knew. For the next three years or more we and our successors would fight the war on the ground, with 120,000 more casualties, without the support of having the enemy's homeland bombed and destroyed if necessary, to force them to desist in their attacks.

There were all kinds of reasons given by our weaker leaders on why the bombing wouldn't work, but the fact remained that these same "leaders" valued world opinion about Vietnamese casualties more than they valued their own men. In 1944 there had been no question about whether it was morally correct to destroy Cologne or Tokyo to back up our soldiers, but this was "different."

The enemy knew all the while with certainty that America had finally turned back from defeating them and seeking victory. Why should they negotiate in good faith? They didn't have to, and in fact, they never did.

On November 1, 1968, along with many other GIs around me, I intuitively knew that we would never win. In my heart I turned against the prosecution of the war. After the sacrifices I had already seen, along with the waste and deceptive weakness of our leaders, I became extremely bitter.

Our military leadership, from battalion and brigade, all the way to Chief of Staff level in the next few years would decry the decline in morale, increases in drug use and fraggings, and general attitude of the troops. What did they expect from men they were supposed to lead by example?

The final total halt in the bombing of the enemy's homeland was to go on for over three more years. All that time GIs like us were to fight and die for a cause already seen objectively at its best as a "stalemate" by our leaders, but in reality would eventually become a defeat. All that time the nation as a whole turned more and more against the cause, and the radicals became more shrill in their support of the enemy and condemnation of our soldiers. During the ensuing respite from reprisal on North Vietnam, 20,000 more American fighting men would be killed in action and many more thousands wounded or maimed for life.

The action of halting the bombing was indeed a civilian order resulting from weakness of will, but I believe our highest military leaders did not take a strong enough moral stand against it, to the point of resigning in protest. That would have been the appropriate step to show their feelings and their concern for the protection and morale of the fighting men in their charge. They did not, in fact, use the most eloquent and powerful protest at their disposal.

In Vietnam, of course, we had to just swallow our bitterness and keep on humping and fighting.

On that same first of November, I remember an APC track of the mechanized infantry blew up near us, hit by a mine or RPGs and one more American soldier was killed in action. After hearing that Delta Company of our battalion was in contact with the enemy, that night at about eleven we spotted enemy movement from our night position and opened fire into the woodline, first with M-79s and then our rifles. The enemy returned fire, "probably dug into a goddamn berm." We called in artillery fire which came in as Willy Peter. White phosphorus, huh? We're screaming now, "Yeah! Get some, Arty! Cook these sons-of-bitches!" When enemy fire ceased, we advanced into the blown-up smoking mess, rifles at ready. Drag marks from enemy bodies, one shell-shocked, burned, and shaking prisoner captured. Under questioning he revealed his squad had been carrying 44 mortar shells to attack Fire-base Moore.

"They was probably gonna celebrate the goddamn bombing halt." We smashed his lantern, too; we hated the obnoxious things, the Viet Cong were always blinking them in the dark around us, signaling our positions to each other. It was near midnight when Charlie Company of our battalion came on the radio requesting an urgent dust-off for shrapnel wounds from a booby trap. They were still calling at 12:30 in the morning.

About the second or third of November, we heard that Bravo Company was down in choppers on a hot LZ. They had one dude hit in the legs and a chopper pilot wounded, too. A little later on they got in heavier contact and killed five Viet Cong. In Alpha Company we made enemy contact that day, too—snipers. All we got for our shooting was two heavy blood trails where the enemy had dragged their dead off once again.

Sitting in the dirt about this same time in November at Firebase Moore, eating C-rats, I was shocked wide awake by a tremendous explosion just outside the wire. Right in front of me, beyond the perimeter on the road, lay the smoking wreckage of a five-ton U.S. Army truck; American GI bodies lay blown out on either side. Within seconds my squad was ordered out on line past the smoking wreck to stop anyone else from entering the right of way. The Rat Patrol and Engineers came with their minesweepers and gingerly began their work. They made it to the other side safely. At the other end "volunteers" were called and an Engineer Corps five-ton front loader started crawling towards us. Halfway, there was another huge explosion, *KA-BOOOOOoom!* Pieces of the vehicle, driver, and guard were blown in all directions right in front of our eyes.

Medics and other dudes from the perimeter ran towards the scene, a medevac chopper was called in for the casualties. There was a burst of screaming and yelling from the wounded, the medics, the grunts, the engineers, and the lifers. New names to be added to the weekly "score." The sight of that huge vehicle blown in the air was astonishing.

We fingered our rifles, snapping the safeties on and off, eyes darting around; "There's gooks around, man, I can smell the sonsabitches!" somebody said near me. The engineers minesweeping the road again reached our end, shaking, but safe. "Volunteers" were called for again. There's another flurry of GI activity, the sound of voices, cursing, comes to us. Meanwhile, we're still spread out in a thin line, amid the smells of warm muck and burnt explosives. This time it's a deuce and a half, a GI 2½-ton truck; they'd loaded it up with sandbags, too. Halfway to the earlier craters and another big *Whooooom!* explosion, dust and debris and pieces of metal flying, disbelief and horror were on everybody's face; the same thoughts hit all of us at once: "It's gotta be command-detonated!" At that moment two figures start to run from a ratty little hootch out past the paddies and just that quickly we fired short bursts on full-automatic, leading the bastards. Maybe we hit them, maybe we didn't, but they still got away, disappearing into the bush. Some lifer REMF behind us was yelling, "There go the sons-of-bitches! Get 'em!"

"Yeah, O.K., man, you try an' knock down a running dink at that range that quick."

We stood there mad with our smoking rifles in our hands. The other squads are called out, perhaps it was my whole company now. We're put on line dragging our feet through the watery muck. Everybody's muttering to one another, "Gawddamn, did you see those fuckin' mines?" We're on edge, tense, don't know if there's more gooks around, more mines, or maybe booby traps.

Feeling with his hands in a paddy dike, one of the dudes finally catches a wire. "I got it, man! Here's the detonator wire!" The gooks have been crawling out at night, setting those big Chi-Comm plastic high-explosive mines under the hardpan of the road by digging under from the rice paddies, right under our noses. That rock, clay, and laterite made damned fine shrapnel, too.

Well, a REMF "chaplain," who appeared from somewhere, came wheeling up in a jeep now that was all over and safe. He's going to be a hero, we can tell by his calculated pose. He drove slowly to the end of the cratered road, got out, hands on his big, fleshy hips and smile over at us slouching, lean, filthy grunts. It's like he's waiting for applause or something. We hated that son-of-a-bitch, too; he didn't give a damn about those blown-up, mangled GIs. I bet he got together with the colonel and had himself written up for a medal for gallantry that same day. I bet right now, fifteen years later, he's still telling the story of how sad he was for "his boys" and how brave he was, maybe blushing a little for effect. Next comes another leech, the major we hated so much, driving the same route in another jeep. It was like a weird REMF orchestra. Hatred and bitterness swept over me, damn near a feeling of despair at the pure folly of it all.

It wasn't until later in the evening we heard from the RTO that Bravo Company's hot LZ and firefight today had cost them another GI killed and two more wounded.

We keep on humping and about now we heard that Nixon has been elected president after promising to "end the war with honor." By now, the GI response to the news is a mirthless, snickering snarl. We're still out here in the bush; and sure enough, under our new president, the war dragged on for four more years, with tens of thousands more boys killed and wounded.

On another operation, all of them part of what the Army called "Operation Quyet Chien," we were working with ARVNs. Maybe Ruff-Puff militia or maybe the 12th ARVN Regiment from Cai Be. This time we were set up in a long line along a wooded bush area, and the Viets are sweeping through the jungle towards us, starting maybe a mile on the other side. I'm sitting at an OP in a pretty little glade with my rifle ready, smoking my pipe a little, trying to rest, enjoying the dry greenery and peace for a moment.

Suddenly an ancient-looking Vietnamese man with a white beard like Ho Chi Minh popped out of the bush on a little trail straight at me, "like a fuckin' jack-in-the-box." He was muttering and clucking to himself real loud like an old rooster toward the bush and jungle we're facing, the place he just came out of. He was making so much noise and acting so weird, I know damned well he had been pushed out on point by the Viet Cong in there to outline our positions for them. A split second later, we spotted two or three enemy soldiers with AK-47s between our OPs and open fire on them. They were a point element of the Viet Cong force. Even as I'm shooting my rifle at them, the jungle seems to absorb them; they vanish, we don't know whether we hit them or not. We kept blasting out a wall of fire.

The old patriarch was standing up beside me, smiling through all this ripping-roar.

"Probably his damned son's in there," I thought.

He was still jabbering away, loud into the foliage, pretending to be senile or something. Some other day I might have shot the old son-of-a-bitch on the spot. This time, however, I reached out my hand like a steel claw and jerked him down to the ground beside me. He felt as though he weighed no more than seventy-five pounds, like an old skeleton. I motioned to him for silence and stuck a fresh American cigarette in his mouth to shut up his babbling, even lit it for him. He sat in perfect calm for a few minutes with the uproar of shots and explosions going off out through the jungle in front of us and smoked the Kool down to the filter. While I was reloading my still-warm rifle, I stared at his old, worn, lined face, thinking how he's seen the French Foreign Legion come and go those many years ago; "Probably used to be a Vietminh, huh old man?" I wish he could have told me his real story—how many firefights he's seen, how many hundreds of times he has done this thing.

Abruptly he stood up; maybe he felt I wasn't going to hurt him, smiled his thanks to me; nodding, polite as can be, he shuffled off down the line of worn, tired American infantry, still chattering and clucking into the bush.

"Never say die, huh, you old bastard?"

Nobody shot him or messed with him or even appeared to notice him. It was one of those days when we collectively didn't give a damn about anything. He eventually disappeared as magically as he'd come.

It was almost a "normal" day, as we later advanced and pushed into the ARVNs, blowing up and destroying some bunkers and food caches, finding eight dead bodies of Viet Cong between our two forces. One thing was different that day. There were seven live enemy prisoners captured by the ARVNs, besides the usual many Viet Cong suspects. The prisoners had the military white-sidewall haircuts and NVA-VC uniform—shirts and bandoliers.

The treatment they got I had seen before, but it was still terrible to behold. They were taken to some nearby village and forced to kneel, where they were kicked, beaten, stomped on, teeth crushed out, and finally their heads smashed in by rifle-butts of the ARVNs, Ruff-Puffs, and the "White Mice," the Vietnamese National Police. Some of us, marching by all this in long lines through the village, are invited to join in the killing; not feeling vengeful as a group that day, we keep plodding on, trying not to notice the screams and cracking noises in that little square by the canal. They were beaten to death as we were moving out of sight and sound. I was glad to see my old rooster wasn't with them, "the decrepit old survivor."

It was somewhere between the 6th and 9th of November, but we had lost track of time. We had been marching all night across the endless swamps and rice paddies. Occasionally we crossed tree lines, approaching them with tense caution or waded through chest-deep canals and waterways between berms or dikes covered with hedgerows. Hour after hour, strung out in long lines, we dragged our feet through the water and deep, clinging muck. We were trying once again to catch a known local Viet Cong force by surprise, working in unison with some kind of ARVN battalion. During that long night we came to a small hamlet, for once undetected. I was the point-man for my platoon, along with a newer dude, perhaps Winters.

The other platoon file was parallel to us in column; on a high mud bank overlooking miles of water, we stopped short. We whispered together: "Fuck this night-walkin', I wish somethin' would happen."

The four of us leading the whole company of infantry slide up dripping wet and filthy, real quiet. We were listening to the splashes of paddles in a waterway just thirty feet in front of us. Down that canal between two paddies glided a long sampan-canoe loaded with enemy soldiers carrying AK-47s and piled high with equipment. We held our breath; here was a target we couldn't miss. We got our weapons trained on them and whispered hoarsely on our PRC-25, "Got three Victor Charlies point-blank." Our little noise was covered by the loud splashing of the gooks hurrying along. Back came the answer from the Ell Tee, harsh over the radio, "Don't fire! Repeat, don't fire! We're after bigger things!" Like stupid fools we gnashed our teeth and followed orders. The three enemy soldiers, probably sensing or hearing us by then, paddled away quickly, loved by the gods, the bastards.

That's the night I about started hating that Ell Tee myself. We had these three Viet Cong cold turkey; we could have blasted them, halted the horrible marching, got a nice long break. But no, he had some big-time lifer strategy to follow, do what that colonel wants. Later on, I quit feeling angry, "Ah, hell, he's jus' out here humpin' with us, too, an' the battalion commander prob'ly ordered him not ta fire. Th' whole damn things turnin' inta nothin' anyway."

It was the same night we were sneaking in to take some enemy-controlled village.

Sloshing and squishing, wet and cold, eaten alive by insects and leeches, a compound agony in long lines. Sometimes I wonder how or why we kept going. We reached our objective; in the earliest light of the approaching dawn, from my position I see GIs moving towards a gate. I felt like yelling, "Don't you go near that fuckin' thing!" but I was so exhausted no words came out. Next thing, there was the orange flash of an explosion, dudes were yelling. I don't know what's going on. I don't care.

Later, I snap awake. "Must have fallen asleep!" The sun is shining, our clothes are drying a little, and in our positions surrounding the village, we're quick-stuffing Cs down our throats. The settlement is awake in there, too. Come the sergeants' cries, "Saddle up, Move out!" We got up and went in carefully. There are Viet Cong flags nailed to trees, even a picture of Ho Chi Minh in one spot. Every hootch and building is searched and ransacked, while the people cower, saying, "No VC, no VC!" They have seen nothing, know nothing.

In one falling-down little hootch, hidden somewhere, we found a wounded Viet Cong soldier. The grotesque, untreated bullet holes and furrows seemed to bother us more than him. He had to be a casualty of one of our nighttime sniper shootouts. Another dude and I were ordered by the lieutenant to sling the son-of-a-bitch in a poncho-liner and carry him along with us. We wanted to waste him, to put him out of his misery, but "Oh, no! Not that!" After a half mile or so of humping that cripple through the Delta mud, he got so heavy that we started dropping him, over and over. It had gotten to be almost like an experiment. He just winced in agony, never screaming. I was just about totally fed up, so we threw him down on the first road we came to. He was done for, anyway.

We went past a village, thinking the operation we were on was a failure. We advanced on line through more paddies to another dirt road running along a river or deep canal. On the other side was a marshy jungle area, and the 12th ARVN Infantry guys were advancing through it towards us in a surround, squeezing the enemy between us. We filed out along the dusty road reveling in its dryness. I looked at Brackett as I passed saying, "God, Almighty, what a relief, huh?" He was grinning, too. "I just love this damn dust!" he says. We took up firing positions in a long thin line.

On the other side, about fifty meters away, rifle firing suddenly broke out in a popping crackle, then dies away. The RTO yelled out, "Two VC killed right in front of us! They're running!" Then things quieted down. At my OP in the line, I have two new guys with me who are real wide awake. The guy on my right was a pretty good dude named Winters. I had already spotted a hootch behind us across the road and gotten one of my weird urges to go visiting Viets. I shuffled over and squatted down; the family handed me a bowl of rice and sauce. I was eating away, when across the road and canal came the crash of rifle and machine-gun fire. *RRRRRRPPPPP! ZZZZZ Beow! Pop! Pop! Pop! Pop! Craaack! Craaack!* The Vietnamese family's bowls went flying, as they ran off shaking. I snatched up my rifle, diving towards the sound of shooting and the road. There was a firefight right across from us, with the Viet Cong pinned between us and the ARVNs. Ten yards to my right, Brackett and Barnett spotted an enemy soldier across the canal and cut him down with automatic fire. They shouted about it. Somebody else yelled, "There's more gooks in there!" Some of the other dudes were firing their rifles; enemy bullets were snapping and whizzing by, and our machine-gun was going.

Down the canal to my right, there was a huge explosion; *Whoom-Boom!* as a sampan loaded with VC ammunition exploded after being hit by tracers. Other sampans were tied to overhanging branches along the water's edge, but they looked empty.

I was down flat in the dust, tight-ready, finger on the trigger of my rifle, searching with my eyes, staring at each bush and clump, watching for movement, knowing the VC are being pushed towards us. Our RTO was yelling, "There's eight more enemy dead! There's U.S. casualties! Somebody's calling a dust-off!" Just at that moment I spotted a Viet Cong with an AK-47 across from me and fired a long burst directly at him on full-automatic, in case there were more around him. Right in the middle of my burst, a sampan-canoe shoots straight out from the bank on my side down below me and into the thick of my rifle fire. An old man and a mama-san paddling and a pretty young girl of about seventeen sitting in the middle. In that split-second image, I see one of my bullets slam into the girl's head and she topples over sideways, trailing a gush of blood into the water. I stared transfixed.

"Where did they come from?"

There's thick bush down along both banks.

"Were they hiding in there all this time?"

The father and mother stared into my eyes in that next split second, still paddling fast, and in another second they were out of my sight, dragging the body of their girl in the water. I jerked a look sideways at the men on either side of me.

"Did they see? Was it my fault?"

I felt sick at the feelings in me about what I've done. Winters is hugging the ground with his rifle in firing position, looking off to our right, more towards Brackett and our machine-gun position. The dude on my left is so new I don't even know who he is. I'm shook up bad, more than usual.

"Shot at an enemy soldier and hit that little girl. God, oh God! This place!"

I still see those eyes, that scene, today—more than fifteen years later.

Between the 3rd and 11th of November we were in almost daily contact with the Viet Cong. It was described as "light and sporadic." It was also nasty, vicious, filthy, and exhausting. The tension was ever present, day and night. The area we were operating in around the villages of Cai Lay and Cai Be was in western Dinh Tuong Province, bordering the Plain of Reeds, about twelve miles south of the village of Ap Bac. It seemed a strange coincidence that I was here so close to the place that figured in my first news of the Vietnam War. Ap Bac was the site of the battle in January of 1963 in which three American advisors had been killed. John F. Kennedy was still president, and I was in high school. Now, after five years of fighting in the same area, it was still primarily under enemy control, except for brief interludes when American or ARVN operations swept through. This province, this area could be taken as typical of our failure. Ho Chi Minh's or Vo Giap's prophecies that they would outlast us in the war were coming true. In the meantime, though, we were here, we had our orders to follow, and we kept trying. We operated with the three other companies of our battalion in surrounds. Our average "paddy strength" from late October to early November was eighty-five men in the company actually out humping in the field. On the 3rd of November, battalion records reported Alpha in enemy contact twice, including mortar fire. Bravo was in a firefight nearby, killing two Viet Cong, capturing a Russian carbine, and losing one GI killed and two wounded.

From the 4th to the 11th of November we had hit the enemy several times. My memory of that whole week is one of me marching, shooting, jumping, and rolling. On the 6th we were in a long firefight by a canal and killed several enemy whose bodies we found with weapons, laying beside others we knew had been dragged away. Delta and Charlie were both fighting that day, too, and took casualties.

In the 9th Division newspaper, *The Old Reliable,* there is a report of an action by our battalion on the 6th of November, when seventeen Viet Cong were killed and eleven weapons were captured north of the village of Cai Lay. Later I found out there were nine GIs killed and wounded that day in our area. Was it the day by the canal in the firefight when I killed that poor girl? It all runs together in my memory of this place, day after day, week after week.

On the 7th I remember coming in to a hot LZ on one of our very rare helicopter assaults. It's an indescribably helpless feeling being in an aircraft inexorably descending into enemy antiaircraft fire. After we hit the ground, we put such a heavy volume of fire into the hootch that AK fire had been coming from that it burst into flames. During that same week we got the constant feeling that we were surrounded all the time by a hostile population.

Vietnamese civilians lay moaning and crying, wounded by our shell fire, small arms, or airstrikes, staring at us as though we were animals. Blinking light signals were around us night after night in the wet, slimy dark. Sudden enemy fire when we least expected it; instant reaction by us and a report by radio back to the lifers:

02:23: Alpha is reporting blinking light signals.

05:09: Bravo is under heavy enemy fire.

14:40: Alpha is in contact with the enemy at XS218535 returning fire on six Viet Cong west of canal, two killed, rest running.

Later: Three more Viet Cong reported killed by 5th/60th troops. Captured this day: three AK-47s, two M-79s one B-40 RPG.

So, which canal was this? We were near canals every single day. We marched along them, blew bunkers with demolitions beside them, and waded across them up to our necks with our rifles over our heads, expecting every second the *Pop! Crack!* of an AK bullet.

On the 8th of November in another blocking operation with Alpha and Delta along still another canal, we killed five more Viet Cong while the 12th ARVNs killed eight. In all these operations, there was a steady small number of American casualties, too.

The days were also spent combing through the seemingly numberless hamlets and villages, working sometimes with half-assed ARVNs or RF/PF militia. The ARVNs always seemed to mince around like little fairies. Compared to us, who were out in the bush day and night for weeks on end, they seemed as clean as a bunch of young school girls. At night they hurried back to their little camps and forts, where they could wash up, hide-out, and live good off the American dole. We detested most of them, but every so often in 'Nam you'd run into a good, tough unit of them, maybe because of a good commander or the American advisors with them.

Even when there were ARVNs on an operation, though, we operated independently of them, just pushing in from different directions on a surround and mingling with them at the end for a little while. They seemed to idolize us or seek our approval, but we never paid much attention to them.

We would get alternately infuriated or gentled by the village people's unbelievable indifference or false meekness to us. We could feel the hand of enemy control in those places. The VC might leave and hide-out for a little while during our searches and surrounds, but they came right back and were there controlling the hamlets, directing the people and the progress of the war for most of the time. For our part, sometimes we'd speak softly and hand out part of our rations to the villagers; at other times, maybe after a bad march, we'd bust in, kick and push them around, slashing things. Those times would terrify the women and children and the ancient papan-sans whose young dudes were off with the Viet Cong or maybe the ARVNs; we never knew which.

After the times where we took out our tiredness and frustration on them, we would be appalled by our own actions, each in his own way, never by general discussion or argeement. The result would show in the next search, where we would exhibit a new feeling of sympathy and understanding for these wretched but strong people who knew so much about us and, at the same time, so little. The net result with all the men that I knew was an even more depressed feeling than the solitude of the northern jungles had given us.

I'll always remember the recurring feelings when we surrounded and searched hootches in the typical rice paddy hamlet. I recall the mud sliding up the embankment they were always perched on above the muck. We'd be dripping wet, exhausted. Feeling the presence of a family in fear inside, we would burst through the door, sloshing and swinging in like some great, green water creatures emerging from their most terrible dreams. The slim, black automatic rifle menacing, safety-off, on automatic, hand on the pistol grip, finger laid by the trigger, ready for the one-in-a-hundred chance that the Viet Cong would be there. We have a license to kill, and they know it. What god gave us that right? Why should we petrify them so? The older women and gray-bearded patriarchs drawing together with the young mama-sans, the wide-eyed terrified little children moaning to each other and to us. The quick rooting, kicking searches, one of the braver of the family always holding a smoky, open oil lamp for us to check the mud and brick bombshelters underneath. We'd pull apart the lofts, and tear down wall hangings or room dividers, little trinkets and keepsakes and bags of seed cascading down. I got so sick of it sometimes I almost cried when I saw their faces. At times my thoughts seemed to merge mistily with theirs. It shook me to think of my own home and family so far away.

"Old mother, grandpa, little ones, don't you know me?"

Sometimes I could even see in their faces that they do know me. Their own sons are our brother-enemies in this thing called war, just wearing a different uniform. Sometimes even our enemies' families feel our tension, fear, and loneliness. But meanwhile here in our own area of operations, Americans are being killed and wounded almost every single day around us. The GI bitterness builds and often the only target is these same people.

Another time, that same tension will build up in you and you can't stop yourself. Maybe tomorrow night in the next hamlet you will explode and strike out, kicking or pushing them around because one gave you a hateful look. And they will remember the huge, vicious foreigners, "the Americans." It will convert a few more to the enemy side, reinforce the feelings of those who are Viet Cong already. All the people will remember when the enemy moves back into the village the next day. It will give them a little more determination and strength during the next bombing raid or infantry operation that will inevitably come. It will reinforce the Viet Cong's teachings and recruitment.

As a leading power in the world, if our country learns and remembers anything from the long and bloody Vietnam War and the earlier French experience, it should be this: If we draw the line against our enemies somewhere again and say "no farther" and we are pushed into another war, as we surely will be someday, let us pick the battleground with the greatest care. Let us make sure there's a clear-cut enemy and we can fight to win. Our enemies will do everything they can to ensure that we don't get this chance, as they are doing today in the peasant-filled mountains of Central America or the teeming slums of the Middle East.

Let us as a people remember our lessons, though, written in American blood; and if today there are Soviet-Cuban tanks and warplanes and submarines in the Caribbean and on the mainland of the Americas, we'd better take a long look at what has transpired since our withdrawal from Indochina and we'd better redefine what constitutes success in the next military operation we're forced into.

The days and incidents have run together in a mixed-up mess until we were suddenly back at Fire Support Base Moore. We got orders to guard the perimeter-bunkers for a day while the battalion REMFs packed up their papers for moving to a new AO in Long An Province to the north of us.

We were finally stopped, looking out from a perimeter wire at that hated country, talking it over and listening. They informed us that in all these endless night and day marches, surrounds, and fire fights, something like sixty Viet Cong were killed in our area in these first twelve days of November alone. About twenty weapons and five Viet Cong prisoners were captured along with several hundred suspicious Vietnamese rounded up and "detained" as suspects. There have been thirty-eight GIs killed and wounded in these last few days of what the Army calls "Operation Quyet Chien." They also report over 300 enemy bunkers, thirteen buildings, and forty-one sampans destroyed in the same fortnight.

Our battalion was in the last action of the 11th when the chopper of our own 3rd Brigade commander, Colonel Hemphill, was shot down and he and a door gunner were wounded. Six Viet Cong were killed that day.

We are so worn out from the endless humping-marching, we hardly care about any of it, except that we're alive.

Now all we want is a chance to get wasted or laid or rest while we've got a few hours break. And instead, the high ranking brass and the other lifers chose this time to start harassing us again. The big-shot colonels and majors or career lifers were rarely seen out in the slimy muck. Instead, they screamed at us on radios or back in the camp where they were always comfortable. That way instead of maybe coming out on our ordeals of night swamp-marches to set an example or share a little in the burden, they could always be on hand if a chopper landed with some more important lifer or general, or better yet, maybe a correspondent/reporter who could get their names in the papers or on the TV "news."

As usual around fire support bases and night defensive positions, we had a small army of camp followers, whores, half-breed and orphan kids out around us. A day or two stand-down guarding perimeter was a small chance to relax, get laid or loaded, and visit with our weird troupe of Vietnamese gypsies. Not with our self-righteous commanders, though. Instead, we stood at attention in the sun to hear that we had to straighten up our appearance and salute them in a military manner when we're inside a fire base and base camp. Our first break in weeks and we got harassment instead of relaxing of tension.

Later in the day, six of us guarding two gate bunkers saw two of the worst harassers sneaking towards some of our buddies who were bouncing around out in front of us getting laid by a couple of girls. We shouted warnings but they were so into their thing they just kept boom-booming while those lifers crept up on them and caught them in the act. They were screeching at two combat soldiers like a couple of old women: "Stand up! Stand up! Get to the position of attention, troops; you've been caught in an unauthorized position, and you're going to be disciplined!" Right at that instant it wouldn't have taken much for us to have shot that screaming major. They wouldn't sneak around with us outside the wire, hunting gooks like that; it might be a little too real for them. Did they both have pretty little hootch girls taking care of them while we were out in the bush? Here they give these combat-worn, jittery GIs Article 15 punishments for trying to get a little relief. They had to get those "brownie points" with the big-brass and, of course, the whole tone of the battalion had for months.

Soon after this lovely holiday, the entire battalion was loaded up on a big chopper airlift about the 13th of November and moved via Dong Tam many miles north to Long An Province for a new operation. Third Brigade Headquarters moved into Tan An, and we moved into the village and fortress of Rach Kien.

13   Long An

*"I think we understand what
military fame is: to be killed on
the field of battle and have our
names spelled wrong in the newspapers."*
— *General William Tecumseh Sherman
(to veterans of the Union Army)*

Long An Province is divided into seven districts, one of which is Rach Kien. There are more than 300 hamlets and in 1968 the population was close to 400,000. The province is level, with rich, rice-producing land in the eastern part along with plantations of other crops. The majority of peasants here again were tenants or sharecroppers on property owned by landlords. In the northwest part of the province began the Plain of Reeds and this led directly to the Parrot's Beak sanctuary of the enemy inside the Cambodian border. Down through the middle of the province runs the Vam Co Dong River, which flows south out of Hau Nghia province. In the first Indochina war against the French, there had been a strong Viet Minh guerilla force here with local guerilla forces and Communist "Committees of Resistance and Administration." After the French withdrawal and the departure of some Communist cadres for North Vietnam in 1954, purge of the remainder took place in the 1950s and into the '60s during the Diem regime. A large number of the Viet Minh were arrested, imprisoned, or shot, many of them having previously been regarded as heroes by the peasants here.

The new Viet Cong insurgency officially began in 1960 at Ben Tre and with attacks in Long An. The fighting had been continuous ever since.

In 1968, it was estimated that four thousand Communists and supporters had been killed in the province, but two thousand still remained, and it was classed as one of the three most "insecure" provinces in the country (the other two being in the Mekong Delta), even though the enemy guerillas there were only 1 or 2 percent of the population. The counter insurgency warfare we were a part of involved the same aspects I'd seen in other places. The Americans were used as maneuver elements in long patrols, ambushes, and sweeps of "suspect areas." American artillery batteries and air units were positioned here and there to provide fire support. The artillery continued the country-wide policy of H & I. This shelling of "suspect areas" or "free fire zones" continued constantly, day and night, keeping up the intensity of warfare, general destruction, and peril to local inhabitants. I never believed in it because of its inherent message of insensitivity toward the population. A constant brigade presence of U.S. troops was kept supposedly at about 3,000 men, but a "brigade" in 'Nam was often lucky to have three battalions of 400-500 grunts actually out humping. Fourteen thousand ARVNs, mostly Ruff-Puff militias, were available, but their hopelessness was legendary. The Viet Cong attacks continued.

Because the area was a breadbasket of food production and covered one of the western approaches to Saigon, it was considered by the brass to be of prime importance, as was the capital until the end of the war, and the major target of the Communists. The area was one of the most populated parts of the country and, by extension, pivotal to the entire war effort. Yet it seemed that in this part of Vietnam, we were fighting a small core of revolutionary-Communist Viet Cong, armed and reinforced from North Vietnam, yes, but still largely recruited locally despite their continuing heavy losses. A significant thing, looking back on it: an enemy who believed totally in what they were fighting for, (a unified, independent country) and Communist by choice or default for lack of any strong opposition. Actually, a small proportion of the population imposed their will on the rest by their tenacious commitment.

Rach Kien, our new instant home in November, was one of the outposts defending the capital from attacks by the VC/NVA from the Parrot's Beak to the west through the Plain of Reeds down the Vam Co Dong River, or from the surrounding province. It was part of the same ring of forts and fortified towns that extended in a wide circle around Saigon—Phu Loi, Di An, Cu Chi, Duc Hoa, Tan Tu, and others. It was a good-sized village with several wide streets and a maze of dirt roads and tracks in the vicinity. It had a large and crowded population, including permanent residents and shopkeepers, along with hundreds of war refugees, orphans, prostitutes, dope-pushers, and half-breed American street children. It reminded me of a big Tan Phu Khan or a smaller Phu Cuong—just one more fine little Vietnamese town.

In our first hour there, we had counted and visited six whorehouses and had decided to stay in the last one. That same damned old major we hated burst in a little later. In the middle of the floor over which we were spread was one of the beds used for trade, with a kind of raggedy curtain hanging haphazardly around it. When that major came through the door, we were already drunk and stoned, draped around a floor littered with empty bottles of cheap gook booze, the air heavy with smoke. The bed meanwhile was bouncing and swaying terrifically to our cheers. Deep-throated grunting and shrill screeches were coming from the GI and the whore using it. The enraged man turned purple at the sight and sound. He was shouting, "You're animals! You're animals! Pigs!" We're nodding and laughing, "Yeah, yer right, asshole, you got it, there it fuckin' is, lifer." He got hold of himself, maybe because he suddenly noticed we were all armed with our M-16s and pretty wild, edgy. "This place is off-limits," he squealed out now, like the mouse that he was. "Clear out of here, right now!" He backed out, eyeballing his own crazy command nervously.

Keeping it "off limits" soon proved to be unfeasible, however, separated as it was from the military fort by only a few strands of wire and with GIs from our own unit guarding the gate. With the brothers taking the lead that same night and the rest following, business was soon back to normal.

We had been told there'd been a Viet Cong attack on this camp sometime before we arrived. They had blown through one of the gates and killed all the GIs up in one of the watchtowers, causing a number of casualties in the infantry compound itself before being driven out. We were careful and smooth when we went out on a long patrol past the wire the next day. In those first few days out of Rach Kien, we made light contact with the enemy—a few sniper rounds and booby traps found before they detonated. The VC tried to avoid our patrols and ambushes, probably figuring they had already put the fear of God into the Americans in this crowded camp. Our company did root out one of their little base camps of a few tunnels and bunkers and captured a good cache of Soviet and Chinese recoiless rifles, rockets, and mortar shells that otherwise would have come shrieking in on us some night. However, the Viet Cong were still around and on the 14th, the nearby ARVN compound came under a ground attack; we took about twenty rounds of incoming enemy fire on the Rach Kien perimeter, and Charlie Company of our outfit ambushed and killed one Viet Cong.

Meanwhile, between the 14th and 16th, the track company of APCs we usually operated with, Alpha Co. of 2nd/47th Mechanized Infantry, pulled off an ambush, killing ten Viet Cong. Grunts of A and B Companies, 3/39th Infantry, took part in helicopter air assaults called "Eagle Flights," and we soon had our turn at these. Fifteen GIs were killed and wounded while seventeen of the enemy were killed in this fighting. During these operations, ten more Viet Cong were killed by our helicopter air support company, Alpha, of the 3rd/17th Cav.

Back in the camp on our own little stand-downs between patrols, we were real happy with our new setup. We moved into genuine wooden hootches. They were raggedy and falling apart, perched out on stilts over some slough of slimy water, but beautiful to us. Furthermore, we were immediately inundated with crowds of refugee women and children, poverty-stricken and begging to be allowed to wash our clothes, get a little food, sell smoke or gook booze, or be of any other service. It was a little like heaven to all the dudes of the company after the last weeks of horrible humping in Dinh Tuong Province. Right around this time, I was told to report to our lieutenant. He told me I had been chosen to "volunteer" for the Phoenix Program, which was a kind of combined recon-intelligence-assassination operation controlled by the CIA.

I told him, "Okay, man, sounds all right. I guess I'll do it." I didn't know or care why they had picked me, I just figured it couldn't be any worse than the other weird things I'd seen and done. He didn't tell me when I was supposed to go or report or whatever; just told me he'd let me know and to keep on humping with my platoon.

Owens, my half-crazy black bro since my first day in the Michelin plantation, came back to us from the hospital after recovering from his sniper-bullet wound in the upper arm. He showed me the scar, wiggling and laughing as always: "Look at tha' lil mo'fuckah, man, cheap-ass li'l dink bullet. Goddamn, man, Ah though Ah'd getta' sham outta' that, man, but they jus' fix it up so quick Ah didn' even getta' chance ta' do nothin'." I whip out a number and light up, and he's smirking, "Good dude, you know wheah it's at." He nodded his head, cleaning his rifle and checking his field gear and magazines. Bro' Brown from Chicago comes strolling over, and now we have a little party going.

"I gotta red candle, man," somebody else says. We set it up on my little table by an empty widow overlooking the water, and it was damn near romantic-looking. I had my rack sectioned off with a raggedy old piece of cloth for privacy. We were rapping about "back in the world" again. They were saying, "It's gotta change, man; black people been down too long. We gotta come up now, even we gotta fight like old Huey Newton doin'." I didn't know anything about their life back there, really; I just knew I was for them. They were my number-one bros and if they believed it was so bad, it had to be changed. I figured they knew what they were talking about.

I thought it was ironic that we who were fighting a revolutionary Communist uprising in Vietnam seemed to have the seeds of one of our own germinating in the Army. It was eye-opening, the mixing of us all together for months and months. The black dudes talking about their trip, Chicanos like Ramos telling us about their lifestyle, the dudes of every race and nationality and state, all thrown together, closer and more dependent on each other than brothers, learning from one another and surviving. The main thing here and now was that no one cared much about Vietnam or its fate anymore.

I had a Chinese AK-47 assault rifle for a wall decoration and a few other trinkets. I did some good visiting in my little pad, it attracted my buddies with its "own room" feeling. Phil, Ramos' partner, was still making it, too, in Sergeant Loften's platoon, getting a little weirder, like carrying a Viet Cong flag tied to the barrel of his rifle, but "still gettin' by." "Shot" Shotkowsky and Troutman from Missouri were still in our platoon, along with Pancho Carrera, Bergy and Welch, and some of the other dudes who were getting short now, like Truby Gaddy. Our new guys like our "Doc," the medic with whom I came out from Dong Tam (and can't remember the last names of now) formed partnerships with one another. And there were other dudes like our new RTO—Fowler, Winters, Reising, Hardcastle, and some others.

Some of the dudes didn't like the Ell Tee, saying they didn't see him out in the bush as much as others we'd had. He seemed to be feverish sickly to me, but otherwise I didn't pay much attention to him. One of my oldest buddies from Lai Khe hated him like no one else, though, and kept talking about "greasing him." One of my last days at Rach Kien, my dude got himself messed up; seeing the lieutenant on the road behind the hootch, he went for him with a grenade with the pin already pulled. It looked like a "fragging" about to happen. What had finally flipped him out was the lieutenant's order to stop using the "artillery's showers." They'd been complaining they didn't want us "filthy infantrymen" dirtying them up. Probably some first sergeant or lifer-officer over there bitching. Well, the lieutenant backed them up when he should have been sticking up for his own men. A small thing now, perhaps, but after weeks of living in filth and on top of a long list of real or imaginary grievances it took my dude over the hill. He was going to "take him out, right fuckin' now." But, another dude and I saw him throw the pin away and rushed out, but we couldn't let him do it. There wasn't anything to warrant killing for. We jumped him and wrestled around, but the goddamn activated grenade got away. I grabbed it and threw it into a deep, watery ditch just before it blew up. The lieutenant had already stalked off out of range, knowing nothing. He came hustling back and yelled, "Who set off that grenade? What's the matter with you men, are you crazy?"

Other dudes were running up, some with weapons. "Hey, hey! What's happenin'?"

"It's nothin', man, nothin'," we said, "just an accident. Sorry about that shit." The lieutenant went away threatening and muttering at us, little knowing. In any case he was sick, probably with malaria, and soon reported to the hospital with "fevers and chills."

By now most of us do have fever and chills—and the runs and dripping sores, rotting feet, the shakes and God knows what else. It comes with the country. I never saw the lieutenant again, but I heard from at least one guy a long time later that he turned out all right and got home alive.

Meanwhile, we were breaking in another "instant NCO," a school-trained sergeant named Wilbur Gordon from South Carolina. It's funny to me now; I'm a point-man, I'm an E-4, a fire-team leader, and I'm trying to teach another one a few tricks. The Army just keeps sending over new "shake 'n bake" sergeants. He turned out to be a special good dude. Tall, slim, and soft-spoken, reminding me of my dead friend "Pete" Norris.

After long day-patrol operations in this area, we got some nights off—something we can't remember happening for weeks. It gave us a chance to visit with dudes from the other platoons who'd been around a long time but hardly ever got a chance to see us. I remember bullshitting with Sellman, my old Arizona buddy, and with Charles Pace, Ammons, Lockwood, Tharp, Garcia, and Packer. Sergeant Dennis Phillips was over from 1st platoon to visit Brackett, along with Zorba "the Greek" Galimatakis. I think Newall was still humping with us, too. We compared memories and experiences and mostly speculated on what the next few days would bring. It was hard to think farther than that.

14   Eagle Flight

"The name of the game is air."
—American pilot involved in bombing of Laos

On the 17th of November we took our turn at Eagle flights. This was just the local term for helicopter-borne infantry assaults of the whole company. Each day the target was picked from the latest military intelligence. The several platoons were usually landed strategically to try and trap the enemy. It worked and it didn't work at the same time. It came down to the classic axiom of a guerilla war: "If pressed too hard, hide your weapons and disappear among the people." Still, we kept catching them and hitting them, which kept their combat units fragmented into more or less platoon-sized forces.

The problem was the basic problem of the whole Vietnam war; it could go on endlessly. As it was turning out, the American people had started to question the sense of the war, the mounting casualties, and the repeated assurances by their military and political leaders that a settlement was in sight. Most grunts in the heavily populated areas of the Mekong Delta could easily see how inexact this "negotiated settlement" would be.

On the morning of the 17th, as we prepared to go out on a combat assault, the following order came out from "the Major," the executive officer of the 5th Battalion/60th Infantry:

"08:50 hrs. All weeds are to be cut in the battalion area, all trash is to be policed, and the entire area is to be raked."

We got a late start that day; at the airstrip waiting for the Eagle flight, I visited with one of the RTOs. A report came in that one of Silver Spur's choppers had been hit by antiaircraft fire and had gone into Tan Tru with one WIA on board. Silver Spur was the code name for our air cavalry support troop (A/3/17th). I knew right then we were going to hit gooks today.

We went into the CA with Charlie Company of our battalion. It wasn't really a hot LZ but damn near. Viet Cong were running as we hit. We in Alpha took them under fire and started getting shot back at. We moved ahead and overran three wounded enemy soldiers, capturing one AK-47. I think one prisoner was a woman. The men had white-sidewall haircuts and NVA uniforms. They were shot up pretty badly, two of them writhing around, one of them as good as dead already. We were still taking sniper fire and had one of our dudes in Alpha wounded by a bullet. I was out on the line, shooting. We called in a dust-off for the three enemy and our own wounded, and it came clattering down about seven p.m. One of the NVA later died from his wounds.

Our target for that day had been the 2nd Company of the 12th NVA Rocket Battalion. We were far up the Vam Co Dong River, just south of the village of Duc Hoa, near the border of Long An and Hau Nghia Province. We were still trying to protect those REMFs in Saigon from being rocketed. We got the word from MI a few days later that two of our prisoners had just infiltrated in as reinforcements from the Parrot's Beak of Cambodia, twelve miles to the west.

We remained overnight in this position in the slimy muck and leeches, muttering to each other a little in low, whispered grunt talk. At about one the next morning, the enemy began firing at our company, first snipers and then bursts of automatic fire. We held our fire as the bullets snapped by or thudded into the mud. It continued off and on until four in the morning, when we opened fire back in a sudden, heavy volley. We kept our fire low and grazing, trying to skip the rounds into the bastards. I don't remember anyone hit on our side, and we couldn't tell what damage we were doing to them. At nine in the morning we swept the area in front of our night position and captured a wounded VC/NVA officer of the company we'd been shooting it out with since the afternoon before.

About the middle of the day the choppers came thumping down to pick us up and take us into Rach Kien. When we got back I learned that one of the prisoners we'd captured the day before had revealed that another officer had been killed by our first shooting in the firefight.

We became the division ready-reaction force on the 19th, standing guard in Rach Kien waiting for a call out. At about 2:30 in the afternoon our gunship air support made some passes over our firefight area of the day before, catching five Viet Cong in the open and killing them by aerial fire. On the 20th we were called out in the morning and airlifted into another intelligence target, the C/3 Company of the Viet Cong Ben Thu Battalion. This time we headed southwest to an LZ between Tan An and Can Duoc. We made contact with the enemy about an hour and a half after hitting the LZ. It was light small-arms and automatic-weapons fire, and I don't remember any casualties. We captured two more wounded prisoners after the firefight, both in green uniforms and wearing NVA web gear. We also blew up any enemy bunkers we overran and had one dude injured by an explosion.

Studying old records years later, I found that there is no report of POWs captured that day by 3rd Brigade, only three VC KIA. Maybe they accidentally fell out of a helicopter or perhaps MI overdid it with them in trying to get their life stories.

We were lifted off back into Rach Kien again that night from near the mouth of the Vam Co Ta River. Still, we were fulfilling our reason for being: to capture or to kill Viet Cong without taking casualties ourselves.

The last couple of days I was in combat I remember as if it were only yesterday. On the night of the 20th, I heard a report that a five- or six-man LRRP team in our area had made contact and killed a Viet Cong in a shoot-out. The next morning, before dawn, we were awakened in our hootches with orders to "saddle up!" Then for a couple of hours we did the "hurry up and wait" routine so familiar in the Army. We lay in the dust with our weapons, gear, and ammo on, speculating to one another on the next Eagle flight. At least we didn't have to wear those damned heavy helmets anymore and hadn't for a long time. In the jungle heat most of us wore the soft bush hats, though from time to time some "lifer-policy" would take hold for a little while, forcing us to put on steel pots. We always had to shuck every possible ounce of weight just to be able to keep making it in the heat.

We'd been told that we were looking for elements of the Viet Cong 1st Long An Battalion, which had been ordered to "stop U.S.-ARVN operations in the Can Duc-Rach Kien area." Both our military intelligence and the ARVNs were reporting the spotting of "between a platoon and a hundred enemy troops in the vicinity of XS 7006," our target area of that day.

Finally a clerk came running and yelled to us, "Make it to the strip.

Choppers are coming in!''

I quickly crammed food down to level out and get ready for a hard day's humping. Next the Hueys were roaring in on line, sending dust and debris—and Vietnamese kids selling soda—flying. We loaded in, some of us hanging our feet out of the open doors. I was about to give the gunner a dirty look for being so snug and comfortable in his seat until I remembered sitting there myself what seemed an age ago. I smiled at him instead, and he gave me a thumbs-up sign for good luck. Then we were up and out in another cloud of dust and heading for the CA. The villages thinned out below us; everything was starting to look more war-tainted.

Bombing and defoliation scars were showing; the country was raggedy. We were heading west towards the Plain of Reeds.

We circled over one area like a swarm of hornets for maybe half an hour until somebody gave the pilots the word where to insert the grunts. I was thinking, ''You dudes are sure giving these gooks plenty of time to run or get ready!''

Suddenly we were going down, hitting the ground, and then we were out and running in a bombed-out hamlet/farm area that looked all overgrown and wild, bisected by a depressing amount of deep-looking waterways and old canals. There were untended rice paddies and wild-reed, jungle swamps spreading out in every direction. At the LZ we set up defensive lines and a few minutes later we formed up and moved out in the direction they wanted us. I'm point-man for my 1st Squad and have my new guy, Winters, as my slack. We're still doing our Delta thing today, with two dudes of each squad up front, keeping spread out and parallel so we've got firepower if we hit the enemy. My main man, Gaddy, is point-man for the second squad, with Welch and Bergy pretty close. We slogged through a bombed-out village with a few people hiding in it. We ran into one old man there, cowering in a ruined hootch and whimpering, ''No VC, no VC,'' his hands gesturing as we prod him with our rifles. ''More lyin' bullshit,'' somebody muttered. The place smelled like goddamn VC.

Out into the overgrown marshes and stinking muck we splashed, seeing a few hootches ahead after crossing a deep canal up to our armpits. They were nearly hidden in the bush; the second squad took the left and our first, the right; we're only about 400 meters from the LZ. As I led the approach to my hootch with Winters right near me, the silence grew loud. You can feel it sometimes just before it blows—maybe it's the eyes of the enemy on you, but sometimes you get a split-second warning or feeling. Suddenly, we were taken under fire by an automatic rifle shooting from the hootch straight in front of us. With bullets cracking around us close, we've already hit the ground and opened fire.

Thirty meters to our left, the second squad came under machine-gun fire from another enemy position at the same instant; Bergy screams, doubles up in the middle, and goes down shot. Gaddy was firing, Welch ran up shooting. Winters and I were shooting the hell out of the enemy position in front of us on full-automatic. I see him out of the corner of my eye; he's turning out good.

Somebody screamed, "Medic!" off to my left, and he ran to Bergy. Our opposition was silenced by our heavy fire now, and I was so enraged that Bergy had been hit, I jump up and start charging towards second Squad's point where the firing is still going on. I splash through the water firing my rifle on automatic into the VC position. Enemy rounds are snapping by behind me and my new, almost-cherry squad leader Sergeant Gordon screamed, "Get down, Brown, get down!"

As I moved and fired, I almost laughed to myself, "Hell, man, I don't give a fuck anymore. Gordon, you big, nice new South Carolina good-ol' boy. I love you, too, but I don't give a damn; I've been dead a long time."

I continued to move forward, shooting, joining up with Gaddy and Welch who are blasting away too. The firing died down and the Viet Cong retreated, dragging their casualties, of course—the same as we do for ours. We found blood trails and messes and empty shells in front of both point positions in little, dug-in spider hole fighting trenches.

We called in a medevac for Bergy, who's moaning, hit bad by several bullets across the middle in his hips and thighs. I was worried about whether he's hit in the balls. "Doc" was working on him as we threw smoke grenades for the dust-off. Bergy was groaning, "Uhhhngg, uhhngg." I can't tell from my position if anyone else has been hit.

We were told by some brass over the radio to hold our position while other platoons are moving in from different directions. The RTOs yelled about "bodies of enemy killed between us," and more U.S. casualties. We heard intense shooting in the distance. After a while the company commander says to send up four men to check out one of the VC hootches on the left. Sergeant Garza, who was our platoon leader again today because our lieutenant wasn't with us, called out for "volunteers" and I yelled out to get in on it. I think it was Gaddy, Brackett, Welch, and me. Pancho Carrera, Reising, Winters, and a few other guys are close, waiting in case we need help. We were all sweating, alert, eyeing each other, and gettin' ready.

We moved into the foliage cautiously—there was bush-jungle trees and tall palms with clumps of real thick bamboo between. In one thicket Welch and I found two dug-in, fighting positions with some blood and empty AK-47 shells. Suddenly firing from AKs broke out again where Brackett has gone; *Pop! Pop! Pop! Craack! Craack! RRRRPPPPPP!* Seems like about five AK-47s.

I yelled: "Goddamn, they got Brackett!" We call out to him and get no answer except another *BBBBBBBBBRRRRRRPPPPPP!—Crack! Craack! Craack!* burst of enemy fire. We ran for a big, huge mound of dirt, maybe fifteen feet high, bullets snapping through the air. It looked like an enemy OP. We took cover behind it and opened fire on the Viet Cong position. An LOH chopper with machine-gun mounted zooms in low overhead, firing at the same instant. It's "Silver Spur." They radio down, they've killed one VC in a blue uniform with an AK-47.

Under all this covering fire, Brackett streaks back to us out of the bush, real low, giving us a big, sickly grin when he makes it. He turns around and shows us two long, black bullet burns across the back of his jungle shirt. His glasses were a little steamed up, I noticed. He'd been pinned down in there all this time, they damn near got him for good. And him our No. 1 good Sarge! "Fuckin' gooks!" We started to advance towards the enemy position now without orders; we were roused and pissed off.

"Let's get those bastards!"

Welch and I were on parallel-point, spread out, shooting a burst of covering fire every so often as we advanced. I came to a deep drainage ditch. Out of the corner of my eye I could see Welch crossing about fifteen meters to my left. Just as I came up over the other side, sliding real quiet, there was an enemy, a Viet Cong. He was in a khaki-brown uniform with an NVA magazine bandolier across his chest and an AK-47 rifle across his knees in his hands. He was crouched, leaning against a tree and looked wounded, but he was looking right towards Welch as though he'd seen him. Catching him in my sights for that split second, I aimed my rifle, staring in amazement at this enemy. Is he the last one stopping us or are there others in here? He didn't see me. "I can't take no chances!" I opened fire quick-shooting off the top of his head with a ten-round burst at point-blank range. Brains and blood spatter all over the trunk of the tree. He jerked and toppled over sideways, the rifle spilling out of his hands. I grab it, holding my rifle ready to fire one-handed in case there's more of them. Welch had run up and wanted the AK, so I handed it over and he carried it back to the company. The chopper claimed six Viet Cong kills from the air, too, by radio, but I think several of these were bodies of VC we'd killed in the first firefight.

As I was stripping off his ammunition and grenade belts, I looked into the remains of his face. I had gotten his blood all over me. Even though I hated him, I felt a sick feeling. It was the same as other times before: a sense of loss to the world of this young dude, my enemy, but a grunt like me. I shook myself, mumbling, "Ahhh. . .it ain't nothin', ferget it!" I reloaded my rifle, snapping in a fresh magazine, and walked on out out of there, leaving him in his peace. I was the last one out of there. I humped my way back to the platoon, thinking, "Just drive on, man, do yer fuckin' time, dude, and get out of this crazy place for good; go home and make kids!"

The rest of that long day we humped and searched and sweated, constantly tense and ready, but the enemy had retreated; in the late afternoon we straggled back to the LZ and formed up for the helicopter extraction in the old paddies near the shot-up village where the old man was saying, "No VC!" this morning. Just before the choppers came in, some of the M-79 grenadiers moved up and opened fire into the place. Then some of us started shooting our rifles. The grenades and bullets exploded and cracked, pieces of hootches were flying through the air, the little trees swaying. I muttered to myself, "Ahhh. . . don't mean a goddamn thing."

The choppers came in with a roar and we loaded up. They lifted off with our feet dangling out; the cold wind rushing in felt so fine. From up high the country looked so green and pretty, the rivers like little winding snakes. And God was watching, too.

Back in Rach Kien that night we were laid back relaxing when they told us that thirteen enemy soldiers had been killed that day in our area, and four motorized sampans sunk by A Troop-, 3rd/17th Cav, our air support. We were the machines, the animals they wanted us to be. We would be going out again next morning early. We muttered together a little, wondering if Bergy was O.K. in some hospital, and knew by now that two other GIs had been killed that day and one other wounded somewhere around us.

The next morning early, the 22nd of November, we were lying in the dust of the airstrip again, waiting for the choppers. I heard we're still looking for the enemy 1st Long An Battalion. We waited and waited. I checked through my gear, making sure my rifle and ammo were clean and ready. I started to go through the two claymore bags that I carry all my personal junk in and then my pockets. I found the latest letter from home, wrapped in the tattered six-inch-square American flag I've been humping for almost fourteen months now. The letter was small talk about what this brother and that sister were doing. "Cousin so and so is at Princeton University, isn't that wonderful!" I snarled to myself and spat in the dirt, shading my eyes from the glaring sun to look around me. My grunt brothers were all ready, too. There was a total of seventy-nine of them today in A Company. They lay around calmly like me, equipment and weapons squared away, mumbling a little to one another. I looked at their sunburned, haggard faces. They were all young, mostly white, with a sprinkling of the other races that make up America. I thought to myself, "Here sits the best there is."

Gordon was near me, muttering a little now about "the goddamn army, wait and wait, huh?"

I shit-smirked at him a little, "S'all right, Gordon, no sweat, man, the gooks'll still be there."

I saw the choppers coming and heard their whining "thwack-thwacking" roar. Everyone was heaving to their feet around me as the birds settled in on line, door guns pointing toward the ground. Soon we were airborne again in the same direction as yesterday, west of Rach Kien and Tan Tru, towards the Plain of Reeds. The area near where we started slanting down was wild-looking swamps and nippa-palm jungles. It looked as though there had been airstrikes and bombing recently, maybe yesterday, out around us.

As we came clattering in for the CA all I could see is a last sorry-looking little hamlet, a nearby river or waterway, reed swamps, and jungle. Then we leaped out past the door-gunners who look tense and ready. I catapult myself towards the nearest cover. Already I didn't like the look of this place. Artillery fire exploded somewhere to the southeast, *Whump! Carrump! Carrump!* The choppers were up and off and the next lift was coming down behind our perimeter, another platoon of Alpha. I didn't think the whole company was coming in here; the word is one platoon's staying behind as a ready-reaction force.

We fanned out wide, sweeping through the village. The people were nasty-surly, some of the worst I've seen in Vietnam. Anyone of us could tell this was a real enemy-controlled village. They gave us flat, hateful stares, and we arrested and detained several Viet Cong suspects, young and tough-looking dudes with military-type white-sidewall haircuts. It brought another sneer to my face to think that Americans were over here fighting and dying "to save these people from Communism." One whom I grabbed myself with one hand while holding my rifle with the other was backing out of a hootch towards the bush. He gave me such a filthy look I pointed the rifle at his head and started to squeeze the trigger, when something inside me said, "No!" But I was getting to the end of my rope, hating them. I dragged him by the hair over to Minh, our ex-Viet Cong "Tiger Scout." Minh was a real tight, tough little dude who went everywhere we went. We got used to him, gradually. It was eerie at first, having a Viet Cong with us who knew everything about both sides. He snatched my prisoner and started interrogating him.

A few minutes later Minh said, "There beaucoup VC there!"

He was pointing to the thick woodline just beyond the hamlet, past a raggedy-looking little bit of rice paddy. We moved up to this, spread out on line like we're back in the Civil War or something. A single sniper round pop-cracks over us. We held up and after a few minutes' delay got orders to open fire in there, "Recon-by-fire!" "Mad minute!" We cut loose with a single, huge volley. Twigs flew, branches fell, leaves fluttered through the air with the ripping roar of shots. Captain Anderson called in our light observation chopper with a machine-gun mounted to strafe the area ahead of us. He didn't like the look of it, either. It was a real ominous-looking nippa-palm swamp-jungle.

I could see my old buddy Sellman over there, talking on his radio for "the man" and waved at him, grinning. We moved to the edge without receiving fire. Off to my left I heard dudes yelling, "There's bunkers in here, watch it!" I could hear grenades going off over there as another of our platoons moved up beside us, blowing them. There was a sudden, bigger explosion from one of them.

"Sounds like a secondary explosion from VC ammo cooking-off." Then somebody yelled, "One guy hit by shrapnel over there; callin' in a dust-off."

A few minutes later there was a burst of firing, somebody over on the left yelled again, "Gooks! There's gooks in there runnin' with weapons, keep yer damned eyes open."

The word was passed to watch where we walk because one of the explosions had been a booby-trapped 60mm mortar round that was blown in place by our guys. A chopper clattered above the trees in front, firing machine-guns on a strafing run. The tracer ammunition is like a streaking lance. Our RTO picked up a transmission from the LOH gunship of Silver Spur ahead of us that they've "killed two VC by air at XS732619, and the enemy are moving east." The grunts of our company over there were by the riverbank and had killed one VC by throwing grenades in the water around him. They'd also captured an AK-47, but the 3/17th Cav chopper of Silver Spur was "claiming that kill, too."

As my platoon moved up alone into the bush where they wanted us to go, I was near Minh again. He pointed out a sign on a pole to us that had crude writing on it in English and Vietnamese. "To enter is to die." I stared at it, snarling, "Fuckin' VC."

Minh said, "No go in there, beaucoup VC, there maybe forty VC there!" He's real uptight, agitated, sure of himself. As sick of it all and blank-eyed as we were, all we could say was, "Well, we gotta go anyway, Minh."

I was peering ahead into flooded nippa-palm jungle, the wilderness. I was mumbling to myself or anybody near who might listen, "Ya' don't see that stinkin' major out here now, do ya??"

Our platoon leader again today was old Sergeant Garza, our E-7 lifer who had come to us back at the end of the Song Be Operation and was still out here humping the bush with us. Our lieutenant was in the hospital again, ill with fever and the shakes. He probably had malaria. There was no way a grunt got out of that line without evidence of continuous high fever. It was 9th Division policy.

I was point-man again and nervous today, but we were unopposed after we smoked that first sniper as we entered that watery jungle. In a long, heaving column strung out behind me, the platoon was dragging through the two-foot deep, grey, clinging muck and water-flooded bush. I was ordered to change our direction by the compass, over and over by radio from the Company CP, which was trying to match our other platoons and maybe the battalion's other companies, coordinating them over a wide AO. We felt lost even from our own company headquarters, where Sellman was humping Captain Anderson's radio. Out on point alone in this ripping thick bush, thorns, bamboo, and muddy swamps with enemy soldiers lurking up ahead, I missed him. It got to be like hell on earth, hour after hour, hair-trigger for hundreds of minutes. I knew we were going to hit the enemy, but I didn't know where or when.

After maybe two hours, everyone was getting worn out; the expenditure of nervous tension took its toll. One by one, the men began relaxing their guard and paid less attention to each thick clump of bush in the jungle reeds or mounds of dirt that might conceal enemy bunkers. All of a sudden I broke out into the open and led us into a clear area with some hidden small rice paddies and two concealed hootches. "A hidden enemy area, sure as hell!" At the first edge of that little clearing, we took a short break and I traded off the point-man position with my buddy Pancho Carrerra; he and I were taking turns on point.

Back in the middle of the platoon, soaking wet, muddy, and exhausted, I snapped a C-rat can of peaches and smoked a cigarette quickly, flipping the burning butt towards a large pool of water. The son-of-a-bitch came down through the air and landed balanced on a twig in the middle of all that water, smoking merrily. I seized on this as an omen, as soldiers will do, saying to myself, "Well, hell, I'm gonna' get hit today, but I ain't gonna' get killed!"

Just about then, Pancho Carrera, who had moved up front, yelled back, "I'm gonna' check out that hootch," pointing to the closest one with his rifle. The enemy were watching him already.

Another hootch was off to the left. We were in a flooded swampy clearing in the middle of a big "V" at the apex of which was the closest hootch that Pancho was moving toward. The squads had gotten all mixed-up on that awful march, but we're spread out pretty well. Just as Pancho got close to that right-hand hootch, the hidden and dug-in enemy force on both sides opened fire on him and us with small arms and automatic weapons. The bush exploded around us in a crackling rattle, *"Pop! Pop! Pop! Craack! Craack! ZZZZ! RRR-ppppp! Pow! Pow! Pow!* Pancho was hit! He screamed loud and went down; in that split second I saw him open fire on the enemy with his rifle, one-handed.

Our men in the "V" were under an enemy cross fire and the whole platoon was pinned down low trying to crawl for cover with enemy bullets cracking in from all around. I was firing my rifle at the enemy, and I could see Reising in my fire-team start lobbing in grenades with his M-79 "pig." *Thump-boom! Thump!boom!* He was firing from up on one knee, he was new, but he was doing good. Just that second, he was hit! He went down with a scream and a splash to my right. Our new medic, whom I'd first met in Dong Tam during that rocket attack, unhesitatingly exposed himself to enemy fire by jumping up and running towards Reising with enemy bullets splattering and popping around him. I fired off another magazine at the enemy to help cover him, and then

I heard him scream, ''Reising's hit by the heart! He's dying!'' There was a ripping storm of rifle fire from the platoon around me, but our machine-gun crew isn't firing yet, I don't know why. I heard other shouts, ''Medic, medic!'' Maybe other guys were hit. Then I heard Pancho scream again, hit another time in front of me. I look quick left — right; there's a lot of new guys around me, they don't know what the hell to do!

It's my turn now. I'm the old dude, I'm thinking, like Joe Miller back at Tan Phu Khan. ''Do it!'' I'm up and running towards the enemy, firing my rifle on automatic into their positions in long bursts. VC bullets are snapping by, spurting, hitting all around me. I'm ejecting magazines, slamming new ones in, firing again, dodging, moving forward, quick-praying, ''Yea, though I walk through the Valley of the Shadow of Death, I will fear no evil.''

''I'm gonna get Pancho outta there,'' I'm thinking. I didn't know it then, but my new squad leader, Sergeant Gordon, has jumped up behind me, charging and firing, too, good man that he was. As I was still running towards the enemy position, bullets started to tear through my jungle pants, one ripping a hole by my balls. Pancho's hit again, right in front of me, less than fifteen feet away, for the third time. I fired again, another magazine of twenty rounds, and I heard a loud 'Uhhhhhhhh!'' grunt and a splash behind me, as Gordon is hit in the chest by bullets and goes down on his face.

I reloaded and fired another burst crouching and moving; suddenly I see an enemy in a hidden firing position beyond Pancho. He was covered with palm leaves for camouflage and looked like a moving bush with an AK-47 rifle. I shot half a magazine into him as he fired directly at me in the same instant. One of his bullets hit me in the lower arm and wrist, knocking me around and shooting the rifle out of my hands. It sank, lost in the muddy water. My whole right arm went numb like it had been hit by a sledge hammer as I splashed down and rolled over and over in the water quickly. More bullets were coming in bursts: *Pop! Pop! Pop! BBBRRRPPPP! Crack! Crack! Crack! Crack!*

I was just behind Pancho and I heard the medic scream out next, ''I'm hit, Jesus, I'm hit!'' He was over to my right. Fear started to sweep over me. ''This is it,'' I thought. ''This is the end; they got me in a tight spot, no way out!'' Then I got hold of myself, and said, ''Fuck 'em, I'll make it, I gotta help my man up there, he's shot up worse than me.''

Garza was back in the rear and had sent this young soul brother, a new guy named Fowler, crawling up with the radio to call in an airstrike. He was showing some guts, firing his rifle and yelling out, "Airstrike comin', throw smoke! Captain Anderson's called in Lofton's platoon from Rach Kien to back us up!" I looked up from my rolling and dodging, trying to blacken myself with mud for camouflage, and brave Pancho, who'd never lost his cool, was feebly rolling out a colored smoke grenade to mark the American line. Just then, he was hit again by a bullet in the top of the head, and he swirled around facing me, his back to the enemy, beyond caring. I remembered my grenades. I pulled pins and threw, using my good left arm. My last one blew up directly on the enemy position in front of Pancho, exploding loud and silencing it. I never knew how well I could throw with my left arm 'til then.

Immediately after that moment, the first Cobra helicopter gunships of the "Sting Rays" came clattering in overhead, firing machine-guns and rockets as I crawled up to Pancho. A new guy named Joe had come snaking up out of the woodline to help. We dragged Pancho back together, still dodging bullets, as the choppers overhead blasted the enemy position into a blazing hell. We slapped some compresses quickly on Pancho as he lay in the muck on his back. Up until then I hadn't known how many others had been hit besides the guy hit earlier in the day by shrapnel and Pancho, Reising, Gordon, "Doc," and me in our firefight. I knew I'd heard a dust-off coming in under fire behind us during the worst shooting. The Viet Cong were still firing through the exploding rockets and smoke marking the edge of our line. I lay there in the shade of the trees near Pancho, who was delirious. The CP group of the company had by now made their way to the area behind the firefight and called in another dust-off. Sellman was talking on the radio for Captain Anderson again and smiled over at us, nodding his head a little while we waited for the next dust-off. Lieutenant Lee's platoon of the company had moved up in support, and heavy firing continued in front of us. Sergeant Lofton's platoon had been alerted at Rach Kien and air assaulted in as a blocking force to the northern edge of the firefight zone. They were calling in now, they'd killed two more Viet Cong at point-blank range retreating from us.

I heard that Bravo Company was being CA'd in to help us out any minute, and that one of our other platoons had lost three more casualties across the canal from us during my platoon's firefight. They had already been medevaced and I couldn't find out who they were. Gordon, Reising, and "Doc" were already gone, too.

Shooting kept breaking out and lulling out in front of us. A few stray Viet Cong bullets clipped through the leaves above our heads. It was nice to be back here waiting and knowing a chopper was coming to take Pancho and me out. An armed spur LOH was still buzzing around out there, firing a machine-gun every so often. The heavier Cobra gunships from the airstrike by "Sting Ray" were long gone now. The company advanced to find some of the enemy bodies and weapons of our fighting, about seven dead Viet Cong and five AK-47s by the time we left (thirteen more enemy KIA were found by the next morning). Enemy fire still cracked out now and then. One of the medics was working on Pancho as I sat beside him; it looked to me like he had about four or five bullet wounds. I helped "Doc" with the bandages, and he stuck an IV for a blood bag. My buddy was moaning and groaning, slurring his words from the morphine shots. They'd tied a compress around the wound on my lower arm and hand, too. My wrist was shot open pretty good, bleeding a lot, numb and aching.

By then it was about 4:30 in the afternoon, and the next medevac was thumping in. I said a quick good-bye to Sellman, Brackett, Bro-Brown, and a few other close dudes. I missed Truby Gaddy—didn't see him or Winters anywhere. I looked quickly to try and spot them out beyond somewhere—them or Barnett or Welch—but they were probably all up front still fighting.

The dust-off came down in a spray of muddy water behind us and, with two guys carrying Pancho, we slogged across that last stinking swamp to our own little freedom bird. I could still hear small-arms and automatic-weapons fire behind me. As the crew of the medevac pulled Pancho in and laid him unconscious on the metal floor, I climbed in and turned around to look at what was to be my last sight of smoking, burning hootches and jungle, the ruin of war. I was holding a compress on my arm between my legs and had my other arm around my buddy. I felt ready to cut it all loose.

That LZ was still a little hot as we lifted off and soared into the air, green tracers from AKs went whizzing by. Then our own brave dust-off pilot twisted around in his seat, flashing a smile to us. I smiled back and held on to Pancho, praying he'd make it.

15   U.S. Army Hospitals

"They gave me a Bronze Star...and
they put me up for a Silver
Star. But I said you can
shove it up your ass...I
threw all the others away.
The only thing I kept was the
Purple Heart because I still
think I was wounded."
—Vietnam veteran

In a kind of daze, I felt the dust-off descending in a thumping swirl of rotor-wash at the medevac hospital. Medics were running towards the chopper, already alerted by radio that they had a priority-critical coming. They loaded Pancho on a stretcher while the blades were still spinning. Blood oozed from wounds all over him. I stood watching, kind of shaky, feeling him going out of my charge. It felt good. "They'll take care of him." A couple of medics put their arms around me and helped me into the nearest door. I was feeling dizzy, maybe in shock. Inside the door they cut off my NVA ammo/web gear that I'd humped so many miles since Tet, and I heard it crash to the floor. I'd been carrying twenty magazines totaling 400 rounds, and had shot off about half of them. I could hear screaming and crying near me. They undid my pistol belt and bolo knife, and stripped off my muddy, wet and bloody jungle fatigues. They steered me naked into an operating room and laid me on the table. As they were bent over examining my wound, I could hear Wilbur Gordon next to me, groaning and bubbling from the bullet holes through his chest and lung. I kept thinking, "Don't mess around with me, I'm alright, you gotta save my man." I could hear Pancho Carrera nearby, too, moaning in pain, and the other guys. There was a feeling of frantic work going on by the surgeons, medics, and nurses. I found out shortly casualties from the 9th Infantry, 1st Infantry and 1st Cavalry divisions were there all at once. From where I lay, I could see blood and wound dressings all over the floor. I could hear them talking about giving Gordon morphine to quiet him down so they could work on him. As they were cleaning out my wound they gave me a shot of morphine, too, which mellowed things out, gave me a feeling everything was cool and being taken care of. I looked over at my lower arm and saw that the wrist and hand were split wide open by the path of the bullet and bleeding a lot. Then I must have fallen asleep.

I woke up in a big ward lined with racks on both sides, full of dudes from just about every division. Focusing my eyes I could see it was morning; there were American round-eyed nurses moving around the beds and haunting faces of fear everywhere I looked. Grunts with legs blown off by mines, dudes with bloody bandages over bullet holes, IVs going, wheel-chaired GIs visiting others, the wreckage of war all around.

My first thought was, "Did my dudes make it all right?" I swung my legs over to the side of the bed and stood up, weaving. My arm was throbbing and aching under its big bandage as if it had been crushed in a vise. I held it up against my chest and worked my way to the nearest nurse, asking her how I could find my buddies. She told me which ward they were in, and I moved outside into the hot tropical sun. Entering their ward, I could see immediately it was for critical or intensive care. A ward master-type dude confronted me until I told him I had "to see the guys from my own infantry squad."

The place looked like intensive care, lit up and stuffy, two rows of shot-up men not bothering to look as I entered. Chest wounds, abdominal gut wounds, IV bottles, chest tubes, nurses and doctors hovering over lean, gaunt-looking soldiers whose eyes seemed to stare at nothing. The ward master told me to "make it short" and let me go in.

I found Pancho Carrera and Wilbur Gordon side by side. Pancho was completely still and swathed in bandages from his head down, with blood seeping through all over. He smiled a little, trying to focus his eyes on me, while Gordon was wheezing and groaning and lifted his hand to me. I sat down between them. For a second we just looked at one another and then I said, "Well, we're alive." They both kind of nodded. Gordon whispered hoarsely to me, "You did all right, Brown." Those words from a fellow grunt were the ultimate compliment. We talked a little about how Reising and our medic must be dead, whether others had been hit, and wondered how the platoon and company were making out. I could see they were too tired to talk much, and let my eyes wander around the ward. There were GIs with catheters in their necks, blood dripping in, guys all covered with compresses, groaning, beds with curtains around them so nobody could see in. I felt tired of the whole business of 'Nam, looking around me. "All this suffering every day, every week, every month, every year, and nobody sees it."

I smile good-bye to my buddies to let them rest, and wander back to my bed. There I was awarded the Purple Heart medal, which says on the back, "For Military Merit." The paper that comes with it says, "For wounds received in action, 22 November 1968," and "Instituted at New-burgh, New York, in 1782 by George Washington." I lay there thinking and wondering how many millions of Americans have been wounded or killed in the name of their country since that Revolutionary War, so long ago.

The GI across from me is from the Big Red One, shot through both legs by a machine-gun. He was from the 2nd/28th Black Lions. He'd been hit the same day I was after three days of fighting at Firebase Rita. Twenty or thirty guys in his unit had been killed or wounded. We're talking, kind of sleepy, when a beautiful blonde, blue-eyed nurse comes up and asks us, "Are you hurtin'?" and we both answer, "Yeah" in unison. She shoots us up with some fine stuff, and soon we're just floating. He'd been shot near Loc Ninh, not far from the Cambodian border; the guy from the 25th Division on the other side of me had been hit by RPG shrapnel near Tay Ninh. We all lay back muttering to each other about the "craziness of 'Nam and the politicians," and gradually fell asleep.

When I woke up, I decided to write my family from 'Nam for the first time in more than three months. Using my left hand, it came out as an unfamiliar scrawl.

24th Evac. Hospital
R.V.N.
23 November 1968

Dear Family,

You will have to excuse the handwriting since I cannot use my right arm.

I was wounded yesterday in a firefight in the "Plain of Reeds." The bullet went in at the base of my thumb and came out through my wrist and lower arm. It's not bad, though it aches. I was moving up to help a wounded buddy, firing my rifle and throwing grenades when they got me. Another guy came up to help me and we pulled him back. I'm in good shape so don't worry about me. I'll probably get a month's sham out of this. They never put us on the boats like they said, just plain old infantry, still.

Love,
John

Late that afternoon I was sitting outside on a bench in a courtyard between the wards. Around me were crowds of walking-wounded GIs and dudes in wheelchairs. We had on blue bathrobes and hospital pajamas, and we're passing a mellow pipe in the sun. The surgeon had just told me that I might have a "million-dollar wound" with tendon and nerve damage that wouldn't heal or function for a while. I was thinking, "That's O.K. with me because I'm real tired of 'Nam."

I could count up over thirty-five guys killed and wounded in my company in the last five weeks or so, and in the six months of June to November my battalion had lost over 250 men killed and wounded out of an average field strength of about 400-500 grunts actually out humping in the boonies. When I added in the dudes hit in the platoons I'd been with over the past year, it came out to a hundred percent casualties if averaged out against the usual strength of a platoon. That's kind of bad odds any way you look at it.

I got up and shuffled around the hospital, listening to new dust-off choppers clattering in with fresh casualties and watching the frantic medical activity of moving around and handling wounded, crying and groaning noises. There were the silent ones, too—the GIs who hadn't made it and were unloaded dead or died of wounds, the body bags. I continued to explore this sad and sick concentration of war. In one part of the hospital, right near all the wounded GIs was a crouched group of wounded, captured enemy soldiers. I was astonished to see them alive, and squatted down near them, Vietnamese-style, staring at their lean, hard faces and bloody bandaged wounds, ignoring their armed MP guard. They shit-smiled at me with their snaky-looking killer eyes. I was daydreaming as I watched them, moving back and forth between a feeling of empathy towards them and the enjoyable thought of rolling a frag grenade into the middle of them at the same time.

The MP started stalking back and forth glaring at me. Finally he burst out, "Don't you know these are captured enemy prisoners?" I was jerked out of my thoughts of either a beautiful explosion or a weird combat-comradery and stared up at him, with the Viet Cong-NVA staring, too. We looked into his pink, cherry, empty REMF face, and he didn't know shit. ''Fuck it, don't mean nothin'.'' I eyeballed the enemy up close one last time, eased myself up and split. The gook eyes are still following me as I leave.

I drifted back to Gordon and Carrera's ward, and they're awake again. Gordon's still having trouble breathing but he's telling me again I did a good job and wants to put me in for a decoration for valor.

My mind runs back over all the times in the last year I've stood at attention in formations in the sun watching award ceremonies. Each time there'd be a handful of combat soldiers getting a star or two, and each time also groups of majors and colonels who'd recommended each other in careful language for heroic acts. Repetition of it had finally reduced the quality of decorations to a low point. I sat back thinking and smiling at Gordon and finally said, ''Thanks, Sarge, comin' from you it sounds nice, but I bet nothin'll come of it.'' I told them what was going on out around them, and what I'd just seen. They were too spaced out to care, but it looked like they're over the hump—they were going to make it. Every so often a medic pushed through the door, rolling in a new bed with some horribly wounded GI on it. One time they came in with a severely wounded Vietnamese, moaning and crying. With those on the ward who can see watching, they picked up the dude from the rolling stretcher and threw him on to a stationary rack. He let out the most awful groaning shriek, and the REMF-medics grinned, wolflike. The wounded GIs all around, the audience, can't move. Everyone stared at the remaining medic, but he thought it was like applause and grinned some more. He doesn't know we've all done that kind of thing, but right now we're different, we've changed, if only for a little while. It doesn't matter anyway, we're all just little cogs in a big machine. I was feeling kind of guilty because I can move around, and these hundreds of men around me couldn't. I said good-bye to my buddies and drifted out again, back to my ward and to sleep.

For the next couple of days I lay back and visit a little. I was always watching the other patients' expressions and faces. I didn't know most of them, but we were all close. Another big run of casualties came in, a lot of them from the 4th Infantry Division and the 101st Airborne. It was like a continuous war story around there, talking to one grunt after another about firefights all over 'Nam, over and over again.

The nurses are kind, wonderful girls and look like the ones we all went to high school with. I loved them for their tenderness to all my wounded brothers.

One of the nurses comes over to me now, pretty and soft-looking, and asks me if I'm hurting. I say, "Yes," and she shoots me up and it floods over me and I don't give a damn.

In a couple of days I wrote another letter home:

> *26 November, '68*
> *U.S. Army Hospital*
> *V.N.*

Dear Family,

It's now four days since I was wounded and they say they are evacuating me to Japan, so I guess the bullet wound was more serious than I thought. It kind of messed up the tendons and bones where it went through. The nerves seem to be dead. There are other guys from my squad here, too. My squad leader, Staff Sergeant Wilbur Gordon, put me in for the Bronze Star for Valor. He was hit bad, but he's going to make it. Another old buddy, Pancho Carrera, is here, too. He was hit real bad, but he made it.

You can stop worrying about me though, as they say my shooting days are over, and I will be leaving Vietnam around the beginning of December. I feel like some peace and quiet, and I'll let you know where they send me.

> *Love,*
> *John*

The next time I went down to see Pancho and Gordon, they were both gone, taken to another hospital, and I never saw them again. It was like a chapter of my life had been closed with a thud, seeing their beds filled with new casualties lying there.

It was around December 1st, 1968, and after having been moved to another hospital near Saigon, and then to Cam Ranh Bay with its thousands of shiny REMF GIs, I was loaded onto an Air Force cargo lifter. Along with over a hundred other wounded soldiers, I left Vietnam for good. I didn't know it, but U.S. strength in Vietnam that day had reached 536,100.

After stopping at Clark Air Base in the Philippines, we ended up in a large hospital on the "Rock," the island of Okinawa. I stayed here for about three weeks after they operated on me again. My arm was hanging from a pole by the bed for a while, hurting like hell; but I still felt lucky looking at the dudes all around me from every combat unit in Vietnam, hundreds and hundreds of them. A whole flood of new casualties was coming in from the 1st Cavalry Division then fighting in the Song Be-Loc Ninh-Tay Minh area. They had reinforced the Big Red One and 25th Division that had been defending the Cambodian border from NVA attacks for years. I didn't know at the time that Bear Banko, who'd transferred to the Cav from the Phu Loi Recon platoon in August, was one of the casualties. He'd been severely wounded and medevaced about this time in December when his company of the 7th Cav, Custer's old regiment, was wiped out in a massive LZ ambush.

The army has also sent a telegram to my family, telling them I've been hit, and here in Okinawa I got them on the phone and tell them I'm fine.

After my arm's off the rack, I'm up and around my ward again, visiting the more severely wounded and helping the nurses do medic-work. I also had a nice bit of dew that I smuggled out of 'Nam wrapped up in the big bandage on my arm; I had a little tea party going on the roof of the hospital with a group of walking wounded every afternoon.

The doctors came by the beds each morning making their rounds, talking to each one of us and looking at our wounds. One day my orthopedic surgeon says to me, "How you doin', Brown? You wanta go back to your unit, back to 'Nam??" For a moment I just stared at him. I'd been expecting this, even though my lower arm, wrist, and hand wouldn't move yet. Then he said, "You know, back in the old days, you would've lost your lower arm from that bullet, but you're looking pretty good now."

I said, "Well, O.K., Doc, whatever you say, man. I'll go back over if that's what's in the cards."

He looked at me and said, "That's all right, Brown. I was just curious about what you'd say. I've found out you've been in 'Nam long enough. Right now, you're going to be sent to the 'Indian Head,' the 2nd Infantry Division on the DMZ in Korea." He smiled as though he was giving me a big, joyous Christmas present.

I said to myself, "Thanks a lot you son-of-a-bitch. That's just what I want to hear. I get to go from a slimy, stinking swamp full of gooks to a frozen bunch of snowy hills full of gooks; big difference!"

He looked at my hand, wrist, and lower arm again, seeing how it wouldn't bend, turn, or flex and said, "Well, you might have to have another operation on those tendons anyway." He walked to the next bed-ridden GI, muttering a little to himself.

I was lying in my bed later on, thinking about this, and talking to myself. I'd just gotten stoned with my bunch of wounded GIs up on the roof. Who came sweeping into the ward but Ann-Margret, the movie actress. She was going from bed to bed, one GI after another, leaning those beautiful boobs over them, whispering to them, taking their hands, kissing them. I watched all this, kind of fascinated with her body, so coveted and so photographed. She gets to me now and says, "Hi, how you doin', soldier?" I motioned to her to lean forward, like I'm so screwed up I can't move; she bends over to give me a little peck and I kissed her full on the lips, wrapping and squeezing my good hand around one of those lovely projections of her body. She was startled for a second, but hardly bats an eye. She straightened up with a stage smile on her face, nodding at me with a look that said, "This animal," and moved on to the next dude. I was grinning to myself, thinking about how these celebrities flock around the fucked-up riffraff of war. "Hell, woman, you came here, you put yerself into our trip, don't let no little soldier-joke bother ya'."

The dude next to me is giggling insanely and says reverently and admiringly, "How did it feel, man, any different??"

I looked over at him laying there so shot up and said, "Hell, no, man, she feels jus' like any old cow."

On a reading table at the hospital I ran into a stack of Army newspapers including one from the 9th Division, *The Old Reliable* of the 7th of December 1968. There's a front-page report of the firefight in which I was wounded. The Viet Cong body count total had turned out to be twenty enemy killed by the grunts and cavalry gunships working together. The thing that seemed a little strange was the mention of only four GIs hit by enemy fire. I could count more than that by name myself, besides three more hit in one of our other platoons, one other guy hit by booby-trap shrapnel earlier in the day, and two more hit after Bravo Company reinforced us.

Years later I found that brigade, battalion, and company records all differed in reports of the action, but at the time I just sat wondering about this report and the way history is written and recorded.

I shuffled on back to my ward to try and forget about it all but I couldn't.

I lay in my rack lost in thought, reliving my last month in combat, mumbling out loud to myself, "Really lucky, huh, man? Never got wiped out, jus' on and on, day after day. It's like some big, endless Indian uprising except these Indians got automatic weapons and rockets, Huh?

Yeah. Twenty more killed and wounded out of the company since that mine blew up on the 23rd. About twenty confirmed Viet Cong killed by Alpha Company alone, ten or fifteen more dragged away, twenty or thirty more killed 'by the choppers'; fourteen enemy weapons captured. Where's this all goin', huh? What the hell are we doin' in 'Nam? They ain't even bombin' Hanoi and Haiphong anymore and look at this here.''

I ran my eyes up and down the long rows of beds full of suffering, wounded American soldiers. ''Here's the ones who go when they're called, the ones who believe in the flag; look at 'em now an' it ain't fer nothin', either, jus' words, an' swamps across th' ocean.''

One day, some doctor made the decision to quit bothering with me, and I was sent on my way via transport aircraft through some hospital near Tokyo, Japan, back to the U.S.A.

It was Christmas Eve, 1968. The big Air Force Hercules crowded with wounded American soldiers hit the runway with a screech and rolled up to Elmendorf Air Base, near Anchorage, Alaska. A loud collective sigh of relief rose like a hiss around me. Alaska was American dirt. Frozen-up, maybe, but still U.S. territory. We had developed engine trouble halfway across the Pacific, and everyone was terrified as the aircraft gained and lost altitude, along with the pilot's gloomy announcement. A wounded marine next to me had started crying, saying, ''I knew I'd never make it home, anyway.'' The plane was half-full of priority-stretcher-cases, which were unloaded fast in the freezing air. All us walking-wounded stood shivering in our blue hospital robes, watching the frantic shuffle.

All around in the twilight were jagged, snow-capped mountains surrounding the town. To me there was a sudden unreal peace in finally being out of Asia, out of the war, with no possibility of being sent back to it. The mountains spoke to me of peace and solitude. I had dreaded the thought of ever returning to the crowded eastern seaboard, and the sight of this rugged country inspired me immediately. Ever since that Christmas eve returning from the war, I have had a strong attachment to Alaska, the closest part of our country to Asia—a frontier, both in the American pioneer sense and also in the international meaning. I knew the state was still a vast, mostly unsettled wilderness, and that first night I felt a longing to live there some day on the edge of man's civilization.

People came out to meet us from the airbase in Alaska that night, bringing us little Christmas presents and welcoming us home. They were mostly middle-aged ladies, mothers and wives, and their faces were really smiling. It gave all of us a feeling of gratitude that I never have forgotten. Yet after so many long months in combat in Vietnam and the bloody field-hospitals, they seemed almost magically clean, virginal, and unscarred—a weird feeling about people back in the world that was to stay with me for many years.

Christmas in that hospital in Alaska, then another transport-flight to McGuire Air Force Base and a bed in Walson Army Hospital at Fort Dix in New Jersey. The hospital is the same as all the others, full of wounded soldiers yearning to be out of the army and free.

So, it's the end of the bloodiest year of the Vietnam War for the United States, but by no means the last. I was home. I didn't know it then, but from January to December of 1968, there had been 14,592 Americans killed in combat in Vietnam and something like 75,000 to 80,000 wounded, around 25 percent of the casualties of the entire war. During my year with the Big Red One, the Division had suffered over 5,000 casualties.

I was given a few days' medical leave and rode home to my family's house in Pennsylvania in my dress uniform on a Greyhound bus, my arm bandaged in a sling. Changing buses in Philadelphia in the cold damp air, I threaded my way through crowds of civilians, moving smoothly and carefully, watching every face and movement. Most people seemed to avoid my eyes or even avoided looking at me or the other returning veterans nearby. Young student-hippie types cast hostile glances. Muttered words like "baby killers, murderers" drifted to us. We stiffened and glared, tensing for action. The words subsided to patronizing whispers and smirking head shaking. I felt that hatred and bitterness flooding over me again. "Welcome home, huh, buddy?"

The crowds, traffic, bus and train stations, and the flashing neon lights seemed unchanged. It was me, us, who were different and had changed. People strutting by in their clean new clothes enraged me. People driving their shiny new cars enraged me. Shoving, pushing, sloppy, scuzzy, careless civilians all around enraged me. Advertisements twenty feet high for some kind of whiskey or new paint enraged me. "A whole damned country full of millions of draft dodgers, REMFs, and cherries, an' over there the GIs are dyin' fer nothin'."

And all the time I was moving along tight-careful, watching every place I put my feet, still methodically searching the sides and front of the trail ahead of me for danger, outwardly appearing as calm as could be.

About the 1st of January, I was sitting in my parents' house staring at the wall, listening to meaningless chatter about nothing. My mind was on 'Nam again—as usual; on this dude or that guy or "How'r they doin'? Wonder if Gaddy and Brackett and Sellman are O.K.?" What happened some night or day, long ago.

Everyone in the family and in the upper-middle-class neighborhood seemed so untouched, unscarred. I kept muttering to everyone who would listen, "The war's still goin' on over there, ya' know?" The most they'd do is nod their heads a little, solemnly, and say, "Well, yes, that's true, isn't it?" or "It's really a very unattractive situation, I must say." or "How did we ever get involved in a war over there? I simply don't understand. Our generals must be insane."

And I'm daydreaming about that Tonkin Gulf incident four and a half long years before. Johnson's and McNamara's scheming and lies, the frantic shuffling of Bundy's and Rusk and Rostow to escalate the war purposefully, to manuever and encourage Johnson into sending in the line battalions while the old, battle-scarred leaders, "the war-mongering generals" like Ridgway and MacArthur urged and begged their civilian masters not to do it.

And now most of these same culpable fools with the blood of thousands of my brothers on their hands were "doves." They were against escalation. They were searching for an alternative. Negotiations were in order. We could afford to refrain from bombing the enemy. We could afford to lose "moderate casualties" (of GIs) while we prostrate ourselves and said to the impassive North Vietnamese Communists, "Our army is bogged down in your country's jungles and villages because we have tied the hands of our soldiers. We have never saturation-bombed your civilians into surrender, and now we've stopped our surgical strikes. We've showed such admirable 'restraint,' let us negotiate now."

And I keep thinking of exploding grenades, flashes of RPGs, bursts of automatic rifle fire, incoming rockets, screams of "Medic!" over and over and over. I can't sleep, can't rest, nobody knows nothin'.

My father is proud of me but aloof, as if he's seen it all, but I know he hasn't. He was in the rear, back in World War II. My mother, she's really glad and thankful that I made it home alive, as mothers are. She doesn't have to maintain a facade. But she doesn't know anything, either. And I had girl friends. One was Amy, with whom I was sleeping before I went overseas. I wrote from 'Nam and told her, "Forget me," and she did. She's gone, I don't know where. Another one I've got now, she looks good, but she's into clothes and college and "Middle Ages

History, the Medicis and Leonardo da Vinci.'' ''Well, that's O.K., my goddam pass-time is up anyway.''

Back at the army hospital at Fort Dix, the orthopedic surgeon studies my arm, the way the wrist, thumb, and lower arm don't work correctly. He tells me I'll have to have another operation. The medical doctors examine me, telling me I've lost a lot of weight according to my records. The tests show I have amoebic dysentery, malarial-type fevers and shakes, and a heavy infestation of hookworms. And all around me were guys so much worse off, I feel sick about them. Worse gunshot-wounds, single and double amputees, shrapnel blasts by grenades, mines, or rockets. The war, the whole scene, spread out around me and us, day after day.

One morning who came tripping between the hospital beds of our ward, but this famous pop-singer who calls himself ''Tiny Tim.'' He was strumming his ukulele ahead of a trail of giggling ''groupie'' girls. He was singing in his high squeaky voice about ''tip-toeing through the tulips.'' I stared with fifty other hard-faced old men-boys at this apparition from outer space. He was a huge thing, despite his name. I thought to myself, ''You ought to really look around you, pig, and think about what yer singin'.'' These dudes from the 25th and 4th Divisions next to me didn't have any legs to tiptoe on.

The other guys in the ward are shouting and screaming now, catcalling, throwing water pitchers, drowning the idiot out. He kept up his fake stage smile while retreating, the blank-eyed ''groupies'' backing up in shock, the nurses running in to quiet the animals down.

I got another medical leave for a while, but didn't feel like going ''home.'' In my dress uniform again, arm in a sling, ribbons, CIB, and Division patches, I took off wandering. It was early 1969, and damned if I didn't wind up on the streets of Washington during Nixon's presidential inauguration ceremonies. I was mellow and wandering around in the crowd, when suddenly there was Nixon and all the new bunch of big shots, Ehrlichman, Mitchell, Haldeman, and others in limousines. The old Democratic big shots, whom I hate more than I ever hated the Viet Cong, who like to forget that they put us into this war, are cruising along luxuriously, too, smiling their comfortable, satisfied, powerful smiles, deigning to glance now and then at the crowds on either side. They'll go to the inaugural balls and parties tonight in rich apparel, eating and drinking and gabbling in rich abundance. The sight of all the plump, dressed-up-pretty fat cats made me physically sick. I wish with all my power that they could be grabbed up, put in the line with a pitiful little plastic-stocked rifle, and sent in against a dug-in company of Viet Cong or NVA Regulars. I wish to Christ I could hear them cry or pray. For a second I dream of a fiery ambush.

I was standing there in a glowering rage: "The dudes are still over there in '69, my platoon, my company is still out there, where these pigs put them, dressed in rags, in the slime and mud, with rifles in their hands. The shooting, the AK-47s, the rockets, the ambushes, the shot up GIs screaming—it's all going down right this minute, while this fuckin' carnival's going on."

On the other side of the street from me in a park, a crowd of "hippies" was inaugurating a pig for president, a real pig. The cops were pushing and hassling them, the shoving crowd around me was yelling again, and I can see more limousines and cars coming. It's another part of the inauguration parade; the vehicles were full of cheering, blond-haired, blue-eyed, all-American preppies and kiddies, draft-deferred college students, plus a few "token" blacks. They were riding along singing, "Up, up, with people, you meet 'em wherever you go!" They held up happy signs, and grinned with glee; and I hated them. Them and their 2-S draft exemptions and important careers to pursue, their carefree ignorance of the realities of 1969.

To my mind the great parade should have been led by an honor guard of jungle-uniformed combat soldiers, flown in from every division fighting in Vietnam at that moment. But it wasn't, it was just more bullshit, drivel, and pretension. And that was the moment that I looked at the "war protest movement" in a whole new light. They wanted to end this war right now, this war that the politicians were losing. Here I was a man of lost illusions, but still a patriotic veteran American combat soldier, and I suddenly wanted the same thing, too. Maybe my reasons were different, but I began to see them as allies. The upper class, the politicians and bureaucrats and their sons weren't doing it; they had their exemptions or cozy, token military jobs or more important things to do. They had stopped bombing North Vietnam while we were fighting and dying in the field; they hadn't backed us up, but the GIs were still over there dying in combat that day, everyday. I wouldn't be able to rest while it continued. I suddenly had had it with the whole crooked thing in early 1969, and I was still in an Army uniform.

At the same moment, back in the Mekong Delta my battalion was in contact and taking more casualties and the enemy was attacking Can Tho, where Tommy Donaghue was stationed after going back for a second tour.

After returning depressed to Walson Army Hospital, I finally had my scheduled operation. The tendon-bone pain was back; my arm hung from the pole again for a week or so. The whole damn thing seemed like a waste of time because manual dexterity didn't return.

16   Politics No!

*"War is therefore a continuation
of policy by other means. It is not
merely a political act but a real
political instrument, a continuation
of political intercourse by
other means."*
—Karl Von Clausewitz

For the next four months after recovering from the operation, I served as an acting medic in the hospital.

I worked on two wards of more severely wounded men. My job consisted of going around every day, doing all sorts of chores with the more shot-up soldiers, helping the nurses to change wound dressings and bed pans, getting things, doing favors for dudes who couldn't move. I got a long, concentrated rerun of the consequences of the war. Every day was a reminder of my own past, a reminder that the fighting was grinding on under Nixon. When one is surrounded by suffering and pain and with no belief in the reasons and methods causing it, medic work can be more radicalizing than combat. The hospital was full of dope—legal and illegal. If your wound hurt after an operation, they would shoot you up with Demoral or real morphine. After my second operation, I developed an allergic reaction to Demoral so they had to give me the real thing. If you were supposed to be officially beyond pain, there were medics and oddball GIs cruising the wards selling other kinds of dope.

One night I went off base with another GI into the nearby little town of Wrightstown, New Jersey. The streets were lined with cafes and cheap jewelry stores that prey on soldiers—the same as outside any Army camp. Outside one joint selling junky "diamond engagement rings," I eyeballed two tinhorn salesmen strutting back and forth on the sidewalk hawking their wares. In the window was a large cardboard poster with a long list of names. On top was a headline, "Vietnam Honor Roll."

Below in smaller letters, it read, "The following listed soldiers have been killed in action. As our contribution to their memory, we will not bill their families for the remaining principal and interest they owe us on jewelry they purchased here on our time-payment plan!"

The same old wave of sick disgust rolls over me, as I look at this obscenity and listen to these two hovering sharks, true war profiteers, starting their cheap-assed sales pitch at us. "Same as fuckin' Saigon, same as that goddam inauguration, it's all the same."

I ended up wandering into this off-base GI coffeehouse serving "free refreshments and doughnuts to soldiers." It looked the same as all the other fronts in the ville, except the whole place was full of young people my own age. There was coffee and all, and a scattering of tables and chairs; I sat down stiff and alert in a corner with my back to the wall, watching and listening. I looked at this tough-sounding but pretty girl in a short skirt, hair cut close. She was sounding off about the war and how wrong it was. I sat there gazing at her and listening. I could feel across the room that she was tense and strung-tight as I am.

She was yelling and arguing, not backing up; she's the first person I've really listened to about anything in a long, long time. She was the first girl I'd ever seen back in the world who cared, who knew and felt that our American GIs were dying every day, that it wasn't working, that something was wrong with the whole thing. Suddenly, I really looked at her and she seemed beautiful to me, and I loved her instantly. I jumped to her defense when one of the new GIs, still in training and a total cherry, argued back at her. I'm in my dress uniform, still proud, but definitely wired out, ready for anything. My rank, medal ribbons, Combat Infantry badge, and division patches brought instant authority to my voice and silence to the room full of fifty people, mostly trainees.

After I defended her position on the necessity of ending the war, I moved over and sat close to her. I've been with her ever since. Josie Duke has been my wife for fifteen years and has borne five children, living a rough, scrabbling life on the edge of the wilderness. So I guess it really was love at first sight, and my life changed for the better. I had finally found someone to live for, someone who cared about what was eating at me and shared all my feelings and memories of Vietnam.

The next day I could hardly wait to get through my work at the hospital to return to the coffeehouse. As soon as I came through the door, I saw her and she smiled and came over to me.

All through my war service, I heard so much about the antiwar movement that I was curious to learn everything I could from Josie.

We sat together and started to talk; the warm glow of having found someone is in both of us. She talks like a GI herself, clipped, to the point, no frills. She tells me all about the Columbia uprising of '68 and her part in it.

The main radicals had gone on to tear SDS apart with political infighting, but she and a small group had decided to do something specific to end the war. She had identified the same political and bureaucratic perpetrators of the war that I had, during the same year. Starting first by distributing leaflets to soldiers home on leave, they ended up at Fort Dix living in an old farmhouse off-base and starting their "coffee house" in a vacant store front to bring to the Army their opposition to war. Over the past year and a half, she had been in many demonstrations and confrontations with the police, some of them violent. The violence against the protestors caused a feeling of hopeless rage that they were able to convert gradually into radical answers to problems.

She was talking again now. "You were on the wrong side in this war; the Viet Cong are the freedom fighters and patriots. The National Liberation Front, the NLF, is the true government of Vietnam; the Saigon government is only a puppet one. It was set up by the Americans and has no support among the people at all."

I sat gazing at her, my mind running back over the real images. Thousands of South Vietnamese soldiers killed fighting the Viet Cong. The chopped off heads and dead bodies of civilians assassinated by the Communists. The ARVN Cavalry Battalion that stood and fought the 273rd VC Regiment on the 13th of February, killing eighty of them after our Tet Offensive ambush. The Ruff-Puff ARVNs who betrayed us or ran away at Tan Phu Khan in the May Offensive. The months and months of not seeing ARVNs at all in the jungles north of Lai Khe. My Vung Tau family and the draft dodgers, dope-pushers, and whores of Saigon, Phu Cuong, or Rach Kien. The phlegmatic 12th ARVN Regiment around Cai Lay and the thousands of Mekong Delta farm families, faces of fear, understanding, hatred, welcome, the intense eyes of Minh, our ex-Viet Cong tiger scout, the sardonic smirks on the faces of the wounded Communist prisoners at the med-evac hospital, all the confused sides.

"Wrong damned place to be," is my half-strangled, muttered answer.

She's sure of herself, though. "We're there in Vietnam so the big defense corporations can make money off the millions of bombs, the support of our huge army, and to take control over the whole Indochinese peninsula for its raw materials. It's a big capitalist and government plot.''

I was thinking to myself, "Bombs, huh? Bombing the jungle—they ain't bombing Hanoi or Haiphong. There shouldn't even be any Hanoi or Haiphong left if our GIs are fighting and dying over there. 'Bout like if they'd stopped bombing Germany in the middle of World War II.''

Out loud I'm saying, "We gotta pull our troops out now, this year, 1969.'' Some of the Vietnamese will fight us forever, the war will go on indefinitely and our government won't use its full power against the Communists to win. I hate to think all our casualties have been fer nothing, but I'm beginning to believe it. I don't know why we went into Vietnam; who the hell knows the real truth? All I do know is the war has to be fought out by the Vietnamese and if the Soviets and Chinese are arming one side, we shouldn't do anymore than arm the other side.''

She laid out her position again. "The Viet Cong and PLO, the Cubans, the IRA, and the worldwide socialist movement are all one force, one brotherhood, marching towards the victory of the oppressed peoples of the world over the great beast, Imperialism. We have to join them in the struggle or be destroyed!''

This type of heavy thinking set me back a little, but it was fascinating. I'd seen the incredible, vicious fighting ability of the VC; their never-quit attitude was legendary among combat GIs. I let my mind wander over what I'd seen of the South Vietnamese officials in their palaces and villas with their Citroens and Mercedes. God, I'd hated the bastards. The always-clean and shiny generals and colonels in our own Army, hounding us for "body-counts," and the presidential inauguration of Nixon, the fat cats and high brows, the limousines and Cadillacs, the gay, happy throng while the war continued that very day. The bitterness in me was huge. Here I was a trained, veteran soldier, an accomplished killer, a survivor, skeptical, tired, lean, capable of instant violence, and I was utterly captivated by her assurance, vitality, and confidence. I looked at her and I knew I'd found the right woman, at least one who cared enough to get radical about it.

She told me about one of her early demonstrations against a meeting of the Foreign Policy Association in New York when Dean Rusk, the secretary of state, an architect of American involvement in the Vietnam War, was present. She and the protestors had marched into the driveway chanting and trying to block the fancy automobiles and fine people from entering the meeting and were pushed back by the police several times. Finally they threw bags of cows' blood that burst all over the cars, while news reporters took pictures. In my own bitter state of mind at this time, I loved hearing about it. The milling, yelling crowds, the well-fed, untouched "policymakers" getting their nice evening shook up, the blood spattering on their limousines—all while American GIs fought and died in the mud for the empty words of politicians that same night on the other side of the world.

Then she told me of another time when, after hanging President Johnson in effigy and then burning the dummy, she was arrested and taken to a small precinct to be booked. Since there wasn't a woman cop to frisk her, she was shut into an interrogation room until one could be found. Unfortunately, she still had a bottle of flammable liquid in her pocket and was expecting a heavy bust. Along comes this old black janitor, working a push broom and sawdust and a wheeled trash can, humming to himself. Without appearing to even notice her fear, he paused next to her while she dumped the incriminating evidence into the police trash of old cigarette butts and coffee cups and then shuffled on along. It was silent communication with no words spoken.

So my new education began in what had happened to the rest of my generation while I'd been overseas. The days at the hospital went on and the nights at the coffeehouse. There was a feeling of danger for me in even going there from the army base, a dread that it was going to lead me into the stockade when I was almost finished with Uncle Sam.

About the third night of my attendance, a radical group from New York SDS came down. They had just returned from a "national conference" in Chicago.

Mark Rudd was sitting on a high stool among a crowd of GIs, both recruits and veterans. He was stocky built, light-haired, had an outthrust jaw and an immediately noticeable domineering manner.

I had heard of him back in May of '68 in Vietnam in news accounts of the Columbia student uprising. I settled down in a corner near Josie to hear his statement:

"You guys are in the Army, and you've either been to Vietnam or you're going. The point I want to make tonight is that the main struggle going on in the world today is between American imperialism and national liberation struggles against it; in the American army you're one of the oppressors."

There was absolute silence in the room as the audience of mostly working class GIs tried to absorb this version of their world. Rudd went on in his harangue, warming to his crowd control and to the sound of his own voice. I was already somewhat skeptical and bored but I kept catching parts of the current SDS line:

"Where do you stand with regard to the United States as an oppressor nation?"

"The oppressed people of the world are the ones who have created all the wealth in America around you; your cars, your televisions, your houses, your supermarkets, your clothes—all of it belongs largely to the oppressed people of the world. In Vietnam you will only be fighting to keep it all."

"The ultimate goal of the revolution is the destruction of American imperialism, and stopping the immoral war in Vietnam is the first way to begin. We in our affluence are living on the labor of the Vietnamese, the Bolivians, and all other colonized peoples..."

And so he went on and on for perhaps two hours, until most of the soldiers were half-asleep, their real questions about Vietnam unanswered. It was the beginning of my exposure to the intensely Communist politics of the Weatherman faction of SDS. There had been political in-fighting for control and direction of the organization since the winter before at Boulder, Colorado, and Ann Arbor, Michigan. Josie had gone to both of these national council meetings and had come away confused over their objectives and determined to do something concrete to end the war. The overall radical leadership had an idea for almost everybody. Acquaintances connected with the Institute for Policy Studies, a radical think-tank in Washington, DC, had started creating antiwar movements around military bases. It was a way to channel young idealists into a new attack on the system.

For Josie, moving to Fort Dix was part of her answer to the extreme Communist tone of the SDS at the time, but the extremists came down occasionally to try and raise the political fervor.

Rudd was still preaching:

"What we need is the creation of two, three, many Vietnams, as Che Guevara said. The many Vietnams include the black uprising of Detroit in '67 and Cleveland in '68. We need to bring the Viet Cong revolution back home to America!"

This was decidedly not what the GIs were gathered to hear, and vague rustlings and rumblings of discontent arose.

"Ah, hell, what's the dude talkin' about, man? He's not talkin' about endin' the war in 'Nam, he's jus' a Communist."

The extreme radical nature of this and other speeches I heard kept discontent in the Army fairly low.

Josie looked uncomfortable, too, but there was still the tie with Columbia of '68, and a loyalty that went with it. I didn't push the issue later; we were already beginning to understand each other's true beliefs and motives.

In this atmosphere of political storm, Josie and I soon became lovers—very close and intense. My free time out of the hospital was spent entirely in her company. I came to know the other activists who ran the place: Beth, Saul, Ron, Herby and Margaret, Bob, and others. They were all sincere and dedicated in their beliefs. Their influence strengthened my feelings against the war.

Saul and Beth seemed to be the radical-intellectual guiding lights of the coffee house staff. They had both been friends of Josie at New York SDS and Columbia.

Saul spoke to me as though my relationship with Josie made me a believer already.

"What we're doing here is educating GIs to accept the correctness and inevitability of Marxism. The common ground for all dissent and radicalism occurring right now is really existentialism. It's what makes all the hippies scream, 'Revolution for the hell of it!' or 'If it feels good do it!' What we want them to begin saying is 'Power to the people!' or 'Off the pigs!' or 'NLF is gonna win!' When they do, we've won."

I said, "What d'ya mean by existentialism?"

"It's an old theory or a philosophy that relates well to twentieth century life. A gut-level rejection or revolt against anything that appears absolute like giant corporate capitalism, for one thing. The theory is that there are no absolute binding moral laws or values, that there is no God, and that man alone creates legal and moral rules on earth, that man is individually temporary, and we exist in a world devoid of purpose.

"It's too apolitical for us, but it can lead people into accepting our real theories. Existentialist ideas have become naturally popular among kids, what they're calling hippies now, but we think they're too disorganized and lack a purpose for bettering society.

"We believe in socialism and we are trying to channel the existentialist antiwar feelings in other young people into a socialist movement."

I said, "O.K., I understand, but when you say 'socialism' don't you mean communism?"

"Yes, I do. I believe in communism, but I say 'socialism' so I don't turn people off and to differentiate between our new left ideas and old-style Stalinism.''

"I can see what yer sayin', Saul, but to me socialism and communism are the same anyway, and I don't think Americans will ever believe in it. Too many people here are comfortable an' the Vietnam War ain't botherin' them enough to go Communist over it. I'm among yer group here because I'm tired of the dudes gettin' killed over the 'Nam fer nothin', but I'm not a Communist, and I know God exists.''

He answered with a smile, "It's O.K., John. You'll understand and you'll believe after a while.''

In meetings I often listened to the ex-students talking about the Columbia uprising and other demonstrations. They seemed to be almost amazed at the violent reactions of police. It was as if despite all the talk of revolution they didn't understand yet that the power structure was not going to just suddenly give up and turn control over to them. I tried to describe to them what real revolutionaries were like—how five or six Viet Cong would sometimes attack a whole platoon or company of Americans to protect their retreating comrades.

My attempt at portraying the reality of revolutionary struggle was usually seen as ignorant soldier-admiration of enemy proficiency, not evidence of the realities of Communist revolution.

All of a sudden, the surgeon at the hospital decided to operate on my hand and arm again—to "give it another try." The next day I became a patient once more, with all the other dudes "back in 'Nam again.'' After the operation, my wound is pulled and wired together tightly and hung from the old pole-stand again. I'm getting morphine shots, I'm stoned, laying in that ward, and staring at all the fucked-up GIs around me again. But now I had somebody, Josie. She came to the hospital all the time, sat by my bed, kissed me, and loved me. She could feel and see the war all around her in those wards. The guys so shot-up they couldn't move who cried quietly in their beds. The dude from the 1st Cavalry Division with no legs who played a wind-up "laughing box" all day long, staring at nothing. The wounded guys nearby begging the nurses for more dope to kill the pain in their bodies and in their minds. Josie did them all favors and brought them coffee and looked into their eyes. She stayed with them and with me and got a little firsthand dose of 'Nam. During some of our hospital hours together I tried to convey to her my constant feelings of luck-guilt, of making it through O.K. while I remembered the ambushes, snipers, firefights and rocket attacks, at maybe a hundred GIs hit close by me—killed or wounded—besides many others a little farther away.

After I was able to be up and around and back to doing hospital medic work, the doctor decided he had fixed my arm as well as he could. I was finally released from Walson and assigned to the basic training cadre at Fort Dix. I served now at Pro Park testing the combat proficiency of troop trainees heading for the war. It was the summer of 1969. The Army had, of course, reneged on its deal of giving me an early out because I'd been wounded and "hadn't served my whole second tour in Vietnam."

I had already moved into Josie's room at the farmhouse, forcing myself into the cozy little student-radical "collective." This was the cause of an all-night meeting. For hours and hours I lay in an upstairs bedroom listening to the haranguing voices rise and fall.

"But you have a revolutionary responsibility to put your private pleasure aside. You can't have him here!"

"Well, if he can't stay here what's the point of our coffeehouse, he's a soldier, isn't he?"

"But these GIs don't understand anything about the complexities of the struggle!"

"Chairman Mao said that revolutionary guerillas must be fish swimming in a sea of people!"

"Josie! You have to listen to reason. If we let him in, they'll all want to move in!"

"That's too damn bad, huh? Isn't that the whole purpose of our work here!"

"But Fidel would say. . ."

"According to Lenin. . ."

I finally fell asleep in my new double bed waiting for her—my defender, my girl.

We eventually won the struggle, a true proletarian victory, and from then on we became a counterforce to "bourgeois student elitism." Over the next few months more and more GIs, some of them combat veterans like myself, moved in and gradually the "elitest" complexion of the place changed. In fact, some of the radicals even left. It was becoming a "GI movement." In the meantime, though, Josie had to learn and adapt to the army-wife routine.

When the alarm started ringing at 4:30 or 5:00 a.m., I'd jump up, throw on my uniform, and report to headquarters company on the base for reveille. My bunk in the barracks stayed unoccupied and clean; a buddy covered for me there. While I ran the trainees through combat testing all day, Josie worked on the writing and layout of the antiwar newspaper, *Shakedown*, put out by the coffeehouse staff for distribution to the soldiers of Fort Dix. After I drove off base, I'd spend six or so hours every evening with her in the joint, talking to GIs, answering questions about Vietnam and the war, sometimes to the same trainees I'd just been testing. And right then, the same thing was springing up or occurring outside Army and Marine bases all over the United States. It was a major development in the antiwar movement, leading to the founding of "Vietnam Veterans Against the War" and eventually to "Vietnam Veterans of America"—organizations whose existence reflected a feeling of betrayal among many combat veterans. I was to find out later that money to pay all the activities, living and traveling expenses came from tax-free foundations in New York, Boston and other places. Every few weeks Beth would go on a trip to collect it. One of the important connections was Cora Weiss, who was married to a radical attorney named Peter Weiss of the Lawyers' Guild, and was also the daughter of Samuel Rubin of the Rubin Foundation. The army didn't like what was happening at all, even if we were just telling the truth about what we'd seen "over there." It was part of the crumbling process, a new worry for them and the foolish politicians who had started it all. GIs from the base constantly drifted in at night when they were off duty. Some agreed and some argued, but the original coffeehouse activists were happy anyway because at least they were in contact with the real America instead of only with students in a surreal world.

A communal lifestyle was carried on in the farmhouse, with acid rock, dew, pictures of Chairman Mao and Ho Chi Minh, and all. It was impossible for me to look at those pictures myself, but I tried to ignore them, because they seemed so important to everyone else. They appeared to need heroes. It was as though everything learned as children had vanished and a "new revolutionary life" was at hand. Nonbelief in anything America had stood for was the only position to take. I felt more like an observer than a participant, like I was an old man watching kids growing up. Fighting the Viet Cong on the ground for so long had trained me not to accept anything at face value.

The waving of the enemy flags in Washington or New York or San Francisco and the chants of "Ho! Ho! Ho Chi Minh! NLF is gonna win!" had taken something out of every soldier who fought in Vietnam and had left a legacy of bitterness.

"Man, if those idiots back there are waving Viet Cong flags at home and cheering the gooks, what the hell are we doin' here?" I heard that statement or something like it many times out in the jungle or huddled in some NDP under fire. And now I was home alive, bitter about the whole thing myself, trying to learn the other side of it, and to understand the other half of my own generation while the war still raged on. A growing existentialist renouncement of all authority was going on in the larger sweep of the movement among the people our own age. Demands for legalizing pot and acid together with crazy rock concerts and collective living all took up equal time with the movement "to end the war." It showed me how unreal the war was to most of them. At the same time, political radicals aspired to a discipline to equal the commitment of the NLF.

For Josie and her group, more strongly committed than many, it became a frantic race against time. Gradually, more radical renouncement of the whole American way of life took place, including free-enterprise captialism, which they saw as having caused the war. No countering of the overall view of the dialectics of world power struggle was permitted. This ignored the possiblity that even if the whole world was socialist-communist there would still be ideological or territorial differences leading to wars (such as the Soviet-Chinese conflict). Instead, along with their frustration over Vietnam, came an increasing feeling that they were revolutionaries, too—brothers and sisters of the revered Viet Cong and Cubans, who could do no wrong in the eyes of the "New Left."

The mass movement to end the war rapidly spread to universities and colleges across the country despite the extreme leftist politics of the organizers. Because these were the sons and daughters of the decision makers and bureaucrats and the upper and middle classes generally, they received more headlines and attention in the media than the sacrifice and heroism of soldiers far away. In fact, combat heroism or militarism of any kind extolling American fighting men had become first a sore subject and later an object of joking scorn. At the same time the growth of antiwar feeling spreading within the military services in 1969 enraged the lifers and brass. They, of course, wouldn't admit officially that we'd all been used for a no-win war; all they could do was hate their fellow soldiers who were saying it out loud.

One day I was made forcibly aware of this when I was pulled in by the CID for interrogation about "subversive associations." They started with the old tough-cop routine, threatening me with a court-martial and stockade time for "association with communists." By this time I was so jumpy and wired out from the events of the past year and a half that I exploded. I screamed at them, almost driven to tears of rage, "I'll blow you all away with a goddam grenade one of these nights!" I must have shocked some sense into them because they suddenly stopped. I couldn't stop: "You rear-echelon mother fuckers, you better watch yer asses or I'll come back and cut you to pieces with an M-16."

One of them actually backed up to the wall and showed that he carried a pistol, right there in his paper-filled office. I was unarmed. After that, they spoke quietly to me, trying to calm me and ease me out of the building. They must have known from my records I'd just gotten out of fourteen months in Vietnam. I was still shaking with rage and emotion when a few minutes later I was ordered to report to a military psychiatrist. This shrink was a REMF, too, in my book. I looked into his clean, unlined face, his wandering eyes, and instantly hated him. In the Vietnam War it had become fashionable in his profession to no longer recognize "combat fatigue" or "shell shock" of previous wars. He was chattering at me like a trained monkey in a green suit. "Ahh hell," I thought, "I'll tell this guy what I really think."

"Those CID and my CO and you, too, asshole, all got fat bellies, an' I keep dreamin' about blowing 'em all apart with a '16. I wanna see 'em splatter like big, ripe red tomatoes. An' I could low-crawl up to any goddamn office full of pigs on this base an' heave a grenade in an' ain't nobody gonna even see me. That's what I think about, man, so how does that grab ya?" The shrink cherry-stared at me for a long moment with wide eyes, and I saw my chance and started right in again with some more plans I had.

He finally calmed me down and said, "I'm going to give you an immediate thirty-day leave for medical reasons. I think you ought to get off this base real soon."

I said, "That's fine with me." He nodded, smiled wimp-like, and politely dismissed me. I headed off base right away, smirking to myself a little now. I told Jose what had happened, and we packed what little stuff we had for a month-long trip.

It wasn't until years later, thinking about these events, that I was able to reflect calmly about that incident, to realize and admit that even the U.S. Army that I was so tired of by then was a reflection of the still-free society we lived in then and now. That I could completely lose my control and insubordinately threaten the lives of my superior officers, whether out of combat fatigue or not and not be court-martialed, was an example of tolerance that took me fifteen years to admit. It was an extension of the same freedom and tolerance that allowed the student radicals to wave the flags and slogans of the enemy our country was fighting, without fear of imprisonment—the very greatness of the tradition of American liberty that I would fight to defend again today.

In the meantime, we headed to my parents' house in Pennsylvania where they got to know Josie. Everthing was fine for a few days until we started to talk politics. They were shocked by my new radicalism, having no real idea of the long trail of bitterness that it came from. Soon, we hurried off to New York to visit Josie's father.

I first met Anthony Duke in his office in a building full of black street kids from Harlem. The place was called ''Boy Harbor'' and is essentially a school-camp-educational institution that he'd founded thirty years before in an attempt to answer some of the problems of the country's ghettos. He's a straight, short, squared-away-looking dude with eyes and face that command attention. He appears to be in perfect condition at fifty years of age. He impressed me by the way he embraced Josie with such evident love—the war and radical scene had estranged and divided so many families. Next, he sized me up while I did the same to him, and we got a little superficial history from one other. I soon heard from him that he'd commanded an LST in many beach landings, including Normandy and Okinawa of World War II. I'm thinking to myself, ''Well, maybe he's got some idea about what's going on in the jungles of 'Nam right now, I don't know. An officer in the Navy at sea on board a ship, popular support from home, a national desire for unconditional victory.''

He invited us out to the family house in East Hampton on Long Island. We agreed to meet him there and left. On the noisy, crowded streets of New York, I asked Josie to marry me again for the second time since we left Fort Dix. She agreed by asking me the same, and we hug and kiss and feel good.

Out at East Hampton later, we are in their large and fine house overlooking the water. Josie's father took us speeding around in his boat. He had this Naval Commander look on his face now—the same one that he always gets on a boat. I'm standing there beside him, watching all these fancy yachts and happy weekenders, thinking about 'Nam again, still popping and blowing right this minute. I jerk myself back to the business at hand.

"Mr. Duke, I'd like your permission to marry your daughter." He looked at me for a while as if perhaps the conventionality of it was a little unexpected. Then he said something graceful like, "That's very considerate of you to ask. Of course, you may." He then began to tell me the history of his family, of which he's obviously proud. I have a feeling that he doesn't have any idea where my mind is at presently, how crowded it is with dark violent thoughts, savage and bloody memories. We had a pleasant stay with my prospective father-in-law for a few days and somehow our radical anger didn't come between us. We stopped for a short visit with "Abuela" Cordelia, the wise and understanding matriarchal grandmother of the Duke-Biddle clan. There we met Josie's first cousin, Tony Biddle, who alone is upholding a family tradition by entering the U.S. Navy from Cornell. He mused about being the only person in his large university circle to put on a uniform in these strange times. It was apparent to both of us that the class born to leadership positions was renouncing the responsibilities of service.

We headed out again on a long drive to Florida to visit Josie's mother. As soon as I met her, I immediately sensed a combativeness and a feeling that I've got some ulterior motive. I backed off, thinking, "Let it slide." Mostly I looked around Florida at all the plump, relaxed people skating along, oblivious to all the bloodshed and stink still going on every day in Indochina.

The big news in May had been the bloody assault by the 101st Airborne Division on Ap Bia Mountain, Hill 937, near the Laotian border—called "Hamburger Hill." After suffering hundreds of casualties while capturing the position, the Army abandoned it a week later. Perhaps this was the ultimate demonstration of the futility of Vietnam. The war and progress of the fighting was still constantly on my mind; the Big Red One was still fighting the NVA up along Thunder Road and the 9th Infantry Division was still slogging through Viet Cong ambushes in the dirty Delta. With each piece of war news, I felt like I was still there.

Every day those young GIs over there were still fighting and winning their part of the war. Cutting through the jungles, slogging through the swamps, digging bunkers and holes, ambushing and fighting off the enemy, humping the ammo and serving the guns, rescuing and bandaging their wounded buddies, doing their time in the line. I was still proud to have been one of them, and I couldn't figure out what to believe in anymore.

For months the army routine dragged on, with me testing new troop-

trainees and Josie working at the coffeehouse. The whole Fort Dix Army
movement thing had become constantly more GI-centered. The antiwar
feeling was visible at every major military base in the United States;
the feeling had even spread to Vietnam, where the brass were beginning to have serious problems with troops. Units refused to assault specific objectives or disobeyed orders, fragging or attacking hated or
distrusted officers, widespread racial disorders, large-scale hard-drug
usage all increased.

And yet, amazingly the combat-heroism still continued "over there."
The troops returning to Fort Dix told the same stories we veterans had
lived through. Professionalism in firefights, rescuing wounded buddies,
and killing the enemy, to the constant reminder of "America doesn't
care." My feelings of loyalty to these fellow soldiers combined with
my desire to see the war ended left me in a quandry.

The Army was having its own problems with image that year with
the sensational revelation of the My Lai massacre of several hundred
civilians. The incident had occurred at the end of the Tet Offensive of
1968 in 1st Corps.

The eventual publication of gruesome photographs and eyewitness
stories led to an uproar in the country and a further boost to the antiwar movement. The American response and handling of the event further impressed on me the difference between our free and responsive
society and the Communists, who had conducted and hidden their far
larger massacres for decades. I had a feeling of revulsion at the close-
range murder of women and young children myself and didn't think that
those responsible should get off free. It was as though the thousands of
times we GIs had withheld our fire in civilian areas were all in vain.
The term "baby-killing GIs" came even more into vogue.

At the same time, I had my own clear memories of shooting into villages, either in response to enemy fire or by accident and once in revenge at long range in the May offensive at Tan Phu Khan. The people
at home who hadn't experienced a guerilla war could hardly be expected
to understand the long chain of circumstances brought on by the very
nature of the fighting that led to incidents like these. I was in the same
dilemma as many other military men and Americans in general over
civilian killings in Vietnam. What made My Lai so different was the
point-blank nature of the event and the extended mass murder of helpless victims.

In a characteristic manner, the military absolved all officers of responsibility except a platoon leader, Lieutenant William Calley. From the America Division commander, General Koster, down to a company commander at the scene, no one else was convicted. For me, remembering the constant insistence by higher-ups on a "body count" should have been enough to reduce Calley's sentence.

The incident further polarized the American people on the war and made our continuing ground presence there even more untenable.

A subsequent irony to me was the eventual awarding of the Pulitzer Prize for journalism to Seymour Hersh for his role in publicizing the event. It was the only such award for written journalism to come out of the entire Tet Offensive reporting on combat heroism by American fighting men, that had cost 23,000 U.S. casualties.

Although the several hundred GIs affected by the coffeehouse student activists had their anti-Vietnam War feelings strengthened by the association, the process was also working the other way around, too.

The vivid reality of Viet Cong actions described by us veterans had a subtle effect on those radicals who remained in close contact with us. There was a leveling-off process in the down-with-America aspect of their rhetoric. This brought them closer to less marxist groups, like the "Mobilization to End the War," then planning large national demonstrations.

At the same time, their former comrades in Columbia or in the New York regional SDS who had remained in small affinity groups of elite student intellectuals went farther to the left. The most radical elements of the Revolutionary Youth Movement branch of SDS had recently formed themselves into a militant Communist group called "Weathermen" (a name taken from a popular song of the time by Bob Dylan).

In the late summer and early fall of 1969, small groups of these self-proclaimed Communist revolutionaries came to Fort Dix and inflicted themselves on us. They always insisted on chanting that "the Viet Cong are gonna win!" and glorying in any bad news from the Vietnam battlefields. Whenever we veterans heard such news, it hurt. We knew all too well what it meant in human terms. The radicals were far beyond that. They waved the hated Viet Cong flags in our faces and preyed on our equally fervent desire to see American combat troops withdrawn from the endless war. Mark Rudd, the "Columbia Comrade," came to the coffeehouse again; he struck me as egotistical and smooth—a manipulator. He had been practically created by the news media as the leader of SDS, but, according to Josie, the real planning and brains came from Bernardine Dohrn and Jeff Jones in Chicago. These Weathermen had finally come up with the line that "America is made up almost entirely of pigs, except the blacks," and should be "occupied by a foreign power of the World Communist Revolution."

Time and again, I or my combat-veteran buddies had to swallow bitterness and hatred and either look away or leave the presence of the most vehement radicals.

A low-key antiwar demonstration had been planned for Fort Dix in late September, with participation by more carefully calculating antiwar groups like "The Resistance," led by Judy Chomsky from Philadelphia, the daughter of Noam Chomsky, a radical M.I.T. professor who was head of the anti-draft organization "Resist."

There had been several planning meetings, but I was keeping at arms' length because of my military duties. By then, I was having problems about even being in the same room with some of the most radical pro-Viet Cong types.

One day I got a shock at Pro Park when I ran into a young sergeant from my battalion, the 5th/60th, 9th Division. He was a dude from Bravo Company. We greeted one another like survivors; I asked him what happened after I left the battalion at the end of November. He told me that the next few days after I got hit the battalion kept running into the Viet Cong. Bravo was attacked two days later on the 24th to 25th, taking casualties. On the 30th, they were attacked again and had seven more GIs killed and wounded. My own Alpha Company had gone into combat again on the 6th of December, capturing a large cache of enemy weapons and ammunition and killing several Viet Cong in ground fighting. He didn't know what casualties Alpha had taken in the weeks after I left, just remembered that incident and those involving his own company. He also told me that our sister battalion, the 2nd/60th, was attacked on the 13th of December by NVA Regulars and Viet Cong, losing forty-seven GIs killed and wounded and killing thirty-two of the enemy. The final month he was there just before he rotated home in February, our 5th/60th Battalion hit the enemy several times, taking casualties and got in a big firefight on the 26th, losing another twenty GIs killed and wounded.

For the rest of the day I was back in 'Nam again, worrying and wondering if Gaddy made it home to North Carolina alive, and about Welch and Owens and Brown and Sellman and Barnett and Winters and Brackett, who had eight months to do when I left. All the other dudes, too, that I had imagined as being alive and well, just as I'd left them, and now I'm wondering and it's eating at me.

It was hard to explain it to Josie that night so I sat with my new friend Denny Johnson in the coffeehouse, mumbling about "fuckin' 'Nam." Together we can almost work ourselves into tears about it. Denny's this heavy-set, solid dude who has been coming in. He came back from the "Tropic Lightning," the 25th Infantry Division. His platoon was overrun in an NVA ambush near Tay Ninh; he was one of the few survivors and he was hit badly. He had just gotten out of the hospital, but he had so much RPG shrapnel moving around in his neck and body that the doctors told him he could "die any time, sudden-like." We've got so many memories in common we're becoming friends; sometimes we'd get drunk on beer and rail at the extremes of the student radicals.

That same night there happened to be another hours-long meeting between the coffeehouse staff and a group of visiting radicals, including a few Weathermen. The visitors are emphasizing the slogan "Revolution has come, time to pick up the gun."

Denny and I ended up getting drunk again together in a true "working-class pig manner." In the middle of the night, we burst into the farmhouse full of freaks, packing an M-1 carbine with a thirty-round banana clip. We opened fire at the bannister running up to the second floor, stitching the rounds close and neat, the bullets blasting through the wood and out through the wall. The house was echoing from the gunfire while Denny and I staggered over into a corner laughing, for another round of booze. Then we passed out. Josie found us lying amidst a stacked-up pile of empty beer cans.

Two of the Weathermen whom I knew well were Teddy Gold and Dave Gilbert. Teddy was an old Columbia comrade of Josie's, who struck me as slightly insane. When he'd sit talking to me he'd jabber so quickly and frantically, I could barely understand him; I was definitely impressed by his feeling of urgency and dedication.

He had just returned from a trip to Castro's Cuba, where he had met with Communist cadres of the Viet Cong and their "Provisional Revolutionary Government." The VC message to visiting American radicals in 1969 was that they needed allies inside the United States to end the war with a victory for the Communists.

Teddy Gold said that we were "living inside the monster, and we must assist the Viet Cong in defeating American forces." He told me, "Once the United States was defeated by a worldwide Communist revolution,

America would be run by an agency of the people of the world.'' It was the official Communist line in September of 1969. I was astounded.

Reflecting on it much later, I realized that it is still the official Communist line, and undoubtedly will be until the struggle is decided.

During the summer, Dave Gilbert used to come down to the Fort Dix coffeehouse and talk sensibly and clearly in a quiet manner. I remember discussing politics with him for hours and never feeling any hostility, actually admiring his intellect and liking him. Josie told me later she remembered that he'd been a bright student with a great sense of humor, but by September of '69 he was also part of the Weathermen and incapable of rational discussion.

The rapid change in his personality to a mindless orator against America and supporter of revolutionary violence was alarming to us. After going underground as a Weatherman, he ended up years later in prison for a murder that occurred during an armored-car robbery in New York.

With both families attending, Josie and I were married that same September in a traditional church wedding. We decided to go along with the wishes of our parents on the wedding, since how and where it occurred seemed so much more important to them than it did to us. Along with a couple of Army buddies, I chose to wear a full-dress Army uniform. They included Chuck Solish, who'd given me my first machete back at Phu Loi during the Tet Offensive.

For myself, it was both a matter of pride-in-service, and a way of announcing that combat soldiers and antiwar protestors were really ''getting it together.''

Immediately after our wedding reception, we left the happy family gathering to rush back to Fort Dix. A large meeting had been planned about the Fort Dix demonstration, and representatives from a number of groups were expected to arrive on September 21st.

At the coffeehouse, our first confrontation occurred when a group of Weathermen burst through the door chanting ''Ho! Ho! Ho! Chi Minh! Viet Cong are gonna win!'' They were carrying Viet Cong flags, and these symbols of the enemy became the issue over which the coffeehouse staff and the Fort Dix GIs would finally confront them.

The Weathermen were boasting they'd been running around New York supposedly picking fights with ''working-class dudes'' of the Bronx and talking about their plans to ''go into the factories and confront the workers.'' For some reason none of them had made it to an assembly-line job yet, though.

Now one of the female Weathermen, Karen Ashley, came shrieking through the door: "All GIs are objectively pigs! All GIs are pigs!" The male Weathermen seemed to hide behind the females in the confrontation. Perhaps they realized that I and the rest of the soldiers in the room were getting fed up with their slogans, long-winded bragging, jive talk, and four-dollar words. Only our common commitment to ending U.S. involvement in the war kept us from attacking them on the spot.

The "meeting" adjourned to the old farmhouse; here it continued for several days and nights, as various groups came and left.

The major issue remained the Viet Cong flag. Karen Ashley, Lew Cole, Shinya Ono, Ted Gold, a different, crazy Dave Gilbert, and a number of other Weathermen insisted that they planned to come to Fort Dix "to attack the MPs and the American Pig Army, carrying the glorious banner of the Viet Cong."

They talked and raved for hours, dominating the crowded rooms and raising the level of violence. The Fort Dix coffeehouse staff and we GIs present took a final stand refusing to permit the enemy symbol and announced that the demonstration was cancelled.

In the crowded, smoky rooms, chaos reached an even higher pitch. The final straw for me personally was some fanatical bearded radical screeching in my face, "The pig role of the GIs must be confronted with the banner of the glorious Viet Cong!"

I punched him in the throat with a knuckle jab and he fell on the floor rolling and gasping. The room went into an uproar as people grabbed at my arms, shouting "no violence." I shit-laughed grunt-style. "No violence, huh? All I've been hearin' about is revolutionary violence for hours. The hell with all of you." I pushed my way out through the crowd into the darkness outside. On the other side of the house, a campfire had been started by radicals from Resistance or PL or the "Mobe." I walked out into the farm fields followed by a few other GI buddies. We sat in the dirt, shared a smoke and some beer, staring at the stars.

Somebody said, "It's the same stars that shine over the 'Nam, dudes, know what I mean?" We all nodded. "Hey my man. Ain't none of it means nothin'."

By now, I was enraged with the radicals. The non-Weathermen were going to hold their demonstration at Fort Dix on October 12 to conflict with the Weathermen's "Days of Rage" in Chicago. That was the plan, but I didn't care anymore and didn't want to take part in it. I just wanted to get through the Army and keep my new wife Josie with me.

I was beginning to feel that it wasn't wise to express feelings against American involvement in the war on an Army base where we still had to follow orders or be imprisoned. I felt the center of government was a better place to express dissent—a tradition that went back to the time of the Revolution. In October and November of 1969, Josie and I went to several demonstrations. At the Washington Moratorium the main speaker was a radical named Richard Barnet. He had once been in the government as a member of the Disarmament Agency, but was now a director of the Institute for Policy Studies or I.P.S., which acted as theorticians for the radical movement.

We attended the main mobilization demonstration on November 15, 1969, in Washington D.C. from Fort Dix along with several busloads of off-duty soldiers and Vietnam veterans. The enormous crowds of up to half a million people there showed how widespread the war-weariness was in America. Most of those present were peaceful average Americans and their goal was simple and just.

The Weathermen came again, though, to forment violence purposely and cause the police to retaliate against the crowd. Thousands of people carried signs saying "Give Peace a Chance," but the Weathermen carried Communist flags. Starting at Dupont Circle, they led a screaming mob to attack the South Vietnamese embassy, breaking windows, smashing cars, and setting fire to a police motorcycle. Even in trying to avoid a confrontation with them, we were pushed around and tear-gassed.

The radicals continued on their spree of window-smashing and destruction, trying to raise the level of violence. On the second day, the Weathermen attacked the Justice Department, smashing windows and exploding red smoke grenades to symbolize their support of the Communists.

Eventually they pulled down the American flag from the pole in front and raised the Viet Cong flag. The police drove them out of the area again, and they headed off on another destructive spree.

I left Washington with Josie early. I no longer wanted to be part of what was occurring and no longer cared what people around us thought.

For the next two months at Fort Dix, I reported for duty at the Basic Training Center, but word of my associations had spread to the lifers. They began to harass me, trying to get me to "disobey a lawful order." I just kept following orders and doing my time. At nights I was still wrapped up with Josie's coffeehouse. On weekends we went to a few more demonstrations, rallies and teach-ins at Rutgers, Yale, and CCNY.

I looked out over shouting crowds with their Viet Cong flags fluttering, and the sight of the enemy symbols gave me a vicious feeling of hatred. I stared at these thousands of privileged, allowanced, well-taken-care-of young people and felt sick.

"What did they know about it anyway? What did they have to worry about?" Not the war, really, not with their deferments. Not a year in the infantry in the jungle. Not a KGB prison or total disappearance. Why wave the Communist flag? Why chant about Ho Chi Minh? Every time I heard it, I had to bite my lip as I remembered my dead and wounded buddies and tried to quit imagining about tossing a grenade among them. The demonstrations seemed too happy, anyway. The music, the laughing and giggling references to the "pigs" or "baby-killing GIs," and the cozy little joint circles—it was all superficial. I gradually began to pull back inside myself, more bitter than ever; Josie retreated with me, beginning to see things in a different light herself, as she shared my experiences.

I agreed only with the demand to end American troop involvement in the war. I tried to understand the frustration of the most radical, dedicated activists that could lead to their identification with the Viet Cong, whom they saw as a brave group of fighters against a great power, but I couldn't. I also knew first-hand that many Vietnamese did not want to live under communism. I could never reconcile myself to our radicals' expressed hatred of their own country and support of the enemy. Perhaps we had made a mistake by going into Vietnam to preserve the freedom of a people who wouldn't fight hard enough to defend it themselves, if we weren't willing to go the limit ourselves.

But what was the record of the Communists towards their own populations? What about the freedoms here that we all seemed to take for granted that enabled us to protest without being shot or disappearing? What about our two-hundred-year tradition of freedom of the press, something denied in every Communist society in the world? I couldn't find it in myself to embrace the ideals of a philosophy whose actual practices always turned out so differently from its promises.

I had a feeling of disgust with my own country's leadership but not disloyalty to the nation or the ideals that it stood for. Josie moved her political position with me, and perhaps it was our forced association with the Weathermen of SDS that made us see things more clearly. We were, in effect, driven out of the anitwar movement by their pro-Communist, pro-Viet Cong stand.

The undenied resentment of many veterans, including myself, towards the student-protesters stemmed not only from their radical excesses, but from the lack of any real danger or threat of service through most of the war. The class stratified 2-S and graduate-school deferments kept them from having contact with the war as we had. If anything, it prolonged the war by not sweeping into the ranks large numbers of this part of the population and involving their families in the reality of it. That, in turn, probably prolonged by several years the national turn against it and negated the chances of a call for total victory.

During the war years, approximately fifteen million men of my generation were deferred or disqualified from the draft, mostly by college deferments. At the same time, out of some eight million who served in all the armed forces during the conflict, three million served in Indochina and two and a half million in Vietnam. Out of this number, perhaps one million saw some form of combat.

In the future formulation of our national policies, this must be remembered. In the event of a return of the draft, if the armed forces are not drawn from all classes, there will be the same class divisions, the same disunity, the same exclusion of intellectuals and their eventual disloyalty, with working-class sacrifice and bloodshed. An elite, technologically-oriented armed forces, recruited from "mostly underprivileged citizens," loyal to their pay and benefits, along with a small oligarchic power clique in the government, could become a danger to our future as a free society. All citizens should serve their country when need arises, whether they are gifted students or the children of politicians, business men or workers. This would keep our democratic republic just that, and spread out the burden, sacrifices, and morality of our actions.

For Josie and me, the fall and winter of 1969-70 was the beginning of a sense of expatriation from our own society. We shared a feeling of frustration at the seeming endlessness of the war, combined with dissolution over the evermore radical rhetoric of the peace movement's leadership.

In January of 1970, it was all partly solved for me by ETS from my three-year Regular Army hitch. A long line of old-looking boys, blank-eyed, decorated combat veterans, were handed honorable discharges; it was almost like some big, community-college graduation. Just different "courses" and a practically worthless "degree" that later became almost a stigma or mark of the beast: "Oh! A Vietnam War veteran are ya? Huh?" Smirk-sneering looks of gut-shot babies, gleeful burning, dark drug scenes.

The cops were there at our mass discharge graduation ceremony, though. Another set of blank-eyed dudes themselves representing many of the big-city police departments, recruiting. They must've figured that Vietnam veterans would make fine police to handle riots and racial disorders in the "black ghettos." I took one long look at them and said to myself, "Uh-unnnnnh. I ain't goin' from one war to another, specifically when there's a lot of my black grunt bros out in them streets, pissed off." I slid on by that one.

We left the Fort Dix farm house-coffeehouse scene the day after my discharge, saying a hasty good-bye to everyone and everything.

During the next month and a half we traveled back and forth between New York and Philadelphia, staying with friends and relatives. We tried to avoid the subject of the war. The disagreements we felt over the continuing death of American GIs and with the leadership in the radical peace movement made this necessary.

Several times in New York we stayed at house-collectives of movement activists, but often got into arguments.

There were rumors of planned bombings by Weathermen, some of whom had gone underground already.

On one occasion we ran into Teddy Gold in a place near the old New York SDS headquarters on the Lower East Side. He was as hyper as ever and told us that the time for revolutionary violence was finally at hand. He was wearing a Superman cape and was with several other Weathermen. He seemed elated at the prospect of action and chattered so furiously I had trouble following him. He sensed that Josie and I did not share his political ideas, and spoke to her as though she were a traitor.

In early March, Josie had one last contact with her former Columbia comrades. Her oldest and best friend, Diane, who had joined the Weathermen, was in jail and begging for bail. She had been busted for assault in the "Days of Rage" demonstration in Chicago and again later.

We met with attorneys of the radical "Lawyers Guild" and discussed her situation. We were on the Lower East Side on the 6th of March, 1970 when word came of a large explosion nearby on West 11th Street.

We went to the scene and saw a huge gaping hole where a fancy New York townhouse had stood. Barricades in the street stopped all vehicles, while police and bomb squad personnel sifted through the dusty, smoking rubble.

Teddy Gold, along with Diana Oughten and Terry Robbins were dead.

They were blown to pieces by explosives stored in the building while preparing to bomb symbols of American power. All three were well known to Josie and the incident drove home the point that her radical former comrades were beyond the point of reason. They were in a pathetic way, "bringing home the War."

We were both completely fed up with everything to do with the peace movement. We wanted to go off alone and live a little. After a few false starts in Pennsylvania and stays with my family for a while, we realized there was nothing in the East for us at all. We had to get away from anyone close to us because there was so much bitterness erupting we couldn't stand to be around anyone but ourselves.

Crossing the country slowly, camping along the way, we were in Ohio during the U.S. invasion of Cambodian base camps.

When I first heard about the invasion, I silently cheered the GIs who were carrying out the fighting, and the President, despite my bitterness and confusion over the war. The only problem was that the Parrot's Beak and the Fishhook should have been overrun four or five years before. Meanwhile, not far away, a crowd of 600 students egged on by radicals were protesting the "widening of the War." After the demonstration escalated to violence and rock throwing, four of these Kent State University students were shot and killed by National Guardsmen. Four hundred universities across the country went on strike and more bombings occurred. We felt even more sickened over it all; it seemed like the country was tearing itself apart over the war that spring of 1970.

All the way across the United States to California, we found division, argument, and bitterness. It was obviously getting to the point where America as a whole was feeling the war. Now almost everyone we met knew somebody "who'd been there," and had strong opinions about the war, mostly negative.

In California, we headed towards the Santa Cruz, Monterey, and the Big Sur coast. Josie had a younger brother living there, who had come to our wedding and was now approaching draft age. John is young, somewhat impressed by my experiences and feelings on the war, and Josie loves him—which was reason enough to hang around the area for a while. We drifted down to Fort Ord a few times out of nostalgia. There was a GI antiwar movement coffeehouse scene there, but we found we really have little in common. We ran into Tom Hayden there during the planning of some demonstration. Even though he'd been an acquaintance of Josie's in SDS and instructed her on Communist politics at Columbia, he ignored her now. He was trying to remain the center of attraction. Despite my own quandry of feelings about Vietnam, I couldn't help but dwell on his five year long, steady support of a Communist victory there while thousands of my brother GIs had been dying to prevent it. I looked bitterly into his eyes thinking and mumbling, "Well, you're winning aren't you, like they never let us win; I guess it feels pretty good, huh?"

While talking to him his eyes kept wandering around searching for someone more pliable or important to expound to. He found such a person when he teamed up with Jane Fonda, a famous visitor to North Vietnam during the war. She threw her support first behind the enemy and eventually behind Hayden's political career.

That same day, our prisoners of war in Hanoi and elsewhere continued their lonely vigil, often under torture or in solitary confinement, awaiting the end of the fighting—their stories and suffering still unknown. They were verbally attacked, demeaned, and criticized by other pro-Communist visitors to the enemy's homeland besides Jane Fonda and Hayden, even by a former American attorney general, Ramsey Clark.

Meanwhile, there at Fort Ord were the long marching rows of young soldiers, M-16 rifles on their shoulders, heading for Vietnam with "duty, honor and country" in their hearts. Those words were part of my soul, too, but my heart cried at seeing them, and beside me my new wife Josie cried, too.

All the hopeless rage and bitterness at the wrongs on all sides reached a crescendo for us that summer of 1970. One day we loaded up our truck and headed north for Alaska. I remembered the solitude of those northern mountains on that Christmas Eve medevac flight from Asia in 1968 and decided to discover what lay beyond them.

Sources, Bibliography
and Recommended Reading

$\mathbf{I}$n writing this book I primarily used the forty or more letters home, a journal and eyewitness memories of mine and my wife Josie's. However I have over the years also studied numerous published works and unpublished records on the subject to add to my knowledge and understanding. Rather than include notes on the very numerous sources used to verify my personal records and memories on the various military actions, political moves, news media reports, and antiwar activities, I have assembled a list of pertinent military records and a bibliography by category.

John M.G. Brown
Port Lions, Kodiak Is.
Alaska 1985

Military Records (unpublished)
O.R.L.L.s   *Operational Reports and Lessons Learned*
             Quarterly Reports and After-Action Reports
             Daily Journals and Logbooks and unit reports of
             radio transmissions

Primary Sources: **Fall of 1967 to Tet and May Offensives of 1968**
— Phu Loi, R.V.N.

1st Aviation Battalion, 1st Infantry Division Sept.'67-July '68
1st Squadron/4th Cavalry, 1st Infantry Division Sept. '67-July '68

2nd Battalion/2nd Infantry (Mechanized) 1st Infantry Division
2nd Battalion/16th Infantry/1st Infantry Division
1st Battalion/26th Infantry/1st Infantry Division
1st Battalion/28th Infantry/1st Infantry Division
2nd Battalion/28th Infantry/1st Infantry Division
1st Engineer Battalion/1st Infantry Division
H.Q. Battery, 1st Infantry Division Artillery, Phu Loi, R.V.N.
701st Maintenance Battalion, Phu Loi, R.V.N.
35th U.S. Infantry Platoon, Scout Dog
61st U.S. Infantry Platoon, Combat Trackers
Long Range Recon Patrol, Co. F./52nd Ranger Infantry
7th Squadron/1st Calvary Air Cav., Di An and Phu Loi
2nd Squadron/34th Armored Cavalry, Di An and Phu Loi
A Battery/5th Bn./2nd Artillery/IInd Field Force (Duster Guns)
234th Radar (for enemy's rocket and mortar attack launch positions)
11th Combat Aviation Battalion

Primary Sources: **May Offensive of 1968 to Sept. '68**
                 Quarterly O.R.L.L.s, Daily Journals, Logs,
                 etc.

H.Q. 1st Infantry Division, Lai Khe R.V.N.
1st Battalion/16th Infantry (Rangers) Lai Khe, R.V.N.
1st Battalion/2nd Infantry/2nd Batallion/2nd Infantry (Mechanized)
1st and 2nd Battalions/18th Infantry
1st/2nd/and 3rd/Squadrons/11th Armored Cav. (Blackhorse Trp.) Xuan Loc and
  other locations, R.V.N. June-Aug. '68
147th Aviation Co. "Hillclimbers" (Chinooks) July '68 Vung Tau R.V.N.
3rd Brigade Aviation, 1st Infantry Div. (L.O.H.s) July '68
1st Aviation Battalion, Radio Transmissions, June-Sept. '68
1st Squadron/4th Cavalry, 1st Infantry Div., Radio Transmissions

Primary Sources: **Mekong Delta, October to December, 1968**
                 O.R.L.L.s and daily journals and logbooks

5th Battalion/60th Infantry/9th Infantry Div. Dong Tam,
  Firebase Moore, Cai Lay, Rach Kien, R.V.N.
H.Q. 3rd Brigade ("Go Devils"), 9th Infantry Div. (Quarterly O.R.L.L.s)
2nd Battalion/47th Infantry (Mechanized)
2nd Battalion/60th Infantry/9th Infantry Div.
6th Battalion/31st Infantry/9th Infantry Div.
3rd Battalion/39th Infantry/9th Infantry Div.
3rd Squadron/5th Cavalry, Armored/9th Infantry Div.
2nd Battalion/4th Artillery/9th Infantry Div.
Troop A. 3rd Squadron, 17th Air Cav. ("Silver Spurs")

Published Military Organizational Record

Vietnam Order of Battle, Shelby Stanton U.S. News & World Report Books, Washington D.C. (1981)

Newspapers and Periodicals

Pacific Stars and Stripes, Newspaper for U.S. Armed Forces overseas (1967-1968) Published in Tokyo, Japan
The American Traveler, Newspaper for the 1st Infantry Div. in Vietnam (1967-1968)
Danger Forward, Journal of the Society of the 1st Div. (1967-1968)
The Old Reliable, Newspaper for the 9th Infantry Div. in Vietnam (Sept. 1968-Feb. 1969)
The Observer, Newspaper of "MACV", Military Assistance Command Vietnam (1967-1968)
The Army Reporter, Newspaper of "USARV" U.S. Army Vietnam (Feb.-May, 1968)
and other various periodicals and newspapers.

For the United States military view:

A Soldier Reports by Gen. William Westmoreland, Dell Publishing (1980)
The 25 Year War, America's Military Role in Vietnam by Gen. Bruce Palmer Jr., University Press of Kentucky, 1984 and Simon and Shuster, NY
On Strategy, A Strategic Analyses of the Vietnam War by Col. Harry Summers, Presidio Press, Novato, CA
Battles and Campaigns of Vietnam by Thomas Carhart, Crown Publishers, NY (1984)

For detailed and realistic view of combat in Vietnam:

Ambush! by S.L.A. Marshall (A.U.S. Ret'd.) First published 1969, Nonfiction, The Battery Press, Nashville (1983)
Everything We Had by Al Santoli, Random House, NY, (1981) Nonfiction
Charlie Company by Goldman and Fuller (Co. C, 2nd Battalion/28th Infantry/1st Infantry Div., 1968-69) Wm. Morrow, NY, (1983) Nonfiction
365 Days by Ronald J. Glasser, George Brazillier, NY, (1980) Nonfiction
Home Before Morning—An Army Nurse in Vietnam by Lynda Vandevanter, Warner Books, NY, (1984) Narrative
Dear America—Letters Home from Vietnam, W. W. Norton, (1985) Nonfiction
Fields of Fire by James Webb, Prentice-Hall, Englewood Cliffs, NJ, (1975) Novel
The 13th Valley by John M. Del Vecchio, Bantam, NY, (1982) Novel
Close Quarters by Larry Hieneman, Popular Library, (1977) Novel

For better understanding of guerilla war in the Vietnamese countryside see the following books (of varying political views):

Silence Was a Weapon by Col. Stuart Herrington, Presidio Press, Novato, CA, (1982). (Vietnam War in the villages, late in U.S. involvement period.) Nonfiction

War Comes to Long An, Revolutionary Conflict in a Vietnamese Province by Jeffery Race, Berkeley (1972)

The Endless War, Vietnam's Struggle for Independence by James Pinkney Harrison, McGraw Hill (1983)

My Lai 4 by Seymour Hersh, Random House, NY (1971)

For analyses and reporting on the Tet Offensive of 1968 see:

The Big Story, How the American Press and Television Reported and Interpreted the Crisis of Tet 1968 by Peter Braestrup, Westview Press, Boulder, CO (1977) and Yale Univ. Press

Tet! by Don Oberdorfer, De Capo Press, NY (1971)

Front Page Vietnam, As Reported by The New York Times edited by Keylin & Boiangin, NY (1971)

For an in-depth overall study of effect of news media on U.S. policy see:

Bad News, The Foreign Policy of the New York Times by Russ Braley, Regnery Gateway, Chicago (1984)

For views of United States political leadership and political/military decisions on the Tonkin Gulf, escalation and conduct of the war, Tet Offensive and bombing of N. Vietnam:

The Pentagon Papers, Sen. Gravel edition, Beacon Press, Boston (1971)

The Pentagon Papers published by the New York Times, Neil Sheehan, Fox Butterfield, etc., Bantam Books, NY (1971)

Papers on the War by Daniel Ellsberg, Simon & Shuster, NY (1972)

The Best and the Brightest by David Halberstam, Random House, NY (1965)

The Unmaking of a President by Herbert Schandler, Princeton Univ. Press (1977)

The Lost Crusade by Chester Cooper Dodd, Mead (1970)

Truth is the First Casualty by John Goulden, Rand McNally (1969)

Tonkin Gulf by Eugene Windchy, Doubleday, NY (1971)

How We Lost the Vietnam War by Nguyen Cao Ky, Stien and Day, NY (1978)

The Limits of Intervention, An Inside Account of How the Johnson Policy in Vietnam Was Reversed by David McKay, NY (1969)

J.F.K. & L.B.J.: The Influence of Personality upon Politics by Tom
   Wicker, Wm. Morrow, NY (1968)
*Delusion and Reality, Gambits, Hoaxes and Diplomatic One Upmanship in
   Vietnam* by Janos Radvanyi (a communist-bloc defector) Gateway
   Editions/Regnery-Gateway, Chicago/South Bend (1978)
The Communist Road to Power by William J. Duiker, Westview Press,
   Boulder, CO (1981)
No More Vietnams by Richard Nixon, Arbor House, NY (1985)
Also various articles in *Foreign Affairs,* the journal of the Council on
   Foreign Relations, NY

For views on effect of "limited" or "selective" bombing of North Vietnam see:

In Love and War by James and Sybil Stockdale, Harper and Row, NY
   (1984); Bantam (1985)
The Prestige Press and the Christmas Bombing 1972 by Martin Herz, Ethics
   and Public Policy Center (1980)
How "Rules of Engagement" Lost the Vietnam War by J. Terry Emerson,
   Human Events (May 18, 1985)
Congressional Record Barry Goldwater (March 6, 14, 18, 26, 1985)

For an understanding of how writing sympathetic to the communist cause in Vietnam influenced the media and the population see:

The Vietnam Reader by Marcus Raskin, Random House, NY (1965)
U.S. Political Warfare: The 1968 Hue Massacre by Gareth Porter, Indo-
   china Chronicle (June 1974)
Proletariat and Peasantry in Early Communism, Asian Thought and
   Society, by Gareth Porter (Dec. 1976)
The Crimes of War by Richard Falk, (Professor of International Law),
   Princeton Univ. Press (1971)
Behind the Lines: Hanoi, Harrison Salisbury (of the New York Times),
   Harper and Row, NY (1967)
At War with Asia by Noam Chomsky, NY (1970)
Big Victory—Great Task by Vo Nguyen Giap (Gen., Peoples Army,
   N. Vietnam), NY (1968)
Also: *Banner of People's War,* New York (1968)
      How We Won the War, Philadelphia (1976)
The Village of Ben Suc by Jonathon Schell (Iron Triangle), Alfred Knopf NY
   1967)

Trip to Hanoi by Susan Sontag; Farrar, Strauss & Giroux (1968)
Vietnam Will Win by Wilfred Burchett, NY (1969)
Catapult to Freedom by Wilfred Burchett, Quartet Books (1978)
*Target America—The Influence of Communist Propaganda on the U.S.
   News Media* by James Tyson (with preface by Reid Irvine), Regnery/
   Gateway, Chicago (1981)
On Genocide by Jean Paul Sartre, Beacon Press (1968)

For a further understanding of the conversion of idealistic middle class students to radicalism see:

Diana (Oughten), *The Making of a Terrorist* by Thomas Powers,
   Houghton-Mifflin, Boston (1971)
The Battle for Morningside Heights, Why Students Rebel (Columbia
   University S.D.S.) by Roger Kahn, Wm. Morrow & Co., NY (1970)
Weatherman (Dedicated to the Vietnamese People), edited by Harold
   Jacobs, Ramparts Press (1970)
Miami and the Siege of Chicago, the Republican and Democratic conven-
   tions of 1968 by Norman Mailer, Signet Books, New American Library,
   NY (1968)
also: *Armies of the Night* (1967)
Harvard Hates America, The Odyssey of a Born-again American by John
   Le Boutillier, Gateway Edition/Regnery-Gateway, Chicago (1978)
The Berkeley Archipelago by Joseph P. Lyford, Regnery-Gateway, Chicago
   (1982)
Up Against the Ivy Wall by Jerry Avorn, Atheneum, NY (1969)
The Strawberry Statement—Notes of a College Revolutionist by James
   Kunan, Random House, NY (1969)

Recommended general analysis:

Long Time Passing, Vietnam and the Haunted Generation by Myra
   MacPherson, Doubleday, NY (1984)
The Wounded Generation, America after Vietnam edited by A. D. Horne,
   Prentice Hall, NJ (1981)
Vietnam, A History by Stanley Karnow, Viking Press, NY (1983)
Why We Were in Vietnam by Norman Podhoretz, Simon & Shuster, NY
   (1982)
also: *The Present Danger,* Simon & Shuster, NY (1980)
The Real War by Richard Nixon, Warner Books, NY (1980)
Dictatorships and Double Standards by Jean Kirkpatrick, American Enter-
   prise Institute, and Simon & Shuster, NY (1982)
How Democracies Perish by Jean-Francois Revel, Doubleday and Co.,
   Garden City, NY (1984)

YBARRA HIDALGO · VIRGIL L HITER · JAMES C HOUGHTON · FATHIES KELLY Jr ·
R KING · WILLIE KNOWLES Jr · KENNETH D KRALICK · KENNETH H CARPENTER ·
NALD T STOKES · PATRICK R ROY · STEVEN T RUNYON · MARCOS SOSA Jr ·
OMAS E PRIESTHOFF · JAMES T TAYLOR · JAMES M THOMAS · JOHN W VASILOPULOS ·
S W WEST · WILLIAM G WILKINSON · DEAN J CRAIG · RICHARD A HOUSE ·
G McDONNELL · HENRY L OLSON · BARRY L RUNYON · MARVIN SMITH ·
B WEARING · GUADALUPE NATAL ZUNIGA · DOYLE L BELL · JAMES D BLANDEN ·
RICK C CASSIDY · EDWARD L CLEMMON · ROBERT J GRANDE · THOMAS HUBBARD ·
AY · JOSEPH MORGAN Jr · MARSHALL L RITZ · GEORGE X ROCHA ·
L SENZ · LARRY D TRAASETH · BENNIE ALSTON · DAVE E ASHFORD ·
D BOBIAN · JAMES L BROWN · WALTER O BROWN Jr · ANTHONY V CAMPANIELLO ·
ES CARPENTER · GEORGE P COLANGELO · ROGER D EVANS · LEROY EVERETT ·
LVIN A GREENE · THOMAS E GRINER · DONALD P HAMILTON · LARRY A HANKE ·
MAS S HENSHAW · CHARLES R HOLLAND · JOHN F HOLZ · RODNEY HULL OLESON ·
KLOPMEYER · RAY TAYLOR · JEROME F LE VASSEUR Jr · JUNIOR E LOT
RICHARD E MEHL · EUGENE MILEY · GREGORY McCRAY · WILLIE
NORMAN · LOUIE PETE PINA · RANDALL B PURDY · STEVEN N RADU ·
IEGEL · JUNIOR L SCHRINER · WINFIELD A SPOEHR Jr · BRUCE W St LOUIS ·
IE L LANCASTER · MURRAY D VIDLER · THOMAS M WEBSTER · JIMMY LEE WOOL
DAVID ANTOL · TERRENCE D BECK · GLEN D BELNAP · WILLIAM A CARTER ·
MURRAY · GREGORY GORE · JOHN H HOLMES · CHARLES L HOUSLEY ·
FFERSON · HORATIO L JONES · WILLIAM C JONES · BERNARD P MEINEN Jr ·
RD F GIITTINGER · JEREMIAH D McGARRY · MORRIS G McPHAIL · RICHARD J PAY
ERTS Jr · TERRY ROBERTS · BARRY A THOMPSON · RAFAEL A VALPAIS-MORALES ·
LPH J BILLIOT · JAMES H BROWN · FRANK H BUCK · DANIEL S BUKALA ·
COPELAND · MITCHELL J DUNCAN · MICHAEL J FEAGAN · LARRY E GONZALEZ ·
ICHARD J JANSKI · RICHARD A KASKE · CARROL G KEEHNER · WILLIAM H KENNEDY ·
LAMBERT · EUGENE MANIGO · ROBERT D MASON · THOMAS R MATTY ·
VID W MILDE · WILLIAM C MOORE Jr · DAVID R MYERS · RICHARD H McHAM ·
McMASTER · LES H PASCHALL · DONNIE D PRESLEY · LEE D SCURLOCK Jr ·
E SMEDLEY · DONALD L SMITH · MURRAY L SMITH · CHARLES F SORROW Jr ·
HOKE · DANIEL A VERDUGO · ROBERT L WALLS · FREDERIC P WEBB ·
M H BORCHART · WILLIAM E BRIDGES Jr · TED W BURROUGHS Jr · PETER B BUSHEY ·
R P COOK · ROBERT W COOPER · MARIAN J DOMINIAK Jr · STANLEY W DRIZA ·
ER · ROBERT A HANSELMAN · RODGER D HASTE · MERLIN C HOLLENBACH ·
LEY R HUTCHISON · ROBERT L LONG · STEVEN W MUELLER · PETER E NARVARTE Jr ·
RLES C PETERSON · LARRY P BLACK · TIMOTHY H RINEHART · THOMAS D ROBINSON ·
HWARTZ · JOSEPH L SEEKFORD · MICHAEL M SENGER · GEORGE C SIGALAS ·
CKEL · MICHAEL E SUNIGA · EDWARD RODRIGUEZ · ANGEL VEGA ·
N G WELLMAN · DENNIS P WOOD · FRANK G ANTONE · RICHARD E BOURNE ·
N CLEMONS · MICHAEL J DI NAPOLI · HUGH G WILLARD · CARL R GOODFELLOW ·
NE H HARRIMAN · DUDLEY C HUGHES Jr · ROBERT R JACKEMEYER · LEE B ZOELLER ·
E MADDOX · THOMAS L NELSON · ANIBAL OYOLA-RABAGO · JOHN R PHILLIPS ·
HOLAS G WALZ · RAYMOND C EUBANKS Jr · LESTER L WILLIAMS · JOHN L WULFFERT ·
LERIJA CHULCHATSCHINOW · WILLIAM D DICKSON · DAVID MIDDLEKAUFF ·
A PARSONS · LARRY W PIERCE · VERNIE H POWERS · TRAVIS R SUTTON ·
EL B SWEENEY · MATTHEW J AGUGLIARO · RICHARD W BUDKA · FREDERICK J BURNS ·
NY W JETER · BERNARD D JOHNSON · TERRY T KOONCE · BILLY E LANKFORD ·
O LEWIS · JOHN D MORRIS · CHARLES D McCLURG · LARRY H OERTEL ·
CHIE OXENDINE · DONALD W RICHARD · FRANCIS E SANDERS · PETER W SCOTT ·
ERS · JOE T SHUMPERT · RONALD J SIENGO · EDGAR J UDELL · HAROLD D WILLIAMS ·
CE B BARTON · MICHAEL E BERDY · WILLIE T BRICKHOUSE Jr · SAMMY BUFFINGTON ·
OSEPH T CLARK · TOMMY L DANIELS · ROGER A ELLIS · DANIEL C FAULKS Jr ·
AMBLE · DARRELL D GEHRKE · DAVID R HAEFNER · TIMOTHY J KENNEDY ·
GONS · MATTHEW P MALCZYNSKI · DONALD F McDOWELL · LARRY LEE ORCUTT ·
EL R RICE · GERALD L ROWEN II · JAMES L RUSS Jr · RENNY D SCHOEL ·
M VAN ZANDT · BERNARD F POBLOCK · ROBERT E WOODS · CARL E ABNER ·
C ALFRED · RONALD P ALLEN · HOWARD D ANDERSON · JOHNNIE ANTONIO Jr ·
HN R ARRINGTON · RICHARD W BANNISTER · LAWRENCE M BARNES · GEORGE BINKO ·
ARSCH · DAVID L BOGGS · WILLIAM J BROWN · GEORGE M BROZ ·
WILLIAM A CASON · THOMAS E CAST · KENNETH L CHAPPELL · BOYD E JONES ·
ONALD J CRUDEN · GORDON T DALTON · RICHARD N EDDY · JUDSON W EMMONS ·
L GABRIEL · FRANCIS D GREENWOOD · BRUCE HALL · MOSE HEGLER Jr ·
E HENTSCHEL · TED D HOLLIMAN · DONALD C HOPEWELL · ALBERT L HORNER ·
HELL HUGHES Jr · ROGER B INNES · THORNTON I JACKSON · JAMES L JAKO ·
MICHAEL L JONES · RONALD L KESLING · DONALD R KIRBY III · GUY D KISTNER ·
KLINDT · IRVILLE J KNOX · DAVID N LAFFERTY · LEONARD M LEE ·
EWIS · VERNON R LIPINSKI · GEORGE E LONSDALE · JAMES E LOUDERMILK ·

IRA H HULL
JOHN D PE
GREGORY E
DAVID L CH
CLARENCE
PETER KRET
PHILIP A TIN
TERRY W BL
KENNETH B
ELDON GA
WILLIAM T
FREDERICK
JAMES W M
JAMES A PR
S K
CHARLES
CHARLES
RODN
RIC
W
RT L C
RICHARD H
JAMES B HA
LOWELL JO
MICH
JAM
DWI
ROBE
THEO
GEORG
JOSE CA
FREDIE RA
WILLIAM
JOHN T G
EDDIE H H
GENE RAY
JOSEPH LI
ROBERT W
SHELDON
ROBERT G S
WILLIAM J A
KENNETH B
JOHN M G
WILLIAM E
JUAN H MA
JAMES P RO
JAMES P TU
JERRY W WI
BRIAN P AH
LOUIS W BR
KENNETH D
STEPHEN E
FREDDIE D
RAUL G GU
SAMUEL F H
TERENCE P J
ARTHUR L L
WILLIAM A
MICHAEL J A
LOUIS G PE
WILLIAM G
ANDREW I